GOTHAM UNBOUND

JAMES B. JACOBS

with Coleen Friel and Robert Radick

GOTHAM UNBOUND

How New York City Was Liberated from the Grip of Organized Crime

New York University Press • *New York and London*

NEW YORK UNIVERSITY PRESS
New York and London

Library of Congress Cataloging-in-Publication Data
Jacobs, James B.
Gotham unbound : how New York City was liberated from the grip of organized crime / James B. Jacobs with Coleen Friel and Robert Radick.
p. cm.
Includes bibliographical references and index.
ISBN 0-8147-4246-7 (alk. paper)
1. Racketeering—New York (State)—New York. 2. Mafia—New York (State)—New York. 3. Business enterprises—Corrupt practices—New York (State)—New York. 4. Organized crime investigation—New York (State)—New York. I. Friel, Coleen. II. Radick, Robert. III. Title.
HV6452.N72 M345 1999
364.1'06'097471—dc21 99-6341
CIP

New York University Press books are printed on acid-free paper, and their binding materials are chosen for strength and durability.

Manufactured in the United States of America

10 9 8 7 6 5 4 3 2 1

From JBJ to Jan

From CF to Mom and Beth, for all your support, and to the memory of my father, who is so sorely missed

From RR to Mom, Dad, and Lindsay

Contents

Acknowledgments

The seeds for this book were planted in the late 1980s when I was collaborating with the New York State Organized Crime Task Force on its investigation and analysis of corruption and racketeering in the New York City construction industry. It was obvious at that time that Cosa Nostra's entrenchment in the construction industry had analogs in a number of other businesses, industries and economic sectors. I thought then and continue to think now that a single volume laying out Cosa Nostra's role in the New York City economy would provide an important perspective on Cosa Nostra, New York City, and the urban history of the United States. In any event, I owe my friends and former colleagues at OCTF a great debt of gratitude for enlightening me about organized crime and industrial racketeering. Thus, my thanks once again to Joe DeLuca, Ron Goldstock, Wilda Hess, Marty Marcus, Robbie Mass, Toby Thacher, and all the other members of the OCTF team. Ron Goldstock deserves a special expression of gratitude. He has encouraged, stimulated, informed, criticized, and assisted every step of the way—he's an extraordinary friend and colleague.

This book is a product of the Center for Research in Crime and Justice at New York University School of Law. For continuous, generous, and enthusiastic support, I am grateful beyond words to Dean John Sexton. Likewise, I want to express my appreciation for the sustenance I receive on a daily basis from my colleagues, especially David Garland, Ron Noble, and Jerry Skolnick.

A book like this could not be written by a single individual working alone, at least not by me. Fortunately, I have been blessed with wonderful students throughout my seventeen years at New York University. Many of them have made important contributions to this book. During the summer of 1994, Derek Brummer and Robert Tretter undertook the first spadework on some of the industries. Coleen Friel and Robert Radick served as research assistants during the summer of 1995.

They continued with the research, as Leslie Glass Criminal Justice Center Research Fellows, throughout the 1995–1996 and 1996–1997 academic years, right up to the day they graduated. In effect, they functioned as my junior colleagues. They are not only outstanding researchers but also a delight to work with.

I was very ably assisted during the summer of 1997 by Alex Hortis. Finally, throughout the 1998 summer and fall I received terrific research assistance from Lara Bazelon, Raphael Lee and David Santore; I could not have finished this project without them. Other New York University law students who also deserve my thanks for their contributions to this project are Amy Amster, Lauryn Gouldin, Courtney Groves, Spring Hollis, and Mark Tamoshunas.

John Gleeson, Ron Goldstock, Jim Kossler, Marty Marcus, and Brian Taylor read and commented on the entire manuscript, thereby saving me from numerous errors as well as adding important suggestions.

Many busy people took time out from their schedules to be interviewed for this project. I hesitate to name some for fear of leaving out others. But to all of you—a thousand thanks. I hope I can repay your generosity in part by getting this story right.

My secretary, Virginia Singeltary, competently assisted me in moving this project forward all along the way. Sarah and Eliot Marcus's computer skills saved the manuscript at a crucial point in its life. Niko Pfund, editor in chief of the New York University Press, and his whole staff have been a pleasure to work with. My wife, Jan Sweeney, as always, has been a constant and loving source of support and encouragement.

James B. Jacobs
New York City
December 1998

1

An Introduction to the Place and the Players

COSA NOSTRA IS the largest, most sophisticated, most powerful, and most remarkable crime syndicate in the history of the United States. For reasons that this book makes clear, it is unlikely that any other crime syndicate, at least in the foreseeable future, will play anything like the role that Cosa Nostra has played in our nation's social, economic, and political life. Yet, for reasons this book also makes clear, Cosa Nostra's survival into the next millennium, in anything like its twentieth-century form, can be seriously doubted.

This book deals with Cosa Nostra's entrenchment in New York City's economy and with federal, state, and local governments' omnibus and unprecedented efforts to liberate New York City from Cosa Nostra in the last two decades of the twentieth century. Part I spotlights six major businesses or industries in New York City that have been "mobbed-up" for decades, in some cases for most of the century. Part II examines the federal, state, and local organized-crime control strategies that have achieved significant success in purging Cosa Nostra from the city's social, economic, and political life. The List of Names at the back of the book provides the reader a quick and easy way to identify all the criminals and crime controllers mentioned throughout the book.

With respect to organized crime, New York City is not unique. While the names of the Cosa Nostra families and other details differ from city to city, the main themes of the story we tell for New York City could also be told for Boston, Buffalo, Chicago, Cleveland, Jersey City, Kansas City, Las Vegas, Los Angeles, Miami, New Orleans, Newark, Philadelphia, and many other large and small U.S. cities. In every one of these cities Italian organized-crime groups have a long history of extensive industrial and labor racketeering and of having functioned as important players in urban politics and in the urban power structure.

Therefore, we believe that this book casts light on the urban history of the United States, not just on New York City.

Any study of twentieth-century U.S. urban economics or politics ought to include major chapters on Cosa Nostra, yet, in the past, many of them have not, perhaps because there is a brick wall between criminology and political science. We need to tear down the wall and build a bridge. We hope that this book will make it more difficult for urban scholars, whatever their discipline, to ignore the importance of organized crime in the twentieth-century lives of American cities.

NEW YORK CITY

New York City hardly needs introduction.[1] It is and has been, since the early nineteenth century, the nation's largest city in terms of population and urban economy. It consists of five boroughs: Manhattan, Bronx, Queens, Brooklyn, and Staten Island. The organized-crime racketeering recounted in this book took place in all five boroughs. There have always been neighborhoods in each of the boroughs where organized-crime figures live, socialize, and conduct business. Each of the five New York City–based Mafia families operates in all five boroughs.

New York City has a huge and diverse economy. (Its 1997 "gross city product" amounted to a staggering $330 billion.) For most of the twentieth century, it was an industrial giant and waves of new immigrants were absorbed by its factories. By the 1980s, the city's industrial base had substantially declined, and its economy had become postindustrial, dominated by the banking and finance and securities industries. Not only is New York City the nation's financial and legal center, it is also the center for fashion and the arts. It has a huge multibillion-dollar construction sector. Until the 1950s, it had the busiest seaport in the United States. Even today more cargo is shipped through John F. Kennedy Airport than through any other airport in the nation. The wholesale food markets attract retailers from all over the metropolitan area, and even the region. Its service industries, like waste hauling, are also large, lucrative, and complex. Its convention center, while no longer the largest in size, is still one of the country's most important and prestigious.

Politically, New York City is solidly Democratic; Democrats outnumber Republicans by more than six to one. Almost all the city's elected officials (with the significant exception, since 1994, of Mayor Rudolph Giuliani) are Democrats. For most of the twentieth century the local Democratic Party was dominated by Tammany Hall, a powerful political club that thrived on patronage and corruption. In the 1940s and 1950s, Cosa Nostra boss Frank Costello was a major powerbroker in Tammany Hall and in New York City's political scene. Since the demise of Tammany Hall in the 1960s, the Democratic Party has been far less cohesive. Politics is no longer dominated by political clubs and party bosses. As is true of American politics generally, parties are much less important than they once were; that means that interest groups are more so. In New York City, unions are among the leading interest groups. Throughout the twentieth century, New York City has been a union town and there is a very strong link between the unions and the Democratic Party. Labor unions consistently endorse Democratic candidates and contribute money and personnel to their campaigns.

Organized crime has long been a blight on the labor movement in the city. Many union locals and district councils have been dominated or strongly influenced by organized crime for decades. While there is little, if any, evidence that the organized-crime families directly received corrupt favors from politicians in exchange for financial and other support, we suggest that city politicians' and the city government's indifference to the growth and entrenchment of Cosa Nostra in the local economy at least intimates a comfortable modus vivendi. No mayoral administration (with the possible exception of Fiorello LaGuardia's) until the Giuliani administration made organized-crime control an important priority.

New York City, with approximately 310,000 full-time employees, has more employees per capita than any other U.S. city and spends more money per capita than any other. The city's operating budget for FY 1998 is $34 billion, larger than the budgets of all states except California and New York. This city provides more extensive services and engages in more extensive regulation than any other U.S. city. Nevertheless, until the Giuliani administration, the regulatory apparatus never focused on opposing, much less purging, organized crime.

New York City has one mayor, a unicameral city council, and a single police department. Each borough has its own independent district attorneys. Most of the organized-crime prosecutions and civil suits discussed in Part II were brought by federal prosecutors, but of those brought by the district attorneys, the Manhattan district attorney was by far the most active.

THE LAW ENFORCEMENT FRAMEWORK

New York City is home to a number of federal, state, and local law enforcement agencies. The U.S. Department of Justice has a U.S. attorney's office in every federal judicial district in the United States. There are two federal judicial districts in the city and therefore two U.S. attorney's offices: one in the Southern District of New York (S.D.N.Y.), in Manhattan; one in the Eastern District of New York (E.D.N.Y.), in Brooklyn. Each office is run by a U.S. attorney appointed by the president with the advice and consent of the U.S. Senate. The offices are staffed with dozens of assistant U.S. attorneys appointed by the two U.S. attorneys.

For most of the 1970s and 1980s, the Department of Justice also operated a number of organized-crime strike forces around the country; the federal Brooklyn Organized Crime Strike Force is referred to throughout this book. Early on the federal organized strike force in Manhattan was merged into the U.S. Attorney's Office, which thereafter handled organized-crime investigations and prosecutions along with its other responsibilities.

At the national level, the Federal Bureau of Investigation (FBI) is situated within the U.S. Department of Justice but operates more or less independently of the central department and the ninety-three U.S. attorneys. In other words, the FBI is responsible for criminal investigations and the U.S. attorneys are responsible for prosecuting cases; FBI agents do not take orders from U.S. attorneys and their assistants. For an organized-crime control program to operate effectively, both the FBI and the two U.S. Attorney's Offices had to be willing to make it a top priority and to cooperate with one another. In the 1980s, many joint ad hoc strike forces were formed between the FBI, the two U.S. Attorney's Offices, and—sometimes—other federal agencies as well as the New York City Police Department.[2] There are three FBI offices in the New York City area: Manhattan, Queens, and New Rochelle (a northern suburb). Until the late 1970s these offices operated quite independently, but as the organized-crime control program of the 1980s got into full swing, the offices' organized-crime investigations were coordinated under a single authority.

The FBI is a proactive law enforcement agency. It does not primarily respond to victims' complaints. It investigates crimes and crime problems that come to light in diverse ways, that violate federal law, and that are serious, high visibility, beyond the capacity of local law enforcement agencies, or simply outside any other agency's jurisdiction. The FBI has the capabilities to investigate these problems through the use of high-tech forensics, sting operations, undercover agents, informers, electronic surveillance, and financial-data analysis.

The FBI has a great deal of discretion as to which crimes or criminals it wishes to investigate. Unlike a city police department, it is in a position to prioritize, and must by necessity do so. Because it has great discretion in prioritizing, it can concentrate tremendous resources on particular crime problems. For decades, organized-crime control was not a high priority for the FBI. By the mid-1980s, it had become the top priority.

The FBI investigates and the U.S. attorneys prosecute conduct that violates federal law. At the beginning of the twentieth century, there were comparatively few federal crimes and only a small role for federal law enforcement.[3] Federal criminal law has since proliferated so dramatically that the FBI could find a legal basis for investigating a large percentage of crimes. RICO, the 1970 federal racketeering law, provided the FBI jurisdiction to investigate practically all suspected crimes committed by suspected organized-crime members and their associates.

The U.S. attorneys and assistant U.S. attorneys who work in New York City bring their cases to federal courts in either the Southern (Manhattan) or Eastern (Brooklyn) Districts of New York. The district court judges who preside over the courtrooms are appointed by the president with the advice and consent of the U.S. Senate; they have life tenure. Appeals from these federal courts are heard by the Second Circuit Court of Appeals. The only appeal beyond that is to the U.S. Supreme Court.

New York City's five district attorneys, nominated by their political parties, are elected to four-year terms by the citizens of their boroughs. They are independent of the mayor and of the New York State attorney general. In fact, they do not take orders from any higher authority, federal or state, and they are under no compulsion to cooperate with one another. To our knowledge, the five district attorneys, or even any two, have never joined in a coordinated organized-crime control program. Cooperation occurs strictly on a case-by-case basis.

The New York City district attorneys bring their cases to state courts. The supreme court is the highest level trial court; its judges are called justices. The justices are supposedly elected. But appointed "acting justices" outnumber their elected colleagues. Appeals are heard by an intermediate appellate court, the appellate division. Final appeal can be taken to the New York State Court of Appeals.

The New York City Police Department, with forty thousand officers, is by far the nation's largest. Like all front-line police departments, it is mostly reactive rather than proactive. Unlike the FBI, the NYPD must respond to all citizen reports of crime and to many service calls as well. Its top priority is street crime and order maintenance, not white-collar or organized crime, both of which are extremely labor-intensive and expensive to investigate. Nevertheless, the NYPD has more capacity for proactive and complex investigations than any other city police department in the United States. Its Organized Crime Bureau is long-standing and is staffed by some very experienced detectives. During the 1980s, there was unprecedented cooperation between the bureau and the FBI. In addition, it worked on some creative proactive investigations with the Manhattan District Attorney's Office.

In 1970, New York State created its own Organized Crime Task Force (OCTF). Although it had some limited successes during its early years, by the end of its first decade it was essentially moribund. In 1981, it was reorganized with headquarters in White Plains (a northern suburb) and field offices in Buffalo and Albany. Unlike the U.S. Attorney's Offices and the New York City District Attorney's Offices, after its restructuring the OCTF became a hybrid investigative and prosecutorial agency. During the 1980s and early 1990s, the heyday of the OCTF, the agency employed roughly twenty attorneys and fifty investigators, analysts, and accountants, as well as other professional staff, all working directly for the OCTF director.

The OCTF has statewide jurisdiction; it can carry out investigations and, with the consent of the local district attorney, bring state-court prosecutions anywhere in the state, including New York City. Until recently OCTF was independent of other federal, state, and local law enforcement agencies. Nevertheless, many of the organized-crime investigations referred to in Part II involved significant cooperation between the OCTF and federal and local investigative and prosecutorial offices.

OCTF often handed its investigations over to federal or city prosecutors. On occasion, OCTF lawyers prosecuted cases themselves or were "cross-designated" as assistant U.S. attorneys or as assistant district attorneys.

COSA NOSTRA

There is a lively debate among scholars as to whether American Italian organized crime was transplanted from Italy or is an essentially American phenomenon.[4] Those who favor the transplant theory point to the strong Mafia tradition in Sicily and to the role of Sicilian immigrants in developing organized-crime groups in the United States in the first decades of the twentieth century. Those who favor a nativism theory point to the ways in which the Italian American organized-crime groups connect to American society and its economy. There is no reason to treat these as rival theories. It is entirely plausible to hold that Italian American organized crime has its roots in Italian and especially Sicilian society and culture and, over the years, has adapted to American society and taken on an a distinctly American cast.

It should be emphasized that the American Cosa Nostra and the Italian Mafia are not now and never have been a single organization or even two branches of a single organization. During the twentieth century, they operated as separate and distinct organizations, although they have cooperated in certain criminal ventures, principally drug trafficking, as in the famous "pizza connection" case.[5]

It is now common to trace the emergence of the modern-day Cosa Nostra to the early 1930s. Much of this history was revealed in 1963 by Joseph Valachi, the first Cosa Nostra member to go public and the first to explain that the Italian organized-crime groups referred to themselves as "Cosa Nostra."[6] In this book we use the terms *Cosa Nostra, Mafia, mob,* and *Italian organized-crime families* interchangeably.

According to Valachi, in early 1930, Joseph Masseria and his associates decreed a death sentence for any underworld figure who originated from the locality of Castellammare de Golfo, Sicily. The warfare that followed was known as the "Castellammarese War." One faction was led by Masseria and the other by Salvatore Maranzano. Other gangs and underworld leaders linked themselves to one of the two factions. Vito Genovese, Lucky Luciano, Dutch Schultz, and Al Capone supported Masseria. In 1931, Masseria was assassinated on Luciano's orders, just before he could carry out his plan to kill Maranzano. Masseria's death concluded the "Castellammarese War." Maranzano called a meeting of almost four hundred gangsters in order to create a structure and forge rules for the organized-crime groups. The jurisdiction of various organized-crime "families" throughout the United States was recognized. Maranzano himself was assassinated only months after this historic meeting.

In the 1920s and 1930s there were a number of ethnically based (e.g., Jewish, Irish, German) organized-crime syndicates in the United States. Underworld figures like Arnold Rothstein and Dutch Schultz were among the most powerful organized-crime overlords. With the important exception of Meyer Lansky and a number of other Jewish gangsters and a few Irish American syndicates (e.g., the Hill Mob in Boston and the Westies in New York City), the non-Italian organized-crime groups did not make the transition into the post-Prohibition world.

The Italian American organized-crime groups had been infiltrating legitimate business since the 1930s, perhaps earlier. They were active on both sides of the labor struggles of the 1930s and emerged with strong footholds in many important labor unions.[7] By the 1950s, Cosa Nostra had achieved virtual hegemony in the underworld of organized crime. Italian American organized-crime "families" were entrenched in twenty-four large American cities and, to a greater or lesser extent shook down and "licensed" other criminals and supplied illicit goods and services, like drugs, prostitution, usurious loans, and pornography. Perhaps even more importantly, in the large urban areas they infiltrated labor unions, businesses, and industries. In addition, they participated in (usually Democratic Party) politics; the history of the Cosa Nostra is intertwined with the history of the urban political machines.

It is a major thesis of this book that the Italian American organized-crime families have been involved in industrial racketeering since the early twentieth century and that it is this racketeering, and the economic power and social and political status associated with it, that makes these organized-crime groups different from other organized-crime groups in the United States.

In the mid-1980s, twenty-four Italian organized-crime families were identified as active in the United States. Of these, no city had more than one family except New York, which had five: Genovese, Gambino,

Lucchese, Bonanno, and Colombo. FBI Director William Webster testified before the President's Commission on Organized crime (PCOC) in 1983 that there were approximately seventeen hundred "made members" of Cosa Nostra and perhaps ten times that number of associates. (Other estimates are as low as four associates for every made member.)

The 1967 Task Force on Organized Crime asserted that Cosa Nostra was a nationwide syndicate governed by a ruling "commission" comprising the bosses of the nation's most powerful families. In his 1983 biography, Joseph Bonanno also spoke about a nationwide commission.[8] However, other than a mysterious and bungled 1956 conference in Appalachin, New York, which was attended by Cosa Nostra figures from all over the country, we do not think there is empirical evidence to support its existence. It is best to think of Cosa Nostra as a melange of locally based crime families, each of which has exclusive jurisdiction in its territory.

This does not mean that there is no cooperation among the Cosa Nostra crime families. Indeed, electronic surveillance in the early 1980s revealed that the five New York City–based Italian American organized-crime families, or at least four of them, utilized a council or commission from time to time. But that commission's jurisdiction and authority are unclear. It functioned intermittently, like a court called upon to solve occasional disputes. Furthermore, from time to time crime bosses from outside New York City came to the city to consult with Tony Salerno, the apparent boss of the Genovese crime family,* about obtaining the New York City commission's assistance.

Each of the Cosa Nostra crime families is headed by a "boss" who exercises unchallenged authority (within the family) and whose position entitles him to a generous cut of all the members' revenues. The boss provides resources, sometimes including defense lawyers, for members and their families when needed. He also takes care of payoffs to politicians, police, and other officials necessary for keeping the family's operations running smoothly. In addition, he can approve or veto the proposal of one of his family's crews or individuals to embark upon a new criminal venture. Of course, the boss also represents the family at all interfamily "sit-downs" and negotiations.

*Until the end of the 1980s, law enforcement agencies believed that Salerno was the Genovese family boss. In the 1990s, it became apparent that Vincent "the Chin" Gigante had actually been the boss, but preferred to remain behind the scenes.

The second in command, acting as a deputy for the boss, is the "underboss." The third position in the family's ruling triumvirate is a senior advisor known as "consiglieri" or counselor. The boss chooses a limited number of "capos" (caporegimes), each with authority over a "crew" comprising soldiers ("made members" of Cosa Nostra, sometimes referred to as "good fellows" or "wise guys") and associates. All members of Cosa Nostra are of Italian descent and all are male. Associates, often as crew members, work with and for Cosa Nostra members, but they do not enjoy the rights and prerogatives of membership.

In effect (as Ron Goldstock has pointed out), the Cosa Nostra families provide their members a license to engage in various criminal schemes; the boss and the family ensure that other criminals will not interfere. The family provides a dispute resolution mechanism in the event that a member or associate finds himself in conflict with another organized-crime figure. And the family provides force and the threat of force to enforce the members' "legitimate" interests. Finally, the family also provides a limited system of welfare support.

Cosa Nostra is a secret organization that swears its members to omerta, a code of silence. Cosa Nostra does not hold open meetings or issue earnings statements. It does not maintain corporate headquarters or offices; it does not keep meticulous books and records. Thus, until Joseph Valachi defected from the mob and went public in 1963, no Cosa Nostra member had ever admitted to the organization's existence, much less described its history, structure, rules, and activities. With the exception of Ianni and Reuss-Ianni,[9] sociologists and criminologists have not been able to carry out case studies of Cosa Nostra; nor does the subject lend itself to quantitative analysis.

Cosa Nostra's longevity can be attributed to the ability of each family to seek out, develop, and exploit a range of criminal opportunities, including but not limited to the corruption and control of national and local labor unions, the creation and enforcement of cartels (through bribery and extortion), the supplying of illicit goods and services, and the carrying out of thefts, frauds, and hijackings. Cosa Nostra's foothold in both the criminal underworld and the upperworld of legitimate business, unions, and politics distinguishes it from other United States organized-crime groups that may participate successfully in illicit markets but have been uninterested or unable to entrench themselves in labor, business, and politics.

PART I

THE "MOBBING-UP" OF NEW YORK CITY

Part 1 consists of seven chapters. Chapters 2 through 7 each explain how Cosa Nostra infiltrated, wielded power in, and profited from a particular industry. Chapter 8 generalizes from the chapters that precede it and draws conclusions about Cosa Nostra's industrial racketeering.

We do not mean to leave the impression that the six industries are the only industries in New York City that have been infected with mob-orchestrated racketeering. Over the course of the twentieth century, Cosa Nostra has extended its tentacles into dozens of New York City–area industries. A 1930s investigation of organized crime in New York found a pervasive mob presence in the following industries: bead, cinder, cloth shrinking, clothing, construction, flower shops, Fulton Fish Market, funeral parlors, fur dressing, hod carriers, ice, kosher butchers, laundry, leather, live poultry, master barbers, milk, millinery, musical, night patrol, neckwear, newsstands, operating engineers, overall, paper box, paper hangers, shirtmakers, taxicabs, waterfront workers, and window cleaners.[1] Many of these industries no longer exist, and some that do still exist may no longer be influenced by the mob. It is clear, however, that organized crime's involvement in legitimate industry sweeps broadly and stretches over nearly a century.

The absence of a chapter on Cosa Nostra's notorious role in the International Longshoremen's Association (ILA) and the loading and unloading of seaborne cargo on New York City docks requires a word of explanation. The six industries examined in this book provide a portrait of New York City's organized-crime families in the city's economy as of the 1980s. In short, we chose to shine a light on racketeering in New York City at a single point in time rather than provide the reader with a pastiche of racketeering at different times throughout the century. Chapters 2 through 7 might be thought of as a series of case studies of industrial racketeering. But the chapters ought to be read holistically: taken together, they aim to portray the status and activities of New York City's five organized crime-families circa 1980–1985.

Still, Cosa Nostra's notorious role in New York City's waterfront is worthy of mention. In the 1940s and 1950s, the Port of New York handled more tonnage by far than any port in the United States. The pinnacle of the mob's domination of the docks was the 1930s–1950s. The story was immortalized in the famous film *On the Waterfront* (1954; produced by Sam Spiegel and starring Marlon Brando). In addition, the mob's control of the docks was brilliantly analyzed by Harvard sociologist Daniel Bell in his classic essay "The Racketeer-Ridden Longshoremen."[2]

Cosa Nostra's waterfront power base was the ILA. In the 1940s and 1950s, Brooklyn Local 1814, the largest ILA local in the country, was headed by Cosa Nostra capo Anthony "Tough Tony" Anastasio, brother of Albert Anastasia,[3] boss of the Gambino crime family and the "key waterfront crime boss in Brooklyn."[4] When Anastasio died in 1963, control of Local 1814 passed to Anthony Scotto, a son-in-law, who flourished in the union, in organized crime as a capo in the Gambino crime family, and in New York City political circles. Cosa Nostra used its influence in the ILA to determine who worked on the docks and, most important, which boats were unloaded and when, and which of the waiting trucks were loaded and when. Shippers had to pay off the mob to ensure that their ships were loaded and unloaded and to avoid labor unrest. Furthermore, Cosa Nostra orchestrated extensive and systematic thefts from the shipping.

In the mid-1950s, the New York and New Jersey Waterfront Commission was established to purge the Mafia from the waterfront and to clean up other abuses.[5] The commission was not successful; FBI investigations in the 1970s found that organized crime dominated the ILA locals up and down the East Coast. Today, in part because of Cosa Nostra's racketeering, very little shipping business remains in New York City.

Cosa Nostra exercised power in many other sectors of the economy. Historian John H. Davis, who has written extensively about organized crime, concludes that by 1965 Carlo Gambino, boss of the Gambino crime family, had amassed a conglomerate of interests in the legitimate business world:

> Gambino gained a lucrative foothold in Castro convertible furniture (exclusive control of mattresses used in Castro beds, and the trucking of Castro furniture from factory to showroom to retail outlets), Pride Meat supermarkets (run by his cousin and brother-in-law Paul Castellano), fuel oil trucking, pizza parlor equipment concerns, meat-packing companies—the list was endless.[6]

In 1979, *Wall Street Journal* reporter Jonathan Kwitny published *Vicious Circles*,[7] detailing Cosa Nostra racketeering in legitimate industries, including meatpacking, cheese importation, lunch carts, trucking, securities, alcohol, waterfront, cargo operations, and clothing manufacture in the metropolitan area. Kwitny described the intricate system of physical intimidation and economic coercion and cooperation that enabled the Cosa Nostra organized-crime families to establish themselves as integral players in the core industries of the city.

Even in the 1980s, the six industries covered in chapters 2 through 7 were not the only New York City industries or business sectors with an organized-crime presence. Had we unlimited space and the reader's unlimited patience, we could have included chapters on the moving and storage industry, linen service, restaurants, and nightclubs. Recently, Cosa Nostra has been active in street fairs and even in the securities industry.

The Feast of San Gennaro has taken place in Little Italy since 1916. It is New York City's largest and best-known street festival.[8] In 1996, following a joint investigation by the New York Police Department (NYPD) and the Federal Bureau of Investigation (FBI), a federal grand jury indicted nineteen members of the Genovese crime family for participating in the affairs of an enterprise (i.e., the family) through a pattern of criminal activity. The predicate offenses included fraud and extortion related to the annual San Gennaro festival. The indictment charged that the defendants skimmed money from the rent paid by vendors to the organizers of the street fair and defrauded the city on taxes.[9] While the indictment was pending, the Giuliani administration forced the San Gennaro Society, the festival's sole sponsor, to submit to review by a city-appointed monitor, John C. Sabetta. In his official report to the mayor, Sabetta charged that the society was not a genuine not-for-profit organization, that it violated the city's permit provisions, and otherwise failed to comport with its charter as a charitable organization.[10] In August 1996, the mayor replaced the society with a new sponsor and requested that the Roman Catholic Archdiocese oversee San Gennaro's finances to ensure that profits were donated to schools and parishes in lower Manhattan. Ultimately, James "Little Jimmy" Ida, the Genovese consigliere, and Nicholas Frustraci, a Genovese soldier, were convicted and sentenced to long prison terms.

In the 1990s, some Cosa Nostra members set their sights on Wall Street. High-ranking members of the Bonanno and Genovese crime families shook down the employees of a small brokerage firm to obtain large stock holdings at basement-level prices from a company called HealthTech. Allegedly, with the cooperation and support of HealthTech's CEO, Cosa Nostra members proceeded to inflate the trading price of the security and resell the shares to unsuspecting customers to whom the brokers had recommended the stock.[11] The scheme, called a "pump and dump," resulted in a $3 million loss to investors in seven states when the stock price fell precipitously. In 1997, the United States attorney for the Southern District of New York indicted seventeen individuals in a ninety-seven page, twenty-five count indictment for securities fraud, bank fraud, and extortionate activity.[12]

Having said that chapters 2 through 7 do not exhaust Cosa Nostra's activity in New York City's economy, we emphasize that Part 1 deals with the most important examples of Cosa Nostra's industrial racketeering. We aim to explain and document how Cosa Nostra relates to the unions and businesses in each of these industries, how it pulls money out, and how its operations flourished for so many decades without significant interference.

2

A Cosa Nostra Outfit

Seven Decades of Mob Rule in the Garment District

The maintenance of right conditions in New York's great garment industry has required eternal vigilance—not only of public officials but of labor organizations. . . . Despite the efforts of these agencies, some segments of the garment trade have become the spawning grounds for racketeers intent to make an illicit living off this enterprise. These elements sometimes gain a strong foothold in certain sections. . . . At times, violence and intimidation have donned the honorable cloak of unionism for the purpose of betraying it.[1]

—Justice Samuel H. Hofstadter's opinion in
Barton Trucking Corp. v. O'Connell (1958)

CHRONOLOGY

1920 Organized-crime boss Arnold Rothstein emerges as a major force in the Garment District. Clothing designers pay him to fight against labor unions, and labor unions pay him to derail company strikebreakers. When Rothstein is murdered in 1928, Louis "Lepke" Buchalter and Jacob "Gurrah" Shapiro take over his rackets and expand their power base to include ownership of design companies and control of trade associations and truckers' unions.

1950s The U.S. Justice Department investigates and prosecutes several trucking companies on antitrust charges. *United States v. Cloak and Suit Trucking Ass'n., Inc.* results in a consent decree, but enforcement is negligible and results unimpressive.

1957 Midlevel city employee in the Office of the New York City Commissioner of Licenses denies license renewal to mob-dominated trucking firm. The city wins the ensuing court battle, but the agency does not follow up this regulatory initiative.

1972 The New York City Police Department wages an aggressive parking-ticket campaign against the trucking cartel. Gambino sues New York City for violating his Fourteenth Amendment due process rights. The ticket campaign is dropped as part of the settlement.

1973 Federal and local law enforcement agencies launch Project Cleveland, a sting operation that reveals the role of the International Ladies Garment Workers Union (ILGWU) Local 120 and the Master Truckmen of America in maintaining Cosa Nostra's trucking cartel in the garment industry. New Jersey mobster Anthony "Tony Pro" Provenzano is convicted, but other cases fail.

1982 New York state senator Franz Leichter issues a report detailing Cosa Nostra's control over New York City's garment industry. He charges that Joey Gallo, the Gambino crime family consigliere, controls the Greater Blouse, Skirt and Undergarment Association.

1987 Joey Gallo is convicted of bribery and given long prison sentence.

1988 The Manhattan District Attorney's Office launches a sting operation by establishing a Garment District trucking company and a Chinatown contracting company. Investigators record incriminating conversations between the Gambino brothers.

1992 In mid-trial, Joseph and Thomas Gambino plead guilty to a single antitrust count. They agree to pay $12 million in fines, leave the industry permanently, and allow a "Special Master" to monitor the sale of their companies and to monitor the industry. Former New York City police commissioner Robert McGuire is appointed special master for a five-year term. He and Michael Slattery institute major reforms, set up a victim's compensation fund, and closely monitor garment industry operations.

1993 Thomas Gambino is convicted of racketeering, loan-sharking, and running illegal gambling operations in Connecticut and sentenced to five years in prison.

1997 Robert McGuire's five-year term as special master ends. He cites significant drops in trucking costs in the garment industry.

1998 The U.S. Attorney's Office for the Southern District of New York brings two separate indictments, both alleging the continuation of mob-run labor racketeering in the Garment District. One indictment charges the acting boss of the Lucchese crime family, Joseph "Little Joe" DeFede, and six other defendants, including New York attorney Irwin Schlacter, with imposing an annual "mob tax" of nearly half a million dollars on contractors and designers in exchange for labor peace. The second indictment charges five defendants, including a capo from the Genovese family and a capo from the Gambino family with extorting payoffs from a garment factory and its affiliates from 1991 through 1994.

Since the second half of the nineteenth century, the garment industry has been an important component of New York City's economy. The "needle trades" played a crucial role in absorbing millions of immigrants over the past century and a half. While tens of thousands of immigrants labored in sweatshops for minimal pay, many of them viewed employment in the Garment District as an opportunity to settle into American society and pursue entrepreneurial ambitions. Over time, the ethnic makeup of the workforce changed: in the 1840s, Irish and German workers dominated the garment trade; by the mid-nineteenth century, Jewish immigrants from Germany and Austria-Hungary were entering the industry in ever-increasing numbers. Russian and Polish Jews succeeded them, followed by Italians, African Americans, Puerto Ricans, Dominicans, and Chinese.[2]

In 1890, New York City's Garment District employed 83,000 people, and capital investments in the industry amounted to $630 million; in 1914, New York City employed 62 percent of the women's-apparel workers in the country.[3] The Garment District saw its heyday in the middle of the century, when it employed more than 300,000 people. While an expanding market for low-priced imported clothing eroded the city's dominant role in the decades that followed, the industry still employed 86,000 people in 1993.[4]

From the early twentieth century to the present day, the garment industry has proved fertile soil for organized crime. Arnold Rothstein, the first dominant organized-crime figure of the twentieth century, became involved in the industry when designer companies invited his thugs to crush emerging unions.[5] Rothstein ultimately played both sides of the fence by providing muscle to the unions. Following his murder in 1928, Louis "Lepke" Buchalter and Jacob "Gurrah" Shapiro took over his labor rackets and eventually gained full control over trade associations, truckers' unions, and designer firms.

Buchalter's and Shapiro's power was brought to the attention of the public by Thomas E. Dewey, who served as special prosecutor of the State of New York from 1935 to 1937, and as the Manhattan district attorney from 1938 to 1942. One of Dewey's biggest cases was the prosecution of Buchalter and Shapiro for extorting tens of millions of dollars from businesses.[6] Shapiro was convicted of extortion in the baking industry, another mob-dominated sector of the local economy. Federal prosecutors first tried and convicted Buchalter for racketeering in the fur industry; later, Dewey successfully prosecuted him for racketeering in the baking industry.[7] Ultimately, Brooklyn District Attorney William O'Dwyer convicted Buchalter of murdering Joseph Rosen, a truck driver in the garment industry who had cooperated with Dewey's investigations. Buchalter was executed in 1944.[8]

After the demise of Buchalter and Shapiro, Italian American organized-crime figures rose to power in the New York City garment industry. Among them, the seven most important were Thomas Lucchese, James Plumeri, Dominick Didato, Natale Evola, John "Johnny Dio" Dioguardi, and Thomas and Joseph Gambino.[9] Although Dewey prosecuted and convicted Plumeri and Dioguardi for extorting money from truckers working in the Garment District, the two served only brief jail sentences. Dewey referred to Dioguardi as a "young gorilla"[10] and "a racketeer on a long way up to 'success' in organized crime."[11]

Cosa Nostra maintained its power over the Garment District by operating a trucking cartel, which it enforced through control over a trucking trade association, the drivers' union, and a contractors' association. Profits derived from extortion and from ownership interests in trucking companies and designer firms. In the 1980s, capo Thomas Gambino and his brother Joseph were the most important Cosa Nostra figures in the

LINCOLN TUNNEL
GARMENT DISTRICT
0 miles 0.5
42 Street
39 Street
34 Street
Fifth Avenue
Eleventh
Tenth
Ninth
Broadway
N
MANHATTAN
14 Street
14 Street
HOLLAND TUNNEL
Houston
Broadway
CHINATOWN
Canal Street
WILLIAMSBURG BRIDGE
MANHATTAN BRIDGE

Garment District. Ultimately (as we shall see in chapter 9), they were brought down in an elaborate sting operation executed by the New York County District Attorney's Office.

HOW THE GARMENT INDUSTRY WORKS

New York City's Garment District consists of three major components: designers ("manufacturers") in midtown Manhattan (the "Garment District"), contractors in lower Manhattan's Chinatown, and trucking companies. All three of these businesses have been controlled or influenced by organized crime since the early decades of the twentieth century.

"Manufacturers" are businesses that design women's and men's fashions, contract for their production, and sell the finished goods to retailers. The term *manufacturer* is misleading, since most of these companies design but do not actually manufacture clothing. They include such household names as Liz Claiborne, Calvin Klein, and Donna Karan,[12] and numerous smaller and lesser-known companies.

Designers first assess the fashion trends and develop designs for the clothing they will sell for that season. Second, they purchase large rolls or bolts of fabric known as "piece goods" from suppliers from all over the country, which are delivered by the colorful "pushboys" who are a Garment District institution. Third, designers employ cutters,[13] who use electric knives or heavy shears, to cut the fabric into individual pieces of a dress or blouse that, when sewn together, result in the final product. Fourth, designers send this cut-work to contractors, who might be thought of as manufacturers. They sew the cut-work together into a finished product and affix the designers' labels. Finally, the designers place their apparel with retail outlets. Throughout this process, timeliness is essential because the clothes have a narrow window of marketability; today's trend-setting garments are tomorrow's castoffs. If apparel is not delivered on schedule, a season's business may be lost, or stores may fill up their racks with other items. Thus, designers are highly vulnerable to threats of delay.

Contractors essentially are sewing factories, which receive raw materials from the designers and make them into finished garments. In recent decades, the majority of contractors are located in Chinatown "sweatshops," where Chinese women, some of them illegal immigrants, use sewing machines to stitch cut-work.[14]

Trucking companies transport the cut-work from midtown designers to Chinatown contractors. They also take finished apparel back to the Garment District for inspection or transport it directly to retailers. Over the years, the Gambino crime family expanded its garment interests to New Jersey, where additional sweatshops, trucking companies, and warehouse outlets are located.

COSA NOSTRA AS BANKER

Cosa Nostra served as a bank for many garment industry participants. All five New York City Cosa Nostra crime families engage in loansharking.[15] Many designers and contractors are undercapitalized. If costs escalate sharply, orders dry up, or fashions change, firms find themselves short of cash.[16] Given the precarious nature of the business, and the sudden vulnerability of the companies when cash needs arise, banks are not often a viable option. Moreover, many firms, especially Chinatown contractors, are not considered good risks.

Organized crime kept a steady supply of cash flowing in the garment industry, in effect serving as its covert financier and banker. Capos distributed cash to soldiers charging interest of perhaps 0.5 percent a week. The soldiers then distributed the money to street-level loansharks, who lent it out at rates of approximately 3 to 5 percent a week. At such high rates, the interest ("vigorish," or "vig") added up rapidly so that the borrower paid interest as high as 222 percent a year.[17] Companies that could not meet their payments were sometimes forced to place a few "no-show" workers on the payroll, or share or cede ownership of their firms to organized-crime figures.

Financial services often provided Cosa Nostra's first contact with new design firms and contractors; other services followed. The design firms needed sewing services, the contractor shops needed raw materials, and both needed trucking services. Cosa Nostra's trucking companies often provided the only means by which contractors could obtain orders from designers. A new contractor would ask a trucker to help the contractor secure sewing work from the midtown designers; the trucker would oblige and transport a shipment of cut-work from midtown to

Chinatown. Having once accepted the assistance, that sewing factory was "married" for life to that trucker, who would provide all future shipping services.

Manufacturers had the same experience. For example, when Aaron Freed opened his sportswear firm, the Gambino brothers helped him find contractors to do his sewing work. When he had trouble paying bills, the Gambinos let his credit run for months. Even when he used a "gypsy" trucker, as he did occasionally, he still had to pay his assigned trucker as if the latter had performed the work.[18]

COSA NOSTRA'S TRUCKING CARTEL AND THE "PROPERTY-RIGHTS" SYSTEM

The mob's power in the Garment District stemmed from its control of the trucking companies and influence over their drivers. Members of the trucking cartel provided essential services to the midtown designers and Chinatown contractors. The coercive marriage of contractors and designers to truckers constituted an elaborate "property-rights" system enforced by the trucking cartel. In reality, the truckers themselves decided which trucking company would service each Chinatown contractor and Garment District manufacturer. Cosa Nostra–controlled trucking companies treated their customers as property.[19] The property-rights system became so institutionalized that trucking companies, through front organizations described below, signed *written* agreements allocating territories and customers.[20] Fixed prices were maintained and competitive behavior was suppressed through financial penalties and violence.

The sanctity of "marriage" was enforced through economic coercion and, occasionally, through intimidation and violence. For example, if a contractor sought to terminate its relationship with its trucking partner, the truckers' cartel would ensure that the firm received no work from midtown designers—in effect, an economic death sentence. The unhappy contractor would have no choice but to return to its former partner. On occasion, a contractor was so anxious to break free of its trucker that it shut down in one area and reopened elsewhere. If this ruse was discovered, the contractor would be forced back into the arms of its original marriage partner. If a designer tried to divorce its contractor, no contractors or truckers would come courting; the only options were to reconcile with the original trucker, close the company, or appeal to Cosa Nostra bosses to work out a solution.

In addition to price fixing, truckers had two other lucrative schemes. The first involved the billing system. The designers had to pay up front, not after services were provided. Thus, when a Chinatown contractor received an order from a designer, the designer subtracted its trucking cost from its payment to the contractor.[21] Contractors, frozen out of the pricing process, never knew exactly what it cost to have cut-work shipped to and from Chinatown.

"Round-trip pricing" also enriched the truckers. Cut-work had to be transported from the contractor's shop back to the Garment District or directly to retailers. The designers had to pay for the round-trip, regardless of whether the trucker actually moved the finished apparel. A contractor who needed to rush finished goods uptown might not be able to wait for its assigned trucker.[22] If the contractor delivered the goods personally, or employed another person to do so, the assigned trucker still had to be paid. In fact, by billing designers rather than contractors, truckers ensured that the latter would not have an opportunity to object until after such payments had been made.

THE MASTER TRUCKMEN OF AMERICA (MTA) AS CARTEL ENFORCER

Cosa Nostra relied on a trade association to enforce the cartel. The Master Truckmen of America (MTA), controlled by the Colombo family, policed and managed Cosa Nostra's trucking cartel. Any "alien" truckers who tried to break into the industry faced an array of anticompetitive practices. The MTA would inform would-be entrants to the Garment District that they could not do business there; some lucky or connected firms were allowed to join the cartel, but unless they had bought out a cartel member, they would have no customers. If a trucking company refused to join the MTA, or failed to pay its dues, the drivers—who were all members of the International Ladies Garment Workers Union (ILGWU) local—would strike. If that was insufficient to bring the rebel trucker into line, trucks would be vandalized or stolen. Cartel truckers also engaged in "monopolistic parking practices,"[23] blocking curbs or entire streets so that an "unconnected" firm could not deliver its shipments. Thus, the trucking cartel ensured that the marriage system would not be subverted and that Cosa Nostra's domination of garment trucking remained absolute.

COSA NOSTRA'S POWER OVER THE TRUCK DRIVERS: ILGWU LOCAL 102

ILGWU Local 102, which represented the truck drivers, was another base of Cosa Nostra's control in the garment industry. While the ILGWU as a whole had remained mostly free of racketeering throughout its history, the garment industry's leading trade magazine, *Women's Wear Daily,* called Local 102 "an active tool of labor racketeers." Sol C. Chaikin, the president of the ILGWU in the 1970s, admitted that "we have never been able to control 102."[24]

Local 102 served the mob in three critical ways: it helped the MTA preserve Cosa Nostra's trucking cartel; it ensured that Cosa Nostra trucking companies avoided labor disputes with other ILGWU locals; and it prevented any other union from entering the industry.[25] If a trucker refused to join the MTA or to succumb to its anticompetitive demands, the MTA would arrange for a Local 102 job action. Noncompliant truckers were soon brought to heel; there was zero tolerance for attempts to undercut Cosa Nostra's inflated rates in cut-work trucking. This perverse alliance between the employers' trade association and the employees' trade union guaranteed Cosa Nostra's control over the industry. An incident that occurred during the Project Cleveland investigation reveals how Local 102 served the interests of the MTA. As soon as a government undercover agent purchased a trucking company, MTA President Frank Wolf threatened a Local 102 strike unless the new owner paid 10 percent of the purchase price to the MTA.[26]

Cosa Nostra's control over Local 102 ensured that Cosa Nostra trucking companies enjoyed labor peace. If an ILGWU local struck a mob-controlled company, replacement drivers managed to get through the picket lines. Some of the drivers were actually members of Local 102, or it would turn out that union officials had ordered strikers to stay off the picket lines just when the replacement drivers arrived. In either event, the union would lose the strike.

Significantly, not all of the drivers employed by mob-owned trucking companies belonged to a union. Sometimes high-ranking organized crime members like Thomas Gambino ran "double-breasted" shops, employing a mixture of unionized and nonunionized drivers. These mobsters used their favored status as garment industry power players to avoid paying union-scale wages.

Cosa Nostra also used Local 102 to prevent any other union from representing garment truck drivers. In one reported case, Matthew Eason, a union organizer and president of a local affiliate of the United Warehouse Industrial and Affiliated Trades Employees Union, filed a petition with the National Labor Relations Board (NLRB), seeking to have his union represent the employees of two employment agencies. However, Eason ran into complications because the employment agencies were supplying workers to Interstate Dress Carriers, a New Jersey–based trucking company with ties to the Lucchese Family.[27] Eason was soon approached by representatives of Interstate Dress and the union. They offered him bribes to withdraw his labor petition and threatened him with physical harm if he refused.[28]

CONTROLLING THE CONTRACTORS: THE GREATER BLOUSE, SKIRT, AND UNDERGARMENT ASSOCIATION

Cosa Nostra used the Greater Blouse, Skirt, and Undergarment [Employer] Association (Greater Blouse), which represented the interests of approximately one hundred unionized contracting companies, to control the Chinatown contractors.[29] Greater Blouse brokered collective bargaining agreements between the contractors, and the ILGWU and sought generally to resolve labor problems.[30] In addition, Greater Blouse entered into agreements with other trade associations, including trucking companies and Seventh Avenue designers.

In his 1982 report investigating the mob's role in the Garment District, New York State Senator Franz Leichter charged that the Gambino family used Greater Blouse to solidify its domination of labor and expand its infiltration. Joseph N. Gallo, the business representative and de facto head of the association, was also the Gambino crime family's longtime consigliere.[31] Since Cosa Nostra firmly controlled the association and, by extension, labor contracts in the industry, contractors either paid a hefty fee to join Greater Blouse or found another line of work.

A May 1983 intercepted telephone conversation between Gambino crime-family boss Paul Castellano and Thomas F. Gambino[32] indicated that their family shared control of the association with two other New

York crime families. Gambino told Castellano, "You got a third in it [Greater Blouse], the West Side has a third in it and Jerry has a third in it." According to prosecutors, the "West Side" referred to the Genovese family, and "Jerry" was the Colombo family's acting boss Gennero "Jerry" Langella.[33]

In 1976, the Chinese Garment Makers Association (CGMA) brought a lawsuit in state supreme court charging that Greater Blouse's officers had entered into an agreement with a major designer trade association aimed at diverting contractors' profits into mob bank accounts.[34] The agreement required the designers to deduct more than 7 percent of the money owed to the contractors and send it directly to Greater Blouse, which ostensibly used the sum to cover "administrative expenses" before forwarding the remaining amount, if any, to the sewing factories. According to the CGMA, the "administrative expenses" were mob payoffs. The CGMA claimed the scam was even worse than it appeared because Greater Blouse inflated the deducted amount by basing it on the contractors' gross proceeds—the contract price *plus* overhead, transportation costs, and profits. This practice, according to contractors, allowed the association to siphon off as much as $30 million annually from the contractors' shops.

The CGMA also charged that Greater Blouse denied members access to the association's rules, procedures, and financial statements and that contractors were denied their rights and were unable to protect their interests. But the judge ruled against them, stating that the "challenged method of electing the directors did not violate state law."[35]

Cosa Nostra also used its control over Greater Blouse to obtain no-show jobs from member firms. Such "jobs" provided valuable patronage and legitimate cover for racketeers.[36] Cosa Nostra further used Greater Blouse as a cash cow by diverting contractors' membership dues into its own coffers. At $50 a month for each of the seven hundred members, these dues amounted to $35,000 each month, or $420,000 a year.

COSA NOSTRA'S PROFITS: INTERESTS IN TRUCKING AND DESIGNER FIRMS

The Cosa Nostra crime families profited from ownership of trucking companies. Thomas Lucchese, a Cosa Nostra crime-family boss from 1953 until his death in 1967, controlled Champion Trucking and passed it on to his heirs in the Lucchese family. Another major Lucchese figure, James Plumeri, owned Ell-Gee Carriers Corporation and Barton Trucking Company. Natole Evola, a powerful member of the Bonanno crime family, owned Amity Garment Delivery Company and had interests in Trinity Trucking, Belmont Garment, ECCO Trucking, and Milton Feinberg Trucking.[37]

Thomas F. Gambino, widely regarded as the most powerful organized-crime figure in the Garment District, held ownership interests in a number of trucking and design companies. At various times he controlled no fewer than eight garment trucking firms: Astro Carriers, Major Dependable Delivery, Dynamic Delivery, JHT Leasing, Clothing Carrier's Corporation, Greenberg's Express, GRG Delivery, and Consolidated Carriers, the largest hauler of garments in New York City.[38] In 1974, *Women's Wear Daily* charged that all five New York Cosa Nostra families held interests in garment trucking.[39]

Some Cosa Nostra figures also held ownership interests in design firms. As early as the 1930s, Thomas Lucchese was infiltrating design firms through threats and violence. Together with his son-in-law Thomas Gambino, he held significant interests in both Sherwood Fashions and Budget Dress Corporation; when testifying before the McClellan Committee, Lucchese admitted his interests in garment design companies.[40] After Lucchese's death in 1967, his garment-industry companies passed to the new Lucchese family boss, Vittorio Amuso, who allowed high-ranking Lucchese figure Michael Pappadio to monitor and control the family's garment-industry interests until 1989.[41] Other prominent organized-crime figures who have held interests in the garment industry include Carlo Gambino (Arlene Dress Company),[42] and Paul Castellano (G & I Dress Company).[43]

These garment-industry interests were lucrative for Cosa Nostra. For example, in a 1994 racketeering, conspiracy, and murder case against Lucchese figure Anthony Casso, two witnesses testified that from 1987 onward, Casso and Amuso received millions of dollars in cash from the Lucchese family's garment-industry businesses.[44] When, in 1993, Thomas Gambino was sentenced to a five-year prison term for racketeering, loan-sharking and illegal gambling, he was worth an estimated $100 million;[45] much of this fortune derived from his garment-industry interests.

If, however, Cosa Nostra determined that a particular design firm was not worth keeping in operation, a "bust out" (bankruptcy fraud) stripped the company of all its assets and left creditors in the cold. In his 1982 report, New York State Senator Franz Leichter reconstructed the details of a bust out orchestrated by Michael Pappadio. Together with two associates and legitimate garment-industry designers, Pappadio incorporated a firm called Fashion Page. In 1975, when the firm's business began to decline, Pappadio's friends and associates supposedly lent the company $275,000. Soon thereafter, two fires destroyed Fashion Page. The first, in May of 1975, led to an insurance recovery of $300,000, the majority of which went to repaying the Pappadio loans rather than Fashion Page's numerous creditors. Seven months later, another fire destroyed all the company's books and records. Two weeks after that, the business closed for good.[46]

THE U.S. DEPARTMENT OF JUSTICE'S ANTITRUST SUITS

On April 30, 1951, the Antitrust Division of the U.S. Department of Justice (DOJ) filed two separate civil antitrust suits against the garment industry's truckers.[47] One suit attacked the marriage system that dominated the trucking of men's coats and suits; the other targeted the trucking of women's garments.[48] The litigation languished for more than four years until, in October 1955, the parties signed consent decrees that prohibited a range of anticompetitive practices. The garment truckers agreed to open to DOJ attorneys all books, ledgers, accounts, correspondence, memoranda, and other records and documents. The trade associations agreed to submit written reports to the government regarding their compliance with the terms of the settlement. The federal court retained jurisdiction so that if the defendants engaged in the same illegal practices, the government would not have to file a new lawsuit. Instead, the Antitrust Division could merely "apply to the Court at any time for such further orders or directions as may be necessary or appropriate for the . . . carrying out" of the judgment.[49]

The consent decrees raised expectations that were not realized. Rather than driving organized crime out of the Garment District, the decrees merely encouraged the mob to become more surreptitious; written documents that formerly had spelled out flagrant illegal practices were replaced by unwritten rules of cooperation.[50] The marriage system did not change. Nearly thirty years later, garment truckers were continuing to fix prices, allocate customers, prevent designers and contractors from selecting shippers, and to harass and to bar competitors from the industry.

NEW YORK CITY'S REGULATORY FAILURE

Operation of a common-carrier trucking firm in New York City historically required a license issued by the commissioner of licenses.[51] In 1957, for reasons that are unclear, the commissioner briefly used his licensing authority to oppose organized crime. Barton Trucking Corporation, a firm that operated five trucks in the Garment District, filed a routine application for a public cart license.[52] For decades, the commissioner had always granted such licenses upon request. The statute made citizenship the only qualification for a public cartman's license and did not appear to give the commissioner discretion.[53] However, Barton Trucking was controlled by James Plumeri, a former associate of Buchalter and Shapiro and a well-known racketeer in the garment industry. Commissioner Bernard J. O'Connell pointed to Plumeri's prior conviction for extortion and other racketeering-related crimes in the Garment District, found Plumeri to be unfit as a public cartman, and denied Barton Trucking a license.

The decision set off a round of litigation. Plumeri's lawsuit charged that the commissioner's denial deprived Barton Trucking of a valuable property right without due process of law; that the commissioner had acted arbitrarily and beyond his powers; and that public carriers in the garment trucking industry were exempt from licensing requirements.[54]

The trial court rejected all of the plaintiff's claims and affirmed the license denial. Judge Samuel H. Hofstader's opinion decried organized crime's infiltration of legitimate industries: "some segments of the garment trade have become the spawning grounds for racketeers intent to make an illicit living off this enterprise." The judge noted that "the license commissioner, like other public officials, [was] aware that the hoodlum empire extends into many territories."[55] In upholding the denial of Plumeri's license, the court held that the commissioner had the power to consider an applicant's character (or lack of it) when exercising his licensing authority.

Plumeri dominated the next round. In December 1958, the appellate division reversed the lower court's ruling, finding that the commissioner had exceeded his authority under the public cart–licensing statutes.[56] Although the appellate court noted that Plumeri's criminal background might render him unfit to operate in the garment-trucking business, the court found that the licensing commissioner had arrogated power that was not his to wield.[57] However, a year later, the Court of Appeals, New York's highest court, reversed the appellate division and reinstated Hofstader's ruling, thereby leaving Plumeri and Barton Trucking without an operating license. The Court of Appeals held that although the commissioner did not have explicit power to consider an applicant's character, "power to grant a license necessarily implies power to withhold it for good cause."[58] Thus, the commissioner was "not only empowered, but indeed . . . duty bound" to inquire into the personal character of proposed licensees,[59] and Plumeri's criminal record provided a wholly adequate reason to deny Barton Trucking's application.[60]

Unfortunately, city officials did not use this important affirmation of their licensing authority to advance the attack on organized crime. It was not until the Giuliani administration came into office in 1994, that regulatory power was again aimed at purging organized-crime figures from legitimate industries.

THE PROJECT CLEVELAND TRUCKING INVESTIGATION

In March 1973, with the cooperation of William Aronwald, head of DOJ's Joint Strike Force Against Organized Crime in Manhattan, the New York City Police Department purchased a garment-trucking firm known as Gerro Trucking in order to obtain evidence of organized crime's involvement in the garment industry.[61] Law enforcement officials established Herman Goldfarb, an ex-convict, as the president and owner of Gerro Trucking, wired him and his offices with recording devices, and waited to see who might fall into the trap.[62]

Through the duration of Project Cleveland—from March 1973 to approximately August 1974—law enforcement agents taped thousands of hours of conversations, which included incriminating evidence against a number of trucking industry figures. By October 1975, a federal grand jury had indicted eight people on charges of conspiracy and extortion. In one indictment, the federal government charged MTA Director Frank Wolf with extorting a $5,000 payment from Gerro Trucking. A union official was also indicted for allegedly cooperating with

Wolf in threatening to stage a strike against Gerro Trucking if an extortionate payment was not made. Matthew "Matty the Horse" Ianniello, a captain in the Genovese crime family and Frank Wolf's assistant, as well as a business agent for ILGWU Local 102, was also named in the indictment. Project Cleveland eventually led to a labor-racketeering conviction of New Jersey Teamster official and Cosa Nostra capo Anthony "Tony Pro" Provenzano.[63] In its scope, degree of local and federal cooperation, and inventiveness, this sting operation was a promising remedial effort.

But Project Cleveland failed to make a serious inroad against Cosa Nostra's garment-industry interests. Most of the high-ranking organized-crime figures in the garment industry remained untouched. To be sure, Provenzano's conviction was an important victory for federal prosecutors. Yet that case had little relation to mob influence in the Garment District. Among the Project Cleveland defendants directly involved in the Garment District, four men—including Frank Wolf and Matthew Ianiello—were acquitted in November of 1976. This was a major blow to law enforcement efforts because the MTA played a key role in Cosa Nostra's garment-industry operations, and because Wolf was the most important defendant in the case.

Trying to put a positive spin on the government's effort, Aronwald emphasized that Project Cleveland had led to the imprisonment of individual mobsters and spawned similar sting operations that produced additional convictions.[64] While it is true that Project Cleveland disrupted organized crime's operations in the Garment District slightly, major Cosa Nostra figures—the Gambino brothers in particular—remained untouched and the mob's domination of the Garment District remained rock solid.

CONCLUSION

Perhaps no other industry is more bound up with the history and peoples of New York City than the garment industry. Perhaps in no other industry did organized-crime figures operate so openly. This was due to the fact the Gambino brothers and other organized-crime figures owned their own companies and because the garment industry's legitimate institutions were so interwoven with the mob-sponsored truckers' cartel. The MTA, the ILGWU Local 102, and Greater Blouse all collaborated with the mob; each reinforced and strengthened the trucking cartel, and each funneled money into the coffers of organized crime. The marriages of trucking companies to manufacturers and contractors produced a property-rights system enforced by Cosa Nostra through the trucking cartel. While Thomas Dewey's prosecutions in the 1930s and 1940s and the Project Cleveland prosecutions in the 1970s put some organized-crime figures behind bars, the government's best shots were not nearly enough to weaken Cosa Nostra.

The *Barton Trucking* case might have provided New York City with a tremendously important tool to use against organized crime. The New York State Court of Appeals had held that the city could base denial of trucking licenses solely on applicant character. Trucking companies owned or operated by known mobsters could be purged from the industry. No arrests, prosecutions, or long trials were needed; a mob-controlled business could be crippled by an administrative decision. Having established its authority over licensing garment truckers, New York City officials did not attempt to drive Cosa Nostra–owned truckers out of the garment trade. In fact, organized crime only became more entrenched in garment trucking in the ensuing decades. Why then did the city not use its regulatory and licensing power against organized crime? Unfortunately, we can confidently offer no answer to that question. However, we believe that an answer should be sought in the symbiotic relationship between city politicians and Cosa Nostra.

3

Fishy Business

The Mafia and the Fulton Fish Market

[Operating] in a frontier atmosphere . . . the Fulton Fish Market is a sovereign entity where the laws of economic power and physical force, not the laws of New York City, prevail.[1]

—Frank Wohl, court-appointed monitor of the Fulton Fish Market, 1990

CHRONOLOGY

1883 The Fulton Fish Market opens in lower Manhattan.

1923 Joseph "Socks" Lanza establishes himself as the de facto boss at the Fulton Fish Market by controlling Local 359 of the United Seafood Workers, Smoked Fish and Cannery Union.

1933 The U.S. attorney for the Southern District of New York charges Local 359, twenty-four companies, three trade associations, and fifty-four individuals operating at the market with extortion and running a cartel in violation of the Sherman Act. Among the defendants is Joseph "Socks" Lanza, a capo in the Genovese family, Local 359's business agent, and "czar" of the Market. Many defendants enter guilty pleas, including Lanza, who serves two years in prison.

1938 Lanza is convicted on federal racketeering charges; five years later he is found guilty of extortion and remains in prison until 1950. He is returned to prison for violating parole by associating with organized-crime figures.

1968 Lanza, still on the union payroll, dies. He has been the undisputed ruler of the Fulton Fish Market for forty years.

1974 Carmine Romano, Lanza's successor as the Genovese crime family's manager of the Fulton Fish Market, becomes secretary-treasurer of Local 359.

1975 Carmine Romano establishes the Fulton Patrol Association, ostensibly to prevent thefts of seafood. For this "protection," wholesalers pay $1300 weekly to the thieves who regularly stole from them.

Local 359 officials extract payoffs, characterized as Christmas presents, from wholesalers. The money, supposedly earmarked for local members, goes directly to the Genovese crime family.

1979 At the direction of the U.S. attorney for the Southern District of New York, the New York City Police Department, the U.S. Internal Revenue Service, and the U.S. Department of Labor undertake a joint investigation of organized crime at the Fulton Fish Market. The investigation results in the conviction of forty-four defendants and fines totaling $331,000.

1980 Carmine Romano relinquishes his position as secretary-treasurer of Local 359 to his brother Peter. Carmine becomes trustee of Local 359's welfare and pension funds.

1981 Carmine and Peter Romano, as well as Local 359 as an entity, are targeted by federal law enforcement officials in *United States v. Romano,* the most significant case arising out of the 1979 investigation of Genovese operations in the Fulton Fish Market. Both brothers are convicted. Carmine receives a twelve-year prison sentence; Peter, eighteen months.

1982 United Seafood Workers, Smoked Fish and Cannery Union places Local 359 under trusteeship and strips Carmine and Peter Romano of their union positions, but the election of their brother Vincent to the Local 359 presidency perpetuates the influence of the Genovese crime family.

Mayor Edward I. Koch transfers the responsibility for collecting rent payments from wholesalers at the Fulton Fish Market to the South Street Seaport Corporation, but rents are frozen for ten years.

1987 With evidence generated by Operation Sea Probe, a joint FBI and NYPD investigation, U.S. Attorney Rudolph Giuliani files a civil RICO suit against twenty-nine defendants, Local 359, its officers, and the Genovese crime family. One year later, most of the defendants enter into a consent judgment; a default judgment is entered against the rest. The court appoints Frank Wohl to act as the market administrator.

1990 Wohl's report cites continuing rampant racketeering at the market. He imposes fines on companies and individuals for violating the consent decree and calls for comprehensive city regulation.

Eight loading companies earn $5 million annually by charging retailers exorbitant rates to park in city-owned lots around the market.

1995 New York City Council passes Local Law 50, Mayor Giuliani's reform bill, empowering the city to regulate, investigate, license, register, and expel businesses and individuals from the Fulton Fish Market. Despite retaliatory labor strikes, court challenges, and picketing, many reforms are implemented. The city removes six unloading companies from the market because of their connection to organized crime and replaces them with a city-approved company.

The New York City Department of Business Services becomes the landlord of the market; New York Economic Development Corporation serves as agent. A new lease agreement raises wholesalers' rents substantially. The city gains $1.3 million in revenue. Two of the mob-affiliated loading companies are removed from the market.

1996 Six of the eight remaining loading companies are removed from the market. The two remaining loading companies, licensed by the city, agree to reduce their charges by approximately 70 percent.

1997 Local Law 28 is passed to extend Local Law 50's reforms to the city's other wholesale food markets and to expand the city's power to regulate the Fulton Fish Market.

HOW THE FISH MARKET WORKS

The Fulton Fish Market is the oldest and largest wholesale fish market in the United States. It was organized in 1833 to serve fishing fleets on the East River near Fulton Street. However, as early as 1924, some suppliers were trucking seafood to the market. Today, no seafood is delivered directly by ship; rather, refrigerated trucks bring seafood from around the world to the market in boxes of one hundred pounds or less, some of which is flown in from abroad. The market runs from 10:00 P.M. to 10:00 A.M., Sunday through Friday. It consists of approximately seventy "stalls"—storefronts with stand space out front where most of the actual selling occurs. By morning, the stands are emptied and the buildings closed; only a few scattered fish and wooden wholesaler signs remain to hint at the overnight bustle. More than five hundred people work at the market. Approximately two hundred million pounds of seafood are delivered to the market annually. Estimates of the dollar amount of seafood sold annually vary from $200 million to $2 billion.[2]

The fish market occupies two blocks of South Street in lower Manhattan, stretching from Fulton Street north to Peck Slip, underneath the FDR Drive overpass (see map, p. 147). Approximately half the wholesalers' stalls are housed at street level in two rundown, sheet-metal warehouses owned by New York City: the 1907 Tin Building or "Old Market Building," and the 1939 "New Market Building." Across South Street, opposite the two main warehouses, fifteen wholesalers lease separate garage-like stalls in newer, city-owned buildings, and others operate from their own buildings.[3] At the end of 1998 there were approximately sixty wholesalers operating at the Fulton Fish Market.

Wholesale seafood vendors at the Fulton Fish Market, like firms in the garment industry, are extremely vulnerable to threats of delay. Time is of the essence in selling fish. First, fishermen sell their catch to suppliers. The suppliers pack fish in boxes and use freight-hauling companies to transport it to the Fulton Fish Market. Fish from the West Coast and abroad is trucked in from area airports. Beginning at 10:00 P.M., truckers deliver frozen and fresh seafood in vehicles ranging from huge forty-foot refrigerated trailer trucks to small vans.[4] Each week, approximately four hundred vehicles belonging to dozens of trucking companies and suppliers transport seafood to the market. They line up along South Street north of the market and wait to be unloaded.[5]

Prior to the city's 1990s reforms, the unloaders had tremendous leverage over truckers and suppliers.[6] It is tiring, expensive, and frustrating for truckers to sit for hours waiting for a service that they could easily provide themselves. The time at which a truck is unloaded directly affects the day's profit because fish displayed at the wholesalers' stalls by 3:00 A.M. commands a higher price than fish displayed at 6:00 A.M.. Thus, truckers were willing to pay to be accorded priority.

After the seafood is unloaded, it is delivered to wholesalers' stalls. The wholesalers employ approximately eight hundred workers, called "journeymen," who prepare the seafood for display, sell it, and deliver it to their customers' vehicles. Many of these workers are members of Local 359 of the United Seafood Workers, Smoked Fish and Cannery Union.[7]

By 3:00 A.M., the deliveries are displayed and hundreds of "retailers" from restaurants and retail seafood stores begin arriving at the market. Until the recent reforms, eleven loading companies, which were distinct entities from the unloading companies, assigned each retailer to a particular parking area in one of the eleven designated parking zones, located on public property. The retailers had no say in where they would be permitted to park and often were unable to change zones. The retailers leave their vehicles unlocked and walk from stall to stall, selecting seafood from the various wholesaler displays. The wholesalers' journeymen use hand trucks and "hi-los" to take the fish to the retailers' parked vehicles. There the journeymen load the fish into the vehicles. Retailers paid fees ranging from $5 to $50 per night to the loaders to keep their vehicles and fish secure from vandalism or theft.

Suppliers are also somewhat dependent on the goodwill of the wholesalers, who sell their catch primarily for cash, at prices reached in on-the-spot negotiations with retailers and restaurant owners. Prices vary according to quality, quantity, and demand. The wholesalers, who—in effect—operate on consignment or commission, take a fee from each retailer's or restaurateur's payment and remit the remainder to the supplier.[8] Thus, the supplier does not know in advance the price his fish will command and must rely on the wholesaler's negotiating skills and honesty. Although the situation is changing, most of the market's sales involve cash.

HOW COSA NOSTRA CONTROLLED THE FULTON FISH MARKET

The Fulton Fish Market has been a revenue source and a power base for Cosa Nostra since the early twentieth century. The Genovese crime family has influenced every facet of the market's operations since the 1920s. This influence flowed from control of Local 359 of the United Seafood Workers, Smoked Fish and Cannery Union, which represents the four hundred journeymen and twenty wholesalers, managers, and supervisors. However, not all journeymen are union members, and the former loading and unloading crews were not unionized. The Genovese crime family created loading and unloading cartels, maintained interests in some wholesaling companies, operated "security services," and organized and charged for parking.[9] The Bonanno crime family played a lesser role in the market, through ownership of certain unloading companies and by conducting loan-sharking, gambling, drug sales, and protection services on premises.

As with the other mobbed-up industries examined in this book, Cosa Nostra functioned as a kind of legislature, court, and police force for the market. The rules covered competition, prices, labor relations, payoffs, and respect. Businesses and individuals faced threats of violence, property damage, and expulsion from the market for violating the rules.[10]

The Genovese crime family governed through two wholesaler associations, which represented many wholesalers at the market. The wholesalers located in the Old Market Building warehouse were represented by the Fulton Fishmongers Association, and those located in the New Market Building warehouse were represented by the New York Wholesale Fish Dealers Association. These organizations cooperated in market governance and defended market operations to the outside world. For example, the president of the Fulton Fishmongers explained that the low rent paid by the wholesalers was justified by the run-down accommodations in the Old Market Building.[11]

When problems such as theft of fish arose, the associations knew whom to contact. In 1975, the president of the Wholesale Fish Dealers

Association asked Carmine Romano, an associate of the Genovese crime family and the secretary-treasurer of Local 359, for help in preventing thefts. Cosa Nostra established a watchmen's association to patrol the market area; whether this was a protection service or a protection racket was unclear, even to those who paid the premiums. Years later, at Romano's trial on federal racketeering charges the president testified that "if the thieves knew that the union was looking out for us . . . they wouldn't bother us . . . [b]ecause the thieves would be afraid of the union."[12]

COSA NOSTRA'S DOMINATION OF LOCAL 359

Given the perishability of seafood, the market required a reliable labor force. As federal prosecutors noted in a 1981 sentencing proceeding involving several convicted Local 359 officials, "[I]n the wholesale [fish] industry, where competition is fierce and time is of the essence, it is crucial for businesses to maintain the good will of the union and the men who run it. Organized crime recognizes this power and knows how to use it."[13]

Cosa Nostra's influence in the Fulton Fish Market was rooted in its control of Local 359. That union had only 850 to 900 members including the four hundred journeymen at the market who set up the wholesalers' seafood displays and sold and delivered the fish.[14] The Genovese crime family controlled Local 359 since the 1920s; for decades, Joseph "Socks" Lanza, a capo in the Genovese family, used his position as business agent of Local 359 as a power base. Known as the "czar of Fulton Market," Lanza determined who could transact business of any kind anywhere on market premises from the 1920s to the 1960s.[15] Lanza ran Local 359 for the benefit of the Genovese crime family. He accepted payoffs in exchange for the nonenforcement of certain contract terms and for not seeking increased wages and benefits for union members.[16] The result was labor peace and a smooth-running market.

Lanza found many ways to turn power into cash at the market. In the early 1930s, the Manhattan District Attorney's Office revealed that fishing-boat captains were forced to pay tribute in order to have their catch unloaded without problems. To obtain the ice needed to preserve their fish, boat crewmen were forced to hand over bags of scallops to the unloading crews.[17]

In 1933, the Manhattan U.S. Attorney's Office brought a sweeping indictment against Local 359, twenty-four companies, fifty-four individuals (including "Socks" Lanza), and three trade associations operating in the market.[18] The indictment alleged that the wholesalers were running a cartel in violation of the Sherman Anti-Trust Act. The government also charged the defendants with extorting "tribute" from boat captains for the privilege of doing business at the market. Lanza and others entered guilty pleas, and Lanza served a two-year prison term. In 1938, after several failed attempts, the federal government finally convicted Lanza. In 1943, he was convicted again, this time for extorting money from the president of a Teamsters union local.[19]

Paroled in 1950, Lanza was arrested again in 1957, for gambling and consorting with organized-crime figures. After the parole violation was resolved in Lanza's favor, there was a public scandal and two official investigations. The parole decision was overturned and Lanza returned to prison.[20] Nevertheless, Lanza remained on the union payroll and continued to rule the market until his death in 1968.

Over the years, "Socks" Lanza was assisted by Nunzio "Harry" Lanza, a brother, who served as a Local 359 official throughout the 1960s. He too was a capo in the Genovese crime family. In the 1970s, a brother-in-law of the Lanza brothers served as president of the local, and a Lanza son-in-law served as union attorney.[21] From 1974 to 1980, Carmine Romano, whom federal investigators considered to be Lanza's successor as the Genovese crime family's Fulton Fish Market "manager," served as secretary-treasurer, the de facto top position of Local 359. His brother Peter Romano took over as business agent. Carmine Romano served as Local 359's secretary-treasurer until Peter succeeded to that position in May 1980; Carmine then became trustee of the union's welfare and pension funds.

In 1979, the U.S. attorney for the Southern District of New York led a joint investigation into organized-crime operations at the Fulton Fish Market. The investigation produced more than forty convictions. The most important prosecution, *United States v. Romano*,[22] targeted a variety of extortion schemes. The government alleged that the defendants had established the Fulton Patrol Service, which, functioning as a protective racket, collected more than $644,000 (the equivalent of upwards of $1,700,000 in 1996 dollars)[23] from wholesalers from 1975 to 1979. The defendants were charged with extorting Christmas payments from the wholesalers and with forcing them to pay $25 a month to rent useless union placards. Some businesses continued to pay the sign rental fee for years after they had ceased displaying the signs.[24]

The Romanos were convicted of RICO, conspiracy to violate RICO, aiding and abetting violations of the Taft-Hartley Act, and misusing union pension funds.[25] In addition, Carmine was convicted of misusing union funds, and Peter of obstructing justice and perjury. Carmine Romano received a twelve-year prison sentence and a $20,000 fine; Peter got eighteen months. Both Romanos had to forfeit their union positions.[26]

Vincent Romano assumed control of market operations after his brothers were ousted from their union positions in 1981.[27] The Genovese crime family thus maintained the tradition of adapting to criminal prosecutions by handpicking the successors of those who had been convicted. The family continued to extract revenue from the market by receiving bribes in exchange for not enforcing collective bargaining terms. Incredibly, the family also continued its extortionate practices—the protection rackets, the union-shop signs, and the Christmas presents.

THE WATCHMAN'S ASSOCIATION PROTECTION RACKET

As early as the 1920s, Lanza instructed his underlings to steal seafood from wholesalers, and then persuaded the victims to purchase theft insurance from him.[28] In 1931, Manhattan District Attorney Thomas C. T. Crain estimated that gangsters were shaking down fish merchants to the tune of $25,000 a year.[29] One wholesaler testified that he had paid $5,000 to Lanza's watchman's association for "protection." By 1981, the Fulton Patrol Association was collecting $700,000 ($1,180,000 in 1996 dollars) from businesses in the Fulton Fish Market.[30]

The wholesalers did not complain publicly about Lanza or market operations. They maintained that paying Lanza was cheaper and more efficient than other means of preventing thievery. The president of the Fulton Fishmongers Association (the trade association representing the Old Market Building wholesalers) explained that "in almost every instance when someone has missed a barrel or a box of fish it has been returned within a few hours after we reported it" to the protection association.[31] Wholesalers declared that they were not victims of extortion but beneficiaries of theft insurance.

The Genovese crime family continued this racket through the years. For example, in 1975, Carmine Romano established the Fulton Patrol Association to protect the New Market Building wholesalers from thefts of seafood. For this "insurance" the New Market Building wholesalers paid $1,300 ($3,720 in 1996 dollars) a week. Although the association employed only two watchmen, the number of thefts dropped significantly.[32] Perhaps the association instilled fear in would-be thieves; more likely, the wholesalers were paying off the very people who had been stealing from them. Tired of high theft rates, the Old Market Building wholesalers eventually purchased the association's services as well. The most lucrative scam was the association's special service of guarding unsold fish stored overnight for $2,800 weekly per wholesaler.[33]

Loading companies provided their own protection services to retailers. For a fee, the loading crews watched over the restaurateurs' and fish store–owners' unlocked vehicles while they shopped. According to the loading companies, it was not a protection scam. "We help to stack the fish, we make sure it's not stolen, and we allow the retailers to go to all the wholesale stands without worrying about thousands of dollars of fish waiting in their vans." Nevertheless, in a tax-evasion case one loader admitted that he encouraged retailers' payoffs with threats of violence; those who did not pay found their vehicles damaged and their fish stolen. In other words, the loaders were not typical security guards. For example, in 1995, one of the loaders was a Genovese family associate; two others were awaiting trial on federal armed bank robbery and explosives charges.

The prosecution of the racketeers was impeded by witnesses' concerns that testifying would provoke violent retaliation against themselves and their families. Three wholesalers chose to serve six-month prison terms rather than testify against Romano and his associates.[34] Others committed perjury.[35] Local 359's longtime accountant admitted that he lied to a grand jury about Carmine Romano's participation in the Fulton Patrol Service scheme because he feared the Genovese crime family's retaliation.[36] Immediately following the trial, one witness was shot several times in front of union headquarters. No one ever was arrested. At the trial of Carmine Romano, the defense presented 350 letters from wholesalers, union members, and other market participants attesting to his integrity and good reputation.[37]

COERCED RENTAL OF UNION SIGNS

Until the 1980s, Local 359 officials forced wholesalers to "rent" cardboard signs stating that they employed union labor. The Romanos received more than $66,000 ($112,000 in 1996 dollars) in rent from this scam.[38] These sign rentals violated the Local 359 constitution.[39] In 1981, a federal court struck down the practice as violating the Taft-Hartley Act. Soon thereafter, the United Seafood Workers, Smoked Fish and Cannery Union placed Local 359 under trusteeship and ousted Carmine and Peter Romano from their union positions.[40] But the Genovese crime family retained its influence over Local 359 through Carmine and Peter's successor, their brother Vincent Romano.

EXTORTING CHRISTMAS PAYMENTS

Fulton Fish Market wholesalers routinely gave Christmas presents to Local 359 officials. To insulate themselves from Taft-Hartley Act liabilities, union officers used middlemen to collect the funds; occasionally, however, they solicited directly. Throughout the 1970s, wholesalers were encouraged to make a holiday contribution "to the boys in the union." The union members never saw the money, which went directly into the coffers of the Genovese crime family.

Before 1975, this Christmas "gift giving" was informal and irregular. After 1975, it became a systematic extortion scheme.[41] In *United States v. Romano,* the government alleged that from 1975 to 1979, union officials collected $300 per wholesaler each Christmas.[42] In 1979, the Fulton Fishmongers Association gave a lump sum donation of $2,400 ($5,000 in 1996 dollars) to the union, in lieu of individual contributions. The wholesalers apparently decided to overlook the illegality of such payments.

DEFRAUDING SUPPLIERS

Wholesalers received fish from suppliers on consignment, sold it to retailers, deducted a "commission," and remitted the remainder to the supplier.[43] At the time the fish was delivered to the wholesaler, the supplier could not know what its ultimate payment would be because fish prices fluctuate daily. Thus, the suppliers risked being cheated.

The consignment system also made suppliers vulnerable to phantom wholesalers. Such corrupt wholesalers would order increasing amounts of seafood, eventually accepting large quantities with no intention of paying the supplier. The owner of the phantom company would then, often at the same location, establish a new wholesale business under another name and repeat the fraud. Although New York City had the authority to refuse licenses to unreliable wholesalers, it did not choose to exercise it.[44]

In the late 1980s, officials estimated that suppliers lost $6 million as a result of fraud. Most out-of-state suppliers feared pursuing legal remedies because of the market's reputation for being mobbed up. Moreover, phantom wholesalers were hard to locate. Given the difficulty of proving criminal fraud and finding corrupt wholesalers, criminal prosecutions were also rare.

THE UNLOADING CARTEL

For decades, the Genovese crime family operated a lucrative unloading cartel at the market. Genovese soldiers ensured that no companies unaffiliated with the cartel worked at the market. In return, cartel members kicked back a portion of their revenues to the organized crime family. Throughout the 1970s, for example, the unloading companies made cash payments to Carmine Romano every Friday in the back room of a nearby Genovese social club.

The job of the unloading companies was to remove boxes of fish from the trucks and place them on the ground. This simple task required only basic equipment and unskilled labor. In the late 1980s and early 1990s approximately six unloading companies operated at the market; each one employed one "unloading crew" or "gang," ranging in size from two to thirteen employees, to take the fish from the suppliers' trucks to the wholesalers' stalls. In 1992, the unloading companies had estimated combined gross revenues of more than $2 million ($2.24 million in 1996 dollars).[45]

The cartel assigned wholesalers, suppliers, and truckers to particular unloaders. As in the case of the property-rights system that bound Garment District manufacturers to truckers, Fulton Fish Market truckers had no de facto ability to choose an unloading company. Similarly, the wholesalers who paid the unloaders' fees had no say in the assignment of the crews.[46] Truckers, suppliers, and wholesalers all understood that they could not unload their own trucks or choose a particular unloading crew. Indeed, truckers had to wait for the services of their assigned unloading crew, whether or not other crews were available. No unloading crew would solicit customers who "belonged" to other unloading crews.

There was no price competition among the unloading crews; to the contrary, there was a to-the-penny uniformity in the prices they charged the wholesalers: usually $1.35 per one-hundred-pound box and $0.65 per sixty-pound carton.[47] The power of the unloaders allowed them to extract supplemental charges ranging from $10 to $60 per truck. "Jump-up" or "man-on-truck" charges had to be paid in cash when an unloader entered the truck to unload cargo, and, often, even if the unloaders didn't enter the truck. Unloaders in other cities performed this service for the basic unloading fee.

STEALING SEAFOOD

Unloading crews and their associates had many opportunities to steal fish. Unloaders did not sign receipts for the products they handled. Moreover, there was no time to weigh shipments as they passed through the market. Stolen fish were easily diverted to mob-connected wholesalers.[48] Cosa Nostra "skimmed" or "tapped" money by taking a cut of seafood stolen by the unloaders. One undercover agent estimated that, as a group, wholesalers who were not mob controlled lost between two thousand and three thousand pounds of fish a night because of skimming; retailers had to purchase a 115-pound box of seafood to be sure of obtaining 90-pounds.[49] Wholesalers' annual losses added up to an estimated $1.5 million.[50]

THE LOADING COMPANIES' PARKING RACKET

Through the loading companies, Cosa Nostra controlled parking at the market.[51] The parking areas varied in size, each operated by a different loading company. Some companies or their affiliates leased premises from the city for a nominal fee. Others simply appropriated the public streets for their private business without making any payments. The loading companies reaped lucrative profits. Circa 1990, the loading companies charged $20 a night or more for parking, depending on a variety of factors including the size of the retailer's vehicle and often the retailers' ethnicity. The loading companies reaped an estimated $5 million a year ($5.9 million in 1996 dollars) in fees from parking alone.[52] The Genovese crime family received a significant portion of this amount.

NEW YORK CITY'S FAILURE TO REGULATE

Until 1982, the city's Department of Ports and Terminals collected rents at the market. In 1982, Mayor Edward I. Koch's administration transferred responsibility for rent collection to the South Street Seaport Corporation as part of a deal to develop the waterfront area and historic landmark district adjoining the Fulton Fish Market. The South Street Seaport Corporation inherited two main leases in 1982, one with the New York Wholesale Fish Dealers Association (representing New Market Building wholesalers) and the other with the Fulton Market Fishmongers Association (representing Old Market Building wholesalers).

It was anticipated that the transfer of responsibility to the corporation would increase revenues for the South Street Seaport Museum. However, this goal was thwarted because both the Koch and Dinkins administrations prohibited the South Street Seaport Corporation from raising rents while the market's operations were being investigated. In 1992, a government consultant reported that New York City received approximately $268,000 ($300,000 in 1996 dollars) annually in rent from the wholesalers in city-owned buildings, but that the annual market value of the leases was close to $3 million.[53] Politicians remained passive about this loss of potential revenue.

CONCLUSION

From the early twentieth century, the Fulton Fish Market served the Genovese crime family as a base of power and revenue. Businesses and individuals faced threats of violence and property damage if they did not follow the mob's dictates. The Genovese family used its influence over Local 359 to extort money through the collection of Christmas payments and union placards. Cosa Nostra established cartels of loading and unloading companies, controlled parking, and forced wholesalers to pay "insurance" to prevent theft.

City regulation was practically nonexistent. In the 1930s, businesses at the market were required to obtain permits from the Department of Markets.[54] It was alleged that only the approval of "Socks" Lanza, who maintained close friendships with many Tammany Hall politicians, was needed to obtain such permits.[55] Manhattan District Attorney Thomas C. T. Crain, facing removal from office in 1931, testified that he could not explain why he had been lax in investigating and prosecuting organized crime in the market.[56]

The relationship between top-ranking organized-crime figures and prominent politicians continued for decades, and no doubt had important implications for the lackluster efforts of law enforcement to crack down on mob domination of legitimate industries. While a few important mob figures were prosecuted and convicted of racketeering in the 1980s and court-appointed officials were put in place to root out corruption in the market, the overall results were unimpressive. Inaction by city officials and the inability of law enforcement agencies to weaken the Genovese crime family's lock on the market permitted racketeering to flourish. Suppliers, wholesalers, and retailers had no choice but to consider the payoffs as the cost of doing business, which they passed on to consumers through higher seafood prices. For decades, mob rule was an intractable fact of life at the Fulton Fish Market.

Participants in the Fulton Fish Market did not complain. Some observers attributed participants' silence to the fact that the costs of doing business with Cosa Nostra were passed on to consumers.[57] Mob rule had certain advantages. Cosa Nostra prevented competition in the provision of unloading, loading, and parking services. The lack of competition allowed cartel members to set prices higher than any fish market in the country, even controlling for the higher cost of living in New York City. With organized crime firmly in control of the union, labor relations remained peaceful. Other than a strike in 1987, there was no serious disruption of operations or a crisis in getting fish to restaurants and retail stores. It was not until the mid-1990s, under the Giuliani administration's organized-crime control campaign, that the city used its regulatory authority to attack organized-crime racketeering at the market.

4

The Taking of John F. Kennedy Airport

The goods that come into the various airports around New York City . . . truckers have to pick [the goods] up, and take the goods where they are destined. . . . So the truckers have an important and integral part, a key position in the New York area through the fact that they have control over . . . the airport. If it gets into the wrong hands, of course, there can be a stranglehold over New York City.[1]

—Robert F. Kennedy, chief counsel, McClellan Committee Hearings, U.S. Senate, 1957

I don't think he knows in his heart that we rule the airport.[2]

—Frank Manzo, the Lucchese crime family's overseer at JFK Airport, in an intercepted conversation reported by the *New York Times* in 1985, discussing an airfreight executive's refusal to make payoffs in exchange for labor peace.

CHRONOLOGY

1948 Idlewild Airport opens in Queens; in 1963, it is renamed John F. Kennedy Airport. From its inception, the airport is plagued by mob-orchestrated cargo theft.

1956 Teamsters Local 295 is established to represent the clerical employees, dispatchers, truck drivers, and warehouse workers employed by freight-forwarding and trucking companies that service the airport. The Lucchese crime family controls the local.

1958 John "Johnny Dio" Dioguardi, a capo in the Lucchese family, and John McNamara, president of Local 295, are convicted of conspiracy and extortion.

McClellan Committee Report finds that Jimmy Hoffa created Local 295 and several other paper locals to pay off the Lucchese crime family which supported Hoffa's candidacy for the International Brotherhood of Teamsters presidency.

1968 The New York State Investigation Commission (SIC) conducts investigations and public hearings into racketeering at the airport.

1969 Future Gambino crime-family boss John Gotti pleads guilty to charges of truck hijacking at the JFK Airport and serves three years in prison.

1970 The Lucchese crime family supports the establishment of Teamsters Local 851, which represents over two thousand truck drivers and warehouse workers and fourteen hundred clerical employees and dispatchers who were former members of Local 295.

1971 U.S. Attorney General John Mitchell announces two criminal antitrust indictments against thirteen trucking companies, six individuals, and the National Association of Air Freight (NAFA). Most of the defendants plead no contest and enter into a consent decree that dissolves NAFA and prohibits the fixing of airfreight prices.

1978 Robbers take $5.8 million in cash and securities from a Lufthansa Airlines cargo hangar; it is the largest robbery in U.S. history at the time. A mere $100,000 is recovered and only one individual ever convicted; evidence implicates the Lucchese crime family.

1983 The federal Brooklyn Organized Crime Strike Force launches the Kenrac (Kennedy Rackets) investigation, which collects evidence of bribery, theft, and labor racketeering, leading to the convictions of mob-connected officers of Locals 295 and 851.

1985 The Kenrac investigation results in the indictments of eleven people for bribery and labor racketeering; in a separate prosecution, seven people are charged with extortion and conspiracy. Harry Davidoff, vice-president of Local 851, receives a twelve-year prison sentence and $125,000 fine. The other defendants enter guilty pleas, including Frank Manzo, the Lucchese crime family's airport overseer; Local 295 President Frank Calise; and Lucchese capo Paul Vario. They receive twelve-, nine-, and six-year prison sentences, respectively.

1989 Pursuant to a settlement reached in *United States v. International Brotherhood of Teamsters,* Judge Frederick B. Lacey is appointed independent administrator. Lacey initiates the permanent removal of Teamsters Local 295 president Anthony Calagna and the suspension of five other officers.

1990 The U.S. attorney for the Eastern District of New York brings a civil RICO suit against Locals 295 and 851. The complaint targets fourteen individuals, including several members of the Lucchese and Gambino families. In 1992, a federal district court judge imposes a temporary trusteeship on Local 295.

1991 The Kenrac II investigation, launched in 1987, ends with indictments for bribery and labor racketeering against seven individuals, among them Anthony Calagna and Gambino capo Anthony Guerrieri. All are found guilty; Calagna receives a prison sentence and is banned from all union activity for thirteen years.

1992 Local 295 is placed under trusteeship. Judge Nickerson appoints Thomas Puccio, a former assistant U.S. attorney and former chief of the Brooklyn Organized Crime Strike Force, as trustee.

1993 In September, the U.S. attorney for the Eastern District of New York obtains a criminal RICO indictment against seven individuals, including Anthony Razza, secretary-treasurer of Local 851, and Anthony Calagna, the former president of Local 295. The indictment charges them with extortion, labor racketeering, and related offenses. The defendants enter guilty pleas. Razza receives a twenty-one-month prison sentence and is barred from the IBT for life.

In June, Trustee Puccio files a motion with Judge Nickerson seeking to extend his trusteeship to Local 851.

Following Razza's indictment, IBT President Ron Carey ousts the leadership of Local 851, and appoints Curt Ostrander as temporary trustee.

1994 The U.S. Attorney's Office for the Eastern District of New York, Local 851, and the IBT sign a consent decree establishing a bifurcated monitorship over Local 851. Former federal prosecutor Ron DePetris is appointed independent supervisor of Local 851, and Curt Ostrander is appointed to continue as union trustee.

1995 DePetris, on behalf of Local 851, files civil RICO suits against two freight-forwarding companies.

1997 Indictment of eighty-three defendants for participating in an air cargo theft ring.

1998 Both defendant freight forwarding companies settle with Local 851.

Puccio and DePetris remain in place as the union trustee of Local 295 and independent supervisor of Local 851, respectively. The terms of both men are due to expire sixty days after the locals hold free elections and the court certifies the results.

In December, fifty-six individuals and eight corporations are indicted as a result of Operation Rain Forest. The defendants are charged with stealing, fencing, and distributing air cargo from John F. Kennedy Airport.

John F. Kennedy International Airport (JFK Airport), which opened as Idlewild Airport in 1948,[3] is located in southeastern Queens on the shores of Jamaica Bay, fifteen miles from the center of Manhattan. In 1993, it accounted for roughly 30 percent of the total value and tonnage of air cargo imported into the United States and for roughly 24–31 percent of the total value and tonnage of exported cargo.[4] "A city unto itself,"[5] JFK Airport's five thousand acres contain runways, terminal buildings, hangars, warehouses, high-security storage vaults, container stations, and truck depots. The Airport employs more than forty thousand people. The Port Authority of New York and New Jersey operates the airport and derives revenue from the airlines, freight forwarders,

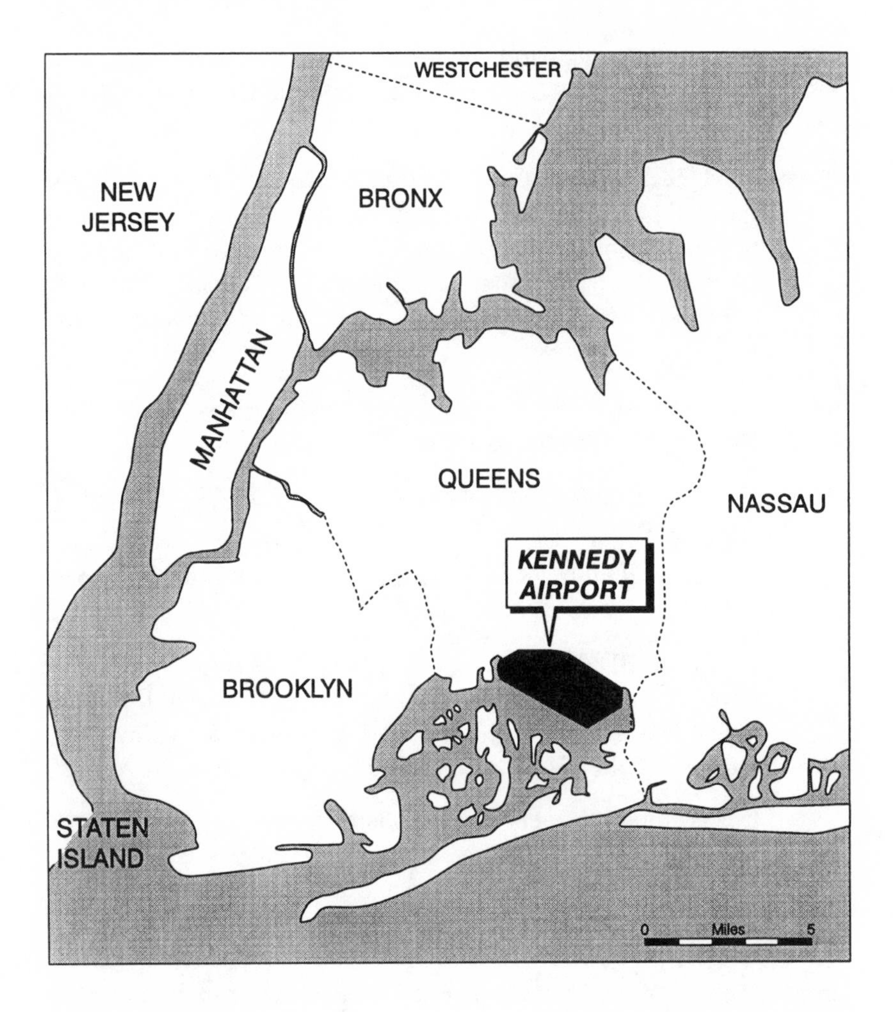

and customs brokers. The land is owned by New York City and leased to the Port Authority.

In the 1950s as freight business moved from ships to airplanes, the Lucchese crime family expanded its operations from the New York City waterfront to JFK Airport.[6] Its primary power base at JFK consisted of two Teamsters union locals, Local 295 and Local 851, which represent employees of freight-forwarding and trucking companies. The Luccheses also exercised control over trucking services at the airport through the Metropolitan Importer Truckmen's Association (MITA) and by maintaining ownership interests in several trucking companies.

The volume and value of the cargo made theft at JFK Airport a highly attractive enterprise for organized crime. Through its entrenched position there, the Lucchese crime family profited from the theft of air cargo and from payoffs by freight-forwarding companies. The union locals also provided jobs for Cosa Nostra members and associates; union officers handpicked by the Lucchese family steered work to mob-controlled trucking companies. Cosa Nostra transformed control of trucking services into revenue through payoffs from members of the trucking cartel and by profits from ownership interests in trucking companies.

HOW THE AIR-CARGO INDUSTRY OPERATES

Importers, manufacturers, and wholesalers located throughout the United States rely on the air-cargo industry to transport goods through JFK Airport to the New York City metropolitan area and beyond. The industry involves shippers, airlines, freight-forwarding companies, and IBT Local 295 and IBT Local 851. Local 295, with over two thousand members, represents truck drivers, helpers, switchers, platform men, motor-lift operators, mechanics, garage employees, and fuellers employed by freight-forwarding companies. Local 851 represents office clerical workers and dispatchers employed by freight-forwarding companies, and has an estimated fourteen hundred members.

The freight-forwarding companies coordinate, arrange, and manage the operations necessary to the movement of cargo. Typically, the freight forwarder, who is employed by a manufacturer or other shipper, secures insurance, warehouses the merchandise, and when necessary, arranges for repacking, marking, and weighing.[7] Approximately three hundred forwarding companies operate at JFK Airport; the majority use their own trucks and drivers. Most are large, national corporations that maintain offices and warehouses at the airport. If the freight forwarder does not provide its own ground transportation, it contracts with a trucking company to drive cargo to and from the airport. The trucking companies operating at the airport range in size from "mom-and-pop" companies to organizations with several hundred employees.

The following example illustrates how an air-cargo transaction operates. The manufacturer hires a freight-forwarding company to ship shoes from a factory in a Miami suburb to a department store in Jersey City, New Jersey. The forwarder hires a Florida trucking company to pick up several hundred boxes of shoes at the shipper's factory and take them to the forwarder's warehouse at Miami Airport. The forwarder packs the shoes into containers that also hold cargo the forwarder has received from other shippers, allowing the forwarder to take advantage of the airline's lower bulk rates. Truck drivers, employed by the forwarder, take the containers to the cargo terminal, where airline employees load them onto the aircraft. At JFK Airport, airline employees unload the containers. The truck drivers take the containers to the forwarder's warehouse, where they are disassembled. Trucking companies, or the freight-forwarder's trucks, take the shoes to Jersey City.

COSA NOSTRA'S CONTROL OF TEAMSTERS LOCALS 295 AND 851

Cosa Nostra's influence in the airfreight industry is well documented.[8] For several decades, the Lucchese crime family played a role in key facets of air-cargo operations through its domination of IBT Locals 295 and 851. The locals' memberships comprised the men and women responsible for the clerical work, trucking, and loading and unloading of air cargo. Control over these unions gave the Mafia control over the shipping operations at JFK Airport.

Hoffa and the Creation of Paper Locals

From its inception in 1956, Local 295 was awash in corruption. Jimmy Hoffa, who attained stature within the Teamsters union as the central regional leader of the major Midwest locals, obtained authorization to charter Local 295 and six other International Brotherhood of Teamsters (IBT) locals in New York City in order to expand his power base into the Northeast.[9] Robert Kennedy, who investigated Hoffa and the Teamsters as chief counsel to the U.S. Senate's Select Committee on Improper Activities in the Labor or Management Field (the McClellan

Committee) scornfully referred to the seven new union affiliates as "paper locals."[10]

At the hearings, the McClellan Committee played intercepted telephone conversations that Hoffa had conducted with John "Johnny Dio" Dioguardi, a soldier in the Lucchese crime family and a notorious labor racketeer.[11] The recorded conversations revealed a conspiracy between Hoffa and Dioguardi to use Local 295 and the six other bogus locals to ensure the election of their handpicked candidate, John J. O'Rourke, to the presidency of the IBT Joint Council, an umbrella organization representing the interests of more than 125,000 rank-and-file Teamsters in the New York City metropolitan area.[12] Senator John L. McClellan, the chairman of the committee, commented that "[t]he fact that one of the nation's most powerful labor leaders, James R. Hoffa . . . used [John] Dioguardi and [Anthony] Corallo[13] in his efforts to capture control of [the Teamsters] in New York City only serves to underline the importance of gangster infiltration in the labor movement."[14]

The power-grabbing scheme of Hoffa and Dioguardi was a resounding success. In 1957, with the support of regional Teamsters organizations in the South, Midwest, and, critically, the Northeast, Hoffa was elected the International President of the Teamsters union. John O'Rourke was elected vice-president.[15] Cosa Nostra's influence now reached to the very top of the Teamsters. In New York City, Cosa Nostra used its power in the Teamsters to infiltrate the air-cargo industry; Local 295 functioned as the Lucchese crime family's puppet until the early 1990s, when it was placed under trusteeship.[16]

In 1970, the Lucchese crime family expanded its power base by forming IBT Local 851, which served as a haven for Local 295 officials under investigation for soliciting and taking bribes from freight forwarders and for various labor-racketeering schemes.

CORRUPT UNION OFFICERS

Once elected IBT president in 1956, Hoffa repaid his debt to the Lucchese crime family for supporting his successful bid for the IBT presidency by appointing Harry Davidoff, a close Lucchese associate, to head Local 295. Davidoff dominated Local 295 for forty years. Two decades into Davidoff's rule, the Senate's Permanent Subcommittee of Investigations characterized him as "a ruthless New York thug, a gangster who gravitated to the labor movement for no other reason than to steal from it."[17] When Harry stepped down, his son Mark and Frank Calise ran the two IBT locals. In 1985, when Calise was convicted of labor racketeering and sentenced to a nine-year prison term, Lucchese member Anthony Calagna and various relatives assumed control of the unions.

LEAD AGENTS AND TRUCK HIJACKING

The lead agent position was a key role in the freight forwarding business. They allocated the job assignments for truck drivers, warehouse workers, clerical workers, and dispatchers. Many of the lead agents at the airport were members of Local 851. Some were associates and friends of the Lucchese crime family. Despite the fact that lead agents played an important managerial function, the freight forwarders had no role in choosing them.

Lead agents were in a position to arrange truck "give-ups" and hijackings, the two most common forms of cargo theft at JFK Airport.[18] In a give-up, the truck driver who is transporting goods to or from JFK Airport parks the truck with the keys in the ignition, then leaves the vehicle for "a minute" to get a cup of coffee or use a bathroom. In his absence, the truck is stolen according to a prearranged plan. Hijackings require a lead agent to tip off Lucchese representatives at the airport about a valuable cargo shipment and its scheduled route. A Lucchese truck-hijacking crew intercepts the truck just outside the airport grounds and wrests it from the driver, using violence or the threat of violence.[19]

Many high-ranking organized-crime figures cut their teeth carrying out truck hijackings and give-ups at JFK Airport. For example, in 1969, future Gambino crime family boss John Gotti was sent to prison for hijacking trucks transporting clothing from JFK Airport.[20] Henry Hill, protagonist of the book *Wiseguy* and of the movie *Goodfellas,* spent much of his criminal career carrying out airport-related cargo thefts. Hill often assisted Jimmy Burke, a notoriously ruthless associate of the Lucchese crime family, who was reputed to be the "best" airfreight hijacker operating out of the airport. Burke and his crew were responsible for the theft of millions of dollars of valuable cargo, which ranged from jewelry, weapons, and securities bonds, to household appliances, meat, shoes, and toys.[21] According to Hill, the secret to Burke's success was his cadre of informants: insider tips flowed in from all sectors of the airport as cargo handlers, truck drivers, and airline employees assisted the thievery in exchange for a fraction of the take. To safeguard his operations, Burke bribed corrupt policemen to alert him to government informants and potential witnesses. Hill remarked that when it came to linking Burke to a hijacking, "[t]here was never one driver who made it into court to testify against him. There were quite a few dead ones who tried."[22]

The Lufthansa Heist

The December 1978 robbery of cash and securities from the Lufthansa Airlines cargo hangar at JFK Airport was, at that time, the most lucrative robbery in the nation's history. The tabloids called it "the crime of the century," and it has inspired several books and films. Armed with detailed information about the complex security system from one of the cargo's supervisors, a Lufthansa employee named Louis Werner, a gang of seven masked gunmen broke into a high-security Lufthansa Airlines building. The robbers rounded up the guards and forced them to open the vault where the shipment was kept. In a little more then an hour, they had stolen an estimated $5 million of unmarked money and $875,000 worth of jewelry.

The robbers' familiarity with the layout of the building and the fact that they addressed several Lufthansa employees by name caused the FBI to suspect an inside job. According to the FBI agent who directed the investigation, the four robbers and mastermind of the theft retained a small portion of the proceeds and passed the rest to Lucchese capo Paul Vario.[23] According to Henry Hill, the mastermind of the theft was Jimmy Burke. But the only individual ever prosecuted in connection with the robbery was Louis Werner, the Lufthansa cargo supervisor who had first tipped off the mob to the existence of the shipment. In 1979, Werner was convicted and sentenced to fifteen years in prison.[24] Of the nearly $6 million stolen, only $100,000 was ever recovered.[25]

THE SALE OF LABOR PEACE

The Lucchese crime family's influence with Locals 295 and 851 secured advantages above and beyond opportunities for lucrative heists. One advantage was the ability to sell labor peace to freight fowarders. Picketing, work stoppages, slowdowns, and misroutings could impose staggering costs on freight forwarders, whose businesses depended upon the speedy delivery of air cargo. For example, when members of Locals 295 and 851 conducted a five-month strike at the JFK Airport against Emery Worldwide in 1989, the company lost $20 million in revenue and eventually went bankrupt.[26] In 1984, the Brooklyn Organized Crime Strike Force estimated that Cosa Nostra received millions of dollars every year in labor-peace payoffs from freight forwarders.[27]

Freight-forwarding companies and trucking companies operating at JFK Airport also made payments to Cosa Nostra to avoid enforcement of expensive contract terms, especially featherbedding requirements. For example, between 1992 and 1993, Kuehne & Nagel Air Freight paid upwards of $100,000 in bribes to Anthony Razza, the secretary-treasurer of Local 851 and an associate of the Lucchese crime family, in exchange for a favorable collective bargaining agreement. Among the advantageous terms in the new contract was a yearlong freeze in pension contributions by Kuehne & Nagel Air Freight for its Local 851 employees.[28] Payoffs purchased additional benefits. For example, union officials assisted forwarding companies in recruiting customers from competitors and granted them immunity from cargo thefts.

For decades, freight forwarders made payoffs to officers of Locals 295 and 851; these were passed along to high-level Lucchese members. When federal investigators intensified their investigations of organized crime in the JFK air-cargo industry, freight forwarders began using intermediaries, usually corrupt union officials who would funnel the money directly to the Lucchese family. Forwarding-company executives would disguise the bribes as payments to labor-consulting companies (run by Lucchese family associates) for services rendered.[29]

The Lucchese crime family used Teamsters Locals 295 and 851 to reward friends and associates with jobs as truck drivers, warehouse workers, dispatchers, and clerical employees. Some union members had to pay off union officers to retain their employment. Union officers, in the usual manner, passed these payments to high-ranking members of the Lucchese crime family.

COSA NOSTRA'S OWNERSHIP INTERESTS IN TRUCKING

Cosa Nostra members and associates held ownership interests in trucking companies in the JFK Airport air-cargo industry. Local 295's contracts with freight-forwarding companies contained a provision prohibiting the use of a trucking company at the airport without the union's written permission. In this way, the union steered freight forwarders to mob-controlled trucking companies, which enjoyed immense advantages over competitors. Cosa Nostra members owned, operated, or received payments from at least twelve trucking companies. For example, Cosa Nostra associate Frank Manzo, overseer of the Lucchese crime family's interests at the airport, owned two trucking companies: LVF Air Cargo, Inc., and LVF Airport Service Inc.[30]

THE ROLE OF MITA

For two decades, the Lucchese crime family controlled the Metropolitan Import Truckmen's Association (MITA), a trade association comprising a dozen trucking companies operated by Cosa Nostra associates from their positions as trucking consultants and troubleshooters. (These positions were less conspicuous than high-profile, upper-echelon MITA positions.) By 1965, according to law enforcement officials, practically every top MITA officer answered to the mob.[31] Through its decades-long domination of this trade association, the Lucchese crime family, with the support of Local 295, enforced a trucking cartel at JFK Airport.

Members of the trucking cartel paid hefty fees to the trade association, which were passed along to the Lucchese crime family. The airlines initially asserted that they should be free to negotiate for trucking services with any trucking company, regardless of whether it was a member of MITA, but they eventually acquiesced to the trade association's membership requirement. Coercion was an obvious factor: unaffiliated trucking companies attempting to operate without cartel approval found that the cargo they were scheduled to pick up at JFK arrived badly damaged or did not arrive at all.

GOVERNMENT RESPONSES

Port Authority

The Port Authority of New York and New Jersey, the government agency responsible for overseeing operations at JFK Airport, took some remedial action to augment airport security forces but was not effective in combating Cosa Nostra activity. In 1987, the head of the Port Authority police force acknowledged that stealing and extortionate activity at the airport, which had resulted in a $3 million loss the previous year, was "getting worse."[32] Five years later, reacting to a 1991 report of the amount of cargo stolen from the airport, Port Authority officials insisted that labor racketeering and theft were not significant problems because the reported $5.4 million loss represented only a fraction of the estimated $80 billion worth of goods transported annually.[33]

In 1994, freight-forwarding companies reported 218 cargo thefts, resulting in losses of nearly $5 million.[34] That same year, twenty-two robbers belonging to crews headed by low-level associates of the Gambino crime family were arrested following a two-year investigation launched by the Queens County District Attorney's Office. Although none of the individual robberies carried out by the crews was large enough to attract the attention of investigators, it is believed that the aggregate impact of the crews' activities resulted in financial losses greater than those incurred from the infamous Lufthansa heist.[35] In the mid-1990s, Port Authority officials tightened security at JFK Airport. In response, the thieves, under Cosa Nostra's direction, began targeting warehouses used by freight-forwarding companies located off airport premises.

DOJ Initiatives

In the late 1960s, the National Association for Air-Freight, Inc. (NAFA), a national organization of trucking companies, absorbed MITA. Subsequently, the federal government attempted to break up Cosa Nostra's trucking cartel in the JFK air-cargo industry. Three antitrust cases were filed, two criminal and one civil, which named as defendants NAFA, several trucking companies, and their officers. In 1974, twelve trucking companies, three individuals, and NAFA entered a consent decree that, among other things, ordered the dissolution of NAFA and enjoined the fixing of prices for ground transportation of imported air freight at JFK.[36] However, the consent decree merely forced mobsters to exercise control over trucking services at the airport through alternative means. The Lucchese crime family continued to dominate the trucking business through Local 295 and Local 851, and through direct or indirect control over several trucking firms. Cosa Nostra's control of airport cargo operations remained firm well into the 1980s.

Operation Kenrac

In 1983, the Federal Organized Crime Strike Force, based in Brooklyn, launched an investigation code-named Kenrac—"Kennedy Rackets." The investigation, which lasted five years and resulted in several important convictions, painted a disturbing picture of the depth and scope of the mob's infiltration of the air-freight industry. By 1985, the FBI had amassed enough incriminating evidence, which included five hundred reels of taped conversations from bugs placed in Lucchese crime family associate and airport overseer Frank Manzo's home and telephone, to arrest Manzo as well as Local 295 President Frank Calise and Local 851 Vice-President Harry Davidoff.

Based on the Kenrac findings, the U.S. Attorney's Office for the Eastern District of New York obtained a twenty-three count indictment charging Manzo, Davidoff, Calise, and eight others with participating in a conspiracy to commit extortion through a pattern of racketeering activity that included shaking down shipping and trucking companies at JFK Airport.[37] Faced with overwhelming evidence against them, Manzo and Calise both entered guilty pleas and received prison terms of twelve and nine years, respectively. Harry Davidoff went to trial in federal district court on a five-count indictment.[38] He was found guilty but obtained a reversal several years later in the Second Circuit Court of Appeals. However, Davidoff was ultimately retried, convicted, and sentenced to ten years in prison.[39]

While the government's victories against top Cosa Nostra–affiliated power brokers at JFK Airport seem impressive, the Kenrac prosecutions failed to make significant inroads into the mob's dominion over the airport. The prosecutions of Davidoff, Calise, and Manzo effectively derailed the criminal careers of those individuals without addressing the partnership between the upperworld and underworld that enabled Cosa Nostra to continue operations after the convictions.[40]

CONSEQUENCES OF COSA NOSTRA'S CONTROL OF JFK AIRPORT

Mob control of the air-cargo industry at JFK has had significant and long-lasting consequences on the economy of New York City. The share of air freight entering the United States through JFK Airport fell from 41 percent in 1977 to 33 percent in 1987.[41] Some commentators attributed the decline, at least in part, to the reluctance of companies to open or expand air cargo operations at the airport because of the presence of organized crime.[42] At least one large freight-forwarding company refused to handle high-value cargo, such as furs and watches, if the shipment had to pass through JFK Airport.[43] In the 1980s, several shippers, including IBM, began to divert cargo to other airports. While labor racketeering and cargo theft were not unique to JFK Airport, these problems were perceived to be most serious there.[44]

Surprisingly, airlines carrying cargo through JFK Airport did not often complain about organized crime; some refused to acknowledge that a problem even existed. The most likely explanation for this silence is fear of adverse publicity. Airlines have a strong interest in maintaining a public image of tight security to attract and retain the allegiance of travelers.

For decades, officials who investigated mob-operated shakedowns of freight-forwarding companies at JFK Airport reported that the businessmen targeted by Cosa Nostra were similarly silent. The victims' reluctance to come forward was often attributed to concerns for physical safety.[45] Another factor was the mob's role in stabilizing the industry by "curbing competition, setting prices [and] allocating markets."[46] In fact, many freight-forwarding companies would not have remained in business if they had to pay union wages and benefits. By contrast, companies that cooperated with Cosa Nostra thrived. The money that freight forwarders saved in labor costs by avoiding strict enforcement of contract provisions—sometimes unionization itself—far exceeded the costs of the payments required to obtain such preferential treatment. Companies paid off top-echelon union representatives to be allowed to use nonunion labor, which is much cheaper. It is unlikely that the freight forwarders passed on any savings to their customers and indirectly to the public. However, schemes like this call into question the existence of a "mob tax."[47]

Union members were the true victims of organized crime at the airport. Their leaders usually failed to aggressively police employers to ensure that proper benefit contributions were paid, and sometimes took (and solicited) bribes to look the other way. In addition, the union officers themselves sometimes embezzled and misused funds.

Yet, members of Locals 295 and 851 did not complain about Cosa Nostra's control of their unions. Many members gained entrance into the union through relatives or friends, often through connections to the Lucchese crime family. Members with ties to organized crime recruited others to perpetuate the connection. Few dared to complain about illegal practices at the airport or within the union. It was in their best interest to remain silent because those who caused trouble were threatened with loss of employment and physical harm. Those who cooperated with union officials received favorable treatment, such as overtime schedules and desirable work assignments.[48]

It seems that the Kenrac investigation, which dislodged from the industry three of the most entrenched and powerful Cosa Nostra figures, would have significantly reduced mob-orchestrated thievery and extortion at the airport. But it did not. Davidoff, Manzo, and Calise were soon replaced by other organized-crime associates. In addition, the Gambino crime family took advantage of the brief period of upheaval following their convictions to take over part of the Lucchese crime family's turf. Five years after the Kenrac defendants were convicted and sentenced, federal government officials sought to have Local 295 placed under trusteeship. In granting the government's request, Federal District Court Judge Eugene H. Nickerson stated, "[The] contention that Local 295 is now free of the influence of organized crime rings hollow. . . . [T]he evidence exhibits [that] Local 295's officers closed ranks against the government's investigation."[49]

CONCLUSION

Cosa Nostra members and associates, journalists, and others familiar with the air-freight industry have long referred to JFK Airport as the mob's "candy store."[50] *Wiseguy* protagonist Henry Hill explains, and a slough of prosecutions and investigations confirm, that the airport's air-cargo operations were thoroughly dominated by Cosa Nostra from the opening of the airport in 1948 until at least the late 1980s.

The mob's power base was Teamsters Locals 295 and 851. The former (along with several other paper locals) was created by Jimmy Hoffa in the 1950s, with the help of the Lucchese crime family, to further his IBT presidential ambitions; the latter was created in 1971 as a haven for 295 officials under government investigation. Through domination of these Teamsters locals, the Lucchese crime family established and policed a trucking cartel. Cartel members made regular payoffs in exchange for labor peace. Cosa Nostra expanded its revenues from the airport by handpicking union officials with the power to exploit their detailed knowledge of valuable cargo shipments to set up truck give-ups and hijackings.

Mob rule came at the expense of rank-and-file union members, unaffiliated trucking companies, businesses that depended upon receiving cargo shipments, and the general public, which was forced to pay a mob tax reflecting the cost of mob payoffs on goods shipped through the airport. Although high-profile investigations since the 1950s have repeatedly exposed the presence of organized crime in the air-cargo industry at JFK Airport, law enforcement officials were unsuccessful in purging or even disrupting organized crime's cartel until the mid-1990s.

5

Exhibiting Corruption

The Javits Convention Center

[Y]ou're buying a pass in and out of here. You can't do that. You know, if we're hitting everybody else, which we are, you know making them do certain things . . . how do you get a pass[?] How could that possibly be? You know what I'm talking about? You understanding what I'm saying?[1]

—Wire-tapped conversation between Robert Rabbitt Sr., the general foreman at the Javits Center, and freight-company president Ronald Muller

CHRONOLOGY

1986 The Jacob Javits Convention Center opens.

Anthony Salerno, ostensible boss of the Genovese crime family, is convicted on federal charges of rigging Javits Center concrete bids and of inflating the center's construction costs by approximately $12 million. The Julius Nasso Concrete Company and the S & A Concrete Company are also implicated in the illegal concrete cartel.

1987 The U.S. attorney files a civil RICO action against Teamsters Local 814, alleging that the Bonanno crime family controls the local and its officers. Pursuant to a consent decree a court-appointed trustee is directed to purge the local of organized crime.

1988 The U.S. attorney files a civil RICO suit against the International Brotherhood of Teamsters and the Teamsters General

Executive Board. The consent decree creates an Independent Review Board (IRB) composed of three court-appointed officers to oversee disciplinary and electoral processes. The IRB begins purging mobsters from corrupted locals, including Local 807, which had become a haven for ousted officials from Local 814. Local 807 members load and unload vehicles.

1990 The U.S. attorney for the Southern District of New York files a RICO suit against the District Council of Carpenters and its chief officials.

1991 Ralph Coppola, chief steward of the Javits Center, is identified as an agent of the Genovese crime family and removed from his position.

1992 Twenty-seven members of the Carpenters union, the Teamsters union, and the Exhibition Employees Union who work at the Javits Center are indicted on charges of theft, extortion, and violence. Twenty-four plead guilty; three are acquitted.

Robert Rabbitt Sr., general foreman of Local 807, is indicted for receiving bribes, larceny, possessing stolen property, conspiracy, and falsifying business records. He pleads guilty to the last charge and serves one year in prison. The same charges are brought against his son Michael, but are dropped pursuant to Robert's plea agreement and Michael's promise to perform one year of community service.

1994 The case against the Carpenters union and its chief officials ends in a consent decree, permanently enjoining the defendants from racketeering or knowingly associating with any organized-crime figures. The court appoints Kenneth Conboy to monitor compliance with the terms of the decree.

Robert Rabbitt Sr. resigns from Local 807 for five years as part of a settlement with the IRB. His son Michael takes his place.

Carpenters union District Council President Frederick Devine appoints mob associates Anthony Fiorino and Leonard Simon District Council representatives at the Javits Center.

1995 New York State Comptroller H. Carl McCall issues an audit report charging Javits officials with mismanagement and toleration of corruption.

The New York State Senate holds hearings on racketeering at the Javits Center.

IBT President Ron Carey, acting on the basis of an IRB report, removes the leadership of Local 807 and places the local under trusteeship.

Governor George S. Pataki nominates Robert Boyle as president and CEO of the Javits Center and Gerald McQueen as inspector general.

Anthony Fiorino faces the first disciplinary hearing conducted under the Carpenters union consent decree. Following testimony by federal investigators concerning his close connection to the acting boss of the Gambino crime family, Fiorino is expelled from the union.

1996 Manhattan District Attorney Robert Morgenthau obtains indictments against several members of Exhibition Employees Union Local 829 for misusing union benefits while employed at the Javits Center.

1997 Gerald McQueen becomes president and CEO of the Javits Center.

In 1969, New York Mayor John Lindsay proposed a new exhibition and convention center to replace the New York Coliseum. The mayor and other proponents promised that a new center would compete more successfully for national trade shows and would stimulate New York City's economy by creating employment and business opportunities. Another benefit would be revitalization of the rundown site consisting of twenty-six acres stretching between 11th and 12th Avenues and from 34th and 39th Streets on Manhattan's west side.

Plans for the 1.8-million-square-foot Convention Center, which was later named for the popular former Republican U.S. Senator, won legislative approval and a $375 million initial construction budget in 1979.[2] Responsibility for construction and development was assigned to the

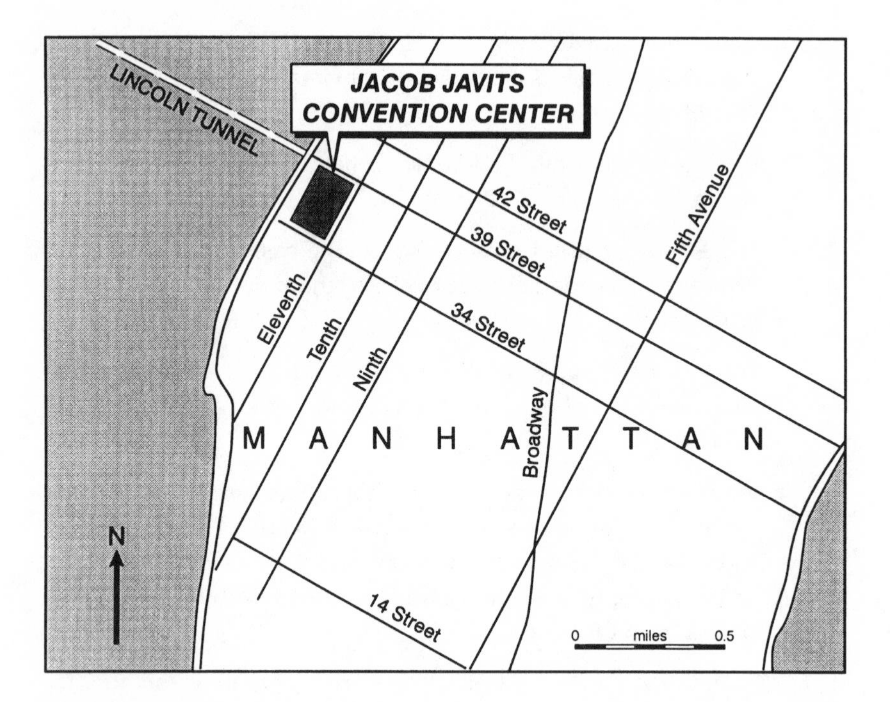

New York Convention Center Development Corporation (CCDC). The groundbreaking ceremony for the convention center, the nation's largest at that time, took place in late 1980. The center opened for business in April 1986.

Since the first concrete was poured for construction, the Javits Center was mired in organized-crime corruption and racketeering. Cosa Nostra bosses and members owned the concrete companies and dominated the union that poured the concrete. The CCDC awarded a major Javits Center construction contract to Julius Nasso Concrete Company and S & A Concrete Company, allotting $30 million for the concrete superstructure of the facility.[3] Both companies were later tied to the concrete cartel run by the Cosa Nostra "commission."[4] Anthony "Fat Tony" Salerno, ostensible boss of the Genovese organized-crime family, was convicted of rigging Javits Center concrete bids and of inflating the center's construction costs by approximately $12 million.[5] Few contractors were willing to complain; retaliation could be swift and brutal. For example, Irwin Schiff, owner of an electrical contracting company doing work during construction of the center, was murdered in a Manhattan restaurant soon after complaining to the FBI about corruption and theft at the center.[6]

By establishing a power base in the Teamsters, Carpenters, and Exhibition Employees Unions, Cosa Nostra crime families infiltrated the center, controlled its operations and extracted millions of dollars annually.[7]

OPERATION OF THE CONVENTION CENTER

Legal and Administrative Framework

The Javits Center is a state-owned facility operated as a corporation by the New York Convention Center Operating Corporation (CCOC), a public benefit corporation.[8] The CCOC is responsible for marketing the center to prospective exhibitors and, since 1991, for its management. The CCOC is run by the thirteen-member Board of Directors, of whom the governor appoints seven and state legislative leaders appoint six.[9] Appointees serve staggered three-year terms without pay; major responsibilities include setting Javits Center policy and appointing key administrative personnel. The governor recommends the chairman of the Board of Directors; the board has always approved the governor's recommendations.

Governor Mario Cuomo played a high-profile role in promoting the center in the early 1980s for its revitalization effects on Manhattan's west side. However, during the mid-1980s his administration referred complaints of exorbitant costs and corruption elsewhere.

Several members of the Board of Directors were large campaign contributors and friends of state politicians.[10] For example, Governor Cuomo appointed one board member who reportedly contributed $24,000 to his reelection campaign.[11] For strategic reasons, as well as because the board positions were unpaid and low profile, there was little incentive for board members to involve themselves in the center's management. William Stern, head of the Urban Development Corporation under Governor Cuomo, observed that the "Board is there to make sure everyone's political interests are met."[12]

Arranging a Show

Trade shows and conventions are scheduled and advertised often several years in advance. Until the 1995 reforms at the center, a representative of a trade organization contacted a show manager to arrange a show date.[13] The show manager arranged the dates for the show, rented space from the center, sold it to exhibitors, and hired decorating companies to prepare the center for exhibits. The decorating companies would use the unions' job referral system to employ workers to assemble and dismantle the exhibitions.* Workers lay carpet, load and unload trucks, install electrical fixtures, and perform other types of manual labor.**

The center operates most efficiently and profitably when shows are scheduled one immediately after another. Thus, Javits management has a strong interest in breaking down and packing up the shows as soon as they finish so that the next show can be set up; as a result, most of the setting up and breaking down of shows occurs at night, under time pressure. Before an exhibition opens, the mainly unskilled or semi-skilled workers may work around the clock loading and unloading trucks and vans, moving merchandise into and out of the convention hall, and assembling and dismantling display stands, tables, and seats.

Collective Bargaining Framework

Several unions represent the men and women who work at the center. The Teamsters (Local 807) represent workers who load and unload the delivery trucks and vans with exhibitors' products and supplies. Members of several Carpenters union locals assemble the booths and electrical stations, and, until July 1995, the Exhibition Employees Union (Local 829) represented the general laborers.

*Before 1995, the Javits Center directly employed approximately three hundred people who carried out routine day-to-day operations like event management (including booking shows, marketing, and operating the facility), administration, maintenance, and security. After 1995, the center put on its payroll workers who used to be employed by decorating companies, this swelled the payroll to two thousand employees.

**The center bills the show manager for rent, cleaning, and electrical services. The decorating company bills the show manager exhibitors. The trade association pays the center, and the center's management pays the decorators who worked on that show. The labor expenses are billed separately; each exhibitor is responsible for the labor expended on its exhibits. The trade association also bills each exhibitor according to the floor space used.

Until the mid-1990s, each union negotiated a collective bargaining agreement with the decorator companies. These agreements provided that 50 percent of the labor force for a particular show would be chosen by the decorator and 50 percent by the union through its hiring hall. Throughout the 1980s, the contracts also specified how many workers were required for various tasks, often many more than necessary. This featherbedding in part accounts for convention costs that were two and a half times those in Chicago and four times those in Atlanta.[14]

Featherbedding

Collective bargaining agreements covering work at the Javits Center mandated featherbedding and exorbitant labor costs. Union work rules required that a licensed electrician be paid close to $80 to plug in a lamp.[15] Unloading a forklift required nine workers; the same job required only three workers in Chicago. Exhibitors paid $70.50 an hour for a general laborer at Javits, and coughed up an hourly rate of $127.50 for weekend work and overtime. The comparable rates in Atlanta and Chicago were $33 and $48 an hour, respectively.

Agreements with decorator companies also gouged exhibitors. During the 1994 New York Auto Show, exhibitors paid $10 for a quart of orange juice, $27 for a gallon of coffee and $12 for a pot, and $10 for a sixteen-ounce bag of potato chips. Javits Center contracting rules foisted these outrageous prices upon the trade shows by forbidding trade associations and exhibitors from providing any goods and services themselves. The New York Auto Show organizers claimed that the cost of a New York show was 60 percent higher than a show in Detroit, Chicago, or Los Angeles.[16]

Cosa Nostra's Influence at the Center

Cosa Nostra exerted control over and extracted money from the Javits Center through control of businesses and labor unions. Members and associates of the Genovese, Gambino, and Colombo crime families held important positions within the union locals. They profited by allowing exhibitors to buy their way out of burdensome contractual requirements, and by placing members, associates, and friends in highly paid positions at the center.

THE CARPENTERS UNION AND THE JAVITS CENTER

Before the late 1990s, there were approximately twenty locals of the International Brotherhood of Carpenters and Joiners in the New York City area, organized under the umbrella of the District Council, which makes major policy decisions for the locals and negotiates the collective bargaining contracts. From the 1960s, the Genovese crime family influenced operations at the Javits Center through its control over the Carpenters union. Vincent "the Fish" Cafaro, a Genovese family member turned government informer, explained that the Genovese family "controlled the hiring of Carpenters union members, first at the [New York City] Coliseum, and then at the Javits Center."[17] Although other Cosa Nostra families exerted influence at the center, the Genovese family was the dominant force.[18]

The Carpenters union job-referral rules dictated that, with limited exceptions, work had to be distributed to members according to their placement on an out-of-work list. Contractors might specifically request a particular union member, but the request had to conform to certain requirements.[19] If a contractor needed a person with a special technical skill, the union was supposed to assign the first out-of-work person on the list with that qualification. In theory, unemployed union members registered at their local union office, which placed them on a chronological list and distributed job assignments accordingly.

In reality, the Genovese crime family ignored the rules and substituted its own criteria for filling carpenter positions at the Javits Center. Typically, a Genovese family associate gave union officials a preferential hiring list, from which between thirty and forty people were selected to work for decorator companies with business at the center. For several years, Cafaro himself had final say over hiring decisions.

Investigations into hiring at the Javits Center, which followed the settlement of a civil RICO suit against the Carpenters union, revealed a preferred "pool list" of approximately one hundred workers who received job referrals before other union members.[20] Many individuals on the pool list had known links to organized crime, mostly to the Genovese family. Sixty pool-list members had criminal records, including convictions for arson and murder. Almost all the listed individuals were Italian Americans; there were no women or minorities. In 1994, approximately half of these men earned more than $40,000, one-third more than $50,000, and six more than $100,000.[21]

During an FBI raid on a Genovese-family social club, agents found a list of fourteen individuals, all but one of whom had worked (or was working) as a carpenter at the Javits Center, and eight of whom appeared on the union's pool list.[22] A former Colombo family capo testified that "most of the people whom the Carpenters union refers to jobs at the Javits Center are either members and associates of the Genovese family, or friends and relatives of Genovese family members and associates."[23] The Genovese family maintained such tight control over who was employed at the center that members of other Cosa Nostra families were at times unable to get jobs there.[24]

The District Council's Ties to Cosa Nostra

The Carpenters District Council's representatives at the Javits Center invariably had close ties to organized crime, especially to the Genovese crime family. Representatives used their power to assign Cosa Nostra members, relatives, and friends to positions with decorator companies. Some jobs were awarded as payment for favors, others to provide legitimate employment for paroled family members. Many positions were treated as "no-show jobs," in which employees who never came to work were carried on the work roster and paid.

Ralph Coppola, an important Genovese associate, began working at the Javits Center in 1987, after his release from prison, where he had served time for arson.[25] He was assigned to the center by then-District Council president Paschal McGuinness, an alleged Cosa Nostra associate. Coppola was quickly promoted to District Council representative and allegedly inducted as a member of the Genovese family.[26] According to Salvatore "Sammy the Bull" Gravano, the underboss of the Gambino crime family who became a cooperating witness, Coppola ran the center on behalf of the Genovese family.[27]

In August 1991, Coppola was replaced at the center after a news article identified him as a Genovese agent.[28] In removing Coppola, Carpenters District Council president Frederick Devine cited Coppola's ties to organized crime.[29] However, Devine himself allegedly had ties to Cosa Nostra. Gravano told investigators that Devine was a puppet of the Colombo family, and another government informant stated that he had seen Devine meeting with members of the Colombo crime family in the District Council office.[30] Federal investigators charged that Devine worked with the DeCavalcante crime family of New Jersey and with the Genovese crime family. (In 1998, federal prosecutors succeeded in convicting Devine on six counts of grand larceny for which he received a fifteen-month prison term.)[31]

In April 1994, Devine appointed Anthony Fiorino and Leonard Simon to be the District Council's representatives at the center.[32] That year, they earned more than $106,000 and $144,000, respectively. The 1995 New York State Senate hearings on operations at the Javits Center uncovered important background information on Fiorino and Simon that demonstrates organized crime's entrenchment at the center.

Fiorino became a member of Local 257 in 1982 at the urging of a Genovese associate.[33] In 1988, the District Council appointed him to the supervisory position of "timekeeper" at the center. Three years later, he was promoted to chief of carpenters at the center, and in 1994, he succeeded Coppola as District Council representative. Law enforcement agencies believed that Fiorino's rapid advancement is explained by his ties to organized crime, especially to his brother-in-law Liborio "Barney" Bellomo, a capo and reputedly, for a time, acting boss of the Genovese crime family.

Leonard Simon had no carpentry skills prior to being employed at the Javits Center. He was an out-of-work taxi driver when he submitted a fraudulent application to the union, swearing that he had five years' experience in the trade. However, Simon had a key connection: his brother-in-law Ralph Coppola.[34] With Coppola's recommendation, he obtained a permanent job at the center.[35] Later, Simon advanced to District Council representative.

There is a dispute over the circumstances surrounding the appointments of Fiorino and Simon. Devine testified at a New York State Senate hearing that he barely knew the two men, and had chosen them on the recommendation of Fabian Palomino, the center's president and CEO.[36] Testifying at the same hearing, Palomino disclaimed knowing Fiorino and Simon, and stated that Devine had appointed both men without his recommendation.

Other Cosa Nostra Families

While the Genovese family has been the dominant Cosa Nostra presence at the Javits Center, other organized-crime families have also played a role. Alphonse "Little Al" D'Arco, former acting boss of the Lucchese crime family, explained the Lucchese family's role in controlling officials of the Carpenters union as "shaking down businesses that employed union members, ghost-payrolling family members, and stealing from employee pension and welfare funds."[37] Salvatore Miciotta, a former capo in the Colombo crime family, claimed to have paid $60,000 a year to the Lucchese, Colombo, and Genovese families so that his exposition company could do business at the Javits Center.

THE TEAMSTERS AND THE JAVITS CENTER

The International Brotherhood of Teamsters (IBT) Local 807 (Trade Show Division) is critical to Javits Center operations. Members of Local 807 primarily load and unload vehicles in preparation for trade shows.

Teamsters Hiring at the Center

Teamsters positions at the Javits Center paid between $21 and $43 an hour, plus generous benefits.[38] The October 1994 contract provided that Saturday and Sunday work would be paid at double the hourly rate; holiday work, triple. Decorators also paid Christmas bonuses of up to $5,000 to Teamsters members employed at the center.

The Teamsters Trade Show Division, through its hiring hall, assigned Javits Center work to *preferred* union members only. The jobs were distributed according to a seniority list consisting of forty-seven privileged members. If the seniority list was exhausted, jobs were assigned to members on the "shape" list of thirty members.[39] "Shape" refers to the process by which union members assemble at either the local office or the place of employment to be selected for work. Union members are usually called by their local and told to go shape at a job site. The general foreman selects members from the shape and assigns them work.

Teamsters who were not on the seniority or shape lists could not work at the center. Many of those on the seniority list were friends and relatives of Teamsters officials and Cosa Nostra members;[40] some had not even belonged to the Teamsters before working at the center. At least eleven members of the seniority pool were relatives or friends of the general foreman; at least fifteen members were relatives or friends of other Local 807 members.[41] One-third of the individuals on Local 807's seniority list had known ties to organized crime.[42]

The Rabbitts and Teamsters Local 807

For almost three decades, the Teamsters Trade Show Division was led by Robert Rabbitt Sr. and his sons Michael and Robert Jr. The Rabbitts created the Teamsters seniority lists, which enabled them to dictate Teamsters hiring at the center.[43]

The elder Robert Rabbitt became a member of Teamsters Local 807 when he was seventeen years old.[44] He was appointed shop steward in 1967, became an officer of Local 807 in 1970, and was subsequently promoted to business agent, responsible for representing the Trade Show Division of Local 807 at the Coliseum.[45] Before the Javits Center opened, collective bargaining negotiations conducted between decorators and the IBT created the position of general foreman explicitly for Rabbitt Sr.[46] As general foreman, Rabbitt oversaw all Teamsters members at the center and served as a liaison between the decorator companies and center management.

In 1985, Robert Rabbitt Sr. was convicted of second degree manslaughter for fatally stabbing a garment shop manager, and sentenced to prison. The court banned him from the union for five years.[47] However, the general foreman's post was held open for him until his release.[48] In February 1992, a New York State grand jury indicted him for conspiracy, receiving bribes, committing larceny, falsifying business records, and possessing stolen property.[49] Rabbitt pleaded guilty to falsifying payroll records so workers could illegally receive workers' compensation benefits and served one year in prison.[50] Afterward, he resumed general foreman duties at the Javits Center. In 1994, IBT investigators threatened to charge Rabbitt with accepting bribes in return for overlooking an employer's use of nonunion trucks and laborers at the center. In the face of these looming charges as well as possible charges for failing to cooperate with union investigations, Rabbitt agreed to a five-year suspension from the union.[51] His job responsibilities were transferred to his son Michael.[52]

The Teamsters collective bargaining agreement with the decorators expired in September 1994, while Rabbitt Sr. was in prison. Michael Rabbitt led the negotiating team bargaining with the decorator companies.[53] As part of the new agreement, the position of Teamsters general foreman at the center was changed to a management, nonunion assignment; thereafter, a criminal record would not be a disqualification. Because the general foreman was no longer a union position, Teamsters reformers were powerless to suspend any corrupt person who held it. The general foreman still managed the Teamsters but was no longer accountable to the membership. The general foreman's contract provided for a $150,000 salary and a $236,000 severance in the event of dismissal without just cause.

After his father went to prison, Michael Rabbitt left the union and took the position of general foreman. Although the Rabbitt family is allegedly mob-connected, the details of the relationship remain unclear. Stories hinting at the power of the father and sons are intriguing but fail to supply hard facts. For example, shortly after his release from prison in 1988, Rabbitt Sr. had a fistfight with a Teamsters member alleged to be a member of the Bonanno family. Such assaults usually trigger serious consequences for anyone who lacks strong ties to organized crime. There was no retaliation against Rabbitt. Further, as general shop steward, Michael Rabbitt selected Armando Rea as assistant general shop steward; the father's involvement in the decision was suspected. A civil RICO suit against IBT Local 814 later exposed Rea as a Bonanno soldier and banned him from Teamsters membership. Michael Rabbitt denied knowledge of Rea's organized-crime connections.[54]

THE EXHIBITION EMPLOYEES AND THE JAVITS CENTER

Local 829 of the Exhibition Employees Union (Expos) is affiliated with the International Alliance of Theatrical and State Employees of the AFL-CIO. A probe by the Manhattan District Attorney's Office found that more than 60 percent of Expos Local 829 workers employed at the Javits Center had felony records.[55] Although the Expos apparently did not maintain a pool list for preferential hiring at the Javits Center, it did use selective criteria. Undercover police investigations revealed that to get one of the handsomely paid jobs at the center—up to $100,000 a year—an ordinary Expos worker had to buy a membership book from union officials for $13,000 to $22,000. Individuals with organized crime connections purchased books at lower cost and enjoyed priority for center assignments.[56]

Exhibition officials also allegedly padded payroll rosters with six ghost employees for small shows and up to twenty ghosts for larger shows. Typically, some of the ghost employees were parolees who used proof of employment at the center to stay out of prison. Ghost employees shared their "salary" with the shop stewards and the Genovese crime family. This scam cost hundreds of thousands of dollars each year.

The Expos chief shop steward, much like the Teamsters general foreman, supervised Expos members at the center. Steven "Beansy" Dellacava and Paul Coscia were chief shop stewards for the Expos at the Javits Center until mid-1995; together, they determined who could work where and when. Coscia was also the vice-president of Local 829; Dellacava began working at Javits in 1990 after his release from prison, where he had served time for selling heroin. Both men were reputedly associates of the Genovese crime family.

Expos officials apparently orchestrated fraudulent legal claims against the center. Injuries sustained in nonwork accidents were presented as workplace on-the-job casualties, which enabled the injuree to file a workers' compensation claim against the center. The worker paid off Paul Coscia, who directed others to stage the accident and serve as witnesses. The settlement was divided among the injured worker, the shop stewards, and mob bosses.

CONCLUSION

From the day construction began, Cosa Nostra was a key player in the life of the Javits Center. The mob, particularly the Genovese crime family, had a stranglehold on three labor unions that represented center workers, and used its power to direct high-paying jobs to members, associates, and friends.

Teamsters Local 807, dominated through Robert Rabbitt Sr. and his two sons, may also have been controlled by Cosa Nostra. While the details of the Rabbitts' connections to organized crime have never been proved, there seems little doubt that Cosa Nostra called the shots with respect to Teamsters interests in the Javits Center. Jobs were given out by the general foreman—Robert Rabbitt Sr. or Michael Rabbitt—based on a preferred list comprised of many individuals with ties to organized crime.

Although the Expos workers did not have pool lists like those of the Teamsters and the Carpenters, they too allocated center jobs selectively. Workers had to buy union membership books for up to $22,000 in order to obtain lucrative center jobs. The Expos union at the center was pervaded by ghost employees, personal-injury fraud, and abuse of security privileges.

Although Cosa Nostra's influence was well known to everyone who transacted business at the center and was reported extensively by journalists, for years politicians and law enforcement officials made little if any effort to attack the status quo. Until the mid-1990s, the mob's power at the Jacob Javits Center seemed impregnable.

6

Carting Away a Fortune

Cosa Nostra and the Waste-Hauling Industry

> [W]e find that garbage collection industry men banded together in associations which eventually . . . invoked monopoly and restraint of trade arrangements with a system of punishments for nonconforming members. . . . In Vincent Squillante we have presented the picture of a man who traded on his association with key underworld characters and his ability to "handle" Local 813, International Brotherhood of Teamsters, to parlay himself into a position where he was the absolute czar of the private sanitation industry in Greater New York.
>
> —McClellan Committee Hearings, 1957

CHRONOLOGY

General History

1947 New York City officials dissolve employer trade-waste associations; associations soon reemerge under different names.

1958 McClellan Committee exposes IBT Local 813 boss Bernard Adelstein's ties to organized crime.

1986 State Assemblyman Hinchey issues report on New York waste-hauling cartel.

1992 Bernard Adelstein, longtime head of IBT Local 813, purged from Teamsters by trustee.

1994 James "Jimmy Brown" Failla, head of trade associations, pleads guilty to conspiring to murder.

New York City Cartel

1974 Brooklyn District Attorney Eugene Gold indicts fifty-five carting firms and nine officials, including Cosa Nostra members; several convictions, but no structural reforms.

1977 Joseph Gambino and Carlo Conti convicted of racketeering and sentenced to prison.

1985 U.S. Attorney Rudolph Giuliani indicts Matthew "Matty the Horse" Ianniello for carting racketeering; he is later acquitted.

1987 Mayor Edward Koch announces support for a plan to create a firm to compete with the carting cartel; the plan is never implemented. The public advocate, Mark Green, later proposes a new version of the plan; it too goes unimplemented.

1989 U.S. Attorney Otto Obermaier convicts Gambino crime-family member Angelo Paccione; he is sentenced to twelve years and $22 million in fines.

1990 Mark Green and Richard Schrader become commissioner and deputy commissioner of Department of Consumer Affairs, and begin using the agency to oppose organized crime and the cartel.

1993 After unsuccessful efforts to break into the New York City waste-hauling market, Browning Ferris Industries (BFI) agrees to assist New York County District Attorney Robert Morgenthau's investigation.

1995 Morgenthau announces state racketeering indictments against twenty-three carting firms and associations.

By 1997, all defendants have been found or have pled guilty.

1996 Local Law 42 passes; Trade Waste Commission created, issues comprehensive rules, including a reduction in the maximum carting rates.

1998 Fear of corporate monopolistic control over the New York City's waste-hauling industry is addressed, as the merger of Waste Management and USA Waste becomes contingent upon the companies' divestiture of three transfer stations in the New York City area.

Long Island Cartel

1984 OCTF Director Ron Goldstock indicts sixteen Long Island carting firms, individuals, and public officials on antitrust charges. Several defendants are convicted, but given light sentences.

1986 Lucchese family capo Salvatore Avellino pleads guilty to state charges of coercion.

1989 Robert Kubecka and brother-in-law murdered by Cosa Nostra for cooperating with law enforcement officials.

U.S. Attorney Andrew J. Maloney files civil RICO suit against Long Island carting cartel; 112 defendants, including 64 Gambino family and Lucchese family members and associates, 44 carting firms, carters' trade association, and IBT Local 813. Leads to federal monitorship.

1994 U.S. Attorney Zachary Carter achieves federal monitorship over entire Long Island waste-hauling industry.

Former prosecutor Michael Cherkasky appointed industry monitor.

New York City residences and businesses produce thirteen thousand tons of trash every day, not including the debris generated by construction projects.[1] Once generated, trash undergoes a two-step process: collection and disposal. Collection is generally a separate industry from disposal; disposal involves providing a final resting place for trash, such as a landfill or incinerator.[2] In New York City, the Department of Sanitation collects residential waste. Commercial-waste hauling—that is, collection—the focus of this chapter, is carried out by approximately three hundred small firms (one to twenty trucks) that together constitute a $1.5 billion per year industry.[3] The drivers and trash collectors are represented by Teamsters Local 813. Most of the firms are members of one of four trade associations.

Although the cartel's precise origins are unclear, New York City officials received complaints as early as 1947 that illegal activities were restricting free competition in the waste-hauling industry.[4] At that time, the cartel controlled only the collection of commercial paper products (the New York City Department of Sanitation picked up most other commercial waste and all residential waste). The city's decision in 1956 to privatize commercial-waste hauling provided a lucrative opportunity for racketeering; suddenly, private carters had approximately fifty-two thousand new customers, a 70 percent expansion of their client base.[5] Restaurants, stores, office buildings, and light industry made up the bulk of the new client base.

Similar cartels operated on Long Island and in Westchester County, just north of New York City. On Long Island, the cartel was established and policed by the Lucchese crime family. The Westchester County carting cartel was run by associates of the Genovese crime family.*

A few very large companies dominated the industry. In New York City, several companies associated with Barretti Carting and several associated with V. Ponte & Sons serviced a large portion of the city. Likewise, on Long Island Salvatore Avellino's SSC Corporation and Emedio Fazzini's Jamaica Ash dominated the industry. But the majority of New York City and Long Island carting companies operated with fewer than five trucks and fewer than ten employees, either as close corporations

*In 1996, following a ten-year federal investigation, RICO and other federal charges (sixty-one counts in all) were brought against seven individuals and fourteen businesses. Prosecutors alleged the defendants maintained a property-rights system and shared profits, which were concealed through sham transactions and false tax statements. On September 30, 1997, five individuals and thirteen waste-hauling companies pled guilty to multiple charges. Among those pleading guilty were Mario Gigante, a brother of former, suspected Genovese boss Vincent "the Chin" Gigante, and Thomas Milo, the sole owner of Suburban Carting Corporation, the country's largest privately held waste-hauling company. Gigante and Milo were sentenced to prison terms of forty-two months and thirty-three months, respectively. As part of their plea agreements, the defendant companies consented to be monitored by former assistant U.S. attorney Walter Mack. Ultimately, all the defendants pled guilty and collectively were fined roughly $17 million. Westchester County has since required all carting businesses placing bids on county contracts to undergo a thorough background investigation. See *United States v. Gigante et al.*, 948 F. Supp. 279 (S.D.N.Y. 1996) (provides some information regarding the indictment); Benjamin Weiser, "Haulers Plead Guilty to Controlling Garbage Routes with Violence," *New York Times*, October 1, 1997, B5; "Waste Hauler Sentenced to 33 Months for Fraud," *New York Times*, February 24, 1998, B2; "Gigante Sentenced in IRS Fraud," *U.P.I.*, April 9, 1998; Alex Philippidis, "Mamaroneck Carter May File Suit Against Former Partner," *Westchester County Business Journal*, 36, no. 41 (October 13, 1997): 5; Donna Greene, "County Includes Integrity as Part of Carting Contract," *New York Times*, May 10, 1998, Westchester sec., 9.

or partnerships passed down from father to son;[6] traditionally, the majority of owners have been Italian Americans.[7] In his in-depth study of racketeering in the carting industry in New York City and Long Island, Peter Reuter hypothesizes that the "ethnic homogeneity" that characterized the carting companies facilitated the Mafia's infiltration of the industry and the creation of a cartel system.

Under the Gambino and Lucchese crime families' influence, the commercial-waste hauling firms, like the trucking firms in the Garment Center, operated a "property-rights" system that bound every commercial customer to one carter for life. The industry was also characterized by bid rigging, inflated pricing mechanisms, and threats of violence.[8]

THE PROPERTY-RIGHTS SYSTEM

Under the property-rights or customer-allocation system, developed and enforced by the Gambino, Genovese, and Lucchese crime families, each customer (or, to be precise, each "stop") belonged to a particular cartel member; no other carter was allowed to solicit or accept the customer's business.[9] The carter owned his stops in perpetuity. When a business changed hands or disappeared, a successor business at the same location remained the property of whichever carter had serviced that stop. Stops taken together were called a "route";[10] stops could be sold to other firms in the cartel but could not otherwise change hands.[11] When disputes regarding ownership of a particular stop arose, they were settled by the trade association. Customers who tried to switch to another carting company quickly discovered that they were unable to get any service. Eventually, disgruntled customers were forced back to their assigned carter, often with penalty charges to drive home the message. (In some cases, the cartel would permit a switch, if the successor carter compensated its predecessor.)

POLICING THE CARTELS: COSA NOSTRA AND THE TRADE ASSOCIATIONS

Through the New York City and Long Island trade associations, Cosa Nostra policed the carting cartels. Outside companies could not participate in the industry and cartel members could not compete with one another. National waste-hauling companies did not seek business in either the New York or Long Island markets. The absence of such companies from these lucrative markets was, according to Reuter, the result of the "effectiveness of the racketeer reputation of the industry . . . and of customer allocation agreements."[12]

The trade associations came under scrutiny as early as 1947, when the New York City Commissioner of Investigation found that "[i]n addition to restricting competition by dividing territory and fixing non-competitive prices, the associations policed the industry in order to maintain their monopoly."[13] To combat the associations' stranglehold over the industry, the commissioner ordered the dissolution of the Greater New York Trade Waste Association, Inc., the Brooklyn Trade Waste Removers' Association, Inc., and the Queens Trade Waste Removal Association. This effort was not successful, for the associations soon reappeared under new names.

The Association of Trade Waste Removers of Greater New York dominated the industry during the period of organized crime's greatest power. Its president for more than thirty years was James "Jimmy Brown" Failla, a capo in the Gambino crime family. Failla held weekly meetings in the association's offices or at a Brooklyn club to assign routes, resolve disputes, and conduct routine business.[14] Other Cosa Nostra–linked trade associations included the Kings County Trade Waste Association (Genovese), the Greater New York Waste Paper Association (Genovese), and the Queens County Trade Waste Association (Gambino). The Long Island carting industry was governed by the Private Sanitation Industry Association of Nassau/Suffolk, which for years was controlled by Salvatore Avellino, a member of the Lucchese crime family.[15]

By maintaining the property-rights system and the cartel, organized crime provided a valuable service to the small firms in the industry. Cartel members charged exorbitant prices and engaged in unconscionable business practices like inflating the amount of waste collected in order to justify higher charges. They did not have to compete for business, and could charge high prices to their customers, who ultimately passed them on to all New York City and Long Island residents. The carters flourished despite inefficiencies that would have been fatal to firms in a competitive industry.

Ownership Interests

A number of Cosa Nostra members held ownership interests in the carting industry. To name just a few examples: Joseph Gambino, son of the onetime Gambino family's crime boss Carlo Gambino, owned several Bronx waste-hauling firms, including the P & S Sanitation Company;[16] Salvatore Avellino, a soldier in the Lucchese crime family and a close associate of crime boss Antonio "Tony Ducks" Corallo, controlled the Salem Sanitary Carting Corporation;[17] Gambino associate Angelo Paccione owned the National Carting Company of Brooklyn;[18] and Matthew "Matty the Horse" Ianniello, an underboss in the Genovese family, ran Consolidated Carting, among other firms.[19]

ENFORCING THE CARTEL

The mob's enforcement mechanisms prevented cheating by cartel members and competition from nonmembers. Monitoring required little effort because the customer-allocation system made prohibited competition easy to spot. Organized-crime figures and cartel members used economic pressure, subtle forms of coercion, and outright violence to punish those who sought to take more than their presliced piece of the pie.

The most common punishments were economic sanctions. If one carter took a customer away from a fellow cartel member, then Cosa Nostra, acting as an instrument of the trade association, would order the wrongdoer to compensate the victim by handing over a customer of equal or greater value.[20] Sometimes, the rebel had to pay a penalty to the wronged carter, as much as sixty-five times the monthly revenue received from the stolen customer. In effect, the trade association functioned like a court with special power to enforce its decrees. Carters who refused to accept the jurisdiction of the trade association found themselves the target of a strike or other job actions by Teamsters Local 813, the only union representing the drivers.[21]

The cartel was so tightly managed and cheating so unlikely to be successful that violence was seldom necessary. However, from time to time the actions of rebel carters sparked violent reactions. Their drivers were beaten, their trucks destroyed, and they themselves threatened and assaulted.[22] The owners of at least one rebel carting company paid with their lives.

In 1982, Robert Kubecka, a rebel waste hauler on Long Island, began cooperating with law enforcement officials. Kubecka had refused to abide by the cartel's property-rights system and recorded conversations with cartel members that aided a number of major investigations. In 1989, Kubecka and his brother-in-law Donald Barstow were murdered. In 1993, Salvatore Avellino pled guilty to conspiracy to commit these murders and was sentenced to an indeterminate sentence of three-and-a-half to ten-and-a-half years. Two years later, Carmine Avellino (Salvatore's brother), Anthony Baratta, Frank Federico, and Rocco Vitulli were indicted in connection with the Kubecka and Barstow murders. All the defendants, except Federico, whose whereabouts is unknown, pled guilty to lesser offenses. In 1998, former Lucchese family underboss Anthony Casso was sentenced to life in prison for conspiracy to commit murders and other crimes, including the murders of Kubecka and Barstow.[23]

ENFORCING THE PROPERTY-RIGHTS SYSTEM

When necessary, Cosa Nostra kept customers in line. Every business, from the smallest bodega to the largest department store, was married to one of the carting companies. Divorce was difficult, if not impossible; businesses that attempted to break away from their partners faced threats and vandalism.[24] When one businessman canceled his waste-hauling contract and started hauling away his own waste, garbage was dumped on his doorstep with a note threatening to bomb his business unless he continued to pay his carter.[25]

Most customers, however displeased with their carter, did not need to be warned twice. When a national hauling firm attempted to break into the New York City market with an offer to cut current carting rates in half, practically no businesses showed interest.[26] One bank executive explained that he refused an opportunity to save 50 percent on waste disposal because he feared the bank's automated teller machines would be vandalized.

COSA NOSTRA'S CONTROL OVER IBT LOCAL 813

Cosa Nostra's influence in the waste-hauling industry was reinforced by its control over Teamsters Local 813, which represented the drivers employed by the carters.[27] For decades, the local was run by Bernard Adelstein, a man whom the McClellan Committee in 1958 branded the "abject tool"[28] of organized crime. Adelstein's reign at Local 813 lasted until he was banned from the IBT in 1992.[29] The McClellan Committee paid special attention to the ties between Adelstein and Vincent "Jimmy" Squillante, a high-ranking official of the New York City Cartmen's Association, and a known mobster. According to the committee, Local 813 was the personal fiefdom of Adelstein, and "far from fighting Squillante . . . [Adelstein] provided vital cooperation as [Squillante] moved . . . to ruthless czardom of the garbage industry."[30*]

Under Adelstein's stewardship, Local 813 served the interests of the organized crime–sponsored cartel. If a carter fell out of favor with Cosa Nostra, members of the local would refuse to work for that company. In 1989, Robert Kubecka had reported that the tires on his trucks were slashed and the windshields broken; a Gambino crime family associate offered to solve his union problems for a $20,000 fee.[31] Jerry Kubecka, father of the murdered Robert, and himself the owner of a rebel carting company, charged that Local 813 threatened his customers with labor problems and violence unless they agreed to be serviced by a firm designated by the cartel.

Years later, in 1989, at a hearing looking into Adelstein's underworld ties, a Gambino-crime-family-underboss-turned-government-witness, Salvatore "Sammy the Bull" Gravano, testified that Gambino capo James "Jimmy Brown" Failla exercised de facto control over Local 813, and that Adelstein "answer[ed] directly"[32] to Failla. A former employee of Local 813 testified that Adelstein and Failla met at least once every two weeks, and worked together in "controlling and manipulating the private sanitation industry in the New York City metropolitan area."[33]

*Following the McClellan Committee hearings, both Adelstein and Squillante were indicted on extortion charges. Adelstein was found guilty, but his conviction was subsequently overturned. Squillante disappeared before trial and is presumed dead. Robert E. Kessler and Phil Mintz, "Feds vs. LI Carters," *Newsday*, June 8, 1989, 3.

Government Responses to Racketeering in Carting

The initial response of law enforcement agencies to the McClellan Committee's reports of mob activity in the garbage industry was ambitious, but in the end little was accomplished. New York State's attorney general sought injunctions against Local 813, three trade associations, and approximately four hundred individuals and corporations involved in the waste-hauling business.[34] He sought to prohibit the defendants from joining the trade associations and from engaging in anticompetitive practices. In 1959, after a protracted court battle, injunctions were granted against the various defendants. It proved to be a Pyrrhic victory, however because state officials left the injunctions largely unenforced.[35]

Information uncovered by the McClellan Committee also led to criminal charges against Squillante, Adelstein, and others. Adelstein was convicted of extortion, but the conviction was overturned on appeal.[36] Squillante disappeared, presumed murdered.[37] In the final analysis, although government hearings succeeded in exposing and bringing a degree of notoriety to a multimillion-dollar racketeering scheme operating in the New York waste-hauling industry, law enforcement efforts were largely ineffective in defeating Cosa Nostra's corruption and racketeering.

MORIBUND REGULATOR: NEW YORK CITY'S DEPARTMENT OF CONSUMER AFFAIRS

The New York City agency responsible for regulating the carting industry was the Department of Consumer Affairs (DCA), created by Mayor Robert Wagner in 1956 to bolster the city government's role in monitoring waste disposal.[38] The DCA was empowered to set licensing requirements, issue carting licenses, and set maximum rates for hauling trash. However, rather than using its licensing authority to keep corrupt individuals and firms out of the industry or to encourage fair economic competition, the DCA simply issued permits on request. The DCA was so promiscuous in granting licenses that in a 1980 interview, one long-time employee could not recall a single license denial in the agency's history.[39] Moreover, the DCA set maximum carting rates that were extremely high—well above the prevailing rates in any other U.S. city—

and cartel members treated the maximum rate as the only rate. Customers, who were not in a position to protest, were told that the exorbitant bills were due to the city-*imposed* rate. Thus, the DCA regulations actually helped to maintain the Cosa Nostra–sponsored cartel.[40] (In the early 1990s, the DCA did reduce the maximum rate, but a lawsuit resulted in the maximum rate's being reset at $14.75 per cubic yard.)

To say that, up until 1990, the DCA failed to exercise its regulatory power effectively would be a gross understatement. For example, in setting maximum carting rates, the DCA's consideration of the waste haulers' costs mocked its role as an independent regulator. To calculate costs, the agency had to factor in the amounts charged by landfills for waste disposal. However, while disposal companies based their prices on the volume of *compacted* waste, carters billed their customers according to cubic yards of *uncompacted* waste.[41] Price monitoring was difficult because of uncertainty about how tightly the carting firms' different equipment could pack waste. If a carter collected 3.5 cubic yards of loose garbage from a customer and could compact that amount into a single cubic yard before taking it to the landfill, then the carter should be able to pass along only the cost of disposing of that single cubic yard. Alternatively, if the carter could compact 3.5 cubic yards into half a cubic yard, then the disposal cost to the customer should have been halved. But carters routinely collected 3.5 cubic yards of loose garbage, compacted it into cubic half yards, and charged their customers for the full cubic yards, thereby passing on two times their landfill costs.

Waste haulers also routinely overcharged their captive customers by billing them for more loose garbage than they actually collected. Because customers rarely measure their waste, it was easy for the carters to exaggerate the amount hauled away.[42] As a result, charges for waste haulage bore little relation to the cost of its collection and transportation to the landfill.

Unhappy customers had two options: (1) confront the carting company; or (2) complain to the DCA. The first option required the complainant to hire a trash auditor, of which there were few, and then confront a company known to be mob-connected—hardly an attractive prospect. DCA did have a complaint procedure and a small number of investigators. And in some cases, customers did obtain restitution. But for the most part, DCA simply would not or could not challenge the systemic corruption and racketeering.[43]

A small New York City business, such as a corner grocery or delicatessen, paid about $15,000 annually for trash removal. Restaurants coughed up $50,000, and large office buildings were charged as much as $1 million per year.[44] While Los Angeles and Boston businesses were paying $9 and $5.30 respectively for every cubic yard of waste hauled away, their New York City counterparts were paying $14.70.[45]

Bid rigging among carters occurred frequently on Long Island, where municipalities would solicit bids for hauling an entire community's waste.[46] However, New York City was hardly immune. When a large customer solicited competitive bids, the waste-hauling firms would collusively decide the low bid and low bidder. For example, in November 1996, state prosecutors indicted several carting companies for fixing bids in connection with the waste collection at fourteen federal buildings, including offices, courthouses, and the FAA control tower at JFK International Airport.

In 1990, Mark Green became commissioner of DCA. He and Deputy Commissioner Richard Schrader (who succeeded Green in 1993 when Green was elected public advocate) tried to mobilize DCA in opposition to the cartel. They moved to revoke Paccione's license, charging price gouging, fraudulent contracts, and intimidation of customers and competitors. When Paccione's company was put into receivership, DCA worked with the trustee, Barrington Parker. Next, DCA launched an expensive and expansive law enforcement effort aimed at voiding illegal waste-hauling contracts. Thousands of citations were issued, and annual reporting requirements were significantly increased. Finally, Green put forward a proposal to create a new licensing authority that would put out bids for companies to service a large area of the city. Each company would have to employ an IPSIG (Independent Private Sector Inspector General) to monitor its operations and report to the government.

SPORADIC LAW ENFORCEMENT

From 1973 to 1974, Brooklyn District Attorney Eugene Gold ran a sixteen month–long undercover investigation of the private carting industry in his jurisdiction.[47] His office set up a carting firm on Coney Island staffed by undercover officers. Although the government carting firm undercut the prices of its competitors by 30 percent, and actively solicited two thousand businesses, it attracted only nineteen customers.[48]

Ultimately, Gold obtained indictments for criminal restraint of trade against fifty-five Brooklyn carting firms and nine carting industry officials, including members of the Gambino, Genovese, and Colombo crime families. The defendants pled guilty in exchange for light sentences.[49] Not one defendant served any jail time; most received insubstantial fines. The DCA imposed its own paltry penalty: $500 per truck.

Meanwhile, New York State Attorney General Louis J. Lefkowitz obtained a court-ordered dissolution of the Brooklyn Trade Waste Association. A Brooklyn grand jury recommended that New York City take over the collection of the waste from commercial businesses located in residential buildings.[50] While considering this proposal, the DCA temporarily stopped issuing new licenses to carting firms with pending indictments, but this show of regulatory muscle was short-lived. Ultimately, every request for a licensing renewal was granted.[51]

The DCA episode illustrated the prevailing view among city officials that the licensing-on-demand policy promoted stability in the carting industry. Leo Pollock, head of the DCA's Trade Waste Division, explained that "we didn't want price wars and chaos in the industry. We didn't think that would protect the public."[52] Although one sanitation commissioner supported a proposal that would have transferred control of fifty thousand stops from privately owned companies to the Sanitation Department, his successor vetoed the idea, and other city officials were equally disinclined to alter the status quo.[53] According to one high-ranking city official, Mayor Abraham Beame "wished the situation would just blow over."[54] Thus, District Attorney Gold's efforts failed to achieve systemic change. If anything, the fizzling of his ambitious prosecutorial effort demonstrated the extent to which political and administrative inertia hindered efforts to destroy the waste-hauling cartel.

Investigation of the Long Island Cartel and Antitrust Suits

In the late 1970s, rebel carter Robert Kubecka, who had long refused to join the Long Island cartel and who had complained to various law enforcement agencies for years, agreed to assist the New York State Organized Task Force (OCTF) in an effort to break the mob's stranglehold on the carting industry. The OCTF, assisted by Kubecka, launched an eighteen-month investigation. In 1982, the OCTF obtained court authorization to bug the automobile of Antonio "Tony Ducks" Corallo, then the head of the Lucchese crime family. The "car bug" turned out to be one of the most productive electronic surveillances of the 1980s.*

Many prominent mobsters and industry figures were caught up in the government's net, including Corallo; his underboss Salvatore "Tom Mix" Santoro; Salvatore Avellino; and James Corrigan, the director of the Private Sanitation Industry Association. Based upon information obtained through the intercepted conversations, New York State Organized Crime Task Force Director Ronald Goldstock indicted twenty-one individuals, including Corallo, and sixteen waste-hauling firms[55] on charges of conspiring to dominate private-garbage collection on Long Island[56] by dividing up territory and stifling competition through threats and agreements, and of conspiring to rig bids on commercial carting contracts.[57] According to the OCTF, this racketeering resulted in overcharges of more than $10 million a year in Suffolk County alone.

The defendants were charged with many offenses, chief among them maintaining a customer-allocation system and conspiring to injure Kubecka. Goldstock claimed that Salvatore Avellino ran the cartel through the Private Sanitation Industry Association of Nassau/Suffolk, which diverted more than $400,000 to the Lucchese crime family.[58] While several defendants pled guilty in 1987 to state charges[59] and juries convicted the remaining defendants in 1988,[60] the impact of the convictions ultimately was undermined by light sentences.[61] Justice John Vaughn ordered the defendants to spend six months in jail or to provide 840 hours of community service by collecting waste for Long Island towns. The guilty carters were fined between $6,000 and $10,000 each. Perhaps in response to complaints over such mild sentences, in 1988 Justice Vaughn imposed $1 million fines on two carting companies found guilty after trials.

OCTF Director Ronald Goldstock, while dismayed by the light sentences, stated that he did not believe that traditional prosecutions could rid the carting industry of the mafia. On January 22, 1985, Attorney General Robert Abrams brought a federal antitrust suit seeking to alter permanently the way carting companies did business on Long Island.[62] The suit alleged that twenty-four Long Island carting companies and twenty-five of their chief executives had violated the Clayton Act,

*Evidence obtained from the Corallo car bug contributed to the conviction of thirty-eight organized crime figures, public officials, and carting companies and to the commission case, the most important organized crime case in U.S. history.

which prohibits unfair trade practices.[63] The suit sought treble damages for the victims of the conspiracy—the municipalities, school districts, and individual customers—all of whom had paid inflated waste-hauling charges for decades, and argued that the defendants should pay a multimillion-dollar fine.[64]

Goldstock called for far-reaching changes in the private carting industry. He sought an injunction requiring that defendants bill customers on a standard unit of measurement—such as a standard container—so customers could compare the rates of different carters. He also asked the court to order carters to publish their rates and the names of their institutional customers, and to provide customers with a written statement that they could cancel their carting contract on ten days' notice. The goal was "to open up the competitive forces in the market place to allow free and open competition."[65]

In 1989, the New York State Attorney General's office settled this antitrust suit for just $3 million in cash and services. None of the proposed structural changes was achieved. However, by targeting the cartels as criminal enterprises, urging structural reforms to a corrupted industry, and focusing on restraint of trade violations, Goldstock provided a model for law enforcement agencies to follow in future attacks on the Cosa Nostra–run waste-hauling cartel on Long Island.

In August 1989, Robert Kubecka and his partner, Donald Barstow, were murdered in the office of their carting company. In 1994, Salvatore Avellino, head of the Lucchese family's waste-hauling operations on Long Island and the de facto head of the carters' trade association, pled guilty to conspiracy to commit those murders.[66]

CONCLUSION

Since the mid-1950s, the New York City area carting industry was dominated by cartels and a customer-allocation system. Two cartels, one in New York City and one on Long Island, were managed and policed by trade associations and IBT Local 813. Local 813 head Bernard Adelstein and Vincent Squillante, an officer of the New York Cartmen's Association and a mobster, forged a relationship that furthered Cosa Nostra's interests in the carting business. The trade association and the union were pawns of the Lucchese and Gambino crime families. The cartels were so strong for so long that any challenges by rebel customers or carters were easily defeated by economic sanctions. Personal violence was rarely necessary.

For many years, the New York City Department of Consumer Affairs seemed to exercise its regulatory powers in a manner that was wholly consistent with the interests of the cartel members and the organized-crime figures for whom they fronted. The DCA essentially gave out licenses to anyone who asked, set high maximum rates, and gave tacit sanction to the property-rights system. In 1988, Commissioner Angelo Aponte, approved an enormous—38 percent—increase in waste-hauling rates. He noted that anyone who believed that free enterprise was a term that reasonably characterized the trade waste-removal industry was operating under an illusion. For the business community, the waste-hauling cartels and the mobsters who sponsored them were simply a fact of life in New York City.

7

Building a Cosa Nostra Fiefdom

The Construction Industry

But we gotta have the strength so that when a fucker comes along and bids [on a contract which is supposed to be limited to members of a Cosa Nostra family–sponsored cartel] tomorrow he's got four gold tooths [organized crime members] in front of him saying "now that [you've got the contract] where are all the workers?" That's the power.

Now, as the Association, we control the [employers.] When we control the men we control the [employers] even better because they're even more fuckin' afraid.

Do you understand me? When you got a [employer] who steps out of line, you got the whip. You got the fuckin' whip. This is what he [one of the crime bosses] tells me all the time. A strong union makes money for everybody, including the wise guys. The wise guys make even more money with a strong union.[1]

—Salvatore Avellino, soldier in the
Lucchese Crime Family

CHRONOLOGY

1970s FBI conducts the Long Island Labor Racketeering and Extortion (LILREX) investigation, which results in prosecutions against drywall racketeer and Genovese family capo Vincent DiNapoli.

1981 Brooklyn Organized Crime Strike Force brings charges against DiNapoli, Carpenters union President Teddy Maritas, and others for running a drywall cartel. One year later, after a trial ending in a hung jury, Maritas "disappears" and the others all plead guilty.

1985 Governor Mario Cuomo requests that the New York State Organized Crime Task Force undertake a comprehensive investigation into corruption and racketeering in the New York City Construction Industry.

1986 President's Commission on Organized Crime gives its report on nationwide labor racketeering, calling for greater use of civil RICO.

Federal prosecutors win one-hundred-year sentences against bosses of four of New York City's five Cosa Nostra crime families for running a Cosa Nostra "commission" as a racketeering enterprise.

Federal prosecutors convict leading members of the Colombo family in the Colombo family RICO case, largely for their role in the concrete cartel.

New York City establishes a city-subsidized concrete batching plant.

1987 Governor Mario Cuomo creates the Construction Industry Task Force, comprising prosecutors, investigators, accountants, and support staff from both the OCTF and the Manhattan District Attorney's Office.

Local 6A and the District Council of Cement and Concrete Workers enter a consent decree. The court appoints Eugene R. Anderson as trustee. His trusteeship extends to 1993. Anderson believed the trusteeship did not have any significant effects due to limited powers, funding, and support.

1988 Federal prosecutors convict leading members of the Genovese family in the Genovese family RICO case, seizing its interests in the concrete companies involved in the concrete cartel.

1989 School Construction Authority is created, partially in response to the corruption associated with New York City Board of Education's construction operations. Thomas Thacher is its first inspector general. It institutes a prequalification procedure to prevent construction companies with mob ties from obtaining school construction contracts.

1990 New York City starts the VENDEX system, a computer database of government contractors.

Federal prosecutors bring charges against the organizers of the window-replacement cartel. The trial, mired with murders, jury tampering, and fugitives, produces only three convictions. But others are later convicted.

Manhattan District Attorney's Office successfully brings charges against the twelve-year-old painters' cartel run by the Lucchese crime family.

OCTF issues its final report on corruption in New York City's construction industry. Its recommendations go largely unheeded.

1993 A four-year Manhattan District Attorney's Office investigation culminates in a series of prosecutions against systemic bribery and payoffs in the plumbing industry. Attempts to place the union under a government monitor are denied by the court when the national headquarters imposes a trusteeship of its own. The trusteeship fails to loosen the Lucchese family's grip over the union.

1994 Kenneth Conboy is appointed as trustee over the Carpenters District Council as part of an agreement settling a civil RICO suit. His efforts lead the international union to oust Frederick Devine, president of the District Council.

Lawrence Pedowitz and Michael Chertoff are appointed as monitor and investigations officer, respectively, over the Mason Tenders District Council as part of an agreement settling civil RICO and ERISA charges brought by federal prosecutors. By 1998, general counsel for the international organization lauds the success of the trusteeship in cleansing the district council of corruption.

1995 IBT Local 282 consents to the presence of a court-appointed "corruption officer" who will work alongside a court-approved trustee from the international organization.

1998 Mayor Giuliani proposes a regulatory licensing system for general contractors.

The New York City construction industry is an entire sector of the urban economy, comprising numerous subindustries such as demolition, concrete, rebar, plumbing, drywall, and masonry. It is much greater in scale than the other industries we are examining. Moreover, unlike the other industries, it is not geographically fixed but rather does business everywhere in the city. There are thousands of construction projects at any point in time, ranging from small renovations to massive public works and skyscrapers. For most of the twentieth century, Cosa Nostra has been entrenched in this multibillion-dollar industry.

The New York City construction industry is a huge, decentralized, fragmented agglomeration of thousands of construction companies and materials suppliers, hundreds of general contractors, dozens of major developers, and many onetime or infrequent builders ranging from large corporations to small entrepreneurs. The city is a union town: nearly one hundred trade unions represent the approximately hundred thousand skilled and unskilled workers in the city's construction industry. Architects, engineers, bankers, insurance brokers, lawyers, accountants, public administrators, and contracting personnel also play significant roles.

Major construction projects require extraordinary coordination. Sites must be acquired and capital (construction loans) secured. Lawyers and consultants have to obtain zoning and building permits. Architects and engineers must develop plans. Once construction begins, time is always of the essence. Delays can add huge costs to a project and can bankrupt contractors and developers.

In most major construction projects, the prearranged coordination of contractors and workers from several different trade unions contributes to the industry's susceptibility to disruption and delay. Consider a typical high-rise construction project. After the initial financial and legal hurdles are cleared, existing buildings on the chosen site must be demolished before it can be cleared and excavated. Next, foundations of poured concrete are laid. The superstructure is then built, using steel, reinforced concrete, brick, or some combination of these materials. Then the interior elevators, stairs, plumbing, electrical systems, drywall, and heating and cooling systems are installed. Finally, carpentry, painting, and the installation of doors, windows, and fixtures complete the project.[2]

There is potential for labor and supply problems at every stage, and any individual or organization that can stop the process has the potential to extract payoffs. For more than fifty years, Cosa Nostra's domination of construction unions enabled it to exploit that potential.

THE LABOR RELATIONS FRAMEWORK

Unions and contractors are connected in a complex web of collective bargaining. A single contractor may be a member of several employer associations that negotiate in his behalf with a single union. Conversely, a single union may bargain with a dozen contractor associations. Furthermore, union locals often dispute about jurisdiction over tasks on a construction site.

Many labor contracts impose featherbedding (more workers than are necessary to carry out particular jobs). Sometimes they contain provisions forbidding efficient technologies (e.g., no spray painting). Some contracts require employers to employ workers whose job is not to work for the employer but to enforce the union's rules and interests (e.g., the working Teamsters foreman who makes sure that every trucker who enters the site is a union member).

Construction firms maintain only a small full-time workforce of managers and foremen. When they obtain a contract, they contact the union hiring hall to get the necessary workers. If a union is unhappy with a particular employer, it can assign that employer incompetent workers. Additionally, each union has the de facto power to shut down a site by striking and picketing as well as by sabotage. Essentially, the construction unions determine which companies can do business and which cannot.

In response to the many craft unions' power to set unfavorable terms and to engage in extortion, contractors and builders have reached out to actors with power to control unions, ensure labor peace, and provide relief from onerous collective bargaining provisions. For half a century, Cosa Nostra has had that power.

As we have seen in previous chapters, racketeers can use union power to create and enforce employer cartels. If the union controls which contractors work in a particular construction niche, it can establish and enforce cartels that permit only certain companies to do business. For most of the twentieth century the New York City construction industry has been characterized by employer cartels enforced by Cosa Nostra–influenced or –dominated unions.

COSA NOSTRA AND THE NEW YORK CITY CONSTRUCTION UNIONS

Cosa Nostra's primary power base in the New York City construction industry has been the construction trade unions. The 1986 Report of the President's Commission on Organized Crime (PCOC) found that more than a dozen construction-union locals "have a documented relationship with one or more of the New York City [Cosa Nostra crime] families, often through the holding of union office."[3] The New York State Organized Crime Task Force's comprehensive investigation of corruption and racketeering in the New York City construction industry, conducted in the mid-1980s, found even more extensive labor racketeering in the industry, including the following examples:[4]

DELIVERY

- Teamsters Joint Council 16, the largest IBT joint council, has had several officers tied to the Genovese and Lucchese crime families. For example, Joseph Trerotola, a mob associate, was both president of Joint Council 16 and a vice-president of the international union. In 1991, Trerotola left the union when charged with mob toleration.[5] Joint Council 16's vice-president for several years was Patsy Crapazano, a convicted extortionist tied to the Genovese crime family.[6]
- Officials of IBT Local 282, which represents the drivers of concrete trucks, has been closely associated with or controlled by members of Cosa Nostra for decades. As early as 1954, Manhattan District Attorney Frank Hogan reported that gangsters were threatening concrete suppliers with labor problems. John O'Rourke, president of Local 282 from 1931 to 1965, was closely associated with Lucchese family members Johnny Dio Dioguardi and Antonio "Tony Ducks" Corallo. From 1976 to 1984, Local 282's president was John Cody, one of the most powerful labor figures in New York City and a close associate of the Gam-

bino crime family. An investigation revealed that Cody paid $200,000 a year to the family boss, Carlo Gambino. In 1982, Cody was convicted of operating Local 282 as a racketeering enterprise through extortion, kickbacks, and bribery.[7] Robert Sasso, the president following Cody, pled guilty to racketeering in 1994 as did Local 282 president Mike Boorgal.[8]

SITE PREPARATION

- Blasters and Drill Runners Local 29 of the Laborers Union was long controlled or influenced by a number of Lucchese crime family members. Secretary-treasurer Amadio Petito was convicted of perjury and contempt for refusing to testify before a grand jury investigating whether President Louis Sanzo had received illegal payoffs and whether Lucchese soldier Salvatore Cavalieri, who was not a union member, actually controlled Local 29 and shared payoffs with Sanzo. The government produced evidence that Sanzo considered Cavalieri to be his boss and that Cavalieri's son was administrator of Local 29's pension and welfare fund. Sanzo was convicted of tax evasion and conspiracy to defraud, based on payments he received as part of a money-laundering scheme involving mob-related construction companies.[9]
- Housewreckers Union Local 95 of the Laborers Union was controlled by Vincent "the Chin" Gigante, boss of the Genovese crime family. In 1984, Local 95 President Joseph Sherman, business manager Stephen McNair, and Secretary-Treasurer John "Pegleg" Roshetski were convicted of labor racketeering.[10]

CONCRETE

- There is a long history of Cosa Nostra involvement with Cement and Concrete Workers Local 6A of the Laborers Union. Until the late 1980s, Cosa Nostra controlled this local, as well as the District Council, through Ralph Scopo, a soldier in the Colombo crime family. Scopo resigned as president of the District Council in 1985 after he was indicted on federal racketeering charges (of which he was later convicted).[11] Scopo's sons Joseph and Ralph continued to be affiliated with both the District Council and Local 6A, with Joseph serving as president of Local 6A, until they resigned in 1987.[12] A court-appointed monitor was placed in charge of Local 6A and the District Council from 1987 to 1992.[13]

- For years, Laborers Local 66 was controlled by Peter "Jocko" Vario (nephew of Lucchese family capo Paul Vario), formerly a vice-president of the local, and a member of the Lucchese crime family. In December 1988, Peter Vario, Michael LaBarbara Jr., the business manager, and James Abbatiello, an assistant business manager, were charged with operating Local 66 as a criminal enterprise and sharing the proceeds of their racketeering with the boss and underboss of the Lucchese crime family. They were eventually convicted and resigned from their union positions.[14]

MASONRY

- Mason Tenders Local 23 of the Laborers Union was controlled, until his 1986 conviction for labor racketeering, by Louis Giardina, a former president of Local 23 and a member of the Gambino crime family.[15]
- Mason Tenders Local 59 of the Laborers Union was controlled by the Pagano faction of the Genovese crime family for many years. In an intercepted telephone conversation, the late Joseph Pagano (a Genovese family member), claimed that Local 59 had "belonged to his family for fifty years."[16]
- Peter A. Vario (cousin of Peter Vario, above),[17] a member of the Lucchese crime family and business manager of Mason Tenders Local 46 of the Laborers Union, was convicted in 1988 of labor racketeering and of taking labor-peace payoffs from contractors.[18] The same prosecution also led to the conviction of Basil Cervone, business manager of Mason Tenders Local 13 as well as an officer and union trustee of the trust funds.
- In 1994, the Mason Tenders District Council (MTDC) and several of its officers were charged in a civil RICO suit alleging that the MTDC was a corrupt enterprise that was closely associated with the Genovese, Lucchese, and Gambino crime families. For more than twenty years the MTDC allegedly had extorted payoffs, embezzled trust funds, engaged in kickback schemes with companies, and allowed constituent locals to do the same.[19] Its former president, Frank Lupo, admitted that Cosa Nostra used its control over hiring halls to handpick him for the "elected" presidential position that his father, a member of the Genovese crime family, and his grandfather had held before him. As president, Lupo's role included using union funds to buy real estate at

highly inflated prices, presumably to profit Cosa Nostra.[20] In 1995, the parties entered into a consent decree to purge the union of Cosa Nostra and corrupt influences.[21]

CARPENTRY

- The New York City and Vicinity District Council of Carpenters has long been used by Cosa Nostra to control the city's drywall industry. Genovese family capo Vincent DiNapoli played a major role in orchestrating the District Council's racketeering schemes. Three recent presidents of the District Council, whose combined tenures span three decades, were charged with criminal activity in association with Cosa Nostra.[22] Government officials believe that members of the Genovese family have had direct control over the District Council's presidents. Theodore Maritas, president from 1977 to 1981, was presumed murdered after a labor-racketeering trial against him and other Cosa Nostra members ended in a hung jury. Paschal McGuinness, president from 1984 to 1991, was acquitted of criminal activity related to Cosa Nostra.[23] Frederick Devine, president from 1991 to 1996, was ousted by the international union for alleged mob ties, convicted in 1998 for stealing union funds, and sentenced to fifteen months in prison.[24]
- Many officials in Carpenters Locals 17, 135, 257, 531, 902, and 608 have been convicted for Cosa Nostra–related criminal activity.[25]
- Vincent DiNapoli, a multiply convicted Genovese family capo, along with several contractors, was responsible for creating Plasterers Local 530 as an alternative labor supply to the drywall-taping union.[26] Local 530 for years was run by Louis Moscatiello, a Genovese family associate. In 1989, Moscatiello was indicted for receiving bribes, enterprise corruption, and other offenses. In 1991, Moscatiello was convicted of receiving bribes and other offenses, though the enterprise-corruption charge was dismissed.[27]

PLUMBING

- Steam Fitters Local 638 of the Plumbers Union was, for years, represented by its business agent, George Daly, an associate of Gambino family boss Paul Castellano and soldier Thomas Bilotti. Daly served as Local 638's business agent until his 1987 conviction for soliciting payoffs to insure labor peace.[28]

- Officials of Plumbers Local 2, the largest plumbing local in the nation, were charged with enterprise corruption and related crimes in 1993.[29] A former president and four former business agents pled guilty. Paul Martello was elected as business agent, despite the pending charges.[30]

PAINTING

- In 1990, present and former officials of the International Brotherhood of Painters and Allied Trades District Council 9 and its constituent locals were charged with enterprise corruption of the Painters Union from 1978 to 1990.[31] Several officials, including Paul Kamen, head of the District Council at the time, pled guilty. Kamen admitted that he was under the direct control of the Lucchese crime family.[32] Kamen's predecessor, Jimmy Bishop, who was president from 1973 to 1989, was allegedly handpicked by the Lucchese family as well. He was shot to death in 1990.[33]

WINDOWS

- In 1994, Thomas McGowan, an official in Local 580 of the Architectural and Ornamental Ironworkers Union, which was responsible for supplying window-replacement workers in the metropolitan area, was convicted for participating in labor payoffs.[34] Local 580 was also implicated as the engine behind a highly publicized bid-rigging scheme for window-replacement projects.[35]

Until the court-appointed trusteeships of the 1990s, once racketeers infiltrated and gained control of a union, it proved impossible to expel them. Corrupt officials of construction unions controlled election procedures, had the power to expel members for "improper conduct," and determined who worked at what jobs.* Additionally, union officials who served as trustees of various benefit funds could use these funds

*Because construction workers are usually hired by employers on short-term bases, the hiring hall was developed as a work-referral system to match unemployed union members with job vacancies. While theoretically efficient, the potential for abuse inherent in such official control is obvious; a member who wants to work must go along to get along. New York State Organized Crime Task Force, *Corruption and Racketeering in the New York City Construction Industry* (New York: New York University Press, 1990), 52 (citing and quoting Robert M. Bastress, "Application of a Constitutionally-Based Duty of Fair Representation to Union Hiring Halls," *West Virginia Law Review* 82 (fall 1987): 31, 36).

to enhance their power as well as their lifestyles. Finally, the presence of so many known organized-crime figures in the industry made the explicit threat of violence credible and implicit threats usually sufficient.[36]

The national and international unions that charter the locals in the New York City construction industry either have been disinclined or unable to dislodge the racketeers. The U.S. Department of Labor has not aggressively dealt with complaints of corruption and racketeering. Likewise, the Landrum-Griffin Act, which was meant to ensure union democracy, has been narrowly interpreted and weakly enforced. Thus, for most of the twentieth century, the Mafia's influence in the New York City construction unions has been secure as well as pervasive.

TRADITIONAL CRIMES AND RACKETS

For many years, Cosa Nostra was so thoroughly entrenched in the New York City construction industry that, not surprisingly, its members engaged in all sorts of criminality and rackets related to the industry. For example, construction sites provide restricted areas obscured from public view, and Cosa Nostra members, with ready access through the unions, have regularly benefited from gambling and loan-sharking on such sites.[37] There has also been systematic theft and fraud of union benefit funds. Union officials often handpick the trustees of benefit funds that control hundreds of millions of dollars. Corrupt officials and trustees defraud the funds by accepting payoffs from employers who wish to avoid making mandatory benefit payments. They also steer contracts for benefit-plan services (for example, medical, dental and legal services) to companies controlled by fellow racketeers or to legitimate companies willing to pay kickbacks to obtain these lucrative contracts.[38] For example, Frederick Devine, the former president of the New York Carpenters District Council, dipped into his organization's assets (estimated at over $1 billion)[39] to pay for personal services such as chartered jets, limousines, and entertainment.[40] He also steered dental contracts to a New Jersey dentist in return for extensive personal dental services.[41]

Perhaps most important, Cosa Nostra's union control facilitated extortion and solicitation of bribes from contractors. With the credibility to threaten labor unrest and sabotage, racketeers extort payments from contractors for whom delay means disaster. In turn, contractors pass these extra costs on to consumers. While some contractors are victims of Cosa Nostra's threats, others are willing partners of a crime syndicate that assures smooth performance.[42] Similarly, with the power to choose not to enforce costly collective bargaining provisions (e.g., overtime pay, benefit-fund contributions, on-site union stewards), racketeers solicit bribes from unscrupulous contractors.

Domination of New York City's construction trade unions not only profited Cosa Nostra, it gave Cosa Nostra members and associates the political and economic influence that made this organized-crime syndicate unique. Union positions and positions with contracting firms provided tax covers and legitimate business fronts. For example, John Gotti was a plumbing salesman with ARC Plumbing Company, and Sammy "the Bull" Gravano was the president of JJS Construction Company.[43] "The ability to take a Cosa Nostra member and make him a union officer . . . gave a criminal caterpillar, you might say, the ability to become a very beautiful but dangerous butterfly. It gave him instant legitimacy, an unlimited expense account, legitimate income for income tax purposes, plus all the money he could steal from union dues, an entree into the business community and an entree to those aspiring for political office."[44] It is difficult to overstate the construction industry's importance to Cosa Nostra, both for power and profit.

COSA NOSTRA AND EMPLOYER CARTELS

Once Cosa Nostra established a power base in one of the construction unions, it was a small step to organizing and policing an employer cartel in the construction niche corresponding to that local union's jurisdiction. For example, control over the local whose members pour ready-mix concrete led to the establishment of a cartel of ready-mix concrete producers. Likewise, control over the local whose members put up dry wall in interior construction led to the establishment of a cartel of drywall contractors.

While cartels were reinforced by Cosa Nostra's control of employers through control of employer associations, and by mobsters who owned some of the cartel-affiliated companies, it was Cosa Nostra's union power that established and maintained these cartels.

The Concrete Cartel

Concrete is the basic building block of the physical environment. Among other uses, it is required for the foundations and superstructure of high-rise buildings.* Concrete can account for as much as 25 percent of the cost of a high-rise building. In the late 1980s, between $300 to $500 million was spent annually on concrete in New York City construction.[45] Cosa Nostra dominated this entire subindustry for several years.

According to evidence presented at the "Genovese family" and "commission" trials,[46] Cosa Nostra controlled ready-mix concrete suppliers and contractors through its domination of Local 6A and the District Council of Cement and Concrete Workers, and of IBT Local 282.[47] The Colombo crime family dominated both Local 6A and the District Council. In 1977, Ralph Scopo, a prominent Colombo member, became president of the District Council. Teamsters Local 282 represented the drivers of cement-mixing trucks.[48] John O'Rourke, an associate of the Gambino family, was president of Local 282 from 1931 to 1965. From 1976 to 1984, the Gambino family controlled Local 282 through its associate John Cody. Some observers called Cody, during the years of his reign, the most powerful labor leader in New York City.[49]

Cosa Nostra monopolized the city's suppliers of ready-mix concrete through Genovese associate Edward "Biff" Halloran.[50] By 1981, Cosa Nostra families had helped Halloran obtain ownership and control, in whole or in significant part, of the three largest producers of ready-mix concrete in the metropolitan area, and the only companies with batching plants in Manhattan: Certified Concrete Company,

*Concrete is a mixture of sand, gravel, crushed stone, and other aggregates held together by cement, which bonds the aggregates when combined with water. Concrete hardens as a result of a chemical reaction between water and cement. There are two ways to use concrete. The first is ready-mix concrete. Ready-mix companies are suppliers and transporters of concrete. They purchase the aggregates and cement from local suppliers of those materials. When called upon by a concrete contractor, they combine the aggregates with the cement and water in ready-mix or "batching" plants, and then ship them out in their concrete-mixer trucks whose spinning drums retard setting. Local batching plants are a must, since the concrete will set in ninety minutes, even in the mixer trucks. The second type of concrete is precast concrete, which is precast by the supplier. See John Sedgwick, "Strong But Sensitive; Concrete Construction," *Atlantic,* April 1991, 70.

Transit Mix Concrete Corp., and the Big Apple Concrete Company (which merged with Transit Mix). Cosa Nostra, through Halloran, controlled the entire New York City supply of ready-mix concrete. In return for the monopoly over concrete production, Halloran kicked back to Cosa Nostra's "commission" $3 per cubic yard of poured concrete.[51]

With power over both the product and labor, it was a simple step to control the contractors who poured concrete.* On all concrete-pouring contracts up to $2 million, the Colombo family exacted a 1 percent kickback. Contracts from $2 to $5 million could be performed only by members of a club of contractors selected by Cosa Nostra's Commission. These favored contractors were required to kick back 2 percent of the contract price to the "commission." Contracts worth more than $5 million were the exclusive province of S & A Concrete Company, in which Anthony "Fat Tony" Salerno (boss of the Genovese crime family) and Paul Castellano (boss of the Gambino family) allegedly held hidden interests.[52] Therefore, Cosa Nostra profited from the cartel both through kickbacks and ownership interests. Throughout the 1980s, concrete prices in New York City were 70 percent higher than in other major U.S. cities.[53]

Cosa Nostra figures, using Laborers Local 66 as a power base, organized a second concrete cartel on Long Island. This cartel paid off union officials to permit the contractors to operate double-breasted (i.e., partially nonunion) shops, avoid employment of union shop stewards, pay union workers below scale, and forgo employer contributions to the union benefit and welfare funds.[54] The cartel, organized by the Lucchese crime family through Local 66 vice-president Peter "Jocko" Vario, rigged bids and allocated contracts. In return for the benefits of membership, the cartel contractors paid 1 percent of the price of certain contracts to Vario.[55]

*Although Cosa Nostra did not have similar control over the supply of precast concrete, its use was limited in the metropolitan area. According to one builder, Sam LeFrak, the precast suppliers had some sort of arrangement with John Cody of Teamsters Local 282. In the $250 million Gateway Plaza apartment complex, LeFrak upset Cody and his associates by using precast concrete. Using Cosa Nostra's muscle in other construction areas, Cody convinced LeFrak to use ready-mix concrete. See Roy Rowan, "The Mafia's Bite of the Big Apple," *Fortune*, June 6, 1988, 128; Selwyn Raab, "Irregularities in Concrete Industry Inflate Building Costs, Experts Say," *New York Times*, April 26, 1981, A1.

The Drywall Cartel

In the late 1970s, the FBI's Long Island Labor Racketeering and Extortion (LILREX) investigation uncovered a club of drywall contractors controlled by Vincent DiNapoli, a Genovese capo.[56] Drywall is used in numerous construction projects as a cheap replacement for plaster. In 1993, this subindustry accounted for more than $100 million in New York City construction contracts, most of which were awarded to club members.[57]

Unlike the concrete cartel, the drywall cartel apparently did not control the drywall manufacturers. However, Cosa Nostra controlled the Carpenters union, owned or controlled the majority of the city's drywall contractors, and ran the Metropolitan New York Dry Wall Contractors Association, the industry's major employers' association.

The club consisted of the twenty companies that were members of the Metropolitan New York Dry Wall Contractors Association. In the late '70s and early '80s, they obtained most of the public and private drywall contracts; only a handful of contractors controlled all the city's drywall contracts over $350,000.[58] In an intercepted conversation, Louis Moscatiello, a Genovese associate, explained that the Metropolitan New York Dry Wall Contractors Association had belonged to the Genovese family for forty-five years.[59] The LILREX investigation also discovered that DiNapoli and his associates profited not only from payoffs but also from ownership interests in Inner City Drywall Corporation and Cambridge Drywall and Carpentry Corporation, two of the largest drywall contractors at that time.[60]

The cartel was enforced by the New York City Carpenters union locals and their District Council. (Made up of an executive board and delegates from its constituent locals, the District Council negotiates, supervises, and delegates enforcement of collective bargaining agreements; it also authorizes picketing). The Genovese crime family had dominated the District Council since at least the 1970s, when Vincent DiNapoli and Peter Defeo, two Genovese family capos, exerted strong influence over Theodore Maritas, the District Council's president.[61] The Genovese family's control over the District Council was reinforced by its direct control over several union locals.[62]

DiNapoli used his labor power to form a club of dues-paying drywall contractors who allocated the majority of New York City's drywall jobs through bid-rigging schemes. Club members paid up to 2 percent of the contract price (which was often inflated to cover that cost) for each job that they were awarded through rigged bids. Contractors in which DiNapoli did not hold interests were charged an additional $1,000 per week in return for labor peace. For additional bribes, contractors could avoid certain provisions of the collective bargaining agreements.[63]

In March 1981, the Brooklyn Organized Crime Strike Force obtained a RICO indictment against Vincent DiNapoli, Theodore Maritas, and several others.[64] Shortly after the trial ended in a hung jury, Maritas "disappeared," presumed murdered to prevent him from cooperating with the government.[65] In April 1982, the other defendants, including DiNapoli, were convicted on guilty pleas.[66] While DiNapoli was serving his five-year prison term, other members of the Genovese family took over his labor racketeering and cartel management responsibilities.[67]

The two succeeding District Council presidents, Paschal McGuinness and Frederick Devine, were both charged with criminal activity associated with Cosa Nostra.[68] In 1996, the national union ousted Devine from office because of alleged mob ties, and in 1998 he was convicted of stealing from the union's benefit funds.[69]

The Window-Replacement Cartel

In 1991, the highly publicized "windows" case exposed another major cartel in the New York City construction industry. A federal prosecution revealed that senior members of four of the city's five Cosa Nostra families (the Bonanno family was not represented) formed a club of window-replacement companies that dominated the public sector of the industry from 1978 to 1990.[70] Over those twelve years, the New York City Housing Authority (NYCHA) alone granted $191 million in window-replacement contracts. The club rigged approximately $150 million of those contracts.[71]

The Lucchese crime family controlled Local 580 of the Architectural and Ornamental Ironworkers Union (Local 580), which was responsible for supplying window-replacement workers in the metropolitan area,[72] through two of the local's business agents.[73] Cosa Nostra used its influence and Local 580's power to extort payoffs, solicit bribes, and police the cartel.

Federal prosecutors charged that Cosa Nostra had imposed a $1 to $2 per window charge on most public and some private window-replacement contracts in New York City. These proceeds lined the pockets of corrupt union officials, housing authority officials, and Cosa Nostra bosses. The window-installation companies rigged bids, enjoyed labor peace, and used nonunion labor.[74] Prosecutors in the windows case asserted that members of the club willingly cooperated because the cartel allowed them to pass along inflated prices to the NYCHA and private consumers.[75] Those who challenged the cartel encountered threats or acts of violence and labor problems.[76]

Peter Savino, a mobster-turned-informant, surreptitiously recorded hours of conversations about the cartel's operation.[77] At the trial he testified about the union's methods of policing the cartel. Competitors would be forced to employ union members at the highest rate, while club members were allowed to use nonunion members whom they paid low wages.[78] Moreover, the union (through its hiring hall) would assign the overcharged competitors low-quality workers.[79] Savino explained in court, "Thirty company workers could do 300 windows a day. If union men were used, thirty men could do only 50 windows a day. That would put a guy out of business."[80]

Cosa Nostra members also held ownership interests in some of the companies in the club, thereby benefiting from company profits, as well as payoffs and kickbacks. Savino testified that the Lucchese family provided him $500,000 to start Arista Windows, and that Local 580 then helped his company obtain contracts.[81]

Control, either by ownership or influence, of installation companies further hindered competition by creating additional entry barriers to the market. For example, when Graham Architectural Products, Inc. (Graham), a manufacturer and supplier of windows, tried to expand into the installation business, its customers threatened to seek other suppliers. Moreover, when Graham sought to escape Cosa Nostra's influence by seeking business from other installation companies, it found that they too were controlled by organized crime.[82]

For twelve years, Cosa Nostra reaped profits from its windows racket while consumers and taxpayers paid roughly a 10 percent Mafia tax on window-replacement contracts.

Painting Cartel

In 1990, a joint investigation by the U.S. Department of Labor, the Manhattan District Attorney's Office, and the New York Police Department lead to state racketeering (OCCA) charges against Lucchese underboss Anthony "Gaspipe" Casso, Lucchese capo Peter "Big Pete" Chiodo, senior officials of Painters District Council 9 and several of its constituent locals, and two painting-company executives for rigging bids on all major painting contracts from 1978 to 1990.[83] Members of a club of painting contractors kicked back up to 10 percent of revenue from mob-allocated contracts in return for labor peace, and for sweetheart deals allowing them to violate collective bargaining agreements.[84]

Corrupt Painters Union officials enforced the Luccheses' domination of the subindustry. The Mafia's control over the union was illustrated by Jimmy Bishop's District Council 9 presidency and murder. In 1973, Bishop was elected council president with Cosa Nostra's backing. Sixteen years later he was forced to resign when the Lucchеses' boss began to serve his hundred-year prison term. The faction that took over the Lucchese family wanted its own men running the union, and replaced Bishop with Paul Kamen.[85] Bishop was later shot to death, reportedly after agreeing to cooperate with the government.[86]

In 1991, Paul Kamen, president of the Painters District Council 9, along with eight other union officials, pled guilty to state enterprise corruption (OCCA) charges, confirming law enforcement charges that the union's executive leadership had been handpicked by the Lucchese crime family. In an intercepted conversation, Kamen described the mob tax:

> You shake somebody's hand, that's it by me. . . . You first got to get 5 to 10 percent, a little higher, then you got it made. That's all you have to do. I'm compassionate, 10 percent. It's not hard.[87]

For twelve years 10 percent of all major painting contracts, especially subway and steel painting contracts,[88] lined the pockets of corrupt officials and the Lucchese crime family.

Racketeering in the Plumbing Industry

Ending in 1993, a four-year investigation by the Manhattan District Attorney's Office uncovered a widespread system of payoffs and bribes throughout the city's plumbing industry. Cosa Nostra, corrupt officials of Plumbers Local No. 2 (Local 2), plumbing inspectors, and more than twenty plumbing contractors were involved in a coordinated system of corrupt payoffs from 1983 to 1993.[89] Local 2's plumbers were involved in every major Manhattan and Bronx construction job over this period; their pervasive presence led to bid-rigging schemes, extortion, and bribery totaling more than $1 million, as well as millions in withheld benefit payments.[90] Louis Moscatiello Sr., a Genovese associate, was suspected of having organized this scheme. Louis Moscatiello Jr. (having taken over after his father's 1991 conviction for labor racketeering in the drywall subindustry), was indicted as a coordinator of the plumbing rackets.[91] Prosecutors alleged that the Moscatiellos and union officials created a "Local 2 Control Group" that used mob muscle and union power to run the plumbing rackets.[92]

For payoffs of up to thousands of dollars by each contractor, the mob-associated union officials offered labor peace and the opportunity to violate provisions of collective bargaining agreements. Contractors hired nonunion plumbers (for whom corrupt officials often provided false union-membership cards), avoided pension and welfare contributions, and evaded taxes.[93] Additionally, Cosa Nostra members held ownership interests in several of the plumbing companies. One major plumbing company, De-Con Mechanical, was so closely connected to the Mafia that it did not need to make payoffs to avoid burdensome collective bargaining contract provisions. At the same time, Local 2 officials hindered new companies' efforts to enter the market by selectively enforcing collective bargaining agreements against them.[94]

CONCLUSION

The Mafia has been active and influential in New York City's construction industry for fifty years. The organized-crime families controlled key union locals and district councils in many crafts and trades, such as the laborers, teamsters, carpenters, and mason tenders. Union power enabled them to set up employer cartels, like those in poured concrete, drywall, and window replacement. Cosa Nostra members, including bosses like Paul Castellano (Gambino), Sammy "The Bull" Gravano (Gambino), and Vincent DiNapoli (Genovese) also held ownership interests in contracting companies. The mob was able to place its members, associates, relatives, and friends in lucrative jobs or no-show positions. Union workers were controlled with threats and regularly cheated out of jobs, contractual benefits, and wages. Cosa Nostra members obtained social and political status as labor leaders, businessmen, and power brokers. Contractors adapted to and often benefited from the mob's presence. New York City taxpayers and citizens paid a hefty mob construction tax.

8

Conclusion to Part I

Whether by violence or by effective mutual understanding, the stability of the market is highly desired in established businesses. . . . The gangster undertakes to effect by illegitimate means what is a normal tendency in legitimate business.[1]

—Joseph Landesco, *Organized Crime in Chicago* (Chicago: University of Chicago Press, 1968; originally published in 1929)

But the Mafioso, however he dresses and whatever he rides around in, is a gunbearing grisly who probably has [killed] and will kill on orders, and almost certainly is engaged in robbing innocent people of their money through force and fraud.

—Johathan Kwitny, *Vicious Circles: The Mafia in the Marketplace* (New York: Norton, 1979)

THIS CHAPTER DRAWS some general observations from the case studies in chapters 2 through 7. We deal first with the light those chapters shed on the nature of Cosa Nostra as a crime syndicate, then on lessons that can be drawn concerning Cosa Nostra's industrial racketeering, and finally on implications for our understanding of the twentieth-century urban political economy.

CONFLICT AND COOPERATION

The image of Cosa Nostra as racked by interfamily conflict over territory and control of rackets does not conform with reality.[2] While there was significant gangland warfare in the 1930s and 1940s, after World War II the relationship among the five New York City Cosa Nostra families was generally peaceful. In fact, our research has identified only a handful of incidents of interfamily violence. Moreover, no single sector of the economy was under the exclusive domain of one particular organized crime family; at least two crime families played a role in each of the industries we have examined.

Contrary to popular myth, the five New York Cosa Nostra families have an impressive record of cooperation with one another in industrial racketeering. How this was accomplished remains a question for future research. Perhaps industrial racketeering simply requires a great deal of cooperating, and crime syndicates heavily involved in industrial racketeering are first and foremost concerned with keeping business running smoothly. While there may or may not have been a functioning nationwide commission of Cosa Nostra families that developed in the aftermath of World War II,[3] there is no question that the Gambino, Genovese, Lucchese, and Colombo crime families participated in an interfamily council based in New York City. The Bonannos, at least for a time in the 1980s, were excluded from participation on the "commission," reputedly because of their extensive drug dealing and perhaps also because they had allowed their organization to be infiltrated by undercover FBI agent Joe Pistone (alias Donnie Brasco).[4] The four bosses held meetings to resolve disputes and coordinate racketeering activities. The concrete cartel, with its complex formula for sharing the spoils, is the best example of an interfamily cooperative enterprise.

ACCOUNTING FOR COSA NOSTRA'S SUCCESS

How were the Italian American organized-crime families able to attain so much power in the business world and what explains their extraordinary success, even more remarkable considering that Cosa Nostra bosses lack formal education in economics, accounting, law, labor relations, and other disciplines relevant to functioning successfully in business? Furthermore, to avoid detection, Cosa Nostra members had to run their operations without extensive bookkeeping and records and, starting in the late 1970s, increasingly without using the telephone. Moreover, seeking redress through the court system was not an option.

Part of the explanation for the mob's effectiveness in the business world lies in the advantages it reaped from its reputation for violence.[5] Although we have uncovered relatively few incidents of serious bodily harm exacted against legitimate businessmen, nonetheless, the threat of violence was omnipresent. The organized-crime families' reputation for ruthless violence guaranteed that individuals and firms would yield to their demands.

One striking example of Cosa Nostra's power to intimidate is provided by Peter Reuter's study of the New York City waste-hauling cartel. Reuter explains that in the two decades during which a Mafia member sat on the grievance committee of the New York Trade Waste Association, no carter ever refused to accept the committee's resolution of a dispute over "ownership" of a customer. According to Reuter, "The implied threat of force provide[d] the ultimate incentive to accept the committee's rulings."[6] Likewise, threats of violence deterred unhappy union members from contesting the mob's control of their unions and deterred would-be competitors from attempting to challenge the monopoly established by a club of mobbed-up companies. In effect, Cosa Nostra's capacity to enforce its will through violence is analogous to the government's power to call upon the police, courts, and prisons to enforce its edicts.

A second important Cosa Nostra asset was reliability, at least in comparison to other gangs and gangsters. Cosa Nostra protected its business partners against extortion and harassment by other less stable and less reliable criminals and opportunists. In Italy, Mafia members called themselves, and were known as, "men of honor." The self-image and reputation carried over to the United States. Businessmen knew or at least had reason to hope that with Cosa Nostra, a deal was a deal, notwithstanding the fact that there are many examples of cheating and double-crossing.

A third Cosa Nostra asset might be called "general business acumen." The Italian American organized-crime families held an entrepreneurial worldview and an aptitude for business. They operated according to the view that what is good for business generally is good for Cosa Nostra. Rather than *taking over* legitimate businesses, Cosa Nostra typically preferred to take a cut and provided a desirable service in return. To adopt an expression that is widely heard in studies of the Sicilian Mafia, Cosa Nostra's business strategy was "to wet its beak" (to take a cut) in as many different enterprises as possible. In general, the mob took a slice, not the whole pie.

The adjectives that best describe Cosa Nostra are *entrepreneurial, opportunistic,* and *adaptable.* Cosa Nostra bosses and members have a knack for finding ways to exploit market vulnerabilities and to satisfy business's desire for stability and predictability. The career of Gambino underboss Sammy "The Bull" Gravano provides an excellent example of the energy, imagination, and entrepreneurship that characterize the Italian American organized-crime families.

Sammy Gravano, a man with only a grade-school education, made millions of dollars in legitimate businesses. He was a consummate mobster-entrepreneur: energetic, imaginative, and resourceful. He advanced from small-time hustler to owner of nightclubs and plumbing, drywall, carpeting, and painting companies.[7] Ultimately, Gravano acquired interests in several parts of the construction industry: concrete pouring, asbestos, floor-inlay, and steel-erection companies.[8] His status in the mob enabled him to carry out contracts and guarantee labor peace to cooperative subcontractors, who repaid the favor with kickbacks ranging from $15,000 to $20,000 per contract. In 1989, he handed over close to $1.2 million in profits from rigged construction bids to Gambino family crime boss John Gotti.[9] Gravano, like many of the Cosa Nostra figures, kept seeking opportunities to make money in one business scheme and racket after another. He capitalized on his reputation as a Cosa Nostra member and on the network of connections that Cosa Nostra membership provided him. In addition, and like many of his underworld colleagues, his outgoing, even charismatic, personality was an asset in dealing with business people who apparently concluded that Gravano was no mobster, but an "underworld" figure who shared their passion for business.

COSA NOSTRA'S RESTRAINED AMBITIONS

After reading chapters 2 through 8, the reader may wonder why Cosa Nostra did not completely take over the garment, construction, and waste-hauling industries, the Fulton Fish Market, JFK Airport, and the Javits Convention Center. Since it had the power to determine which firms could participate in these industries, why did it not purge them of all non–Cosa Nostra participants? Had they so desired, the five organized-crime families could have owned all the waste-hauling firms in the carting industry, all the freight-forwarding firms at JFK Airport, and all the fish wholesalers at the Fulton Fish market. They could have used that control to take over supply companies and they could have continued growing and expanding like many national and multinational conglomerates.

With substantial discretion over prices, it is surprising that Cosa Nostra never priced products or services beyond what the market would bear. There are no examples of the mob's overreaching itself: prices were high but not so exorbitant that large numbers of customers refused to pay and sought alternative markets. Why, for example, did Cosa Nostra charge $12 a day to park at the Fulton Fish Market rather than two or three times that amount? Although poured concrete and commercial waste–hauling prices were the highest in the nation, they were stable and sustainable. In other words, Cosa Nostra did not appear to be searching for the highest price the market would bear or to be focused on maximizing profits. Higher concrete cartel prices would hardly have shut down high-rise construction, and higher carting rates almost certainly would not have triggered a revolt by businesses. Peter Reuter believes, based upon a sophisticated economic analysis, that the Mafia failed to take full advantage of its monopoly power in the New York City carting industry, a conclusion that appears equally true of other mobbed-up industries. It seems fair to say that Cosa Nostra has repeatedly refrained from fully exploiting its economic power.

The Italian organized-crime families did not have a plan or strategy for "taking over" entire industries. Unlike many "legitimate" companies, Cosa Nostra's goal was not to get larger and larger. Indeed, Cosa Nostra had no corporate or collective goal at all. Cosa Nostra should be thought of as a loose confederation of individual entrepreneurs and entrepreneurial cliques franchised and protected by the bosses at the top. Certainly, the mob was not aggressive about expanding its membership: those interested in joining the organization had to apprentice to become "made" members. Very few new members were initiated annually; sometimes the organization was closed to new membership for years. Furthermore, the recruitment pool remained closed to non–Italian Americans. All this leads to the conclusion that Cosa Nostra crime families did not function like a corporation.

While remaining a close-knit and in-bred organization may have maximized the chances of maintaining loyalty and secrecy, it also served as a check on expansion.[10] Cosa Nostra stayed with what it knew best: labor racketeering, labor-peace extortion, theft, and fraud. And, of course, the families also devoted substantial time and resources to illegal rackets and traditional crimes, thereby expending energy that might otherwise have gone into building up their power bases in legitimate industries.

Admittedly, there are counterexamples such as Thomas Gambino. A capo in the Gambino crime family, he devoted most of his time and energy to operating his four trucking companies, from which he amassed an estimated $100 million fortune.[11] And certainly, Cosa Nostra's absolute dominion over the concrete industry through a mob-owned and -operated cartel illustrates an extremely aggressive move to monopolize an entire sector of the economy. But these are the exceptions; the overwhelming majority of Cosa Nostra leaders seemed content to share "their" industries with legitimate businessmen.

INDUSTRIAL RACKETEERING

Part 1 documents the remarkable record of industrial racketeering accumulated by New York City's five Italian American organized-crime families during the twentieth century. While many readers may be surprised, even shocked, by the extent of mob involvement in New York City's core economy, this book is no exposé. Industry participants with eyes and ears open were well aware of the Mafia's importance on and behind the scenes. Public hearings and reports, magazine and newspaper accounts, and indictments made such information available to the general public. Among savvy New Yorkers and interested outsiders, it was common knowledge that, for example, the waterfront, Garment Center, and fish market were all under mob control. Our contribution is the big picture of Cosa Nostra's half century of industrial racketeering in New York City.

For much of the twentieth century, the Italian American organized-crime families were a powerful force in, and strongly influenced, indeed dominated, many of the key industries of the nation's largest city. By "influenced" and "dominated," we mean that Cosa Nostra wielded significant power in the unions and companies that constituted these industries by handpicking staff and exacting tribute through numerous rackets and schemes. Mobsters served as union officials or had substantive input into the appointment of such officials and greatly affected their decisions. Union business agents, shop stewards, and trustees of the pension and welfare funds generally owed their jobs to the mob. Cosa Nostra's influence made itself felt from top to bottom, so that many rank-and-file employees felt obligated to organized-crime figures for their jobs and other favors. Mafia members and associates determined who worked, who got paid to stay home, who got promoted, and who was blacklisted.

Chapters 2 through 7 each have a labor-racketeering component. Cosa Nostra has a long history of involvement in labor unions, a history that began during the 1920s and 1930s when management hired streetwise mobsters to break strikes.[12] Soon the unions were hiring Cosa Nostra members and associates to fight back against management goons. Once the mobsters got into the New York City area unions, they never left. They muscled or manipulated their way into leadership positions and solidified control through threats and favors. Union offices and good jobs were filled with Cosa Nostra members, relatives, associates, and friends. Friends and friends of friends got union cards; those who played along got preference for the best and easiest jobs and for appointments as business agents and shop stewards. Thus, it is not surprising that over time, the mob-sponsored officials came to dominate their unions. Until the civil RICO lawsuits of the late 1980s and early 1990s produced court-appointed monitors to purge organized crime from various unions, we know of no case in which a union that had been taken over by the Mafia was ever liberated.[13] Organized crime's control over a union local or district council provided the springboard for infiltrating legitimate businesses and establishing cartels. Holding office in union locals, district councils, and the parent international unions themselves provided Cosa Nostra members and associates with power and status. These individuals had ready access to politicians and a stock of jobs that could be allocated to members, associates, and friends.

Interestingly, certain mob-connected union officials seemed popular with union members. In fact, some court-appointed monitors found that the rank and file did not seem interested in democratic reform and even supported Cosa Nostra–designated candidates when given a chance to vote in free elections.[14] Some rank-and-file members were obliged to the mob through a patronage system. Others, no doubt, were captivated by the charisma of some organized-crime figures. The magnetic personalities of some mobsters with high-ranking union positions had a powerful effect on what Gambino family crime boss John Gotti called "our public."[15] Often men like Gotti were given the attention and deference normally reserved for movie stars and sports heroes, not simply in their own neighborhoods but also in the national media.[16]

Not everyone benefited from mob involvement. Among the losers were firms prevented from competing and consumers who paid higher prices for goods and services. The rank-and-file members of mobbed-up unions were also victims. Cosa Nostra deprived union members of their right to a democratic union and diverted the best jobs to Cosa Nostra members and their associates. Mob-affiliated union bigwigs sold out their underlings by signing sweetheart labor contracts with mob-friendly companies or, in exchange for bribes, by allowing those same companies to operate as nonunion shops or as double-breasted shops. For officials in mobbed-up unions, Cosa Nostra was the relevant constituency, not the membership. Corrupt union officials took bribes from employers and allowed them to escape their contractual obligation to make required payments to their workers' benefit and retirement funds. Like the proverbial fox in the henhouse, Cosa Nostra members and their associates sometimes sat on the board of benefit and welfare funds.

If a company refused to conform to Cosa Nostra's will and disobeyed its rules, it quickly found itself confounded by labor problems, bereft of reliable workers, or debilitated by sabotage. Inevitably, a rebellious company came to heel. A telling indicator of Cosa Nostra's power is the absence of violence in its dealing with legitimate industries. A constant need to resort to force would have indicated weakness, not strength.

Cosa Nostra as a Rationalizing Force

The mob's powers of intimidation, while impressive, were not the sole reason for the compliance of its upperworld business partners, who were hardly innocent victims. Rather, as sociologist Joseph Landesco insightfully pointed out in 1929, "[T]he racketeer does not always impose himself upon an industry or an association. He is often invited in because his services are welcome."[17] Indeed, something more than fear inspired legitimate businessmen to cooperate with the mob. Membership in Cosa Nostra–sponsored employer cartels had many attractive benefits. Provided that they kicked back a percentage of their profits to the mob, cartel members received protection against competitors and a de facto license to fix prices, allocate contracts, and treat their customers like property.

In its comprehensive study, the New York State Organized Crime Task Force concluded that Cosa Nostra played a "rationalizing role" in New York City's construction industry. The phrase accurately captures reality. In the industries examined in Part 1, the mob functioned like a quasi government by providing protection against competition, conflict resolution, policing, and escape hatches from onerous contractual obligations. Moreover, Cosa Nostra bosses functioned as "fixers" in bringing together disparate actors, brokering partnerships and deals, and guaranteeing that the parties would live up to their promises.

IS THERE SOMETHING UNIQUE ABOUT THESE INDUSTRIES?

Was Cosa Nostra's success in industrial racketeering facilitated by the organization and structure of the particular New York City industries it chose to infiltrate? In addressing this question, one has to be wary of the *post hoc ergo propter hoc* fallacy. That is, *first* selecting only industries known to be mobbed up, and *then* seeking out common traits among those industries to explain why they are mobbed up. A properly conducted study would rank various characteristics of a whole range of industries, some ruled by Cosa Nostra and others not, to see whether the two groups differ significantly on any of these selected characteristics. Even then, inferring causation would still be a problem because mob infiltration might cause certain industries to acquire certain common traits, rather than those common traits' being the cause of infiltration.

Still, on the surface, particular commonalities between mobbed-up industries are striking. Notably, timeliness is of critical importance in all the industries we have examined: garments must be delivered on time or there is no market for them; fish spoils; construction delays can bankrupt a developer. Thus, an actor with the power to impose a delay can extort money in exchange for refraining from exercising that power. But the significance of timeliness is open to question because almost every industry has some "time-is-of-the-essence" feature. Practically all manufacturers, for example, have to ship out their products on time or face the wrath or desertion of their buyers.

Furthermore, while timeliness is important, there is no reason to focus on it as the only variable that provides an opportunity for threatening a firm with costs or injury. There is potential power in being able to impose costs by whatever means—strikes, labor unrest, sabotage.

The New York State Organized Crime Task Force argued that mobbed-up industries are highly "susceptible" to racketeering, meaning that such industries possess a structure and organization that encourages industry participants to engage in racketeering, or that provides opportunities for industry outsiders to control or influence critical industry components. The OCTF also concluded that mobbed-up industries had a high degree of "racketeering potential." That is, large amounts of money could be readily siphoned out of these businesses by exploiting their susceptibility. Although this explanation seems to capture a certain truth, it is also tautological. Undoubtedly, the industries that organized crime successfully infiltrated had characteristics that made them vulnerable to infiltration. But although the OCTF did provide a compelling explanation of, for example, the construction industry's vulnerability to disruptions and delays throughout the building process, it failed to apply this rough conceptualization to a whole range of industries *before* determining whether all of those industries had experienced mob infiltration. Couldn't we construct a similar story to explain, after the fact, why any industry was vulnerable to being exploited by organized crime?

A second problem that arises in trying to explain why certain industries have fallen prey to organized-crime syndicates and other industries have not is a disquieting lack of certainty about which industries the mob does have a foothold in. We cannot be completely secure in an assertion that organized crime is not and has never been involved in a particular industry. As we have seen, organized crime has been present in a great number of New York City industries over the course of the twentieth century.

URBAN POLITICS AND ECONOMICS

Organized crime should not be an exclusively criminological topic but should be of great interest to economists, political scientists, and urbanologists. However, with some notable exceptions, urbanologists have not studied Cosa Nostra's role in shaping the economic, political, and physical environment of America's cities. The oversight is hard to understand. Mafia bosses were unquestionably part of the power elite in Buffalo, Chicago, New Orleans, Boston, Cleveland, Kansas City, Philadelphia, Las Vegas, Providence, and many other cities. Throughout the twentieth century, Mafia dons have mingled in business, labor, and political circles as the friends, advisers, and financial supporters of business executives, union leaders, and political party bosses. Their personal and professional connections to New York City's political and economic power brokers needs to be thoroughly documented.*

The link between organized crime and local politics was strongest in the 1940s and 1950s. For example, New York City organized-crime boss Frank Costello had close ties to Tammany Hall and functioned as a kind of political patron. New York City mayor William O'Dwyer was forced to resign from office in 1950, amidst allegations of personal ties to organized crime. His successor, Vincent Impellitteri, was also accused of having mob connections. However, according to New York City historian Robert Snyder, by "the middle of the 1960s the long-standing ties between organized crime and the city's political machine had been broken."[18] *Weakened* might be more accurate. Although, since the 1960s, there have been no allegations linking New York City mayors to organized crime, that hardly proves that the Mafia crime bosses have failed to exert influence over other city politicians and officials.

One striking example of the symbiotic relationship that existed between mobsters and politicians involved high-ranking Mafia figures Antonio Corallo and Daniel Motto and city official James Marcus, all of whom were indicted in 1967 for multiple criminal offenses arising out of the awarding of a million-dollar city contract.[19] Marcus had been appointed commissioner of the Water Department by Mayor John Lindsay in September 1966.[20] As commissioner, Marcus was responsible for allocating contracts related to the construction of water conduits or the rehabilitation of the water supply for the five boroughs.

*For example, any discussion of New York City's great public works projects of the mid-twentieth century is incomplete without extensive analysis of the role played by five crime families. Because Cosa Nostra controlled the construction unions, it is inconceivable that these massive building projects could have been completed without first obtaining, through financial inducement, the approval and cooperation of the mob bosses. Yet in Robert Caro's masterful Pulitzer Prize–winning biography of Robert Moses, who reigned supreme for decades as New York City's premier city planner, there is no mention of Cosa Nostra or organized crime. See Robert Caro, *The Powerbroker* (New York: Knopf, 1974).

Deeply in debt because of poor stock investments and badly in need of cash, Marcus accepted bribes from Motto and Corallo; in exchange, he arranged for the million-dollar contract to clean up the Jerome Park Reservoir in the Bronx to be awarded to a mobbed-up construction company called S. T. Grand. Marcus awarded the contract in November 1966, just two months after his appointment as commissioner, in exchange for thousands of dollars in personal loans from Motto and a percentage of the contract price as a kickback.[21] Confronted with inculpatory conversations intercepted by electronic surveillances, Marcus resigned as commissioner.[22] Ultimately, he pled guilty to a lesser offense and served as a principal witness in the trial of Corallo, Motto, and Fried, all of whom were convicted of conspiracy to violate New York State bribery laws.[23]

The Marcus story is one of many examples of Mafia involvement in city politics. However, the connection between Cosa Nostra and New York City's political elite has never been thoroughly examined. In many U.S. cities, the Mafia has been active in politics by rallying neighborhood residents behind selected candidates and by funneling significant amounts of money and grassroots organizing into political campaigns. It is impossible to believe that the five families operated so openly for so long without at least an understanding with the city's political elite. The lack of any serious initiatives by city officials to attack organized crime, (other than sporadic and largely unsuccessful prosecutions by law enforcement), supports the hypothesis that for many politicians, Cosa Nostra was at least an acceptable fact of life. For some politicians, organized crime was more than that; it was a crucial ally.[24]

CONCLUSION

At least as applied to Cosa Nostra, the model of criminal syndicates as essentially suppliers of illegal goods and services, and investors or launderers of profits in legitimate business is inaccurate. Since the 1930s (after the repeal of National Prohibition), organized-crime groups in New York City have been heavily involved in industrial racketeering not as a sideline but as a core activity. Industrial racketeering must be seen as the defining characteristic of Cosa Nostra, what makes it unique among contemporary U.S. organized-crime groups. There are other criminal organizations that traffic in drugs, pornography, prostitution, and gambling and that engage in systematic thefts, but, since the 1950s no other criminal organization has controlled labor unions, organized employer cartels, operated as a rationalizing force in major industries, and functioned as a bridge between the upperworld and underworld.[25] To find an accurate parallel, one must look outside the United States to Mafia organizations in Italy, the Yakuza in Japan, and perhaps the so-called Russian Mafia in Russia.

In the 1920s and 1930s, there were very strong Jewish, Irish, and German organized-crime groups. There have been African American organized-crime groups throughout the twentieth century active in "numbers," prostitution, and other rackets, mainly in urban neighborhoods. As the twentieth century draws to a close, we see the emergence of a Russian Mafia, Chinese triads or "tongs," Colombian drug traffickers, and Jamaican posses, to name a few. Crime groups like these clearly have the capacity to mount sophisticated criminal operations and to utilize deadly violence when necessary to further their goals. Yet, Cosa Nostra stands apart. No other organized-crime group has shown anything resembling the business sophistication and acumen of the Italian American organized-crime families. No other group has demonstrated the ability to control labor unions, much less play the roles of peacekeeper, cartel enforcer, and "fixer" for entire industries. None has become a political force by underwriting campaigns and taking control of grassroots party organizations. Cosa Nostra is distinctive, even unique, because it has successfully penetrated labor unions to seize control of legitimate industries. The resulting economic power produced high social status and engendered respect, deference, and fear among businessmen and politicians, thereby ensuring that the Cosa Nostra families would wield significant influence in both the upper- and underworlds. The diverse and successful enterprises of Cosa Nostra, and its resulting power and prestige, justify treating this organized-crime syndicate as a criminological topic in its own right.

PART II

THE LIBERATION OF NEW YORK CITY

Part 2 documents federal, state, and local law enforcement's and New York City government's extraordinary attack on Cosa Nostra's industrial racketeering that, by the end of the twentieth century, has ended or seriously threatened Cosa Nostra's influence and control in the industries we examined in Part 1. We tell the story as a tale of industry-by-industry liberation, thereby keeping the focus on New York City's economy. But the story could be told differently, for example, as the last (or perhaps penultimate) chapter in the history of Cosa Nostra or as a chapter in the history of federal, state, and local organized-crime control.

The battle to purge the Italian American organized-crime families from each industry occurred in the context of a campaign by the FBI and the U.S. Department of Justice, complemented and assisted by the efforts of state and local law enforcement agencies, to decimate the Italian American organized-crime families all around the United States. Up until approximately 1980, federal, state, and local organized-crime control initiatives had been sporadic and ineffective. Of course, there had been successes, like Thomas Dewey's prosecutions of Lepke Buchalter (murder), the only organized-crime figure ever to be executed, and

Lucky Luciano (compulsory prostitution),[1] and the federal government's success in jailing Al Capone (income tax evasion).[2] Moreover, we have seen that powerful mobsters like Socks Lanza (fish market)[3] and Johnny Dioguardi (Teamsters and JFK Airport trucking)[4] were convicted and sentenced to long prison terms. Nevertheless, even these major prosecutions failed to disrupt Cosa Nostra's operations and power bases.

Organized crime flourished in the absence of serious opposition. Local police departments and prosecutors lacked the resources and tools to mount sustained investigations and prosecutions of powerful organized-crime figures and, in any event, individual prosecutions, or even series of individual prosecutions, did not disrupt the crime syndicate's operations.[5] Moreover, a symbiotic relationship between organized crime and the urban political machines insulated Cosa Nostra from sustained law enforcement investigations. That, at least, was the conclusion of the U.S. Senate's 1950–1951 Kefauver Committee, whose hearings revealed friendly relationships between organized-crime bosses and mayors, police chiefs, and politicians in many cities.[6] Perhaps just as important as outright political corruption was the view of honest law enforcement officials that organized-crime control was too expensive, too complex, and even too exotic to be given top priority.

Despite the Kefauver, McClellan (1957–1960),[7] and other congressional committees, FBI Director J. Edgar Hoover would not devote significant resources to organized-crime investigations; indeed, until well into the 1960s, he refused even to recognize the Mafia's existence. This egregious intransigence has never been satisfactorily explained: whether it was due to his desire not to divert the FBI's attention from what he considered "more important" targets, like the Communist Party, to prevent the FBI from being tainted by corruption, or perhaps to Cosa Nostra's compromising him in some way (as some have alleged), has never been established.[8]

The federal organized-crime control program evolved slowly from the early 1960s to full maturity in the mid-1980s. There were many important steps along the way. U.S. attorney general Robert Kennedy (1961–1964) revitalized the Organized Crime and Racketeering Section (OCRS) of the U.S. Department of Justice.[9] The Task Force on Organized Crime of the President's Commission on Crime and the Administration of Justice (1967) produced a frightening (indeed, exaggerated) report on the power and organization of organized crime.[10] In 1967, Congress established, independent of the U.S. attorneys, organized-crime strike forces that reported directly to the OCRS; ultimately, there was a federal organized-crime strike force in each of the cities where there was a major organized-crime presence.[11] The federal strike force in Brooklyn handled many of the cases highlighted in Part II of this book. The strike force in the Southern District of New York (Manhattan, Bronx, Westchester) was merged into the U.S. Attorney's Office in 1972. In 1989, all the organized-crime strike forces were disbanded and merged with the U.S. Attorney's Office in their jurisdictions.[12] The Brooklyn Organized Crime Strike Force became a unit within the U.S. Attorney's Office for the Eastern District of New York (Brooklyn, Queens, Long Island).

Although the FBI engaged in electronic eavesdropping on organized crime after the Appalachin Conference came to light in 1957, the legal status of such activity was ambiguous. The 1968 Omnibus Crime Control and Safe Streets Act[13] provided a standard and a procedure for legal electronic surveillance that, by the 1980s, enabled the FBI to spin a thick web of wiretaps and electronic bugs around the organized-crime families. The inculpatory conversations intercepted by this surveillance provided further leads and ultimately the most effective trial evidence.

In 1970, Congress passed the most important substantive anti–organized-crime statute in history, the Racketeer Influenced and Corrupt Organizations Act (RICO),[14] which, among other things, makes it a crime to acquire an interest in, to participate in the affairs of, or to invest the profits acquired from an enterprise through a pattern of racketeering activity. *A pattern of racketeering activity* is defined as any two federal or state crimes listed in the act that are committed within ten years of one another. *An enterprise* is defined as any individual, organization, or group of individuals legally constituted or associated in fact.[15]

RICO made it possible to bring to a single trial whole criminal groups and families—all those defendants who participated in the affairs of the same enterprise (e.g., a crime family or union local) through a pattern of criminal activity and ushered in an era of organized-crime "megatrials." RICO's penalties are draconian. In addition to twenty-year maxima for violation of both the substantive and conspiracy provisions, RICO also provides for huge fines and for mandatory forfeiture of the defendant's property that is traceable to the proceeds of racketeering activity.[16] Although it took a decade, and the persistent prodding of Professor G. Robert Blakey, the law's principal draftsperson, once the FBI and federal prosecutors began using RICO, and the U.S. Supreme

Court had given a green light to use the law against wholly criminal enterprises, practically every significant organized-crime prosecution was brought under the statute. Rudolph Giuliani, the U.S. attorney for the Southern District of New York in the mid-1980s, brought a RICO suit against the bosses of all the families, alleging that they had participated in the affairs of an organized-crime commission through a pattern of racketeering activity (the "commission case,"[17] probably the most famous and important organized-crime prosecution in U.S. history). The two U.S. attorneys in New York City brought separate RICO prosecutions against the leaders of each of the New York crime families (the so-called family RICO prosecutions).[18]

RICO also contains two civil remedial provisions. The one that gives private victims the right to sue racketeers for triple damages[19] has not been used against organized-crime families or members. However, the provision authorizing the government to sue racketeers for injunctions, restraining orders, and other equitable remedies to prevent further racketeering[20] has been used a great deal, providing the government a powerful tool for purging organized crime from labor unions and industries.

In 1970, Congress also created the Witness Security Program,[21] (popularly known as the Witness Protection Program) which gave prosecutors the opportunity to offer cooperating witnesses a new identity and a new life; for the first time, it became possible for one to testify against organized-crime colleagues and survive. J. Edgar Hoover died in 1972, thereby removing an insurmountable obstacle to an all-out assault on organized crime. The way was clear for new leadership to reorganize and reorient the FBI.

The first half of the 1970s did not see major progress against Cosa Nostra. Following the view of the 1967 Task Force on Organized Crime, the FBI's main organized-crime focus was gambling. But the antigambling program was diffuse and unsystematic; it landed many small-time criminals and many defendants unconnected to the Cosa Nostra families. Consequently, it failed to make a persuasive case for the importance of attacking organized crime. Some U.S. attorneys, juries, and federal judges bridled at the prosecution of defendants who appeared to be nondangerous gamblers.[22]

In the late 1970s, after the disappearance and presumed murder of former Teamsters leader Jimmy Hoffa, the FBI shifted its focus to organized crime's labor racketeering. The labor-racketeering investigations of the Teamsters and Longshoremen's unions led to much greater and more sophisticated intelligence about the operations of the Cosa Nostra crime families. And mounting exposes of Cosa Nostra's control of major unions and industries touched a responsive chord in the media and in Congress.

The FBI offices, especially the New York office, made organized-crime control a top priority and reorganized so that separate squads were assigned to each organized-crime family; each squad's mission was to identify the family's membership, table of organization, and rackets and then to come up with a plan for bringing down the entire family. By the early 1980s, there were some three hundred FBI agents, assisted by one hundred New York City Police Department detectives and officers, working on the organized-crime investigations in New York City alone. The chief investigative tool was electronic surveillance. The FBI became adept at establishing the probable cause necessary for obtaining judicial warrants to conduct electronic surveillance by means of telephone wiretaps and tiny microphones ("bugs"). Extremely productive bugs were placed in the homes, social clubs, and cars of many of Cosa Nostra's top leaders. These bugs allowed the agents to listen to and record details of labor racketeering, loan-sharking, cartel enforcement, crime-family politics, and diverse criminal schemes. In subsequent trials the mobsters could be inculpated by their own words.[23]

The federal organized-crime control program was supplemented and often assisted by state and local law enforcement agencies. The New York State Organized Crime Task Force (OCTF), under the leadership of Ronald Goldstock, made an enormous contribution by reconceptualizing organized-crime investigation along the lines suggested by Blakey. OCTF personnel were responsible for the famous "car bug" that for months allowed agents to listen in on the incriminating conversations of Tony "Ducks" Corallo, the Lucchese crime family boss and for the bug on John Gotti's social club.[24] The Manhattan District Attorney's Office played the lead role in several of the major investigations and prosecutions detailed in Part 2.

Cosa Nostra's much-vaunted omerta (code of silence) melted down under the government's relentless campaign. Until Joseph Valachi went public in 1963,[25] there had never been a Cosa Nostra defector willing to testify about the organization. In the late 1980s and 1990s many high-ranking organized-crime figures were cooperating with federal, state, and local prosecutors in exchange for leniency and placement in the Witness Security Program.[26]

The final piece of this contemporary organized-crime control effort was put into place by Rudolph Giuliani's mayoral administration. As mayor, Giuliani continued his attack on the Cosa Nostra crime families, now utilizing the city's regulatory authority over businesses and industries. The administration's goal was to require firms in mob-tainted industries to obtain business licenses and to deny such licenses to Cosa Nostra members, associates, and friends.

9

Liberating the Garment District

> You can't manufacture anything in New York without using trucks. If you control the trucks you control the industry, and [the Gambino brothers] control the trucks. And their partner is organized crime. They control what factories in the garment industry use what trucks, which destroys competition and destroys freedom to choose. . . . [The defendants] levy a tax that flows through the pockets of Thomas Gambino and Joseph Gambino [who are] known in the industry as members of the Gambino crime family.[1]
>
> —Assistant District Attorney Elliot Spitzer,*
> opening statement in *People v. Gambino,* 1992.

COSA NOSTRA WAS entrenched in the New York City garment industry since the 1920s. The mob was able to establish and police a trucking cartel by controlling the Master Truckmen of America, the International Ladies Garment Workers Union Local 102, and the Greater Blouse, Skirt, and Undergarment Association. The cartel consisted of trucking companies owned or controlled by members of Cosa Nostra families. Through the property-rights system and fixed prices, cartel members derived enormous profits. Prior to the 1990s, government efforts to purge the mob from the garment industry had failed to make much of an impression.

The Department of Justice's 1951 antitrust suit resulted in a favorable consent decree but not in any change in business as usual.[2] In the late 1950s, the New York City commissioner of licenses' successful debarment of Barton Trucking from the industry could have led the way to a major attack on the Cosa Nostra cartel, but no subsequent action was

*Spitzer was elected New York State attorney general in 1998.

taken.[3] Project Cleveland, the joint federal-city investigation during the mid-1970s produced several convictions, but again there was no significant impact on the property rights, the cartel, or Cosa Nostra's influence.[4]

The breakthrough came in the 1990s. The Manhattan District Attorney's Office brought a major criminal case against Thomas and Joseph Gambino, by far the most important Cosa Nostra figures in the garment industry. The trial ended in a remarkable plea bargain that went a long way towards removing the Gambino brothers from the industry and established a court-appointed special master whose efforts to eliminate the trucking cartel appear to have been successful.

THE CHRYSTIE STREET FASHIONS AND LOK-KEY STING

In the late 1980s, Thomas Gambino, a capo in the Gambino crime family, and his brother Joseph were at the height of their power in New York City's garment trade.[5] They owned several garment-trucking firms, including Consolidated Carriers and Greenberg's Express, and held many other interests in the industry. Thomas Gambino's personal wealth was approximately $100 million.[6]

In August 1988, the Manhattan District Attorney's Office initiated two undercover sting operations.[7] The goal was to build a criminal case against the Gambinos and purge the garment industry of racketeering.[8] The DA's office set up a sewing shop in Chinatown. To all appearances, its Chrystie Street Fashions was not different from many other Chinatown contractors.[9] Approximately twenty-five women worked at sewing machines throughout the day, making skirts and blue jeans; they had no idea that their supervisor, Ron Rivera, was a New York State Police officer (no New York City detectives were used for fear that they might be recognized).[10] During Chrystie Street Fashions' one-year existence,[11] law enforcement officials secretly recorded numerous conversations between Rivera and Consolidated Carriers "salesmen" who advised Rivera that Chrystie was a Consolidated shop and that Rivera could therefore not hire any other trucking firm.[12]

The second sting operation involved Lok-Key Transportation, a small trucking company ostensibly headed by David Chan, who was really New York State Police detective Kim Lee. While police videotaped the scene, Lee visited Chrystie Street Fashions when Consolidated salesmen were present and offered his own trucking services to

Rivera; this was a direct challenge to the cartel. Consolidated's salesmen informed Lee that Chrystie was a "Consolidated shop" that Lok-Key could not service.[13]

In addition to these operations, police officers obtained court authorization to install listening devices at Consolidated Carriers' headquarters, including the offices of Joseph and Thomas Gambino.[14] On January 30, 1990, after the bugs revealed enough information to support a search warrant, law enforcement agents seized financial records from ten Garment District trucking firms.[15]

INDICTMENTS OF THE GAMBINO BROTHERS

In October 1990, a fifty-five-count indictment charged the Gambino brothers, two of their employees, and four of their trucking companies with racketeering, under New York's Organized Crime Control Act (OCCA). The OCCA charge alleged that the four men and four companies constituted a wide-ranging conspiratorial scheme that, through at least twenty acts of extortion, prevented garment firms from choosing their own truckers.[16] The indictment also alleged that the defendants violated New York State's antitrust law (the Donnelly Act) by allocating customers and territory.[17] A second indictment charged three Gambino associates and six trucking companies with conspiring to restrain trade by forging an illegal combination with the Gambinos.[18] In announcing these indictments, New York City District Attorney Robert Morgenthau asserted that the defendants had imposed a mob tax on every garment shipped in New York City, reaping tens of millions of dollars in illicit profits, ultimately funded by consumers. Prosecutors contended that the ten trucking companies named in the two indictments handled about 90 percent of the garment industry's trucking routes.[19] Thus, the DA's office hoped that by convicting the defendants and seizing their businesses, it could break up the cartel and the marriage system, eliminate Cosa Nostra's presence in garment trucking, and stimulate competition among trucking companies.

In April 1991, the seven individual defendants and ten trucking companies in *People v. Gambino* sought dismissal of the state-racketeering charge on the ground that the terms "criminal enterprise" and "pattern of racketeering activity" were unconstitutionally vague. Justice Herbert Altman upheld the OCCA, finding that the statute provided fair notice to the defendants that their alleged conduct was prohibited.[20] The defendants also argued that the grand larceny and extortion counts of the OCCA charges could not stand because the right to choose a trucker was not *"property"* protected under New York State law. Justice Altman rejected that argument as well, holding that when an "advantageous business relationship [i]s denied as the result of extortionate acts," the right to create and maintain that relationship constitutes legally protected property.[21] After Justice Altman cleared away these and other arguments, the district attorney was free to proceed to trial.

THE TRIAL OF THOMAS AND JOSEPH GAMBINO

The Gambino brothers' state court trial began on February 4, 1992; John DiSalvo and Raymond Buccafusco were tried as codefendants. From the outset, both the prosecution and defense clashed over whether there was sufficient evidence to establish extortion. In his opening statement, Assistant District Attorney Elliot Spitzer told the jury that "[e]verbody in the Garment district" knew who the Gambinos were and that the defendants "used their reputations as the Gambino crime family as a tool of fear—and they took it to the bank." Spitzer explained that when the Gambino name was not enough, "and when somebody stepped out of line, the velvet gloves came off, somebody was sent to the hospital for six months." In his opening statement, Thomas Gambino's lawyer ridiculed the allegation that his client had ever used threats in operating his garment-trucking businesses. "You will not find any baseball bats. You won't find any broken bodies. This is simply a business case, no matter the names and nasty things [the prosecutors] call Tommy Gambino."[22]

The first prosecution witness was the manager of a dress company who testified that when he was in the shop of a contractor who did not want to use Gambino trucks, several imposing men in trench coats suddenly appeared, silently intimidating the contractor. According to the witness, the message the Gambinos conveyed was that "you don't mess around with Consolidated," and that "you have to accept their control —you have to play the game."[23] At most this incident proved an *implied threat*, and only an indirect link to the Gambinos themselves.

To prove the nature and scope of the marriage system, prosecutors called officer Ron Rivera, who recounted how a Consolidated salesman told Lok-Key's Kim Lee that Chrystie Street Fashions was "a Consolidated shop" and that Lee should look for work in Long Island City. A videotaped recording showed another Consolidated salesman telling Lee that "if I find [another trucker] here I try to get them out." When Lee asked if the contractor had the right to choose its own trucker, the salesman replied, "No they don't. It's like a franchised shop." Rivera explained how Consolidated helped steer him work from designers. However, when he tried to obtain the services of another trucker, he was told that he could not obtain its services; he had no choice but to stay with Consolidated.[24]

The defense lawyers hammered away at any suggestion that the Gambinos used violence or extortion. Defense lawyer Gerald Shargel forced a former Consolidated salesman testifying for the prosecution to admit that he had never physically threatened contractors, and that if a contractor were to ship with a non-Gambino company, the salesman would threaten only to stop finding business for that contractor.[25]

In sixty thousand recorded conversations, there were few actual threats of physical violence, which were essential to the extortion charges. The closest the prosecution came was a statement by a Consolidated employee discussing the activities of Lok-Key trucker Kim Lee. The employee stated: "I don't want to say he's gonna get his ass kicked, but he will, sooner or later. One of the fucking truckers will take him apart. He'll be spending the next six months in the fucking hospital."[26] After three weeks of testimony, no direct threats had been linked directly to the Gambinos. The *New York Times* reported that "there has been no mention of any mob murders. In fact, the evidence shows that Thomas and Joseph Gambino . . . were ever so polite in making sure they did not encroach on truckers controlled by rival organized-crime families."[27]

THE PLEA BARGAIN

On February 26, 1992, Thomas and Joseph Gambino along with their two codefendants joined three other defendants in the second indictment in agreeing to a novel plea bargain. The Gambinos pled guilty to a single felony antitrust count;[28] in exchange the prosecutors dropped the remaining fifty-four charges.[29]

The Gambinos agreed to stop enforcing the marriage system immediately, to quit the trucking business by selling their major trucking concerns under court supervision, to grant the court and a "special master" jurisdiction over their trucking companies, and to have no contact with their soon-to-be former companies.[30] Further, the Gambinos agreed to pay a $12 million fine to the state, which would be earmarked for victims of Gambino-trucking overcharges, the cost of the court-appointed special master, and the costs of the government's investigation and prosecution.[31]

The prosecutors thought the agreement made sense in light of uncertainties in their case. As prosecutor Michael Cherkasky explained: "We knew we had them *legally* cold on the antitrust counts . . . [but] our extortion case was *very, very* weak to begin with, and was only getting worse at trial." Cherkasky feared that a "runaway jury" might not convict the defendants on the antitrust charge if it decided to acquit on the more serious extortion charges.

The prosecutors decided to trade off the possibility of impressive prison sentences against the Gambinos* for the opportunity to conduct industry-wide remediation through a special master. District Attorney Morgenthau argued that although his office had given up on a jail term for the Gambinos, it had accomplished what prosecutors all the way back to Thomas Dewey had not. Referring to Cosa Nostra's role in the in the Garment District, Morgenthau stated, "[T]his takes them out in one fell swoop." According to Ronald Goldstock, director of New York State's Organized Crime Task Force, "It's a terrific settlement. . . . Certainly the public is better off with the garment industry taken from the hands of racketeers than with a person sent to prison."[32]

THE SPECIAL MASTER'S REMEDIAL EFFORT

In April 1992, Justice Thomas Galligan appointed former New York City Police Commissioner Robert McGuire, CEO of Kroll Associates, to serve as the special master called for in the plea agreement. The special master's role was to oversee the Gambinos' sale of their trucking inter-

*Thomas Gambino was unable to avoid prison time as a result of his 1993 convictions on various racketeering, gambling, and loan-sharking charges in connection with running Gambino crime family operations in Connecticut. He was sentenced to five years. See *United States v. Gambino*, 835 F. Supp. 74, (E.D.N.Y. 1993)(motion for new trial); Pete Bowles, "Goodfella Did Good; Still Gets Slammer," *Newsday*, October 30, 1993.

ests and their withdrawal from the industry.* McGuire was authorized to "issue such orders and rules as he deems reasonable and appropriate to eliminate anti-competitive practices and encourage competition" in cut-work trucking.[33] He hired a team of lawyers, accountants, and former law enforcement officers to assist in carrying out the remedial effort.

Under the terms of the plea bargain, the special master was to oversee the sale of Gambino-owned trucking companies, shipping contracts, account lists, and routes.[34] While the Gambinos' attorneys had the authority to negotiate terms of the sales and financing with prospective buyers, these were subject to McGuire's final approval. McGuire made it clear that the Gambinos would not be allowed to sell their interests to family members, friends, or to any company with ties to Cosa Nostra. His team subjected prospective buyers to a twenty-page questionnaire and reserved the right to have forensic accountants look at their financial records.[35]

The defendants' trucking interests were eventually sold to four different trucking companies in the summer of 1993,[36] after the deadline had been extended to conduct final background investigations of the buyers.[37] The special master's office then monitored the operations and ownership of each of these successor companies, as well as the remaining trucking companies named in the original indictment. By conducting quarterly audits, McGuire's staff sought to ensure that organized crime did not reenter the industry and that the successor firms did not employ the same anticompetitive tactics as the Gambinos.[38]

The special master also established a compensation fund for victims of the trucking cartel. From the Gambinos' $12 million fine, $3 million was set aside to compensate those who had been overcharged by the defendant trucking companies. McGuire placed advertisements in the trade magazine, *Women's Wear Daily*, and in three Chinese-language newspapers,[39] aimed at designers and contractors who had been victimized by the marriage system. Despite the longevity of the cartel, there were few claimants. Only $800,000 was paid out. The remaining $2.2 million reverted to the state of New York.[40] Perhaps contractors

*The Gambinos were divested of their interests only in companies that had violated antitrust laws. They still maintained ownership of Dynamic Trucking, an interstate trucking company that accounted for $57.6 million of revenue and $4.2 million profit. See Gay Jervey, "Waltzing with the Wise Guys," *American Lawyer*, May 1992, 90.

who had overpaid for garment trucking were no longer in business, or did not notice the advertisements,[41] did not have the necessary records to verify their claims, or were reluctant to get involved.

McGuire sought to stimulate competition in the garment-trucking industry.[42] New rules for the trucking of cut-work between designers and contractors prohibited trucking companies from (1) entering into agreements with other firms to fix rates or terms; (2) trading customer lists or the rights to customers, except in the sale of an entire trucking firm; and (3) establishing an exclusive relationship whereby a contractor or designer agrees to deal with only one trucking firm. The rules further required that trucking invoices include a written notice stating the rate, and that the relationship between the trucker and the designer or contractor not be exclusive. Finally, in an attempt to end loan-sharking, McGuire required that loans by trucking companies in excess of $250 had to be approved by his office. Justice Thomas Galligan approved these rules, along with other monitoring and enforcement provisions.[43]

The special master's office established a monitoring program for both Seventh Avenue designers and Chinatown contractors; the primary focus was on the latter. Meetings were held in Chinatown, and more than five hundred contractors and manufacturers were interviewed on a continuing basis. The manager or owner was given the "Know Your Trucking Rights" flyer (in English and Chinese) describing the special master's rules, emphasizing the fair-trade practices that now governed garment trucking, and providing a toll-free number to report violations.[44] A former FBI agent and six full-time field investigators monitored compliance on a daily basis. The investigators met with the owners of each shop and asked whether they had encountered trucking company problems. They discovered a number of violations by truckers and apparent attempts to evade the new rules. When violations were discovered, Special Master McGuire imposed the costs of the investigation on the violators. At the same time, McGuire persuaded other trucking companies to submit voluntarily to the special master's jurisdiction.[45]

When his special master's term ended in February 1997, Robert McGuire was optimistic about the future of the industry. He stated that "once the chains [of Cosa Nostra control] are unraveled as they have been, I doubt they will become entwined again."[46]

RECENT ALLEGATIONS OF COSA NOSTRA INFLUENCE IN THE GARMENT TRADE

While driving the Gambinos out of the garment industry was a significant step in eradicating organized crime from the industry, other mobsters continued to engage in illegal activity in the Garment District. McGuire and his chief investigator reported to the U.S. Attorney's Office and the FBI information they had uncovered while serving in their court-appointed positions but had been unable to pursue due to jurisdictional limitations.[47] A joint investigation involving the U.S Attorney's Office for the Southern District of New York, the Division of Labor Racketeering of the U.S. Labor Department's Office of the Inspector General, the FBI, and the New York City Police Department was then launched.[48] On April 28, 1998, the U.S. Attorney's Office obtained two indictments against twelve individuals for extorting garment companies. Seven men, including Joseph "Little Joe" DeFede, the acting boss of the Lucchese crime family, were indicted on nine racketeering and seven extortion counts stemming from a scheme that extorted upwards of $480,000 annually from garment businesses.[49] This indictment alleged that the defendants had established extortionate control over various Garment District businesses by

- identifying members of said enterprise as associates and members of Cosa Nostra or the Mafia;
- threatening labor unrest;
- threatening and causing economic harm;
- using and threatening physical violence; and
- obstructing law enforcement investigations by tampering with potential witnesses.[50]

The first indictment named attorney Irwin Schlacter as an associate of the Lucchese family and alleged that he collected extortion payments from Garment District companies on behalf of the Luccheses.[51] In a wiretapped conversation, Schlacter told a trucker that he would suffer the same fate as Mike Pappadio, a former Lucchese associate who was murdered for skimming extortion payments.[52] Although the indictment alleged the enterprise's ability to "disrupt labor peace and . . . control . . . labor unions,"[53] no specific union was implicated.

However, it is possible that UNITE* Local 102 played a role since it is the primary union operating in New York City's garment industry.[54]

Michael Vuolo was also named as a defendant in the racketeering and extortion indictment. He had pled guilty to criminal solicitation as part of the Gambinos' 1992 plea bargain but had been allowed to retain his garment-trucking company. Vuolo's interest in AAA Garment Delivery and its assets are subject to RICO's forfeiture provisions.[55] All told, the government sought $2.5 million from the defendants, allegedly the proceeds obtained through illegal racketeering activity.[56]

The second indictment charged five members and associates of the Gambino and Lucchese families, including Gambino capo Joseph ("the Kid") Gallo** and Joseph Gatto, a Genovese capo, with extorting Hudson Piece Dye and its affiliate companies.[57]

WILL THE GARMENT DISTRICT EVER BE FREED?

As this book goes to press in early 1999, the trucking cartel seems to be broken. The Gambinos' plea bargain and the special-master's work, freeing designers and contractors from the marriage system and stimulating competition among new independent truckers, constitute extremely significant steps toward purging Cosa Nostra from the Garment District. New truckers are competing for work. More than seventy-five independent trucking firms have entered the garment industry.[58] Prices have declined. By the mid-1990s, the special-master's office estimated that trucking costs had dropped approximately 20 percent. The cost of shipping a pair of jeans had dropped from 40 to 45 cents to 15 to 20 cents. According to Special Master McGuire, "For the first time in decades, customers are shopping for truckers and willing to move if they don't get the right price or good service."[59] *Women's*

*UNITE (Union of Needletrades, Industrial and Textile Employees) was formed in 1995 when the International Ladies Garment Workers Union (ILGWU) merged with the Amalgamated Clothing and Textile Workers Union (ACTWU). See Arthur Friedman, "UNITE Ratified Unanimously," *Women's Wear Daily*, June 29, 1995, 9.

**Gallo's father, Joe N. Gallo, a former Gambino family consigliere, was cited in New York State Senator Franz Leichter's 1982 report as the de facto head of the Greater Blouse, Skirt, and Undergarment Association, through which Cosa Nostra diverted huge amounts of money. Franz Leichter, "Sweatshops to Shakedowns: Organized Crime in New York's Garment Industry" (unpublished, March 1982), pt. 3 38–40.

Wear Daily reported that garment contractors and designers feel a distinct change in the industry, and are no longer married to any trucker or subject to billing for trips that were never made.[60]

Still the battle against Cosa Nostra continues. Although no Cosa Nostra figures have arisen to take the place of Thomas and Joseph Gambino, organized crime still is a presence in the garment industry. Following the latest indictments, New York City Police Commissioner Howard Safir commented, "I don't think anybody . . . is declaring victory."[61] The latest round of indictments show that Cosa Nostra still has enough influence to force businesses to pay extortionate demands, but it also shows law enforcement's perseverance. Robert McGuire urges "vigorous investigation of organized crime's tie to the industry into the indefinite future."[62] If his advice is followed, there is an excellent prospect that the garment industry eventually will be fully liberated.

10

Freeing the Fulton Fish Market

> The [New York City] Council hereby finds that the Fulton Fish Market, the center of New York's wholesale seafood industry located in lower Manhattan, has for decades been corruptly influenced by organized crime. . . . The council further finds that despite the repeated efforts of law enforcement to prosecute crimes there and the presence of a court-appointed administrator for the Market, the problem of organized crime corruption in the Market has persisted. . . . The council therefore finds that . . . it is necessary for the commissioner of business services to have expanded authority to license and/or register businesses in the Market area and to regulate the conduct of such businesses.[1]
>
> —Legislative findings to Local Law 50, 1995.

COSA NOSTRA HAS been entrenched at the Fulton Fish Market since the 1920s. Through its control of Local 359 of the United Seafood Workers, Smoked Fish and Cannery Union, the Genovese family ran a protection racket and forced wholesalers to rent union signs and contribute to a Christmas fund. Some members of the Genovese and Bonanno crime families owned unloading and loading companies that operated as cartels that limited competition and fixed prices. Although the market is located on city property, loading companies paid nominal rent, if any, and profited from parking fees. The Department of Ports and Trade which had regulatory responsibility for the market, made no serious effort to attack the mob's interests. The incarceration of mob czars Joseph "Socks" Lanza and his successor, Carmine Romano, had no impact on organized crime's domination.

In the late 1980s, the U.S. Attorney's Office for the Southern District of New York filed a pathbreaking civil racketeering suit that resulted in the entire market's being subjected to the supervision of a court-appointed market administrator. The administrator had only limited suc-

cess in purging organized crime, but upon the completion of the administrator's term, the city established a comprehensive and aggressive regulatory regime that has achieved impressive results.

OPERATION SEA PROBE AND *UNITED STATES V. LOCAL 359*

In late 1984, a joint task force, made up of twelve FBI agents and twelve NYPD officers, launched Operation Sea Probe,[2] an investigation of the Fulton Fish Market that involved hundreds of hours of undercover operations and extensive electronic surveillance.[3] The investigators followed market racketeers to Brooklyn, Queens, and Staten Island to map their connections to other organized-crime members.[4]

Recognizing that past criminal prosecutions had failed to wrest control of the market from Cosa Nostra, U.S. Attorney Rudolph Giuliani filed a civil RICO suit in October 1987. Unlike earlier civil RICO suits, this case was brought without the benefit of a prior criminal case.[5]

Giuliani analogized this use of civil RICO to the use of the Sherman Anti-Trust Act to break up monopolies in the early twentieth century and to the use of federal court trusteeships to desegregate school districts.[6] The lawsuit sought to place the entire market under court supervision and to appoint a trustee for Local 359.[7]

The civil RICO complaint, assigned to Judge Thomas P. Griesa, named twenty-nine defendants, including Local 359 and its officers, and the Genovese crime family as an entity.[8] It alleged that Carmine Romano, as secretary-treasurer of Local 359, and later Vincent Romano, as de facto head of the local, on behalf of the Genovese crime family had engaged in diverse criminal activity, including extortion, gambling, theft, and loan-sharking, at the Fulton Fish Market. The government charged that the Genovese family used Local 359 to extort payoffs from wholesalers by threatening labor problems. In December 1987, the government moved for a preliminary injunction that would entail appointment of an "administrator" to oversee market operations and to prevent organized-crime activity, and appointment of a trustee to replace Local 359's executive officers.[9]

THE CONSENT DECREE

In April 1988, twenty-five of the twenty-nine defendants, including Vincent and Carmine Romano, entered into a consent judgment. A default judgment was entered against the remaining defendants, including the Genovese crime family. The consenting defendants, most of whom had an interest in the unloading and/or parking enterprises at the market,[10] agreed to injunctions prohibiting racketeering practices and to the appointment of a market administrator. The consent judgment permanently enjoined Carmine and Vincent Romano from having any interest in Fulton Fish Market operations and any contact with Local 359.[11] The consent judgment required six other defendants to notify the market administrator of any market-related interests they possessed and prohibited contact with Local 359.[12] All defendants and all persons in active concert or participation with them were prohibited from participating in any illegal activities, including extortion, theft, and gambling, as well as colluding, conspiring, or agreeing with any other individual to participate in such acts. The default judgment barred the Genovese family from participating in any Fulton Fish Market or Local 359 activities.[13] Judge Griesa retained jurisdiction to try any contempt proceedings arising out of alleged violations.

After the settlement, the U.S. attorney filed an amended complaint, naming Local 359 and its president, Anthony Cirillo, and secretary-treasurer, Dennis Faicco, as defendants. Charging that Local 359 and the two union officers were puppets of the Genovese crime family, the U.S. attorney asked the court to remove Cirillo and Faicco, and appoint a trustee to run the local until a free and fair election could be held. The government listed as RICO predicates wire fraud, extortion, and violations of the Taft-Hartley Act (which prohibits union officials from receiving payments from employers).[14]

In denying the government's request for a trusteeship over Local 359, Judge Griesa acknowledged that the Genovese crime family had ruled the union in the past but expressed hope that the consent and default judgments would be sufficient remedies. He noted that the United Food and Commercial Workers International had placed Local 359 in trusteeship from 1981 to 1983, following the convictions of Carmine and Peter Romano, and that new elections had produced the two current defendant officers. Judge Griesa wrote that "[t]he proof offered by the Government has not been sufficient to support its essential claim—i.e., that the Genovese family currently controls, and in recent years has controlled, Local 359 and its principal officers. . . . [However,] [t]his is not to say that there is no evidence of the presence of organized crime, particularly Genovese family operatives, in the Fulton Fish Market."[15*]

THE COURT-APPOINTED MARKET ADMINISTRATOR

The consent judgment directed the parties jointly to name at least one but no more than three proposed candidates for the position of market administrator. From this list, Judge Griesa appointed Frank H. Wohl, a former assistant U.S. attorney then in private practice, to a renewable four-year term.[16]

*The Second Circuit Court of Appeals affirmed the dismissal of the RICO extortion and wire-fraud charges but remanded for reconsideration of the RICO Taft-Hartley violations. *United States v. Local 359*, 889 F.2d 1232 (2d Cir. 1989). The U.S. attorney has taken no subsequent action against the union regarding the Taft-Hartley allegations.

The consent and default judgments empowered the administrator to take sworn testimony from persons with knowledge about racketeering at the market and to inspect the books and records of individuals, businesses, and other entities operating there. With the court's approval, the administrator could implement rules and regulations necessary to ensure compliance with the injunction. The administrator had authority to impose sanctions on the defendants "or any person in active concert or participation with them," for violating provisions of the consent judgments. Possible sanctions included, but were not limited to, public posting of the violations, fines, suspension, and debarment from operating at the Fulton Fish Market. Permanent debarment or a suspension from the market in excess of one year required court approval.

Judge Griesa retained jurisdiction to "supervise the activities of the Administrator and to entertain any future applications by the Administrator or the parties." The administrator could apply to the court for any assistance or relief that he deemed necessary and appropriate. The consent judgment required the administrator every four months to file with the court a written report of his activities.[17]

The Market Administrator's Struggles

Market Administrator Wohl opened an office near the market. He hired Brian Carroll, a retired New York City Police detective, as his deputy administrator. Wohl carried out the duties of market administrator on a part-time basis; Carroll worked full-time. In addition, the office employed three full-time investigators.[18]

Wohl submitted fourteen reports to the court, plus an extensive 1990 midterm report. In his reports, Wohl stated that his staff conducted *confidential investigations*,[19] but no details were provided. All reports documented the resistance Wohl encountered from market businesses when he attempted to procure sworn testimony, records, and books. According to Deputy Administrator Brian Carroll:

> It is important for us to have these records and ultimately the testimony . . . if we are to effectively monitor them and be in the position to draft meaningful regulations governing market operations. Those from whom we have sought testimony or books and records have generally resisted our demands, and the Administrator has had to seek re-

> course from the Court. . . . [T]he process has consumed valuable time. Moreover, once we have successfully compelled an individual to give testimony, the testifier often invokes his constitutional privilege against self-incrimination and refuses to answer key questions.[20]

The court consistently upheld the administrator's requests for defendants' sworn testimony, records, and books.[21] However, the administrator had no power to grant immunity; thus a claim of Fifth Amendment privilege effectively blocked many lines of investigation.

In his midterm report, filed two years into his term, Wohl observed that racketeering remained rampant.[22] Yet, the market administrator's staff claimed that the existence of the administrator's office had resulted in a marked reduction of "skimming," the systematic theft of fish from each box as it is unloaded.

Wohl continually urged city politicians to play a more aggressive role in supervising market operations.[23] In November 1988, the New York City Department of Ports, Trade, and Commerce appointed a market manager to exercise the city's administrative power at the market. The market manager's task was not to purge organized crime from the market but to improve the market's facilities.[24] The Dinkins administration eliminated the market-manager position in 1991 for budgetary reasons, despite the administrator's claims that additional staff was needed.

Wohl's midterm report criticized city officials for failing to regulate and police the market. Wohl claimed that he had delayed issuing the midterm report in the hope that city officials would be stirred from their lethargy,[25] and charged that despite promises to the contrary, the Koch and Dinkins administrations had not taken sufficient action. Wohl stated that city officials had told him that they feared for the safety of city employees, worried about the corruption of police officers, and blamed the fiscal crisis for failing to act.[26] A spokeswoman for the New York City Office of Business Development responded that Wohl's report of racketeering activities was "old news" and reflected his "inability to correct the problem" despite an annual $1 million budget and a large staff.[27]

It is difficult to evaluate the success of Wohl's $3.5 million monitorship.[28] The administrator's powers were probably inadequate to accomplish the court's objectives. The court had granted Wohl power to impose sanctions on the defendants named in *United States v. Local 359* but not on other market participants, such as the wholesalers. Moreover, identifying and communicating with businesses in the market proved difficult. The city did not even have a list of market participants, and compiling basic information was further complicated by language barriers.[29]

It is unclear why Wohl's office devoted so much time and resources to obtaining business records and books. Perhaps Wohl believed that they would reveal violations of the consent judgment or racketeering schemes themselves, but it seems unlikely that market participants would have formally recorded such incriminating information.

Sanctioning Noncomplying Unloading Companies

In 1990, Wohl's office received information that defendant Dominick Lategano had retaliated against a seafood company for complaining about the unloading cartel. The seafood company experienced protracted delays in the unloading of its merchandise and its employees received death threats.[30] Wohl's office and the New York City Department of Investigation (DOI) started a sting operation that lasted from September 1990 through April 1991, the first time the DOI had played a major role in an organized-crime investigation at the Fulton Fish Market.

The DOI sting operation set up a trucking company, Stingray Express, to determine whether any of the consenting defendants were still operating an unloading cartel.[31] Stingray Express posed as a supplier that trucked small quantities of its own fish to the market. At first, an unloading company headed by Gerard Albanese, an alleged Genovese associate, unloaded the Stingray trucks without incident. When, two months later, Stingray expanded its business by delivering eighty boxes of fish that bore the label of another Long Island supplier, Albanese told Stingray's owners to say that the boxes did not come from the Long Island supplier whose name appeared on the label but from other sources. John Gillio, the head of another unloading company, soon approached the Stingray employees and asked the origin of Stingray's cargo. The undercover agents showed Gillio documents indicating that the eighty boxes were those of a Long Island supplier. Gillio advised the agents that his company handled all trucks from Long Island and told them he would speak to some "people," who would talk to Albanese. When the undercover agents asked Gillio who allocated work among the unloading crews, Gillio replied that there were "people" who made those decisions. Gillio also told the agents that he would need to be paid for the unloading of the cargo, even if Albanese performed the service.[32]

In June 1992, Wohl imposed sanctions on five unloading companies that were defendants in the civil RICO suit on the ground that they had conspired to reestablish an unloading cartel,[33] and that the manner of the conspiracy indicated organized-crime involvement.[34] The fines, varying in amounts, totaled $200,000. Wohl ordered that notice of the companies' violations be posted at the Fulton Fish Market and distributed to all parties doing business there. Wohl also suspended the bosses of each of the three unloading crews from working at the market. These sanctions, which came in the fourth year of Wohl's term, were the only penalties Wohl imposed during his administratorship.

Judge Griesa sustained the findings, concluding that "the influence of organized crime in the market still exists to some extent." However, Judge Griesa overturned the suspensions because they "could impair the functioning of the Market." He expressed hope that the fines alone would serve as a "severe warning" and reserved the right to renew the suspensions "if it becomes necessary in the future."[35] In essence, Judge Griesa was acknowledging the three suspended defendants' and Cosa Nostra's power to disrupt or even paralyze the market.

At Mayor David Dinkins's urging, Wohl petitioned the court to extend his term beyond May 1992, until the city could take over the task of supervising the market. Judge Griesa approved Wohl's request. Wohl also asked that the court order the U.S. Department of Justice to fund the extended term. U.S. Attorney Otto G. Obermaier objected to further payments, claiming that the city was responsible for regulating the market.[36] Eventually, after Mayor Dinkins wrote a letter to U.S. Attorney General William Barr, the necessary funds were allocated.[37] Wohl's administratorship ended later that year.

NEW YORK CITY REGULATORY ACTION: LOCAL LAW 50

Shortly after the release of Wohl's 1990 midterm report, representatives of the New York City Department of Ports, Trade, and Commerce announced a plan for "comprehensive reform" at the Fulton Fish Market.[38] Six months later, no plan had been unveiled; city officials claimed that budget cuts and legal complications were responsible for the delay.

Ports and Trade's 1991 budget was cut $1 million; thirty-five of its two hundred employees were laid off, including five of the nine employees assigned to the Fulton Fish Market. City officials postponed issuing regulations for licensing loaders and unloaders until they could conclude negotiations with the South Street Seaport Corporation (SSSC) to return leases to the city.[39] (The city had previously transferred authority to administer leases and collect rent from wholesalers at the market to the SSSC, an arm of the South Street Museum. Pursuant to the contract, the SSSC kept 10 percent of the rent revenue it collected.)[40]

In 1992, the New York City Council opened hearings into whether the market required city supervision.[41] At a May 1992 council hearing on the "City's failure to regulate the Fulton Fish Market," Wohl testified that the absence of an effective regulatory presence created an environment in which racketeering thrived. Several witnesses testified that a lawless environment at the market prevented merchants from doing business honestly. In fear of the consequences of testifying against Cosa Nostra, several witnesses wore black hoods. One witness, identified as a Brooklyn restaurateur, testified that he was beaten by a gang of men for parking in the wrong spot at the market. A Florida truck driver told the committee that he had been dismissed from his job and blacklisted at the market for complaining about workers who refused to unload his cargo. A North Carolina seafood supplier reported that he stopped doing business at the market after wholesalers had stolen $40,000 and that on a different occasion a wholesaler had pulled a gun on him while he was collecting a bill.[42] Another supplier testified that he had quit doing business at the market because wholesalers did not pay their bills and then disappeared.

Officials testified that the city's failure to collect permit and license fees from unloaders, loaders, and wholesalers, and its failure to negotiate reasonable rent increases with the two wholesaler associations over a ten-year period, cost the city nearly $2 million in revenue each year.[43] A DOI official described the results of the "Stingray" investigation, which had uncovered weapons trading, drugs, and racketeering at the market.[44] An attorney representing unloading and loading firms stated that the allegations of corruption were false and that there was no system of unlawfully assigning trucks to specific unloading crews.

At the City Council's next hearings (March/April 1995), Mayor Giuliani unveiled his plan to regulate the market. The City's Economic Development Corporation would take over rent collection from the

SSSC and increase rents. The Department of Investigation would conduct background investigations of companies and workers. The Department of Business Services (as successor to Ports, Trade, and Commerce) would issue licenses and registrations only to businesses it deemed commercially suitable and of good character, honesty, and integrity.

Several council members questioned the need for background investigations of individuals and businesses, especially the use of fingerprinting.[45] Others questioned whether the Department of Business Services could handle the responsibility of managing the market. The president of the Committee to Preserve the Fulton Fish Market, a group representing businesses at the market, argued that the proposed bill would drive business to New Jersey and other sites. Several business owners argued that there was no need for the city to take action.[46]

Two days after the March 1995 City Council hearing, fire swept through the Old Market Building. The fire commissioner determined that the blaze had been set purposely.[47] Some officials speculated that the fire might have destroyed financial records crucial to the city's inquiry into market operations.[48] The crime has never been solved.

Wholesalers threatened to move out of Manhattan if the city raised rents and implemented licensing; they met with the mayors of Yonkers and other cities to discuss possible relocation.[49] In the ensuing war of words, Giuliani threatened to replace the wholesalers. Chief of staff Randy Mastro sent out several hundred letters soliciting businesses to move their operations to the market to replace any departing businesses.[50]

On June 14, 1995, the New York City Council overwhelmingly passed Local Law 50, the city's comprehensive regulatory plan. In its legislative findings, the council said criminal prosecutions and a court-appointed administrator had failed to purge the market of organized crime. The council pointed to loading and unloading cartels, violence and threats of violence, and the practices of "phantom" wholesalers.[51]

Establishing a Market Manager

Local Law 50 authorizes the commissioner of the Department of Business Services to designate a market manager to provide day-to-day on-sight supervision.[52] The market manager is authorized to promulgate rules and regulations; require licensees and registrants to maintain certain records and periodically to examine those records; make referrals to appropriate law enforcement agencies; and perform other duties that the commissioner deems necessary.

Licensing and Regulating the Unloading and Loading Businesses

Pursuant to Local Law 50, every unloading and loading business must obtain a license from the Department of Business Services. The license specifies the maximum rates to be charged for services. The commissioner is authorized to suspend or revoke any business license, or pursue other remedies for Local Law 50 violations. The commissioner may also promulgate rules to ensure orderly unloading, including a queueing procedure for unloading trucks. The commissioner may designate loading areas, and require loading companies to obtain a city lease or occupancy permit. The commissioner was directed to determine whether a city agency should take over loading and unloading services.

Registering and Regulating Wholesalers and Delivery Drivers

Local Law 50 requires wholesalers to register with the city and to obtain a registration number from the commissioner. The registration scheme is aimed at eliminating "phantom" wholesalers.[53] Wholesalers are prohibited from assigning or subleasing their premises to other wholesalers, unless the assignee or sublessee is also registered with the city. Additionally, wholesalers are required to notify the commissioner of any change in ownership subsequent to registration. Each wholesaler must obtain a stand permit, at a rate to be determined by the commissioner, before placing any seafood on the street. The commissioner must maintain and make available a list of all wholesalers who are registered and have permits.

Identification Cards and Penalties

Local Law 50 requires all principals, employees, and agents of licensed and registered businesses to obtain official photo identification cards issued by the market manager. Applicants for "class A" photo identification cards (issued to all owners, employees, and agents of unloading and loading businesses) must be fingerprinted by a person designated by the commissioner and pay the Division of Criminal Justice Services to conduct a criminal-history search.[54] The market manager may also require any person applying for a "class B" photo identification card (issued to all principals, employees, and agents of wholesale companies) to be fingerprinted where there is ample cause to believe that the applicant lacks "good character, honesty and integrity."[55]

Each applicant for photo identification must provide the Department of Business Services with certain information, including any criminal or civil investigation the applicant has been subject to over the preceding five years. The department may refuse to issue a photo identification card if it deems the person lacking in good character, honesty, and integrity. In making this determination, the department must take into account any criminal conviction, any pending criminal or civil proceedings against the applicant, involvement in racketeering activity, and the applicant's "knowing association" with any person who has been convicted of racketeering activity. The commissioner may require the forfeiture of any vehicle, equipment, or property used in violation of the licensing provisions. The law authorizes the Department of Business Services to investigate any matters that fall under the auspices of the regulatory regime.

Any business required to have a license, permit, or registration is liable for violations committed by its principals, employees, or agents. Violations of Local Law 50 or rules promulgated pursuant to it, are punishable by up to $10,000 for each violation. Operation of a loading or unloading business without a license constitutes a misdemeanor punishable by criminal fines, imprisonment, and additional civil penalties.

Local Law 50 requires the commissioner of business services to submit to the City Council regular reports of its market-related investigations. The reports must provide the number of criminal acts and violations reported, referrals to law enforcement agencies, lists of unloading and loading companies and wholesalers, and other information on applications denied and on revenue collected or outstanding.

The Committee to Save the Fulton Fish Market brought a suit in the U.S. District Court for the Southern District of New York challenging Local Law 50 as unconstitutional and contrary to state law. Judge Griesa dismissed the complaint as "entirely without merit."[56]

THE CITY'S REGULATORY ATTACK

Raising the Rents

In 1994, the South Street Seaport Corporation asked the city for permission to resign as the market's landlord. SSSC officers were frustrated by financial losses. The corporation spent an average of $120,000 annually managing the market and received about $27,000 as its 10 percent share of rent revenues.[57] The New York City Economic Development Corporation, as agent for the Department of Business Services, reached a new lease agreement with the Fulton Fishmongers Association, the lessee of the fire-damaged Old Market Building. Wholesalers, who had been paying $72,000 a year to rent city property, agreed to pay $450,000 in the first year of the new ten-year lease; $550,000 in the second year; and $650,000 for each of the remaining eight years.[58] Shortly thereafter, the other major wholesalers' association, the New York Wholesale Fish Dealers Association, agreed to an increase in annual rent from $90,000 to $675,000.[59] The South Street Sidewalk Association, a smaller group of wholesalers, also consented to a rental increase, from $80,000 annually to $650,000 a year, effective June 1, 1998.[60] The city benefited by almost a million dollars the first year.

Evicting Wholesalers

In July 1995, acting under its authority as landlord, the city removed from the market five wholesalers. Two of these companies were owned by relatives of alleged Cosa Nostra figures. Alphonse Malangone Jr., son of a suspected Genovese capo, and Thomas Gangi, son of the alleged Genovese family boss at the market, Rosario Ross Gangi, were each denied leases.[61] In 1996, another wholesaler with suspected ties to Gangi was denied a license on the grounds of falsified records and refusal to discuss relationships with organized-crime figures.[62]

Eliminating the Unloading Cartel

In October 1995, Mayor Giuliani announced his intention to replace the six unloading companies at the market with a single company chosen by the city.[63] Commissioner of Business Services Rudy Washington claimed that five of the six existing companies had engaged in serious misconduct, and that the sixth was linked to an unloader who had refused to testify in a federal investigation.[64] The city rejected the license applications of all six companies. In one blow, a cartel that operated for more than half a century was gone. The city solicited bids from companies desiring to carry out all the unloading operations at the market. Laro Maintenance Corporation submitted the lowest bid and passed the DOI background check. The city's contract with Laro called for unloading fees 20 percent below those previously charged. Laro agreed to unload trucks on a first-come, first-serve basis.

Laro's debut was disastrous. Four hundred journeymen, members of Local 359, refused to move the seafood from wholesalers' stalls to the buyers' vehicles. The Market was brought to a virtual standstill. The protesters claimed that their action was meant to show solidarity with the forty employees who lost their jobs when the six unloading companies were evicted. Ironically, Laro's workers were unionized, unlike the cartel employees they were replacing.[65]

The wholesalers also protested. They told journalists that Giuliani's ousting of the six unloading companies would produce market chaos and higher seafood prices. The Committee to Save the Fulton Fish Market distributed flyers charging that the new regulations "will destroy your Fulton Fish Market."[66] The committee also sought a court order reinstating the dismissed unloading companies,[67] arguing that the city's denial of licenses was an improper exercise of power and a violation of due process. Judge Griesa denied the petition.[68] Giuliani threatened to shut the market if there were further delays or disruptions.[69]

Two months after Laro took over the unloading function, the DOI discovered that Laro had provided incomplete information on its license application.[70] The company had not disclosed that it had been investigated by the National Labor Relations Board for allegedly refusing to hire thirteen janitors at another location because they belonged to a union that Laro did not recognize. Despite this stain on Laro's character, the DOI concluded that overall Laro has enjoyed a good business reputation and Laro's contract was upheld.[71]

Targeting Mobbed-Up Waste Haulers

The new ten-year leases that the three wholesaler associations signed with the city prohibited them from associating or doing business with organized-crime figures. Nonetheless, in October 1995, the associations contracted with Barretti Carting, a waste-hauling company that had been named in a racketeering indictment filed by the Manhattan District Attorney's Office several months earlier. Prosecutors charged that Barretti Carting was a member of a mob-run waste hauling cartel. The wholesaler associations argued that Barretti had been the main waste hauler at the market for years, and that the associations were contractually bound to Barretti.[72] The mayor gave the wholesaler associations an ultimatum: break the contract with Barretti or face eviction from the market. The associations fired the waste-hauling company. Within days, the wholesaler associations signed contracts with a new carter[73] that charged 40 percent less than Barretti.[74]

Driving Out Corrupt Loaders

In August 1995, Department of Business Services Commissioner Rudy Washington notified loaders that they would have to obtain a license to continue operating at the Fulton Fish Market. Eleven loading companies brought a state-court suit challenging the constitutionality of Local Law 50. They argued that they had previously signed a valid fifty-year lease with the (then-landlord) South Street Seaport Corporation. The court found that no valid lease existed and upheld the constitutionality of Local Law 50.[75]

In December, 1995, the city used Local Law 50 to oust two longtime loading businesses at the market; the owners of both had pled guilty to charges that they were part of a thirteen-member Cosa Nostra conspiracy that robbed four banks and an armored-truck depot.[76] Giuliani then sent in city officials to begin running two of the market's loading zones. Hoping that its presence would deter vandalism and violence, the city provided free loading services. This action set off a work slowdown similar to the one on Laro's first day.[77] It was resolved by reassigning those zones to existing loading companies.

In May 1996, the city ousted another loading company on the ground that its owner had been convicted of tax evasion.[78] In July, the Department of Business Services denied a loading license and a photo identification card to Joseph "Chief" Macario, because Macario's company did not have adequate insurance and because of Macario's knowing "associations with the Genovese organized crime family."[79] Anticipating that the license denial would trigger violence, police reinforcements were assigned to the market immediately following the announcement. Furthermore, Macario challenged the Department of Business Services in state court. The court held that the first ground was insufficient but upheld the denial of the business license and identification card on the ground that Macario had "knowing associations" with recognized organized crime figures.[80]

In January 1997, the Department of Business Services awarded licenses to only two of the six remaining loading companies. Even though these two companies had previously engaged in questionable practices, city officials asserted that they had cooperated with the city's reform efforts. Moreover, no outside loading companies had submitted bids for the loading contracts. The two-year contracts set the maximum rates that these companies could charge for loading, parking, and security services.[81] Parking fees dropped from as high as $20 to a maximum of $4 a night for cars, vans, and most trucks, and $6 for the largest trucks. It was estimated that restaurateurs and retailers would save $2.5 million annually.[82]

EXPANDING THE REGULATORY INITIATIVE TO OTHER NEW YORK CITY MARKETS

In October 1996, Mayor Giuliani proposed a bill that would give the city new powers to remove corrupt union officials from the city's seven major wholesale food markets: New York City Terminal Market, the Bronx Terminal Market, the Brooklyn Terminal Market, the Gansevoort Meat Market, the Brooklyn Wholesale Meat Market, the Hunts Point Produce Market, and the Fulton Fish Market.[83] Deputy Mayor Randy Mastro declared, "Every one of these markets in the past decade has involved not one but several mob families."[84] Mastro stated the bill's immediate targets included officials in three unions linked to Cosa Nostra, including Local 359.[85]

At the City Council's Economic Development Committee's hearings in November 1996, Assemblyman Brian McLaughlin (D-Queens), president of the New York City Central Labor Council, denounced the bill as overly broad and intrusive. However, the following spring, a compromise was reached when it was agreed that an arbitrator would have authority to hear appeals of any union-official removals. The City Council passed Local Law 28,[86] and Mayor Giuliani signed it into law on May 16, 1997.

Local Law 28 is similar in many respects to Local Law 50 in that it requires all food purveyors to obtain licenses and to submit to background checks, thus allowing the city to oust any companies with ties to organized crime. Yet, Local Law 28 is more expansive than Local Law 50 because it gives the city authority to investigate and suspend union officials for misconduct or for knowingly associating with organized crime figures.[87] It also applies to other market businesses, such as suppliers of ice. The effectiveness of Local Law 28, however, remains to be seen.

A LIBERATED FISH MARKET

The freeing of the Fulton Fish Market from Cosa Nostra influence is attributable to the civil RICO suit filed by then U.S. Attorney Rudolph Giuliani and to the comprehensive city regulations that were put into place after Giuliani became mayor. The liberation of the Fulton Fish Market ought to be credited to Giuliani's determination.

The civil RICO suit, *United States v. Local 359,* may not have been sufficient to purge the mob from the market, but it was a good start. It forced several prominent racketeers to leave the market. It also placed an administrator into the market's day-to-day operations. Although the administrator's accomplishments were modest, at least the mob was not able to remobilize as long as the administrator and his staff were on the job. Indeed, their presence signaled that change might be possible. Furthermore, the administrator pressed the city to exercise its regulatory power more aggressively.

Local Law 50 was the decisive breakthrough. The licensing system led to the expulsion of the entire coterie of unloading companies and all but two of the loaders. Practically overnight, the unloading cartel that had lasted half a century was replaced by a company chosen by the city. Laro's fees were 20 percent below the cartel's rate. Jump up fees were eliminated. In January 1997, the Department of Business Services granted licenses to only two loading companies, both of which had cooperated with the city. These regulatory reforms show real promise.

One year after Local Law 50 was enacted, a report credited Giuliani's campaign to remove Cosa Nostra from the Fulton Fish Market with having brought about slightly lower seafood prices (a 2 percent decrease, compared with a 13 percent increase nationwide) and a greater supply of fish.[88] In 1998, city officials claimed that the overall cost of fish has declined 13 percent, and the amount of fish transported to the market has increased 14 percent.[89] Incredibly, the head of the Committee to Save the Fulton Fish Market testified before the City Council in 1997 that the reforms were working and that the Department of Business Services were "vital agencies whose presence provides a safe and comfortable environment in which to do business." Based on the success of this initiative at the Fulton Fish Market, Local Law 50 has provided the model for legislation to oust Cosa Nostra from New York City's other major wholesale food markets and from the waste-hauling industry.

11

Purging the Mob from John F. Kennedy Airport

> This court is satisfied that it is faced with an extraordinary situation. . . . Contrary to the argument of Local 295, vestiges of its old regime are not gone. The record established . . . a consistent and extended pattern of racketeering and extortion. . . . Many of the guilty do not appreciate the gravity of their crimes. None of their associates has displayed any interest in reforming the union. The record shows a smug, almost contemptuous, indifference to the presence of organized crime in union affairs by a number of former union officials and an active effort by many in Local 295 to thwart reform. . . . This court concludes that there is a likelihood of continued corruption and that the court should appoint a trustee.[1]
>
> —Justice Eugene H. Nickerson, *United States v. Local 295*, 1992

ALMOST FROM THE date of its opening, JFK Airport's cargo operations served, in the words of Henry Hill, as a "candy store" for the mob. The Luccheses were the dominant organized-crime family at the airport; their power base was the two International Brotherhood of Teamsters (IBT) locals whose histories are inextricably linked to organized crime, IBT Local 295 and IBT Local 851. The mob used these unions to extract payoffs from freight-forwarding companies seeking labor peace and avoidance of burdensome contract provisions. Lead agents, handpicked by Cosa Nostra, facilitated profitable truck give-ups and hijackings. Cosa Nostra also policed a trucking cartel. Cartel members' trade association dues flowed directly to the Lucchese crime family; the association fixed prices and prohibited noncartel-member trucking firms from entering the JFK cargo market.

Ever since the 1958 McClellan Committee Hearings exposed organized-crime racketeering in the air cargo industry at JFK Airport, federal, state, and local law enforcement agencies have launched periodic attacks, including antitrust suits in the 1970s, criminal prosecutions in the 1970s and 1980s, and civil RICO suits in the late 1980s and early 1990s. Only the civil RICO suits have seriously challenged Cosa Nostra's domination of the airport's cargo industry.

REFORMING THE INTERNATIONAL BROTHERHOOD OF TEAMSTERS FROM THE TOP DOWN

Purging Cosa Nostra from the two IBT locals at JFK Airport took place in the context of the larger remedial effort to eradicate mob influence from the national Teamsters union, at the time the nation's largest union.[2] In 1988, U.S. Attorney Rudolph Giuliani filed a civil RICO suit that charged the Teamsters' national General Executive Board with running the IBT as a racketeering enterprise in collaboration with Cosa Nostra.[3] Pursuant to a 1989 consent decree, a three-person trusteeship was established over the IBT: former federal Judge Frederick B. Lacey was appointed independent administrator; former federal prosecutor Charles Carberry was selected as investigations officer; and labor lawyer Michael Holland was appointed elections officer.* The consent decree empowered the investigations officer to seek the dismissal of corrupt officials from the union and to establish trusteeships for corrupt locals. In the course of three years, the trusteeship removed nearly two hundred union officials from Teamsters locals across the country.[4]

In June 1991, Investigations Officer Carberry charged the officers of Local 295 with breaching their fiduciary duty to the local's membership by failing to investigate rampant corruption and by embezzling Local 295 funds. As a result, six of the seven Local 295 officers were removed

*Pursuant to the 1989 consent decree, an independent review board (IRB) replaced the court-appointed trusteeship in October 1992. The IRB's directive was to investigate and eliminate corruption in the IBT. The three-member board consisted of IBT Independent Administrator Frederick Lacey, former CIA and FBI Director William Webster, and Harold Burke, the former head of the United Mine Workers union. (Grant Crandall, UMW's general counsel replaced Burke in June 1993.)

from their posts. Anthony Cuozzo, the only remaining officer, was soon forced to resign because of "knowing association" with Anthony Calagna, a member of the Lucchese crime family and former president of Local 295. Cuozzo was later murdered.[5] Independent Administrator Lacey permanently suspended Local 295 president Anthony Calagna from the IBT and ordered him to repay $50,000 to the local.[6] The federal district court affirmed these actions and approved the order removing the officers.[7] The ousted officials of Local 295 then attempted to arrange that a special election be held to select their successors.[8] In response, Lacey obtained a court order placing Local 295 under a temporary trusteeship and appointed William Ferchak, a longtime officer of IBT Local 732, temporary trustee of Local 295.[9]

In March 1992, Ron Carey,* the newly elected reform president of the IBT, without prior notice to the IBT independent administrator, announced his intention to replace Ferchak with William F. Genoese, another officer of IBT Local 732. The independent administrator vetoed that appointment, finding that Genoese had a "sad record of inaction in the face of a long history of corruption at [JFK] Airport"[10] and was closely tied to the Lucchese crime family. Carey later stripped Genoese of his Local 732 position, citing a "pattern of malfeasance" in the use of membership dues, and installed a temporary trustee to run Local 732.[11]

The IBT trusteeship also launched a comprehensive investigation of Local 851. In 1990, as the investigation moved forward, Mark Davidoff resigned as secretary-treasurer (the top position in Local 851) and was replaced by Anthony Razza.[12] The 1993 indictment of Razza prompted IBT President Ron Carey to appoint Curt Ostrander, an IBT Local 559 official, as temporary trustee and Brian Kelly, a member of New York City's Mollen Commission (investigating police corruption), as investigator.[13]

*Carey won the IBT's first election under the consent decree with the motto "No Corruption, No Excuses, No Exceptions." His appointment of Genoese stirred controversy. The Department of Justice launched an investigation into Carey's ties to organized crime. Carey claimed that his nomination of Genoese was an "honest mistake." The Genoese appointment haunted Carey's reelection campaign. The opposing candidate, Jimmy Hoffa Jr., claimed that Carey was a puppet of Cosa Nostra. Carey won the election by a close margin. The election was overturned by elections monitor Barbara Zack Quindel because of fund-raising improprieties. In November 1997, Carey was prohibited from seeking reelection, and in July 1998, the IRB banned Carey from the Teamsters for life.

ATTACKING THE TWO IBT LOCALS

The FBI and U.S. Department of Justice were not impressed with the Teamsters' progress in reforming Locals 295 and 851. In March 1990, U.S. Attorney for the Eastern District of New York Andrew J. Maloney filed the most ambitious legal attack ever launched against organized crime in the JFK cargo industry. In addition to Locals 295 and 851, the government named as defendants fourteen individuals, most of whom were identified as members or associates of the Lucchese and Gambino crime families, or as officers and former officers of IBT Locals 295 and 851, including Harry and Mark Davidoff, Frank Calise, and Anthony Calagna.

The complaint alleged that the Lucchese crime family had used its control of Teamsters Locals 295 and 851 to extract revenue from the cargo industry at JFK Airport and charged numerous acts of extortion and labor racketeering. For example:

- Between September 1980 and September 1982 defendants Harry and Mark Davidoff, Frank Calise, and Frank Manzo prevented Union Air Transport from using a specific warehouse and transportation service unless the company paid the defendants money.
- In 1983 and 1984, Harry Davidoff, Frank Manzo, and Frank Calise threatened to organize the nonunionized workforce of Pandair unless Pandair paid the defendants money.
- Between August 1983 and December 1984, Frank Manzo and Frank Calise "threatened a strike, boycott, or other collective labor group action" injurious to Kamino Air Transport, unless the company paid off the defendants.
- Defendants Frank Manzo and Frank Calise threatened to increase Schenkers International Forwarders' labor costs unless payments were made.
- Harry Davidoff, Mark Davidoff, Frank Calise, and Anthony Guerrieri extorted Stair Cargo Services by threatening to force the company to hire workers affiliated with Teamsters Local 295.
- Frank Manzo, Frank Calise, and Richard Schroeder threatened to enforce a collective bargaining contract's provisions requiring pension and welfare contributions to Teamsters Local 851 unless the company made payoffs to the defendants.[14]

In March 1991, U.S. District Judge Eugene Nickerson granted partial summary judgment against Harry Davidoff and Frank Calise, finding that their prior racketeering conspiracy and extortion convictions[15] established the predicate acts needed to satisfy the government's civil RICO case.[16] The court enjoined the two men from participating in the affairs of Locals 295 and 851, their executive boards, or any other labor organization or employee benefit plan. Davidoff and Calise were also enjoined from associating with officers, auditors, and employees of Locals 295 and 851.[17] Furthermore, the court ordered the defendants to repay $961,400* that they had obtained in payoffs from freight forwarding companies.[18] Nevertheless, the court declined to impose a permanent trusteeship over the locals, finding insufficient evidence of "continuing corruption."[19]

Court Approves Local 295 Trusteeship

In 1992, after further motions by Independent Administrator Lacey, Judge Nickerson determined that the IBT-installed temporary trustee was unable to rid Local 295 of corruption.[20] Judge Nickerson cited the local's continuing $2,000 a month payments to Harry Davidoff, despite his criminal convictions and civil sanctions, and the use of union funds to pay attorneys' fees for former Local 295 President Anthony Calagna's defense on charges of extortion and labor racketeering. Pointing to Local 295's history of Cosa Nostra domination and the recent convictions of several of its officers as justifications for close scrutiny, Judge Nickerson imposed a permanent trusteeship.[21] He acknowledged that "Congress considered the appointment of a trustee to run the affairs of a union local as an extraordinary measure," but concluded that the court was indeed faced with an extraordinary situation.[22] Moreover, Judge Nickerson noted that "[t]he implementation of trusteeships under civil RICO is no longer a novel, one-time experiment. It is quickly being recognized as an extremely valuable part of effective law enforcement."[23] The court set no time limit for the trusteeship; it would last until "honest and uncoerced" elections for new officers could be held.[24]

In April 1992, Judge Nickerson appointed Thomas Puccio, a former assistant U.S. attorney and former head of the Brooklyn Organized

*The judge later vacated the amount and ordered further hearings to determine just how much the defendant owed.

Crime Strike Force, as trustee of Local 295. The court granted Puccio broad authority to administer the daily affairs of the local, to investigate corruption, and to oversee the election of union officials. Puccio vowed to use all investigative strategies, including undercover agents and sting operations, to root out corruption.[25] He hired Mike Moroney, a former member of the U.S. Department of Labor's Office of Labor Racketeering and former assistant to IBT's Investigations Officer Charles Carberry, to serve as deputy trustee.[26]

Puccio faced a number of obstacles. His position was part-time, and although he had extensive experience investigating corruption, he had no experience negotiating and enforcing collective bargaining agreements or overseeing routine union matters. Moreover, IBT President Ron Carey was not supportive. He maintained that the fifteen-member ethical-practices board he had created in 1992 was sufficient to deal with Local 295's problems and that further government intervention in Teamsters affairs was unjustified.[27] The Lucchese crime family's continued influence over Local 851, Local 295's sister local, also impeded Puccio's efforts. Puccio claimed that Local 851 encouraged at least thirty Local 295 truck drivers to transfer their memberships to Local 851, in order to elude investigation, notwithstanding the fact that Local 851 represented clerical employees and dispatchers. Forces within Local 295 itself also hindered Puccio's initiatives. A group calling itself the "United Workers Council" distributed newsletters smearing Puccio and his staff.[28]

To foster a democratic atmosphere, Puccio conducted an educational program for Local 295's general membership regarding grievance procedures and union democracy. The trustee's staff distributed copies of collective bargaining agreements to Local 295 members. The deputy trustee published a monthly newsletter describing the trustee's efforts to rid the local of organized crime and discussing other union matters.[29] An advisory committee composed of union members provided the membership with a direct line of communication to the trustee. Puccio also rewrote the local's bylaws to protect union members from corruption. For example, the new bylaws restricted the salaries and pensions of Local 295 officers; required the local's officers to take specific actions against corruption; and provided that shop stewards would be elected, not appointed.[30] Puccio filed a $558,000 insurance claim to recover Local 295 funds embezzled by former union officers. He also sought, on behalf of Local 851 and Local 295 pension and welfare funds, to recover severance and benefit monies paid to former Local 295 officers, including $305,000 paid to Harry Davidoff's daughter, Sharon Moskowitz, a former administrator* of the Local 851 benefit fund.[31] Puccio also warned corporate executives to avoid doing business with a dozen freight-forwarding companies he had identified as controlled by Cosa Nostra.[32]

Puccio's initiatives, however, came at a high price. He exceeded his budget, and spent far more than Local 295's annual income, nearly bankrupting the local.[33] Puccio paid hundreds of thousands of dollars to lawyers and accountants who billed at hourly rates of up to $375. Puccio's salary was $250,000 per year for his part-time services as trustee; his deputy trustee received $150,000 as full-time compensation.[34]

Independent Supervisor for Local 851

In 1992, the U.S. Attorney's Office for the Eastern District of New York sought a court-appointed trusteeship for Local 851. Opposing the motion, Local 851 argued that the election of Anthony Razza as secretary-treasurer had ended corruption. Razza submitted an affidavit claiming that he was committed to a corruption-free union, and that he had succeeded in ridding Local 851 of organized crime. The court again declined to appoint a trustee in the absence of evidence of recent corruption. In September 1993, Razza was indicted on extortion, racketeering, and tax-fraud charges.[35] In April 1994, he pled guilty to receiving unlawful payoffs from Kuehne & Nagel Air Freight and to engaging in a tax-fraud conspiracy with Amerford International;[36] he was sentenced to twenty-one months in prison.[37]

In June 1993, Thomas Puccio filed a motion with Judge Nickerson to extend his Local 295 trusteeship to include Local 851. Puccio asserted that the Lucchese crime family was using Local 851 to frustrate his reform of Local 295. Puccio also alleged that Local 851's president and vice-president had ties to the Lucchese crime family and that local officials had received hundreds of thousands of dollars in bribes from freight-forwarding companies.[38] He later argued that Razza's indictment provided sufficient evidence of current corruption. Local 851 contended that no trustee was needed and that Puccio's expenditures and

*Ultimately, Ms. Moskowitz prevailed, but the pension and welfare fund did recoup some money by means of an indemnification from an insurance carrier.

extensive delegation of duties demonstrated "his unfitness" to serve as a union trustee.[39]

In October 1994, with Puccio's motion pending, the U.S. Attorney's Office, Local 851, and the International Brotherhood of Teamsters signed a consent decree placing Local 851 under a court-appointed independent supervisor.[40] According to the decree, anyone currently serving as a court-appointed trustee or deputy trustee was excluded from serving as Local 851's independent supervisor, thereby preventing the appointment of Puccio or Moroney, whom union officials accused of looting Local 295. Judge Nickerson appointed former federal prosecutor Ron DePetris to the position. DePetris hired David Krasula, a former long-time investigator with the U.S. Postal Inspection Service and the U.S. Department of Labor, as his chief investigator.

Instead of providing for the usual one-person trusteeship, the consent decree created a bifurcated monitorship; DePetris would be responsible for ferreting out corruption; Curt Ostrander, the temporary union trustee appointed by the IBT, would continue to oversee Local 851's daily affairs.[41] The court authorized the independent supervisor to review the union trustee's expenditures, contracts, leases, and appointments. The independent supervisor could veto expenditures, contracts, or appointments that furthered racketeering or knowing associations with members of organized crime.*

The union trustee and the independent supervisor jointly must decide when free and fair elections are feasible. The independent supervisor is responsible for administering the elections. The terms of the union trustee and the independent supervisor terminate sixty days after the independent supervisor certifies the results of the elections to the court. As of June 1, 1999, the local-wide election of officers had not yet taken place.

The consent decree enjoined members and officers of Local 851 from engaging in racketeering, knowing association with any member, associate, or other individuals involved with any organized-crime group, and obstructing the work of the independent supervisor.[42] The consent decree authorized the independent supervisor to investigate

*The consent decree also required a hearing officer, who had to be "acceptable to both [the U.S. Attorney's Office and Local 851] and who has . . . experience in labor-management relations," to review the independent supervisor's vetoes. *United States v. Local 295*, 90 Civ. 1012 (E.D.N.Y. 1992) Consent Decree, 15.

any such acts and, where appropriate, to conduct disciplinary hearings. However, the independent supervisor was authorized to discipline only officers of Local 851 and the other persons named in the consent decree.[43] He could remove officers from their positions and expel them from the union. But he could not discipline members qua members.

When Ron DePetris became independent supervisor, there were no officers to investigate because the IBT had replaced them with temporary trustee Curt Ostrander. As a result, DePetris focused his investigations on Local 851's two business agents and approximately fifty shop stewards, and on lead agents. He later obtained court approval to extend his investigations and disciplinary proceedings to union members who obstructed the work of the independent supervisor.[44] DePetris removed six of the fifty shop stewards from their positions, and he disciplined sixteen lead agents, who were charged with obstructing the work of the independent supervisor.

The independent supervisor's budget was set at $300,000 a year, including salaries, to ensure that Local 851's finances would not suffer the same fate as Local 295's.[45] Under the consent decree the national Teamsters union agreed to support the Local 851 independent supervisor and union-trustee positions, if necessary. Because of the financial straits in which Local 851 found itself at the time of DePetris's appointment, the IBT provided the funding.[46]

DePetris's Effort to Recover Damages for Past Corruption

In an effort to restore the local's financial health, DePetris sought to recover Local 851 assets that had been dissipated or misappropriated. A year into his term, DePetris filed two civil RICO suits against freight-forwarding companies and Anthony Razza.[47] These suits were the first ever initiated by a court-appointed monitor to recover civil damages on behalf of a labor union for past corruption.[48]

Following an extensive investigation by the New York State OCTF, in the first suit, filed in 1995 against Amerford International (now known as Thyssen Haniel Logistics), its parent company, and Razza, DePetris charged the defendants with violating RICO and a New York State labor law[49] by participating in a labor-payoff scheme. In 1990, Amerford was seeking to drastically reduce its labor costs at JFK airport by eliminating many Local 851 positions. However, such terminations were prohibited under the collective bargaining agreement. With the assistance of Razza and others, including Patrick Dello Russo, a shop steward of Local 295 and an unofficial representative of Local 851, Amerford was able to reduce its labor force at JFK by more than twenty employees and maintain labor peace. Dello Russo had previously been given an eighteen-month no-show position as a warehouseman with Amerford that paid him $128,622.

As part of the scheme, the company entered into a consulting agreement with KAT Management Services, whereby KAT received roughly 25 percent of the money Amerford saved because of its reduced labor force. KAT was a front for the Lucchese family; money withdrawn from the KAT account was subsequently distributed in cash to Lucchese members, including Anthony Calagna, then president of Local 295. In all, payments in excess of $500,000 were made to KAT. To conceal the scheme, Amerford disguised the terminations as transfers by offering the terminated Local 851 employees similar positions in Hartford, Connecticut. Razza and Dello Russo told the employees that Teamsters Local 851 supported Amerford's actions and would not be able to assist the workers in fighting the transfers. None of the employees accepted the disingenuous transfer option.[50]

In 1993, Razza, Dello Russo, Calagna, and Andrew Titley, Amerford's chief financial officer, were charged with, among other crimes, participating in an illegal labor-payoff scheme and tax-fraud conspiracy.[51] Harold Niehenke, president and chief executive officer of Amerford, pled guilty to state charges alleging that he had agreed to pay KAT "so that the terms of the collective bargaining agreement . . . would not be enforced . . . and consequently, Amerford . . . terminated . . . over 20 union members, and thereby wrongfully obtained their . . . contractual rights to employment."[52] In April 1994, Titley pled guilty to making unlawful payoffs to Dello Russo in connection with Dello Russo's no-show position. Calagna admitted to (1) conspiring to participate in a RICO enterprise (the Lucchese crime family), which included as predicate acts unlawful labor payoff demands from Amerford, and (2) conspiracy to commit tax fraud. Dello Russo pled guilty to (1) conspiring to participate in a RICO enterprise (the Lucchese crime family), which included as predicate acts unlawful labor payoff demands from Amerford and another JFK freight-fowarding company (K&N), including payment for a no-show position, and (2) conspiracy to commit tax fraud. Razza pled guilty to unlawfully receiving labor payoffs from another company and conspiracy to commit tax fraud.[53]

DePetris, on behalf of Local 851, entered into a settlement with the defendants in June 1998. Amerford agreed to pay Local 851 $1.2 million to resolve the RICO action and $2 million to settle the state labor law claim.[54] The state claim was supposed to be satisfied by funds previously paid by Amerford to the New York State Organized Task Force in 1994, but the OCTF resisted turning over the money.[55]

The second action, initiated in 1997, sought to recover treble damages from Kuehne & Nagel Air Freight (K&N) and Anthony Razza. As the 1988 collective bargaining agreement between K&N and Local 851 was about to expire in January 1992, K&N's vice-president, Chester Calamari, was engaged in negotiations with Razza. Razza advised Calamari to contact Anthony Dello Russo. Dello Russo offered to settle K&N's collective bargaining difficulties for $50,000 in cash and arranged for Calamari to make the payments, disguised as consulting fees, to Group East, headed by attorney Anthony Figoni.

In April 1992, K&N and Local 851 entered into a new two-year collective bargaining agreement. Razza made many concessions, including freezing K&N's pension contributions for up to a year. In return, Calamari paid more than $100,000 to Group East. Figoni then withdrew the monies, and after retaining some to cover taxes, gave most of it to Dello Russo, who in turn paid Razza and the Lucchese family. In a criminal case involving this scheme, Razza pled guilty to receiving labor payoffs from K&N, and to tax-fraud conspiracy.[56]

In March 1998, U.S. District Judge Nickerson denied Kuehne & Nagel's motion to dismiss. He ruled there were sufficient allegations that the freight-forwarding company had been part of a scheme that enriched the Lucchese crime family.[57] Damages, if awarded, would be used to reimburse the International and the Local for some of the costs of the independent supervisor's office.[58]

CONCLUSION

Cosa Nostra's entrenchment in the JFK Airport's freight industry dates back to at least the early 1950s. Although the Kenrac investigations and prosecutions sent many mobsters to prison, Cosa Nostra's influence at the airport was undiminished into the 1980s. Recognizing that additional investigations and prosecutions would not have the desired impact, the U.S. Attorney's Office for the Eastern District of New York brought a successful civil RICO suit against Teamsters Locals 295 and 851. That suit coincided with the sweeping reform effort taking place within the International Brotherhood of Teamsters as a whole under the aegis of the three-person trusteeship led by Independent Administrator Frederick Lacey.

Under the 1989 consent decree between the IBT General Executive Board and the federal government, the Teamsters union launched its own efforts to rid Locals 295 and 851 of organized crime. The IBT removed the officers of Locals 295 and 851 and appointed temporary trustees to run the locals. Seeking to make these trusteeships permanent, the U.S. Attorney's Office filed a civil RICO suit against both locals in 1990. After some reluctance, the district court established a permanent trusteeship over Local 295 in 1992, naming Thomas Puccio trustee. Two and a half years later the court established a bifurcated monitorship over Local 851, consisting of an independent supervisor, Ronald DePetris, authorized to root out corruption, and a union trustee, responsible for managing the daily affairs of the union. DePetris has succeeded in recovering funds for Local 851 and in severing many of the union's ties with Cosa Nostra.

While Cosa Nostra's presence at JFK Airport is diminished, it is not expunged. In May 1997, U.S. Attorney Zachary Carter announced that eighty-three people had been arrested as a result of an FBI sting operation called Kat-Net. The agents had established a fencing operation that attracted gangs of thieves operating at JFK Airport. The agents purchased $13 million worth of goods from the thieves for $700,000. Interestingly, only a few of the thieves had organized-crime (Gambino) ties, demonstrating perhaps that the mob's dominance over thievery at the airport has ended.

In mid-December 1998, Queens District Attorney Richard Brown, head of the New York City FBI office Lewis Schiliro, NYPD Commissioner Howard Safir, and Port Authority Police Superintendent Fred Morrone announced the indictment of fifty-six individuals and eight corporations for theft, fencing, and distribution of property stolen from warehouses in and around JFK Airport. According to Commissioner Safir, Operation Rain Forest led to the recovery of more than $5 million worth of stolen goods. While two of the defendants are IBT union stewards, once again it appears that this organized theft cannot be attributed to Cosa Nostra. It is another indication that the underworld and the upperworld at the airport are changing. It reminds us as well that crime can, does, and will continue even without the Cosa Nostra crime families.

12

Ridding the Javits Convention Center of Organized Crime

> I will put the power of this Governorship behind the prosecutions to sweep out organized crime from the Javits Center. . . . Criminals were given a virtual monopoly on the jobs at the Javits Center. That is wrong, and it must end.[1]
>
> —Governor George Pataki, addressing the New York State Senate Standing Committee on Finance, 1995

FROM THE MOMENT construction began, the Javits Convention Center served as a profit center for the mob. Cosa Nostra's influence was rooted in its control over the unions that represented center workers. The Genovese family's control over the Carpenters union allowed the mob to manipulate the job referral system and place friends and associates in high-paying or no-show jobs. IBT Local 807, led by Robert Rabbitt Sr. and his sons Michael and Robert Jr., also placed many known Cosa Nostra associates in high-paying center positions. Officials of Local 829 of the Exhibition Employees Union padded employers' payrolls with ghost employees, including Cosa Nostra members and associates, and operated a fraudulent workers' compensation racket. The center's Board of Directors and management showed little inclination to challenge organized crime. Efforts to purge Cosa Nostra did not begin until the 1990s. The most important law enforcement initiatives were civil RICO suits brought against the Carpenters union and the Teamsters, and Governor George Pataki's shake-up of the center's management. The law enforcement and administrative reforms show strong signs of success.

ATTACKING LABOR RACKETEERING

The Consent Decree in the Carpenters Union Case

In September 1990, the U.S. Attorney's Office for the Southern District of New York, with cross-designated attorneys from the New York State OCTF, filed a civil RICO suit against the District Council of the Carpenters union and its chief officials, charging that the union had been infiltrated by organized crime and was being operated in a corrupt manner.[2] Predicate offenses included extortion and illegal receipt of payments and benefits. The suit, settled one month into the trial, resulted in a consent decree[3] declaring that "there should be no criminal element or La Cosa Nostra corruption in any part of the . . . union" and that the union should be operated without unlawful outside influence.[4] All members and officers of the union were permanently enjoined from racketeering activity and from any knowing association with organized-crime figures.

The consent decree provided for the Investigations and Review Officer (IRO) to implement and supervise the settlement. The parties agreed on former federal judge and former New York City Commissioner of Investigation Kenneth Conboy as IRO. Conboy's mandate was to review the practices and policies of the union; initiate and conduct investigations into allegations of misconduct; bring disciplinary actions against union members; and if necessary, present evidence of wrongdoing to the Independent Hearing Panel (IHP).[5*] The IRO's decisions could be appealed to Federal District Judge Charles Haight, who retained jurisdiction over all related matters.[6]

In March 1995, Anthony Fiorino, who held various high-ranking positions in the Carpenters union at the Javits Center, became the first union member to face disciplinary charges.[7] The hearing lasted ten days and produced more than two thousand pages of testimony.[8]

Conboy argued before the IHP that Fiorino was the Genovese crime family's agent at the Javits Center. According to Conboy, Fiorino had assigned inactive union members and nonmembers to carpenter

*The IHP is composed of three members of the Independent Hearing Committee (IHC), which consists of the five individuals appointed by the consent decree. The IHP is selected in the usual manner for arbitration panels: the IRO chooses a member, the charged party selects another, and the IRO and the charged party collectively choose the third participant. *United States v. District Council*, 90 Civ. 5722, Consent Decree (1994), 4–5.

positions at the center, ran a corrupt hiring list, and maintained active contact with Cosa Nostra figures.[9] Fiorino countered that his only contact with his brother-in-law Liborio "Barney" Bellomo, acting boss of the Genovese family, was at family gatherings or in accidental meetings on the street.[10] He claimed that the two men never discussed union business or the center and that he did not even know his brother-in-law's occupation.

Fiorino was also charged with threatening a union member who complained about contract violations on a job site in 1984.[11] Gerald Kelty of Carpenters Local 257 claimed that he was set on fire by someone wielding a welding torch and that bundles of ten-foot-long metal studs had twice been dropped on him. (He escaped uninjured.)[12]

The IHP found that Fiorino had knowingly associated with members of the Genovese crime family and had enforced a corrupt employment-referral system that gave preference for center jobs to individuals connected to the Genovese crime family.[13] Fiorino was expelled from the union for life.[14] Judge Haight affirmed the decision, concluding that "beginning in or about April 1994 and continuing thereafter, Fiorino knowingly discriminated against union members by referring for work a small group of favored individuals."[15]

In June 1996, Conboy's investigations culminated in the dismissal of New York City's District Council of Carpenters president Frederick Devine by international union president Douglas McCarron.[16] In a subsequent criminal case, federal prosecutors presented evidence to prove that Devine received payoffs from contractors and that he was controlled by Thomas Petrizzo, a capo in the Colombo crime family.[17] Devine was convicted on six grand-larceny charges stemming from a scheme in which he siphoned money from the union's coffers to pay for lavish winter excursions for friends and family and for personal travel expenses.[18] He was sentenced to fifteen months in prison.[19]

THE CONSENT DECREE IN THE TEAMSTERS CASE

The historic civil RICO complaint against the IBT's General Executive Board (GEB) resulted in a 1989 consent decree providing for an investigations officer, an independent administrator, and an elections officer.[20] In January 1992, the three positions were superceded by an Independent Review Board (IRB), which was authorized to investigate corruption, issue written reports, and hold adjudicatory hearings. The IRB typically investigated, then reported its findings to the Teamsters' General Executive Board, which had the opportunity to initiate corrective measures before the IRB took disciplinary action.

The IRB issued a series of reports recommending the expulsion of certain IBT Local 807 members who were employed at the Javits Center. The IRB charged that Local 807 had become a haven for corrupt IBT Local 814 officials. Pursuant to a civil RICO suit alleging that the Bonanno crime family controlled the officers of Local 814.[21] Arthur Eisenberg, a former regional director of the National Labor Relations Board in New Jersey,[22] was appointed trustee by the court in 1987.[23]

The IRB operated according to the view that "in the absence of direct evidence of knowledge of the organized crime ties of an associate . . . such knowledge may be inferred from the duration and quality of the association."[24] The IRB found that certain Local 807 members had violated the conditions of union membership by bringing reproach upon the union by associating with organized crime figures. Consequently:

- March 23, 1994—The IRB recommended John C. Zanocchio be charged with violating the IBT oath by knowingly associating with members of organized crime. Zanocchio was found to be a member of the Bonanno crime family and permanently barred from the IBT.[25]
- March 24, 1994—The IRB recommended Robert Rabbitt Sr. be charged with bringing reproach upon the union by taking money from an exhibitor at the Javits Center. Settlement on May 31, 1994. Rabbitt Sr. resigned from the union for five years and took a management position as general foreman at the Javits Center.
- May 12, 1994—The IRB recommended charges against Armando Rea, who was appointed assistant shop steward by Michael Rabbitt in 1993.[26] The IRB found Rea to be a member of the Bonanno crime family and permanently barred him from the union.
- January 30, 1995—The IRB recommended charges against Michael Porta Jr. for knowingly associating with members of organized-crime families. FBI agents testified that Porta was a member of the Gambino crime family and that previously he served organized crime's interests as a member of Local 1814 of

the International Longshoreman's Association (ILA). The IRB permanently barred Porta from union-related activities. The federal court affirmed.[27]

- June 9, 1995—The IRB recommended charges against Costabile Lauro for knowingly associating with members of organized crime.[28] The IRB found that Lauro had sustained and purposeful associations with members of the Gambino crime family. Lauro had previously been a member of ILA Local 1814. Lauro was banned from the union.[29]
- February 14, 1996—The IRB recommended charges against Dominic Froncillo for knowingly associating with a member of organized crime. Froncillo testified that for approximately fifteen years he had been friends with Alphonse Malangone, reputed Genovese family capo. Froncillo was permanently barred from the union.[30]

The IRB's March 1995 report documented Robert Rabbitt Sr.'s extensive nepotism and corruption and recommended that IBT Local 807 be placed under trusteeship.[31] Upon review of Local 807's collective bargaining agreements, the IRB concluded that the Javits contract provided union workers with higher wages and benefits than any other Local 807 agreement.[32] It attributed this generous compensation to organized-crime influence and featherbedding. The report also pointed to the criminal records and organized-crime ties of eleven IBT members working at the convention center.

The IRB recommended that union charges be filed against Michael Rabbitt and the other members of the union bargaining team for acting without regard for the union's interest in negotiating the deal that removed the general foreman position from the union. According to the IRB, the transfer of the general foreman position deprived the union of significant influence over how Teamster jobs were carried out.[33] The IRB's March 1995 report spurred IBT President Ron Carey to remove the leaders of Local 807 and to place the local under trusteeship.[34] Johnnie Brown, the newly appointed trustee, was ordered to implement the IRB's recommendations.[35]

State prosecutors brought criminal charges against individual IBT members for various Javits Center rackets, including extorting money from businesses and falsifying bills and general business records. On February 5, 1992, Robert Rabbitt Sr. was indicted along with twenty-six other persons for theft, extortion, and violence related to the Javits Center,[36] and was specifically charged with conspiracy to extort money (by threatening economic harm) from the president of a company doing business at the center.[37] Robert Sr. and Michael Rabbitt were also indicted for receiving bribes, grand larceny through extortion, and criminal possession of stolen property.[38] Other charges against the Rabbitts and other Javits workers included the falsification of business records, making false entries in business records, and concealing the entries[39] with the intent to defraud.[40]

Robert Rabbitt Sr. pled guilty to the falsification of business records on November 9, 1992.[41] Under the plea agreement, all other charges against him were dismissed. His sentence was one-and-a-half to four-and-a-half years. Charges against Michael Rabbitt were dismissed.[42] Another Teamster, Michael Potts, was charged with scheming to obtain unemployment compensation and falsifying business records.[43] He pled guilty to attempted falsification of business records.[44] One other defendant was charged with two counts of grand larceny through extortion, pled guilty to promoting gambling, and was forced to pay a $500 fine. The most important impact of the criminal cases was not the modest sentences but the use of the convictions by the union trustees to remove the defendants from the unions and thus from the Javits Center.

Charges against the Exhibition Employees Union Local 829

The Exhibition Employees Union Local 829, like the locals of Teamsters and the Carpenters, was extensively investigated by local and federal law enforcement agencies. A joint investigation conducted by the Manhattan District Attorney's Office, the New York City Police Department, the U.S. Department of Labor, and the Javits Center's Inspector General[45] resulted in indictments against two Local 829 officers and seven rank-and-file members.[46] Local 829 President John McNamee and Vice-President and Javits Center shop steward Paul Coscia were accused of fraudulently acquiring union health benefits for Genovese family associate John Sullivan, who was not a union member.[47] Several Local 829 members were charged with felonies relating to misuse of union benefits while employed at the Javits Center.[48] There were also charges of loan-sharking,[49] bookmaking,[50] fraudulently collecting unemployment[51] and disability[52] compensation, and conspiring to bribe officials of Teamsters Local 807 in order to get on the hiring list.[53] Most of the charges were disposed of through guilty pleas.[54]

Manhattan District Attorney Robert Morgenthau also investigated a scheme by which Javits Center workers, in collaboration with a dishonest lawyer, filed phony workers' compensation claims on behalf of center employees. From 1992 to 1995, an attorney who was a cousin of an Exhibition Employees Union official admitted filing over a dozen such lawsuits for more than $20 million. This racket no doubt was a factor in the 25 percent increase in the center's 1995 insurance premium.[55]

ADMINISTRATIVE AND POLITICAL INVESTIGATIONS

The Role of the Inspector General

New York State's 1987 Internal Control Act required all public authorities, including the Javits Center, to appoint an internal control monitor.[56] Pursuant to the act, the Javits Center delegated that duty to an inspector general, who also was made responsible for providing the Board of Directors with information necessary to formulate effective policy. In 1991, Javits Center CEO Fabian Palomino selected as the center's first inspector general Henry Flinter, a former assistant inspector general for the Metropolitan Transportation Authority and a former investigator for the New York State Organized Crime Task Force.[57] Subsequently, the position has always been filled by a person with substantial investigative or organized-crime control experience.

In November 1994, Sebastian Pipitone (formerly a New York City police officer),[58] the next inspector general under Palomino, made a significant advance in crime control when he changed the method of distributing paychecks.[59] Previously, union representatives at the center distributed paychecks to center workers. The new rules required workers to come to the center, present identification, and be photographed, in order to pick up their paychecks.[60] Use of this strategy led to the removal of more than two dozen ghost workers from the payroll.[61] When the unions protested and threatened a work slowdown, Pipitone threatened to revoke parking privileges, thereby forcing workers with vehicles to pay $20 a day to park. The unions backed down.[62]

In 1994, Pipitone conducted a surprise search of the center and uncovered three stolen motorboat engines and stolen nautical equipment worth more than $100,000.[63] The equipment had been stolen from the Boat Show and hidden in air-conditioning ducts.[64] According to the Javits administration, surprise searches decreased theft at the center by 77 percent during Pipitone's tenure.[65]

The State Comptroller's Devastating 1995 Audit

State Comptroller H. Carl McCall issued a scathing report on the Javits Center in spring 1995.[66] The audit, covering the period January 1992 through November 1994, charged center officials with tolerating corruption and mismanagement.[67] McCall charged CEO Fabian Palomino with ignoring established management policies and procedures, failing to provide the Board of Directors with sufficient information, and violating employment and purchasing requirements.[68] The center's Board of Directors was accused of rubber-stamping Palomino's decisions and failing to take an active role in the center's governance.[69]

McCall charged Palomino with violating hiring and promotion rules and making personnel decisions without required documentation. Review of personnel files revealed that many jobs lacked a description of employee qualifications and had been filled without a job announcement, in violation of internal control procedures.[70] Most files only contained a letter from Palomino stating that the employee had been hired at a prescribed salary and title. There were also many instances of salary increases and decreases without corresponding performance reviews or explanations.[71]

McCall found that a great deal of security equipment, such as doorknobs, locks, two-way radios, and security cameras, had been purchased but never installed.[72] He also accused Palomino of improperly providing free parking to Governor Cuomo's son.[73]

Palomino was criticized for making purchases and negotiating contracts without board approval. The audit found that 60 percent of procurement contracts, worth $6.7 million, had not been awarded according to the required competitive bidding process.[74] Early in his tenure, Palomino broke a waste-hauling contract with Allied Sanitation, threatening to have Allied employees arrested if they returned to the center. Palomino then awarded the contract to another company, circumventing the bidding process under the guise of an emergency. McCall's auditors observed that Palomino's "unchecked control over most Corporation matters" had permitted inappropriate hiring and vendor favoritism.[75] The audit stated that by consolidating managerial power, Palomino reduced the oversight necessary to prevent corruption.[76]

Despite the extensive authority bestowed upon the inspector general, with a few exceptions, McCall found that the position had been underutilized and ineffective. The state comptroller's audit stated that the inspector general's powers were compromised by lack of autonomy because the inspector general reported directly to the CEO.[77] After the audit, the inspector general was made to report directly to the Board of Directors.

The State Legislature's Hearing Regarding the Javits Center

The state audit of the Javits Center and the reports of the court-appointed trustees in the labor-racketeering cases prompted the state Senate to convene a hearing in March 1995. New York City Mayor Rudolph Giuliani testified that the Convention Center had been losing business, costing the city $500 million in lost revenue and five thousand jobs. He urged that a civil RICO suit be brought against the center and the unions in order to produce a court-appointed trustee with the resources and ability to curtail corruption, and he recommended privatization of the center's management, following the successful model of convention centers in other cities.

Frederick Devine, president of the District Council of the Carpenters, testified that he was willing to renegotiate the union's contract but challenged the charge that the Carpenters union was to blame for high costs at the center. Fabian Palomino, who had resigned as CEO two months previously, testified that he had been aware of organized-crime infiltration but felt that it was law enforcement's job to combat it; he had been responsible for managing the center.

Governor George Pataki also testified at the hearing. He asked the members of the Board of Directors of the center to resign and threatened to close the center if they refused. Pataki insisted that "it is critical that we have a new team in place that is accountable to the public and dedicated to sweeping out corruption and mismanagement."[78] According to the center's incorporation documents, the governor could forcibly remove board members only for just cause.[79] Pataki nominated Robert Boyle for the center's chief executive and Gerald McQueen for its inspector general.[80] McQueen was approved unanimously.

Boyle had served as Pataki's gubernatorial campaign treasurer, was a successful executive in the construction industry, and had been the chairman of the Hudson Valley Hospital Center in Westchester County.[81] The Cuomo board members (who did not resign immediately as requested) objected to Boyle's nomination on the ground he lacked experience, but the nominee was eventually confirmed. Other strong law enforcement figures, like Ronald Goldstock, the former director of the New York State Organized Crime Task Force, and antitrust expert Lloyd Constantine, a former assistant attorney general, were appointed to the board.[82]

BOYLE'S ADMINISTRATIVE INITIATIVES

Robert Boyle, who became the Javits Center's president and CEO in 1995, moved aggressively against organized crime. With Governor Pataki's strong encouragement and support, he implemented a new hiring system and negotiated contracts with the unions. The New York Convention Center Operation Corporation (NYCCOC) articles of incorporation reserved to the corporation the power to "do all things necessary or convenient to carry out the purposes" of the convention center.[83] Boyle eliminated the decorator companies' role in hiring center labor. Henceforth, the Javits Center would negotiate directly with the unions.

In June 1995, Boyle negotiated collective bargaining agreements with each of the labor unions. The new contracts provided that Javits Center management would hire laborers for exhibition and trade shows, allowing the center to control the number of employees on a particular job and thereby eliminating unnecessary and no-show workers. The unions were no longer allowed to pick which members would be assigned center jobs. At the same time the workers became state employees, subject to the Taylor Law that forbids government employees from striking.[84]

On June 29, 1995, Boyle announced that all center employees would have to apply for their jobs the following day. All New York newspapers carried advertisements announcing job openings. On July 1, 1995, between two thousand and five thousand nonunion job applicants assembled at the center, joining more than one thousand union members who had applied for their jobs the previous day.[85]

Based upon the results of a three-page job application (which asked if the applicant had ever been convicted, whom he or she knew and associated with both within the Javits Center and outside it, and the applicant's previous work history) and an interview by a member of Boyle's thirty-person staff, five hundred applicants were hired for permanent staff positions. Only half of the new hires had previously worked at the center.[86] Carpenters union officials Anthony Fiorino and Leonard Simon were not hired.[87]

Boyle organized the new workforce into two divisions: the freight and the erector units. The Teamsters and the Carpenters, the two unions that met the new representational criteria,[88] were recognized as bargaining agents for the freight unit and the erection unit, respectively.[89*]

The Counterattack of the Carpenters Union

In late 1995, the District Council of Carpenters and union member Dominic Claps filed an action in state court seeking an injunction to prohibit center management from discriminating against union carpenters and shop stewards, and monetary and punitive damages. Claps had been designated the general job steward at Javits by the District Council in November 1995. Thereafter, he was only called into work intermittently. The union, on Clap's behalf, claimed that the center was illegally discriminating against union members based on their activity outside the work and union environment. The center cited its right to refuse to employ any individual as long as the decision is made in good faith and complies with the collective bargaining agreements. On February 27, 1996, the court ruled that the Carpenters union must abide by the grievance procedures established by the collective bargaining agreement before petitioning the court and that the union as an entity could not initiate the suit because under New York State law such an ac-

*Unions had to certify that they represented at least 50 percent of the union card–carrying workforce in a particular unit. The District Council of Carpenters had presented bargaining authorization cards from 296 of 390 employees in the erection division, and the Teamsters Local 807 obtained authorization from 91 of 145 workers in the freight unit. However, Exhibition Employees Union Local 829 did not meet the criteria and thus was not recognized as a bargaining agent. "Two Unions Reinstated at the Javits Center," *New York Times*, July 19, 1995, B6.

tion may be brought only by "an aggrieved individual."[90] Subsequently, an arbitrator ruled in favor of the center.

On November 20, 1995, District Council President Frederick Devine announced plans to use the union's $1.5 billion pension and benefit fund to purchase the New York Coliseum in order to provide employment for carpenters ousted from the Javits Center.[91] (The city-owned Coliseum had been largely unused since the construction of the Javits Center and had been for sale for several years.) Mayor Giuliani rejected the idea that same day, citing the District Council's involvement in corruption and racketeering at the Javits Center.[92] Because the city retains final veto power on all matters relating to the Coliseum, the mayor's opposition, in effect, killed the proposal.

LEGISLATIVE INACTION

Governor Pataki and Robert Boyle requested the New York State Senate to consider a law similar to New York City's Local Law 50, which directs the manager of the Fulton Fish Market to require market participants to be fingerprinted and to apply for business licenses. Boyle's proposal would have permitted Javits Center management to fingerprint employees and to require a special license for all businesses operating at the center. These procedures would allow further background checks on all individuals, with the purpose of rooting out Cosa Nostra members and associates. Licenses would be denied to workers with criminal histories or ties to organized crime.

The State Assembly rejected the bill on June 29, 1995, just as Boyle's new hiring plan was being implemented. Both Boyle and Pataki accused the Speaker of the Assembly of being an ally of former Carpenters union President Frederick Devine and of attempting to undermine the Javits Center reform program.[93] The bill, reintroduced in the Assembly the following year, provided for the appointment of a temporary receiver for the center in the event that there was evidence of management corruption, and authorized this receiver to implement licensing requirements and to investigate center contractors and employees.[94] The license application would include the applicant's fingerprints, photograph, and a criminal background check.[95] In passing a watered-down version of the bill, the Assembly noted that the center's history of suspect hiring and employment practices had hurt legitimate employees and workers as well as the economy of the state and New York City.[96] Boyle opposed the bill on the ground that it was too weak and administratively cumbersome. It restored the Carpenters union's power to assign jobs.[97] The bill was ultimately blocked in the Senate. In any event, by this time the changes at the center were so dramatic that the reason for the bill arguably no longer applied.

Mayor Giuliani's recommendation that ownership of the Javits Center be transfered from New York State to New York City attracted attention but little support, especially in light of the center's impressive recovery.[98]

A LIBERATED CONVENTION CENTER?

Concurrent law enforcement and administrative remedial efforts have largely eliminated the organized-crime racketeering that plagued the Javits Center from its inception till the mid-1990s. The Carpenters union and the Teamsters union have each experienced a makeover. The consent decrees in the Carpenters and the Teamsters cases resulted in court-appointed trusteeships. Kenneth Conboy has overseen the purge of the mob from the Carpenters union.

The Independent Review Board, authorized to investigate corruption throughout the IBT, removed many Cosa Nostra members and associates from Local 807. In March 1995, IBT President Ron Carey placed the local under trusteeship. The Exhibition Employees Union avoided a court-imposed trusteeship but was not certified as a collective bargaining agent in 1995 when the Javits Center was thoroughly reorganized.

The revitalization of the Javits Center's management clearly has had an impact. The hiring process, implemented by Robert Boyle,* opened center employment to a large pool of job seekers while simultaneously purging employees with ties to organized crime. A recent report by the Office of the State Comptroller praises the Javits Center for

*In early 1997 Boyle was named executive director of the Port Authority of New York and New Jersey. Inspector General Gerald McQueen then became president and chief executive officer of the Javits Center. Boyle was appointed chairman of the Javits Center Board.

"complete turnaround." The center now has inventory-control procedures, working security locks on all doors, and new guidelines for the approval of contracts.[99] According to Comptroller McCall, "Corporation officials have made major changes, and have fully implemented the recommendations from our prior audit reports."[100]

As the result of law enforcement, political, and administrative efforts, the Javits Center is fully booked for the next two years and is already booking shows for the year 2006. During the fiscal year ending in March 1998, the center earned profits in excess of $400,000, a major improvement from its $1.6 million deficit in 1995.[101] Administrative and personnel costs have decreased considerably, resulting in 10 percent to 40 percent lower exhibition rates.[102] The vice-president of the American Society of Association Executives described the center as an emerging "hot" destination for conventions.[103] The success of the center has even led to talk of its expansion. Governor Pataki and other state officials have discussed doubling its current exhibition space to 1.5 million square feet, an unthinkable idea just a few years ago.[104]

13

Defeating Cosa Nostra in the Waste-Hauling Industry

> Those carters who misused the legitimate business opportunities of this industry besmirched and submerged the interests and welfare of the legitimate carters. The surgery performed by Local Law 42 clearly was essential, overdue and carefully tailored to protect the public interest with measured consideration of the interests and welfare of those who strive only for fair business conditions. . . . The public interest required drastic corrections.[1]
>
> —Justice Milton Pollack, *Sanitation and Recycling Industry, Inc. v. City of New York,* 1996

THE NEW YORK CITY metropolitan area waste-hauling industry was, into the 1990s, dominated by two powerful Cosa Nostra–led cartels, one on Long Island and one in New York City. The cartels enforced a property-rights system through economic coercion, and threats to property and person. The cartels were policed by the Lucchese and Gambino crime families, which controlled the trade associations and unions. Lucchese capo Salvatore Avellino controlled the Long Island cartel through the Private Sanitation Industry Association of Nassau/Suffolk. The Association of Trade Waste Removers of Greater New York, the largest carting employers association in New York City, led by Gambino capo James Failla, limited entry into the industry, fixed prices, and allocated customers. For decades, IBT Local 813, representing the employees of all New York City metropolitan area carters, was run by Bernard Adelstein, a longtime associate of the Gambino crime family. If a carter violated a cartel rule, Local 813 would mount a job action and perhaps threaten the company's customers with violence. In addition, many Cosa Nostra members and associates owned carting businesses.

Prior to the 1990s, attempts to rid the carting industry of mob influence had been unsuccessful. Up until the 1990s the New York City Department of Consumer Affairs, which had the power to establish licensing requirements and set maximum rates, was completely ineffective. Licenses were issued upon request and maximum rates were set to the liking of the cartel, that is, much higher than rates in any other cities. Law enforcement agencies had been unable to bring about any systemic change in the industry. The DCA, under Commissioner Mark Green, began to focus on corruption and racketeering and undertook some important initiatives.

In the 1990s, the combination of criminal prosecutions, civil racketeering suits, a court-appointed monitorship, and a major city regulatory initiative, combined with the willingness of a few large national waste-hauling companies to enter the New York market, has resulted in the apparent elimination of Cosa Nostra from both the Long Island and New York City waste-hauling industries.

ATTACKING THE LONG ISLAND CARTEL: THE CIVIL RICO SUIT

On June 7, 1989, the U.S. attorney for the Eastern District of New York, Andrew J. Maloney, brought a civil RICO suit against the Long Island carting cartel. Maloney charged 112 defendants—including 64 Gambino and Lucchese family members and associates, 44 carting companies, the carters' trade organization, and Teamsters Local 813—with 486 separate acts of racketeering conducted through 46 separate enterprises.[2] The complaint alleged that

- For several decades, the solid waste disposal industry in Nassau and Suffolk counties has been infiltrated, controlled, influenced, corrupted and run by organized crime.
- The Lucchese and Gambino families have been the principal source of such Mafia influence.
- Mafia control of the industry has eliminated competition and . . . cost the residents and businesses [of Long Island] millions of dollars.
- Mafia influence has been accomplished through the use of threats and violence, through the infiltration and control of labor unions,

and through the bribery and corruption of local government officials and employees.

- Finally, [m]embers and associates of organized crime families were and are directors, officers, employees, and . . . shareholders of various carting companies.[3]

According to Maloney, "[T]he relief we're seeking here is to put these people forever and a day out of the carting business." He asked the court to divest the managers of the forty-four indicted waste-hauling firms of their ownership interests, appoint a trustee to oversee the Private Sanitation Industry Association of Nassau/Suffolk, and remove Bernard Adelstein from his position as secretary-treasurer of International Brotherhood of Teamsters Local 813.[4] Maloney also sought to establish a $3 million fund for victims of the Long Island waste-hauling cartel. Shortly after the lawsuit was filed, two of the nation's largest waste-hauling firms, Browning Ferris Industries of Houston and Waste Management, Inc., of Oak Brook, Illinois, announced that they were considering entering the Long Island market.[5]

U.S. District Court Judge I. Leo Glasser dealt Maloney two early setbacks. First, he criticized the suit as "a transparent endeavor to lay claim to the largest civil RICO case ever, with government lawyers multiplying defendants, enterprises, and predicate acts as though numbers were ends in themselves."[6] Second, although allowing the case to go forward, Judge Glasser dismissed the claim for monetary relief on the ground that the RICO statute does not give the government standing to sue for damages.[7]

Wounded but not defeated, the U.S. Attorney's Office, now headed by Acting U.S. Attorney Mary Jo White, moved for partial summary judgment against Salvatore Avellino, head of the Private Sanitation Industry Association of Nassau/Suffolk.[8] Judge Glasser held that Avellino's guilty pleas in the OCTF cases "conclusively establish that he committed at least two predicate acts necessary for RICO liability."[9] Accordingly, he issued an injunction permanently barring Avellino from the waste-hauling industry, and forfeited Avellino's waste-hauling interests as well as the proceeds derived from his illegal actions.[10]* The

*Salvatore Avellino was sentenced to a three and a half– to ten and a half–year prison term for conspiring to murder two carters who cooperated with an Organized Crime Task Force investigation. He was also sued by the estate of murdered carter Jerry Kubecka. See *Jerry Kubecka v. Avellino*, 898 F. Supp. 963 (E.D.N.Y. 1995).

government sought and received similar relief against Nicholas Ferrante, a Lucchese family associate.[11]

The Appointment of an Industry Monitor

In 1994, the parties reached a negotiated settlement. The defendants agreed not to associate with Cosa Nostra members and not to allocate customers by means of a "property rights" system. Avellino's SSC Corporation, now run by his wife and son-in law, and Emedio Fazzini's Jamaica Ash Corporation agreed to be monitored.[12] Waste haulers that were not parties to the consent decree still faced prosecutions.[13] Some of these firms voluntarily signed the consent decree. By January 1998, more than two-thirds of the original defendants had either come under the monitorship or divested themselves of their Long Island waste-hauling businesses.[14] Firms in the former category agreed to be monitored for five years[15] and to pay the costs of the monitoring effort.[16] A method had been found to shift the costs of law enforcement investigation to the suspects themselves.

The compliance officer was to be nominated by the U.S. Justice Department, subject to Judge Glasser's approval. The officer was given broad power to investigate the defendants to ensure that they did not associate with organized-crime figures or violate antitrust and other criminal laws. In the event that the monitor found evidence of racketeering, bid rigging, or customer-allocation schemes, he was to present his findings to either a hearing officer jointly selected by the carters and the Justice Department or to a federal magistrate. Michael Cherkasky, a former prosecutor (a member of the Manhattan DA's team in the Garment Center case against the Gambinos) and managing director of a private investigations firm, was selected to be the industry's compliance officer. His staff includes a former federal prosecutor, two accountants specializing in fraud, and two former law enforcement investigators. The hearing officer, former New York State Supreme Court Judge Leon Lazar could impose fines up to $75,000. The magistrate, by contrast, would be bound by the federal rules of evidence but would have the power to bar people from the waste-hauling industry and to order the forfeiture of illegal profits, no matter how large. The government or a carter could appeal the hearing officer's decisions to Judge Glasser.[17]

Cherkasky set up a twenty-four-hour, toll-free phone number for reporting corruption, racketeering, and anticompetitive practices.[18]

He enforced the settlement against defendant firms and individuals by bringing, or by threatening to bring, charges before the magistrate.[19]

The monitor's most important achievement was opening up the industry to competition. Decades of anticompetitive practices had allowed many inefficient firms to profit because the cartel and property-rights system guaranteed them a customer base. Prior to 1994, no national waste-hauling corporation did business on Long Island.[20] After the settlement, several national waste-hauling corporations bought out defendant carting firms and entered the Long Island market. In April 1997, SSC was sold to Arizona-based Allied Waste Industries.[21] The world's largest waste-carting company, Waste Management, purchased South Side Carting.[22] USA Waste Services, Inc., purchased the assets of Vigliotti Brothers Carting.[23] Jamaica Ash remains the last major carting firm on Long Island not tied to a national corporation. Cherkasky speculates that by 2000, the entire Long Island market will be serviced by national companies.[24] The old cartel has disappeared.

Competition among the new carting companies on Long Island has resulted in lower prices. One large customer's annual bill fell from $360,000 to $170,000.[25] The winning bid for residential waste hauling decreased roughly 50 percent.[26]

BREAKING UP THE NEW YORK CITY CARTEL

The Chambers Paper Fibers' and BFI's Undercover Operations

New York City officials recognized that introducing competition would lead to the break-up of the carting cartel. But Cosa Nostra's decades-long stranglehold on the city's waste-hauling industry was a strong deterrent to outside firms. As late as 1993, New York City was the only major U.S. city in which no national waste-hauling firm operated. Browning Ferris Industries (BFI), a Houston-based company and the nation's second-largest carting firm, with more than $4.3 billion in revenues[27] and business in at least forty-four states,[28] did not service a single stop in New York City. WMX Technologies, Inc., posted upwards of $9 billion in revenues during 1993[29] but stayed out of the city.[30]

To encourage national firms to enter the New York City market, the U.S. Justice Department offered to sell to outside firms the routes it seized from private haulers that had illegally dumped toxic materials. The department scheduled a February 1991 meeting with national waste haulers to encourage and facilitate the sales. As an added incentive, New York City Consumer Affairs Commissioner Mark Green promised that the city would buy back the routes if the new purchasers were driven out by organized crime.[31]

Although none of the major companies accepted the government's offer, BFI eventually decided to test the $1.5 billion New York City waste-hauling market. In late 1991, BFI obtained the contract to collect refuse at Columbia-Presbyterian Medical Center in Manhattan.[32] A BFI spokesperson said, "We're sending a message to Cosa Nostra . . . we're not being run out of town."[33] Cosa Nostra sent back its answer; the severed head of a German shepherd with a note in its mouth: "Welcome to New York."[34] The Council of Trade Waste Associations sued BFI for wrongfully interfering with preexisting carting contracts and for engaging in anticompetitive practices. Judge Diane Lebedeff quickly ruled against the council, upholding BFI's right to compete with local carters.[35] The council then initiated an anti-BFI advertising campaign; it called BFI a predatory pricer and an environmental polluter.[36] One television advertisement mocked BFI's lack of familiarity with New York City by portraying a Texan in a garbage truck staring at a map, trying to find Third Avenue and 75th Street.[37]

The Manhattan DA's office and the New York City Police Department's Organized Crime Investigation Division launched a major investigation of the cartel in 1990. In 1992, an undercover sting was initiated. Detective Richard Cowan posed as a manager of Chambers Paper Fibers Corporation, a Brooklyn-based carting company. During Cowan's three-year undercover operation, he paid more than $790,000 to other carters for the right to service specific stops.[38]

The Chambers Paper Fibers Corporation provided reliable evidence of Cosa Nostra's threats and violence. When Chambers Paper took away customers from members of the cartel, the cartel demanded that Chambers Paper give up its newly signed stops. Chambers Paper's drivers were threatened and beaten (one suffered a severe skull fracture), and a truck was burned. Leaders of the Council of Trade Waste Associations explained that if Chambers Paper paid its dues and stopped stealing customers, the violence would cease.[39]

A year after its entrance into the New York City market, BFI still found local businesses unwilling to change carters, even though BFI's rates were as much as 40 percent lower than those of cartel members. BFI purchased several companies seized by federal authorities[40] but was unable to attract new customers. By 1993, BFI realized that its ability to compete in New York City depended upon the DA's success in purging organized crime from the industry. BFI then committed itself to active cooperation with the Manhattan District Attorney's office, allowing an undercover police officer to pose as one of its employees. For two years as the BFI/District Attorney's Office investigation gathered evidence, BFI's trucks were followed and stolen, its drivers threatened, and its executives subject to intimidating phone calls and letters.[41]

The 1995 Indictments and Plea Bargains

On June 22, 1995, District Attorney Morgenthau called a press conference to report sweeping indictments in New York City's waste-hauling industry.[42]* Charging that organized crime dominated the industry through extortion, coercion, conspiracy, and anticompetitive practices, Morgenthau announced a 114-count indictment against 17 people, 23 carting companies, and 4 trade associations.[43]

The indictment's first count charged that the defendants violated OCCA, New York State's version of the federal RICO statute,[44] by "having knowledge of the existence of a criminal enterprise (called herein the cartel) [and] intentionally conducting and participating in the affairs of the cartel by participating in a pattern of criminal activity."[45] The indictment then listed 113 predicate racketeering acts, including antitrust violations, arson, extortion, coercion, attempted murder, and the falsification of business records.[46] The indictment contended:

*The District Attorney's Office obtained an additional indictment of seventy-four counts on June 18, 1996, against thirteen individuals and eight companies, most of whom had been named in the previous indictment. The new indictment charged the defendants with violating OCCA. The primary racketeering act involved six individuals and five companies controlled by Phillip Barretti Sr. and his sons. Among those newly charged were Joseph and Frank Vitarelli, owners of All City Paper Fibers, and Adriane Paccione, owner of Yankee Continental Carting. David Voreacos, "Trash Industry Crackdown Widens: Bribery Bid-Rigging Charged," *Record*, June 20, 1996, A8.

> The defendants and others banded together as the cartel in order to restrain competition in the private carting industry throughout the City of New York, and to keep carters' price and profits artificially high. The cartel's basic rule was that no carter be permitted to compete for the business of a customer serviced by another carter. The cartel enforced this rule by acts of violence, including attempted murder, assault and arson, and threats of violence, and concerted economic pressure.[47]

The Manhattan District Attorney's Office secured an emergency court order temporarily freezing $268 million of the indicted companies' and individuals' assets, and sought the appointment of receivers to monitor the defendant companies during the pendency of the criminal trial.[48] In December 1995, New York State Supreme Court Justice Walter M. Schackman selected nine receivers to ensure that the defendant carters did not hide or dissipate their assets before a judgment was rendered.[49] The receivers were given broad investigative powers to examine the records and activities of the firms.[50]

As the trial neared, it was revealed to the defendants that more than four hundred of their conversations had been taped by undercover detective Richard Cowan during his three years at Chambers Paper Fibers.[51] Faced with overwhelming inculpatory evidence, ten defendants entered guilty pleas. The most significant plea was that of Angelo Ponte, the longtime owner of one the largest waste-hauling firms in New York City and allegedly a business partner of the Genovese crime family.[52] Ponte pled guilty to attempted enterprise corruption and was fined $7.5 million, sentenced to a prison term of two to six years, and permanently barred from the waste-hauling industry. Ponte sold his waste-hauling assets to USA Waste Services, Inc., now prepared to test the waters of the New York City market.[53] Ponte's son, Vincent, pled guilty to paying a $10,000 bribe to obtain a waste-hauling contract. He was sentenced to five years' probation.[54]

The day before the jury was selected, five more defendants pled guilty to a single felony count of attempted enterprise corruption, and another defendant pled guilty to violating the Donnelly Act, New York State's antitrust law. Only six defendants remained:[55] Joseph Francolino, a Gambino family soldier and business agent of the Association of Trade Waste Removers of Greater New York; Frank Giovinco, the business agent of the Greater New York Waste Paper

Association and alleged Genovese associate; Alphonse Malangone, formerly business agent of the Kings County Trade Waste Association and Genovese capo; Phillip Barretti Sr., owner of the third-largest waste-hauling company in New York City; and Louis Mongelli and his son Paul, owners of a Bronx-based carting company and alleged associates of the Genovese family.[56]

As the trial, which began in late May 1997, was about to enter its third month, and following Detective Cowan's eighteen days of testimony, four more defendants entered into plea agreements. Phillip Barretti Sr. received the most severe sentence: a prison term of four and a half to thirteen years and a $6 million fine. Frank Giovinco was sentenced to three and a half to ten and a half years in prison; Paul Mongelli, four to twelve years; and Louis Mongelli, three to nine years.[57] In October, after twelve days of jury deliberations, the two remaining individual defendants, Joseph Francolino and Alphonse Malangone, were convicted on all counts.[58] Francolino was sentenced to ten to thirty years in prison and fined $900,000.[59] Malangone, five to fifteen years and $200,000.[60] Thus, all seventeen individuals, four trade associations, and twenty-three companies in the original indictment were convicted.

Dismantling the Trade Association

In 1993 and 1994, while the Manhattan District Attorney's Office and the New York City Police Department were gathering evidence on the New York City waste-hauling cartel, federal prosecutors continued their relentless assault by targeting two vital components of the New York City metropolitan area carting cartels: the Association of Trade Waste Removers of Greater New York and IBT Local 813.

In April 1993, federal prosecutors obtained RICO indictments against James "Jimmy Brown" Failla, a capo in the Gambino crime family, who had run the association since 1957,[61] and five other Gambino family members and associates.[62] Failla was charged with four predicate acts: conspiracy to murder and the actual murder of Thomas Spinelli, a grand jury witness who had testified against John Gotti; tampering with a witness; and conspiring to extort money from carting companies.[63] On April 4, 1994, Failla and four of his codefendants pled guilty to murder conspiracy. In return, prosecutors agreed to drop the other charges and to recommend a seven-year prison sentence. Judge Charles Sifton criticized the plea agreement as too lenient. The prosecution responded that the defendants' age and health complications (Failla suffered from high blood pressure and heart problems) justified the plea bargain. Ultimately, Judge Sifton accepted the agreement, thereby removing Failla from the waste-hauling industry.[64]

Purging the Mob from IBT Local 813

In 1992, Charles Carberry, the investigations officer in the national IBT case, began investigating Bernard Adelstein, secretary-treasurer (the top position) of IBT Local 813, which represented employees of New York City and Long Island carting companies. Adelstein's ties to organized crime had first been brought to public attention twenty-five years earlier by Robert F. Kennedy during the McClellan Committee hearings. Throughout his lengthy career, Adelstein had served the interests of organized crime and the waste-hauling cartel. If a carter tried to take over another firm's customer or route, Adelstein would threaten a Teamsters strike against the rebel company.[65]

Carberry sought union discipline against Adelstein on grounds of his close association with James Failla. In permanently barring Adelstein from the Teamsters, Independent Administrator Frederick B. Lacey stated, "Adelstein's associations with the underworld are repugnant. . . . Only by cleansing the [Teamsters] of the likes of Adelstein can the Union ever hope to function as a corruption-free, democratic organization."[66] Adelstein appealed the administrator's decision to the district court, and to the Second Circuit Court of Appeals, but both courts affirmed Lacey's decision.[67] The Teamsters' president, Ron Carey, removed most of Local 813's other officials and appointed a trustee to run the local.[68]

A second stream of reformist pressure on IBT Local 813 resulted from the federal civil RICO suit against the Long Island carting industry. In the 1994 settlement, Local 813 agreed to a court-appointed monitor to root out racketeers and to monitor the reform effort.[69] Judge Glasser appointed Joseph Foy monitor and enjoined union members from engaging in racketeering activities or associating with organized crime figures.[70]

REGULATION WITH TEETH: THE NEW YORK CITY TRADE WASTE COMMISSION

The most novel effort to break the fifty-year-long cartel among New York City carters was the regulatory initiative launched by the Giuliani administration. In furtherance of his determination to liberate the city from the influence of organized crime, Giuliani established a new agency that spun a regulatory web around the carting industry. Giuliani's plan built upon the "exclusive-licensing" model that Consumer Affairs Commissioner Mark Green had proposed in the early 1990s[71] (that model, in turn, built on the licensing program of the New Jersey Gambling Commission and Waterfront Commission) and the licensing system in place at the Fulton Fish Market.[72] The mayor's plan included licensing industry participants, reducing carting rates, and increasing competition.

On November 30, 1995, Mayor Giuliani made a joint appearance with now Public Advocate Mark Green, City Council Speaker Peter Vallone, and District Attorney Robert Morgenthau to announce the proposal that would ultimately become Local Law 42.[73] The law embodies several different strategies of organized-crime control: (1) licensing to bar mob-connected carters from the industry; (2) maximum rates to prevent the cartel from extracting exorbitant profits; and (3) prohibiting contractual terms that facilitated the carters' hold on their customers.[74] The preamble declared that "the carting industry has been corruptly influenced by organized crime . . . [and] fostered and sustained a cartel" and that Local Law 42 intended to "enhance the city's ability to address organized crime corruption, to protect businesses who utilize private carting services, and to increase competition in the carting industry." A Trade Waste Commission (TWC) would take over the regulatory responsibilities of the Department of Consumer Affairs with respect to the carting industry. The TWC was authorized to

- Establish standards for the issuance and revocation of waste-hauling licenses;
- Make individual determinations regarding the issuance, suspension, and revocation of such licenses;
- Investigate the background and fitness of a licensee's employees;
- Appoint independent auditors and monitors;

- Establish maximum and minimum rates for waste-collection and disposal;
- Investigate any matter within the TWC's jurisdiction, including the power to compel testimony and the production of documents;
- Establish service standards for all licensees, including standards for contracts, billing, and compliance with safety and health measures;
- Establish special trade waste–removal districts; and
- Establish fees and rules that the TWC deems necessary for effecting the purposes of Local Law 42.*

The TWC consists of the commissioners of the departments of investigation, business services, consumer affairs, and sanitation. It is headed by an executive director appointed by the mayor. The entire agency is staffed with individuals who have experience investigating or prosecuting organized crime. Edward Ferguson, the first director, had previously served as a federal prosecutor under Giuliani. Thirty New York City police detectives, working out of the Police Department's Organized Crime Control Bureau, are assigned to the TWC to conduct background checks on carting firms and to investigate complaints. The TWC also employs eight auditors and seven inspectors.[75]

The waste-hauling cartel, fighting for survival, launched a legal counterattack. A few days after Mayor Giuliani signed the new law and appointed Deputy Mayor Randy Mastro to serve as acting chair of the TWC, the carters filed a federal suit challenging the law's constitutionality.[76] The plaintiffs argued that the provisions regulating waste-hauling contracts violated the Contract, Takings, and Due Process Clauses of the U.S. Constitution, and that the provisions regarding licensing violated the waste-haulers' constitutional rights to

*Such a regulatory scheme would not be feasible on Long Island because each town has separate licensing procedures and requirements. Long Island waste-hauling Compliance Officer Michael Cherkasky has proposed the creation of an ad hoc committee that would include representatives from the various towns on Long Island, law enforcement agencies, the New York State Department of Environmental Control, the FBI, and the U.S. Attorney's Office for the Eastern District of New York, to address waste-hauling issues. *United States v. Private Sanitation Indus. Assoc.*, CV-89-1848 (E.D.N.Y. 1989), Report VII From the Compliance Officer, January 26, 1998, 7–8.

privacy and association.[77] Mastro responded that "Local Law 42 is an appropriate exercise of the City's police power and authority to regulate local industry to remove organized crime's 40-year stranglehold over the City's private carting industry."[78] In a June 26, 1996, written order, U.S. District Judge Milton Pollack upheld the constitutionality of Local Law 42, stating, "The surgery performed by Local Law 42 clearly was essential, overdue and carefully tailored to protect the public interest."[79]

The carters also failed to persuade the Court of Appeals.[80] Writing for a unanimous panel, Judge Richard Cardamone traced the history of corruption, intimidation, and racketeering in the waste-hauling industry, labeled the waste-hauling cartel a "'black hole' in New York City's economic life," and rejected every one of the carters' constitutional arguments.[81]

Undaunted, the carters next brought suit in state court presenting many of the same constitutional arguments.[82] The state court judge granted the TWC's motion to remove the case to federal court, where Judge Pollack again rejected the legal arguments he had heard only four months before.[83]

The TWC vigorously publicized the new law and regulations. A flyer bearing a large seal of the city of New York and the bold words "NOTICE FROM MAYOR RUDOLPH W. GIULIANI AND THE NEW YORK CITY TRADE WASTE COMMISSION" announced to all waste-hauling customers: "THIS MAY BE YOUR INDEPENDENCE DAY." Local Law 42 declared all carting contracts terminable-at-will by the customer on thirty days' notice. The flyer also explained that the customer was free to void its contract and to negotiate with a carter of its choice. The flyer explained that carting contracts could not extend beyond two years, and that if a customer's contract with one carter was assigned to another firm, the customer would have the right to reject the assignment and select a new carting company. "You will now have freedom of choice and the right to a fair and honest price," the notice stated, exhorting customers to "EXERCISE YOUR RIGHTS."

A waste hauler could seek a waiver from the provision voiding its contracts if it could show that its contracts were fair and that it did not engage in illegal business practices. In determining whether to grant a waiver, the law instructed the TWC to consider "information concerning the business and its principals and the full circumstances surrounding the negotiation or administration of such contracts."[84] In the summer of 1996, when the commission denied the waiver applications of fourteen major carting firms, it gave 10,000 New York City businesses the right to cancel their waste-hauling contracts immediately, freeing them to deal with any waste-hauling firm.[85] Of the 335 carting firms operating in New York City, 212 applied for waivers. The TWC granted only forty.[86]

On September 30, 1996, the TWC issued comprehensive rules. Among them: (1) a carter may not associate with a person whom the carter knows or should know is a member of organized crime; (2) carters may not use trade associations to resolve their disputes over customers, nor to make payments for acquiring former customers of other carters; (3) carters must file their proposed rates with the TWC, to ensure that they are not higher than the maximum allowed by the city; and (4) carters must offer a written contract to each customer; any oral contract can be terminated at will by the customer. Trash haulers convicted of violating the TWC's rules could be fined up to $10,000 and, for operating without a license, sent to jail for up to six months.[87]

On March 26, 1997, the TWC reduced the maximum rate that could be charged for commercial carting to $12.20 per cubic yard of uncompacted waste (down from $14.70 previously set by the Department of Consumer Affairs), and $30.19 per cubic yard of compacted waste (down from $46.70).[88] Giuliani called the reductions the largest tax cut of his administration. Indeed, the reductions were striking. The World Trade Center's annual carting bill dropped 80 percent (from $3 million to $600,000); Columbia Presbyterian Hospital's, 60 percent (from $1.2 million to $480,000); and the bill at 26 Federal Plaza's, 65 percent (from $369,000 to $130,000).[89]

A NEW THREAT TO COMPETITION IN THE CITY'S WASTE-HAULING INDUSTRY

The elimination of the cartel and of organized crime does not mean that competition will reign forever. The Trade Waste Commission has been harshly criticized by smaller carting companies and local businesses that blame it for delays in processing their license applications, thereby ceding the industry to a new cartel of major corporations. In early 1998, a proposed merger involving Waste Management, Inc., the nation's largest carting company, and USA Waste Services, the third-largest, threatened to consolidate 40 percent of the New York City market[90] and 72 percent of the city's transfer-station capacity.[91] By controlling the transfer stations, the new company would be able to increase transfer costs, thereby effectively driving smaller firms out of business and thus nullifying the City's efforts to bring bona fide competition to the industry. At a July 1998 meeting of the City Council's Committee on Consumer Affairs it was reported that roughly 9,500 shopkeepers have experienced a 30 percent increase in their carting costs.[92] Brooklyn Borough President Howard Golden stated in a letter to U.S. Attorney General Janet Reno that New York City was "exchanging organized crime control [over the waste hauling industry] for monolithic corporate control."

By mid-July 1998 a settlement was reached between Waste Management and USA Waste Services officials, and the U.S. Justice Department and thirteen state attorneys general. The settlement allowed for the merger to occur contingent upon the companies' divestiture of three New York City area waste transfer stations.[93]

A WASTE-HAULING INDUSTRY FREE OF THE COSA NOSTRA?

After almost fifty years of dominating waste hauling in New York City and Long Island, organized crime has been routed. The multifaceted remedial efforts of the 1990s, including the creation of the Trade Waste Commission, the Manhattan district attorney's prosecutions, and the Long Island monitorship, appear to have liberated the carting industry and its customers.

As recently as the early 1990s, BFI had no more than 200 clients among the approximately 250,000 commercial enterprises in New York City,[94] and other national carting firms were not willing to compete in the New York City market.[95] By 1997, BFI had more than 500 customers,[96] but it is overshadowed by both USA Waste, which purchased Barretti Carting and began servicing Barretti's nearly 5,000 customers,[97] and WMX, which purchased Resource NE and serves 6,000 businesses citywide.[98] Even more impressive than the entrance and expansion of national firms into New York City's market is the emergence of bona fide competition. Waste-hauling costs for large office buildings have dropped between 30 and 40 percent, and for smaller businesses by as much as 25 percent.[99] According to industry experts, these reductions indicate that there is real competition in the city's waste-hauling industry.[100]

The TWC has been the most creative and important strategy in purging the mob from the carting industry. Staffed by former law enforcement personnel, it functions like a quasi law enforcement agency. It uses its investigative powers and resources to bar firms tainted by organized crime from the industry. As long as the TWC is run by competent and aggressive officials, Cosa Nostra's comeback in the carting industry is unlikely. The true test of the regulatory strategy will come when Giuliani leaves office. Then we will see if the TWC remains vigorous or deteriorates into a moribund regulator.

14

Cleansing the Construction Industry

> We must break the back of corruption in the City's massive construction industry. Price fixing, job extortion, kickbacks and organized crime infiltration and control of legitimate business cannot and will not be tolerated in the greatest City of the greatest State in America.[1]
>
> —Governor Mario M. Cuomo, 1985

THE ITALIAN AMERICAN organized-crime families have been prominent in the New York City construction industry since the 1930s. In the mid-1980s, their influence and power was certainly at or near its pinnacle. Their most important power base was the construction union locals affiliated with the Teamsters, Carpenters, Masons, Laborers, and Plasterers unions. Control of the unions enabled the Cosa Nostra families to solicit bribes, extort contractors, and place members, associates, and relatives in bona fide and no-show jobs with contractors and suppliers; to take ownership interests in contracting and supply firms; and to set up and police cartels in a number of construction niches like drywall, concrete, and window replacement.

Over the years there have been periodic exposés of corruption and racketeering in the construction industry. In the mid-1980s, amid yet a new scandal, Governor Mario M. Cuomo asked the New York State Organized Crime Task Force (OCTF, an independent state agency) for a comprehensive examination of the problem. The OCTF launched the most thorough investigation and analysis of construction-industry corruption in history. Nevertheless, its many recommendations have gone largely unheeded.

Other than OCTF's investigations there has not been an organized-crime control program specifically aimed at the massive construction industry. But there have been a number of important initiatives, especially trusteeships imposed on corrupt labor-union locals and district councils, and efforts by government agencies like the School Construction Authority to police their construction contracts and contractors. In the spring of 1998, the Giuliani administration proposed a regulatory attack on construction-industry racketeering, which, if implemented, would be the most ambitious and comprehensive organized-crime control program specifically aimed at the city's construction industry.

THE OCTF INITIATIVE

In April 1985, in the wake of allegations by the media and conclusions by the New York State Investigation Commission of rampant corruption and racketeering in the New York City construction industry, Mayor Edward I. Koch urged Governor Cuomo to appoint a special prosecutor. Cuomo agreed that the problem was serious, but rather than appoint a special prosecutor, he requested the OCTF (1) to undertake an "intensive and comprehensive investigation into allegations of corruption and racketeering in the New York City construction industry"; (2) to determine "the appropriate prosecutorial and other responses to alleged organized crime activity within the multibillion dollar construction industry"; and (3) to report its conclusions to him and the state attorney general.

Although he had rejected Koch's proposal for a special prosecutor, Cuomo recognized the need to enhance and focus the law enforcement effort. Thus, in December 1987 he created the Construction Industry Strike Force (CISF), composed of prosecutors, investigators, accountants, and support staff from both the OCTF and the Manhattan District Attorney's Office.

The OCTF responded to the governor's request by initiating criminal investigations, designing and utilizing a computer database on construction-industry corruption and racketeering, undertaking an analytical study of the nature and causes of construction-related corruption and racketeering, and embarking upon a broad search for strategies to attack the problem. The CISF produced a number of important investigations and prosecutions involving mobsters, employers, unions, and union officials involved in the drywall, concrete, painters, and plumbers cartels.

OCTF's 1998 Interim Report and 1990 Final Report comprise a comprehensive multidisciplinary analysis of corruption and racketeering in the construction industry, especially the structural, processual, legal, and regulatory variables that make the industry so vulnerable to systemic criminality. Some of the OCTF's primary recommendations were:

- Establish an Office of Construction Corruption Prevention (OCCP)
  As envisioned in the report, the primary purpose of the office would have been to utilize intelligence, information, and industry knowledge (much of which was to be collected by OCTF's research and analysis unit) to design and implement regulations and procedures that bolster deterrence, further incapacitation, block opportunities, and reduce racketeering susceptibility and potential. The office would have combined the Department of Investigation's investigative authority and expertise with the New York City Office of Construction's regulatory authority and expertise. The possibility of creating an OCCP has never been seriously considered.
- Certified Investigative Auditing Firm (CIAF) Program
  The report proposed that the principal contractor on public works projects in excess of $5 million would be required to hire a private-sector monitor and dedicate at least 2 percent of the project budget to the CIAF. The CIAFs would, in effect, function as private inspectors general to insure compliance with relevant laws and regulations and to deter, prevent, uncover, and expose unethical or illegal conduct. This proposal has never been implemented, but CIAFs (often called IPSIGs—Independent Private Sector Inspector Generals) have been utilized on a case-by-case basis by the School Construction Authority, the Trade Waste Commission, and, more recently, by a number of city agencies.
- Office of Union Members Advocacy (OUMA)
  The report saw union democracy as an important bulwark against labor racketeering and hence urged the creation of a new agency to act as ombudsman in advancing the rights of construction-union members. "If rank-and-file union members can make their elected officers responsive to the membership's actual needs and best interests, racketeers will no longer be able to sell out the rights of union members by soliciting bribes and extorting money from contractors."[2] This proposal was never seriously debated, but many of the court-appointed union trustees focused on promoting union democracy.

- State and City Tax Enforcement
  The report urged that state and local tax agencies make construction-industry tax fraud an enforcement priority. "The tax agencies' efforts to audit construction companies, to increase tax compliance, and to recover money from tax evaders would also provide investigative leads for the law enforcement agencies, since most corporate racketeering is accomplished by falsification of corporate books and tax fraud." This recommendation was not implemented.

THE ELIMINATION OF CARTELS

The major organized crime–sponsored cartels, described in chapter 7, each of which lasted for a decade or more, seemed to have been broken up by a combination of criminal prosecutions and civil RICO suits resulting in court-appointed trusteeships over corrupt labor unions.

The Concrete Cartel

Throughout the 1980s, state and federal prosecutions targeted members and associates of Cosa Nostra who controlled the concrete subindustries. In 1982, John Cody, Gambino associate and president of Teamsters Local 282, which controlled the drivers of concrete-mixing trucks, was indicted and convicted on charges of labor bribery and racketeering.[3] Four years later, in the Colombo family RICO prosecution, Ralph Scopo and other prominent Colombo family members were convicted. An important part of that case focused on the lower tier of Cosa Nostra's concrete cartel—the extortion of 1–2 percent fees on all concrete contracts under $2 million.[4] Also in 1986, in "the commission case," federal prosecutors proved the creation and supervision of the concrete cartel's $2–$5 million club. The defendants, senior members of four of New York City's five Cosa Nostra families, including Ralph Scopo,[5] were sentenced to hundred-year prison terms. In 1988, the government obtained a RICO conviction against the Genovese family and its ostensible boss, Anthony "Fat Tony" Salerno (law enforcement agents later came to believe that Vincent Gigante was the boss and Salerno the underboss). S&A Concrete's monopoly of concrete jobs of more than $5 million, the top tier of Cosa Nostra's cartel, figured prominently in that case;[6] half of S&A's assets were forfeited to the federal government. The concrete-producing companies that Cosa Nostra controlled through Biff Halloran were also forfeited.[7]

The federal prosecutors' civil RICO suits resulted in court-appointed monitorships placed over Local 6A and the District Council of Cement and Concrete Workers in 1987, and over Teamsters Local 282 in 1995. The former trusteeship ended in 1993 with reports of no significant change; the latter trusteeship was still in place at the end of 1998.[8]

The prosecutorial efforts were complemented by at least one important mayoral initiative.[9] In 1986, the Koch administration moved against the mob-controlled monopoly on concrete *production* by setting up a city-subsidized batching plant from which all city building projects would have to purchase their concrete.[10] The goal was to break the mob's monopoly by establishing a competitor that would sell concrete at a fair market price, thereby undercutting the cartel. It didn't work out that way. Perhaps not surprisingly, the city had great difficulty finding a reputable business person who wanted to go into head-to-head competition with the mob-controlled concrete companies. Mustapha Ally, a Maryland resident with little concrete production experience, was the only viable respondent to the city's solicitation.[11] His fledgling company, the West 57th Street Concrete Company (West 57th), was plagued by lawsuits from companies alleging unfair competition.[12] Ultimately the city canceled its contract in August 1987, because Ally's company had failed to produce a significant amount of concrete.[13]

F.E.D. Concrete Company bought the contract rights from Ally, and had the West 57th plant producing at full capacity by 1988.[14] However, by then the market price of concrete had fallen dramatically and the city found itself paying more for concrete than private developers. Nevertheless, in 1991 the city renewed F.E.D.'s contract for five more years. Two years into its renewed contract the West 57th plant was bankrupt; F.E.D. subcontracted its New York City contracts to a company that some law enforcement agents suspected of mob-affiliations.[15] This strategy failed to keep F.E.D. afloat, and West 57th collapsed in bankruptcy in 1995.[16] At the end of 1998 the city reverted to purchasing ready-mix concrete in the private sector.

After the Genovese family trial in 1988, in which Certified Concrete and Transit Mix, the two Halloran-owned companies that monopolized production during the cartel's reign, were forfeited to the court and placed under court trustee David Brodsky. By 1990, Certified Concrete was bankrupt. The U.S. attorney began investigating whether Certified Concrete's business had been turned over to Valente Industries, which State Attorney General Robert Abrams feared was well on its way to creating a new monopoly over concrete production.[17] That same year, the court sold Certified Concrete and Transit Mix Concrete to John Quadrozzi with the requirement that there be a seven-year court monitor. Two years later, Quadrozzi was indicted on charges of making illegal payoffs to union leaders and the mob.[18] Although concrete-production and -contracting cartels have been broken up, it remains to be seen whether the Mafia will be purged from the city's subindustry.

Drywall

In the late 1970s, the FBI's Long Island Labor Racketeering and Extortion (LILREX) investigation[19] revealed a club of drywall contractors supervised by Vincent DiNapoli, a Genovese soldier, aided by Teddy Maritas, the Carpenters District Council president.[20] This investigation lead to a 1981 RICO suit by the Brooklyn Organized Crime Strike Force against DiNapoli, Maritas, and several others.[21] The trial ended in a hung jury and Maritas disappeared just before the retrial. Vincent Cafaro, a Genovese member cooperating with the government, testified that Maritas was murdered to prevent his possible cooperation with the government. In April 1982, the other defendants pled guilty. DiNapoli received a five-year sentence; other members of the Genovese family took over his rackets.

Continued federal investigations into the drywall cartel led to the successful prosecution of Standard Drywall Corporation and Prince Carpentry on charges of mail fraud and tax evasion involving schemes to avoid making required union benefit-fund contributions and assisting employees to obtain illegal unemployment benefits.[22] The club of mob-controlled companies was broken up, but Cosa Nostra's presence in the subindustry continued. DiNapoli even remained a significant shareholder in Inner City Drywall, a major contractor, until he sold his shares following his 1988 conviction in the Genovese family RICO case.[23]

In 1987, law enforcement officials began a series of prosecutions and civil suits aimed at purging Cosa Nostra from the drywall industry.[24] Officials of Carpenters Local 608 were successfully prosecuted for extorting payoffs and soliciting bribes from contractors.[25] The most significant government initiative was a civil RICO suit that resulted in a consent decree in which the Carpenters District Council promised to cleanse itself and its constituent locals of Cosa Nostra's influence.[26] Former Department of Investigations commissioner and former federal judge Kenneth Conboy was appointed to monitor the consent decree, and he expelled several corrupt officials and stewards. Moreover, he convinced the international organization to impose a trusteeship that promises significant hiring-hall reform, reorganization of union leadership, and further efforts to purge the union of organized crime.[27]

Window Replacement

In 1990, officials of Local 580 of the Architectural and Ornamental Ironworkers Union (Local 580) and senior members of four of New York City's five Cosa Nostra families were indicted on RICO charges. Among the predicate offenses were extortion, labor payoffs, and bid rigging on contracts with the New York City Housing Authority.[28] The prosecution's key witness was Peter Savino, a Genovese associate, who, as a government cooperator from 1988 to 1989, surreptitiously recorded many hours of conversations regarding the windows cartel.[29] The trial, which played out like a movie, was mired with murder, fugitive defendants, jury tampering, and turncoats.[30]

Vincent "the Chin" Gigante, reputed boss of the Genovese family, was found mentally unfit to stand trial.[31] Vittorio Amuso and Anthony "Gaspipe" Casso, boss and underboss of the Lucchese family, went into hiding. The organizers of the cartel, Venero Mangano and Benedetto Aloi (underbosses of the Genovese and Colombo families, respectively),[32] received significant sentences for conspiring to murder witnesses after discovering Savino's cooperation with the FBI.[33] Peter Chiodo, a Lucchese capo who entered into a cooperation agreement, testified that, on orders from the defendants, he murdered codefendant John Morrissey, a Local 580 business agent and Lucchese associate.[34]

Of the fifteen original defendants, eight went to trial; there were just three convictions.[35] Those convicted were Mangano and Aloi, two of the main organizers of the cartel, and Dennis DeLucia, a Colombo soldier. Follow-up prosecutions succeeded in convicting Thomas McGowan, the Manhattan business agent of Local 580, for receipt of illegal labor payments from a private contractor.[36] Vittorio Amuso was convicted on a superseding indictment of a number of crimes including participation in the windows cartel.[37] Vincent "the Chin" Gigante was convicted in 1997 of RICO and extortion, labor payoffs, and murder conspiracies.[38] Finally, Anthony "Gaspipe" Casso was arrested in 1993 after a two-and-a-half year manhunt, pled guilty in 1994 to racketeering and murder charges, became a government witness, was discredited and removed from the Witness Security Program, and finally sentenced to life imprisonment without parole.[39]

Painting

In the summer of 1990, one month after the windows indictments, the Manhattan District Attorney's office obtained indictments against union officials, contractors, and Cosa Nostra members for operating a cartel in the painting industry.[40] Specifically, prosecutors accused members of the Lucchese crime family with controlling union officials in Painters District Council 9 and its locals and with conspiring with painting contractors in a twelve-year bid-rigging scheme tainting all major public and private painting contracts in the city.[41] By 1991, Anthony Casso was on the run from the windows case, another defendant became a government witness, and others had pled guilty. This was the first successful use of New York State's Organized Crime Control Act against labor officials.[42] Two years later, combined Manhattan District Attorney, FBI, and IRS investigations led to successful charges focusing on the Lucchese family's domination of steel-painting contracts during the same time period.[43] The cartel seems to have been broken up.

Racketeering in the Plumbing Industry

In 1993, a four-year investigation culminated in a series of Manhattan District Attorney's Office prosecutions against Genovese associate Louis Moscatiello Jr., Plumbers Local Union No. 2 (Local 2) officials, plumbing contractors, a major accounting firm, and plumbing inspectors, in an attempt to break up a plumbing cartel of ten years' duration.[44] Louis Moscatiello Jr. was acquitted.[45] Prosecutions against ten union officials led to seven convictions and three acquittals.[46] The district attorney's effort to have Local 2 placed under trusteeship was preempted when the Plumbers Union's national headquarters imposed its own trusteeship over the local.[47] However, progress in eliminating organized crime from Local 2 was undermined in 1997, when Local 2 was merged with the reputedly corrupt Local 1.[48] The prosecution of contractors continues.

LABOR RACKETEERING AND UNION TRUSTEESHIPS

Many of the key mobbed-up construction unions identified in the 1990 OCTF Report have been placed under federal court–appointed trusteeships or monitorships or under receiverships imposed by the parent international union. It would be a stretch to see these trusteeships as part of a single strategic move to clean up the construction industry, but many of the lawsuits that produced these trusteeships were spawned by the construction-industry investigation launched in the mid-1980s by Governor Cuomo and Mayor Koch.

Carpenters District Council

One of the most successful union trusteeships is the one imposed on the Carpenters District Council.[49] Even before the 1994 settlement of the civil RICO suit, the lawsuit itself had prompted anticorruption efforts within some of the District Council's constituent locals. An interim investigation into elections and misconduct charges helped rank-and-file members to oust long-time incumbents in elections at Locals 17 (Bronx) and 20 (Staten Island). The Association for Union Democracy noted that "the combination of government action and rank and file involvement stimulates union democracy against corruption."[50]

As the District Council's IRO, Kenneth Conboy charged several local union officials and members with being associated with Cosa Nostra; most of these cases resulted in permanent bars from union office, retirements, and expulsions from the union.[51] Ousting corrupt officials was only the beginning. Conboy also persuaded the international organization to impose a trusteeship over the union.[52] The need for the parent body's aid was made apparent when Frederick Devine, a Cosa Nostra associate and incumbent president of the District Council, won a landslide victory as incumbent president of the council in 1995.[53] As Conboy wrote in a 1996 report, "[T]he influence of organized crime on the District Council and its locals is pervasive and long-standing. . . .

The only realistic hope of returning the District Council to its membership require[s] the intervention of the International."[54]

In June of 1996, Douglas McCarron, president of the Carpenters International union, imposed an emergency trusteeship over the District Council, ousting Devine from office.[55] McCarron, in cooperation with Conboy, also implemented a controversial restructuring plan for the District Council and its locals.[56] One significant reform is a computerized central dispatch to "conclusively end the tyranny of business agents in dispensing jobs and controlling the livelihoods of rank and file carpenters."[57] Other measures include the implementation of a district-wide out-of-work list for the appointment of job stewards, as well as the use of a labor-management fund to employ liaisons with law enforcement agencies who would act to enforce collective bargaining agreements.[58] While allegations of harassment and job referral violations continue, Conboy believes that "the union is carefully but steadily progressing towards . . . effective self-governance."[59] Locals' elections are planned for the summer of 1999, and District Council elections for 2000.[60]

Teamsters Local 282

IBT Local 282, the mob-controlled union that enforced the concrete-pouring cartel, was placed under international trusteeship in 1992, shortly after Robert Sasso quit as a result of an investigation by the IBT's investigations officer, Charles Carberry.[61] Ron Carey initially appointed Johnnie Brown as trustee. Two years later, after guilty pleas by five former and current Local 282 officials, including Sasso,[62] federal prosecutors brought a civil RICO suit against the local. That suit led to a 1995 agreement whereby a full-time court-appointed "corruption officer" would ferret out corruption and a court-approved trustee from the International would run the union.[63] The court appointed former chief investigator to the Mollen Commission and former police Lieutenant Robert Machado as the corruption officer.[64] Machado is empowered to remove officials and stewards from their positions without a hearing (their cases would then be referred to an IBT review board); within months of his appointment he had removed sixteen officials identified by the U.S. Labor Department as organized-crime associates.[65]

The settlement further required the International to replace Jimmy Brown with Peter Mastrandrea, and later with Gary LaBarbera.[66] Union reformer Larry Kudla praised LaBarbera's appointment as a positive step.[67] But some knowledgeable observers are not yet willing to label the Local 282 reform effort a success story.[68]

Local 6A and the District Council of Cement and Concrete Workers

Local 6A and the District Council of Cement and Concrete Workers, which played a key role in assuring the mob's control over the concrete industry, signed a consent decree that resulted in the resignation of sixteen union officers, including Ralph Scopo Jr., who was president of Local 6A, and his brother, who was vice-president; both men were permanently enjoined from the union's affairs.[69] The union was placed under a court-appointed trusteeship from 1987 to 1993.[70]

In March 1987, Judge Vincent Broderick appointed former federal prosecutor Eugene R. Anderson to monitor Local 6A and the District Council,[71] both of which were reportedly "captive labor organizations"under the Colombo family's control.[72] At the end of his six-year tenure, Anderson concluded that his trusteeship had not made significant headway toward rooting out corruption. He blamed his limited powers, inadequately funding, and insufficient support from the FBI and the U.S. Labor Department.[73]

Mason Tenders District Council

In 1994, a civil RICO and ERISA (Employee Retirement Income Security Act) suit brought by federal prosecutors established a monitorship over the Mason Tenders District Council, which represents twelve locals whose members perform jobs including general labor, bricklaying, masonry, and asbestos removal throughout the metropolitan area.[74] The court appointed former federal prosecutor Lawrence B. Pedowitz and former New Jersey U.S. Attorney Michael Chertoff to act as monitor and investigations officer (IO), respectively. The monitor and IO expelled several members from the union, including a convicted Long Island racketeer, Peter "Jocko" Vario, a Lucchese member.[75] Chertoff also worked with the FBI and Department of Labor to bar corrupt candidates from 1997 elections for local officials.[76] The District Council has also mandated FBI clearances for shop-steward positions.[77]

Just prior to the 1994 consent decree, the Laborers International Union of North America (LIUNA) imposed its own trusteeship over the District Council, naming David Elboar trustee. Elboar signed the consent decree establishing the court monitorship. Steven Hammond, who replaced Elboar in 1995, felt that removal procedures against corrupt officials were delaying efforts to clean up the union. He therefore proposed a restructuring plan to consolidate the District Council's twelve locals into four, eliminating most of the corrupt officials' positions. This plan was implemented in 1996.[78]

Under threat of a civil RICO suit seeking a court-ordered trusteeship, the International union itself agreed to combat corruption to the Justice Department's satisfaction.[79] The International committed itself to job-referral and hiring-hall reforms. Although the Justice Department has been satisfied with LIUNA's efforts thus far, some union members complain that LIUNA is exaggerating its anticorruption efforts to placate the government until the oversight agreement ends.[80] As of the summer of 1998, no significant effects of this agreement have reached New York City's laborers locals.[81]

In May of 1998, LIUNA's general counsel testified to the success of the Mason Tenders District Council's trusteeship, claiming that "all vestiges of corruption and organized crime influence" have been eradicated.[82] However, prominent union-democracy activist Herman Benson believes that further efforts are necessary to eradicate and prevent Cosa Nostra's long-standing influence in the District Council.[83]

Painters

In 1991, in the wake of state racketeering charges against Local 1486 (Long Island) and District Council 9 (New York) alleging a conspiracy with Cosa Nostra to maintain a painting cartel,[84] William Duvall, the International Painters Union president, placed District Council 9 under the trusteeship of John Alfarone.[85] Alfarone, a longtime union official who had opposed mob corruption in a local dry-wall union, was hampered by limited powers and internal conflicts within the International's executive body. Even though state charges led to several convictions and prison terms, some officials who had been appointed by the corrupt regime kept their union positions and their control over job assignments. In 1992 elections, "picked representatives of the old guard took over—took back—all offices, all without opposition except for one." Frank Schonfeld, a veteran Painters Union reformer, noted in the *Union Democracy Review* that without a government presence behind the trusteeship, and without strong backing by the International union, "the overhanging climate of fear and apathy was never lifted."[86] In his view, the union local remains under the Lucchese family's influence.[87]

Ironworkers Local 580

There has been no action taken to place Ironworkers Local 580, the "corrupt engine" behind the Cosa Nostra's window-replacement cartel, under court supervision. Individuals like Thomas McGowan, the union's Manhattan business agent who participated in the cartel, were convicted, but there is no evidence that the union has been purged of corruption. Local 580 continues to have a reputation for organized crime ties.[88]

Plumbers

In 1993, the Manhattan District Attorney's Office launched a major prosecution against officials in Local 2 (Manhattan and the Bronx) of the Plumbers Union.[89] The International union imposed its own trusteeship in 1994, thereby heading off the DA's effort to obtain a court-appointed trustee.[90] The trustee instituted a hiring hall, a positive step because the union had had no job-assignment rules prior to that time. In 1996, the reform effort suffered a setback when an indicted candidate was elected as business agent.[91] Although the trusteeship seemed to be on the road toward reform, its efforts were rendered moot in 1997 when the International organization merged Local 2 with the reputedly corrupt[92] Local 1 (Brooklyn and Queens).[93]

SCHOOL CONSTRUCTION AUTHORITY'S AND OTHER AGENCIES' INITIATIVES

Although no action was taken on its major recommendations, the 1990 OCTF report attracted a great deal of attention. The School Construction Authority (SCA) took the ideas of the report farther than any other public agency. In part, the SCA was created in 1989 because of the corruption associated with the New York City Board of Education's construction operations.[94] The founders of the SCA were determined to keep the new authority squeaky clean. This led them to appoint Thomas D. Thacher II (former CISF director) as the first inspector general. Thacher took the job only after the SCA met his condition that the IG office would have a staff of sixty. Thus, from the outset the SCA made a heavy investment in the control of corruption and organized crime.

The SCA's boldest move was to require the prequalification of contractors who wished to bid on SCA contracts. Contractors had to submit to a thirty-page prequalification questionnaire that included questions such as "In the past ten years has the applicant firm or any of its current or past key personnel or affiliate firms 1) taken the Fifth Amendment in testimony regarding a business related crime?; 2) given or offered money to a labor official or public servant with intent to influence that labor official or public official with respect to any of his or her official acts, duties or decisions as a labor official?; 3) agreed with another to bid below the market rate?" An applicant can be blacklisted as well as prosecuted for a false answer.

The SCA investigators scrutinized the forms and did their own independent investigation. In August 1991, the SCA announced that it was blacklisting for up to five years more than fifty construction companies.[95] More than half the disqualifications were based on purported mob ties or criminality. By 1995, the SCA reported that it had conducted upwards of 3500 background evaluations and debarred 200 firms, "many of whom had ties to organized crime or were the alter ego of firms with prior legal or debarment problems."[96] For example, the SCA debarred the concrete company owned by Nick Auletta's (Genovese crime family) son and the DeCon Plumbing company, which was largely owned by Gerald Fiorino, a Genovese soldier.[97]

Some "problem" contractors were not disqualified if they agreed to hire a private investigating firm (CIAF) (1) to design a code of ethics for the contractor; (2) to implement a corruption prevention program; and (3) to audit and report to the SCA on the contractor's compliance with the code and the program.[98]

The new New York City Charter contained many anticorruption provisions that were meant to respond to charges that the public-construction process was vulnerable to corruption.[99] Under new contract-procurement rules, each agency's contracting officer and chief administrator had to determine whether a contractor or vendor was financially, operationally, and *morally* responsible.

The city also started the VENDEX system, a computer database of government contractors.[100] VENDEX aimed to collect information about contractors' organized-crime ties or other wrongdoing. Would-be contractors and their principals had to fill out an extensive VENDEX questionnaire (twenty-seven pages for business entities; thirteen for principals) about the business, its principals, its tax returns, and its history of government contracting.[101] *Before* awarding a construction contract, a city agency is required to check whether the VENDEX system contains any negative information about that contractor. If so, the agency would be well advised to withdraw the contract or to place some restrictions or conditions on the contractor.

In practice, VENDEX did not work as well as its originators had imagined. For one thing, construction companies disappear and then reappear with new names and owners of records. For another, law enforcement agencies, including the New York City Department of Investigation, were unwilling to share information because information released prematurely could compromise an investigation. Thus, if an executive agency (e.g., Corrections or Environmental Protection) found an indication in VENDEX that allegations had been made against a particular contractor or that the contractor was being investigated, it often could not get any further information. Of course, a risk-averse agency (which most were and are) might wish to stay clear of any contractor whose subsequent indictment might later cause embarrassment.

The VENDEX system and the city's new zeal in keeping itself at arm's length from organized crime did have impact. In one high-visibility case, Comptroller Elizabeth Holtzman persuaded the city to rescind a contract held by a company run by Carmine Agnello, John Gotti's son-in-law, to remove abandoned cars from Brooklyn streets. According to Holtzman, the C & M Agnello Company and its owner had been implicated in a "chop-shop" (stripping down cars) operation in Queens, and Agnello was under investigation for possible jury tampering in a Brooklyn organized-crime trial involving Gotti's brother, Gene.[102] The comptroller also succeeded in blocking a jail-construction project that had gone to a firm whose president owned a majority interest in a concrete company that was operated by a son-in-law of former Gambino family boss Paul Castellano.[103]

THE CITY'S REGULATORY PROPOSAL

In May 1998, the Giuliani administration announced that it was preparing a proposal for attacking corruption and racketeering, as well as safety hazards, in the construction industry that would build on the Trade Waste Commission model. The legislation would require that all general contractors be licensed by a new New York City Construction Commission. The commission would be able to deny licenses to applicants lacking "good character, honesty and integrity," and to prohibit licensees from subcontracting with or employing persons deemed similarly lacking. Certain categories of subcontractors would also require licenses. Alternatively, the commission could require the general contractor or subcontractor to hire a preapproved independent monitor (IPSIG) based on the OCTF's CIAF model.

Critics immediately pointed out several perceived flaws. One, the bill gives sweeping discretionary authority to the Commission to put people out of business. Arguing that the city has not even been able to coherently define who is a "responsible" bidder under the city charter, construction-industry insiders complain that Giuliani's proposal leaves too much room for arbitrary and unfair determinations. Two, the bill is too ambitious. It demands more of the commission than the commission will be able to deliver. Even the Trade Waste Commission has found it difficult to process license requests expeditiously. What will happen to general contractors if the commission's licensing reviews get bogged down? The general contractors will be left in limbo and financially ruined. Three, the bill unfairly burdens general contractors with the duty to investigate and make judgments about the integrity of subcontractors. Such investigations will mean extra costs and delays at the expense of job performance. Four, the bill focuses too heavily on organized crime, overlooking significant issues of technical competence that plague public construction projects. And five, the bill is overinclusive, extending the city's regulatory reach to in-house construction-management divisions of major owners that have never exhibited any problems with corruption, such as New York University and Columbia University.

There are tens of thousands of city contractors, each owned by and employing various numbers of individuals. Is it feasible for the city government to take on the responsibility of investigating and vouching for the moral integrity of even a fraction of these firms? An entire system of norms, rules, and procedures, and a large bureaucracy might ultimately be necessary to implement a fair and comprehensive system to judge the moral eligibility of government contractors. Isn't that the kind of exaggerated ambition that will ultimately come back to haunt government agencies as journalists, other observers, and critics confront government officials with contracts that have been let to all sorts of morally questionable individuals who inevitably will slip through the net?

CONCLUSION

The late 1980s and early 1990s were marked by long-term investigations and the effective use of RICO and OCCA against cartels that dominated the city's concrete, drywall, window-replacement, and painting subindustries. However, even though the government successfully broke up these organized cartels, widespread corruption persists, especially where unions remain under Cosa Nostra's influence.

The Carpenters, Teamsters, and Mason Tenders cases show that coordination between union forces and the government can successfully work toward purging Cosa Nostra. Yet in many of the city's construction trade unions, such as plumbing, painting, and concrete, mobsters continue to suppress union democracy. The case studies demonstrate that trusteeships without a strong government presence fail to inspire the courage and leadership among rank-and-file members required to bring about reform.

Even without the presence of mobsters, widespread and sometimes highly organized corruption exists in the construction industry. In 1998, a Manhattan District Attorney's Office prosecution exposed a cartel of interior construction companies that monopolized the multibillion-dollar office-renovation and -relocation subindustry. The cartel's bid rigging increased the cost of interior office construction by 20 percent.[104] Five of the companies entered plea agreements.[105] Further investigations and prosecutions of participants in New York City's construction industry continue.[106]

15

Conclusion to Part II

> With instability at all levels and with continuing sociological change inevitable, if current law enforcement efforts are maintained in the next five to ten years, the mob is likely to be rendered totally unrecognizable from what it has been for the last sixty years.[1]
>
> —Ronald Goldstock, director, New York State Organized Crime Task Force, 1990

THE SUCCESSFUL PURGING of Cosa Nostra groups from New York City's core economy was not accomplished simply by applying "more of the same" law enforcement medicine that had been administered in previous decades. Success depended upon major innovations and "institution building" in organized-crime control. The introduction to Part 2 briefly sketched the evolution of the federal organized-crime control program. In this chapter we highlight and assess the organized-crime control innovations that have had the greatest impact on industrial racketeering.

CIVIL RICO AND COURT-APPOINTED TRUSTEESHIPS

Traditionally, the only approach to organized-crime control was criminal prosecutions that aimed to send mobsters to prison for lengthy terms. Unfortunately, although a prison term (if lengthy) is a major blow to a particular crime boss, it has little impact on the operations of a powerful, diversified, and entrenched criminal syndicate that can promote replacements from its ranks. Putting mobsters in prison did nothing to eliminate racketeering in unions or companies, or to eliminate cartels. Thus, the defeat of organized crime awaited a different remedy, one that aimed at syndicates and systemic criminality.

Civil RICO provided the means. Most of the key federal organized-crime control initiatives discussed in Part II were brought as civil RICO suits. These suits sought restraining orders, injunctions, and trusteeships to prevent racketeering and to purge Cosa Nostra members and associates from the defendant organization. Civil RICO is particularly well suited to combating racketeering in labor unions and companies, that is, formal organizations that can be monitored. If the individual defendants have previously been convicted of crimes that constituted racketeering acts (so-called RICO predicates), there is no need to relitigate them. The suit therefore turns merely on proof that the racketeering acts were linked to an enterprise (e.g., union or company). Even without previous convictions, it is easier for prosecutors to prove civil RICO liability than criminal liability. Civil RICO suits are governed by civil, not criminal, procedure. Therefore, the government is entitled to extensive pretrial discovery (depositions and documents), which can provide a wealth of information from corrupted companies and unions. The government bears a lesser burden of proof in a civil trial, preponderance of the evidence as compared with beyond a reasonable doubt. There is no requirement of jury unanimity in a civil trial, and, unlike criminal procedure, the government can appeal a verdict in favor of the defendant.

The most important innovation brought about by the extensive use of civil RICO has been the appointment of monitors or trustees to carry out the terms of the court orders or negotiated settlements. In effect, the courts transplanted the techniques and strategies of organizational reform, developed in the school desegregation and unconstitutional prison conditions cases, to the organized-crime domain. Like the special masters appointed to oversee school desegregation or the remediation of deplorable prison conditions, the court-appointed trustees carry out the judge's mandate to transform an organization, for example, purging a union local of corruption and racketeering and restoring union democracy to the rank and file.

Not all of the trustees discussed in Part 2 of this book owed their appointment to a civil RICO suit. Nevertheless, the RICO trusteeships have been the model for other trusteeships, however authorized. For example, in the imaginative plea agreement that resolved the Manhattan district attorney's criminal prosecution of Thomas and Joseph Gambino, the parties agreed to the appointment of former New York City Police Commissioner Robert McGuire as special master to oversee the Gambinos' sale of their Garment Center trucking interests.

The trustee is usually appointed for a lengthy or indefinite term, thus announcing to the mobbed-up union or company, and, more important, to rank-and-file members, clients, customers, and business associates, that the government will not disappear and that the situation will not revert to the status quo ante. A trusteeship signals a remedial *process*, not a one-shot punch. The trustee's specific mandate and powers are shaped by the judge, if there was a trial, or by the parties in the event of a negotiated agreement. The defendants are ordered (or voluntarily agree) to cease racketeering activities and contact with Cosa Nostra members. The trustee's mandate includes the goal of eradicating organized crime (and racketeering, payoffs, kickbacks, bribes) from the tainted organization. The judge maintains continuing jurisdiction and can issue supplemental orders if necessary; recalcitrance and interference can be punished as contempt.

Most of the trustees have been appointed in labor-racketeering cases. Some judges have given a single trustee authority to run the union, as well as a mandate to purge corruption. Other judges have limited the trustee's role to investigations and discipline relating to racketeering.

To assure that racketeering has ceased in corrupted organizations, judges have typically vested the RICO trustees with wide-ranging investigative powers, including authority to subpoena books and records and to compel testimony under oath. Some union trustees have had authority to discipline union officers and members; others could bring disciplinary charges against union officials and members before an independent hearing board or the judge. In either case, union members found to be associated with organized-crime figures could be purged from the union. This is a powerful and effective tool.

The proliferation of RICO (and other) trusteeships has created a new career path for former prosecutors and law enforcement agents. Many of the trustees who have played crucial roles in the liberation of the New York City economy from mob influence had previously served in law enforcement capacities. Such individuals come to the job with a wealth of information about organized crime and significant investigative expertise. They also have close ties to federal, state, and local law enforcement agencies. Of course, although it makes good sense that a trustee whose purpose is to purge organized crime should be drawn

Table 15.1
Court-Appointed Monitors/Trustees

Union/Industry	Monitor/Trustee	Other Positions Held
Fulton Fish Market Local 359	Frank Wohl	Assistant U.S. Attorney
IBT Local 295 at JFK	Thomas Puccio	Brooklyn OCSF
Garment Industry; Special Master over selected defendants	Robert McGuire	New York City Police Commissioner
Long Island Carting	Michael Cherkasky	Division Chief, Manhattan District Attorney's office
IBT Local 851 at JFK	Ron DePetris	Chief Assistant U.S. Attorney
IBT	Charles Carberry Frederick Lacey	Assistant U.S. Attorney Federal Judge and U.S. Attorney
Carpenters District Council	Kenneth Conboy (IRO)	DOI Commissioner; Federal Judge
Teamsters Local 282	Robert Machado (Corruption Officer)	Chief Investigator for the Mollen Commission; Police Lieutenant
Local 6A and District Council of Cement and Concrete Workers	Eugene R. Anderson	Assistant U.S. Attorney
Mason Tenders	Lawrence B. Pedowitz	Assistant U.S. Attorney
District Council	Michael Chertoff	Assistant U.S. Attorney; New Jersey U.S. Attorney; Special Counsel for the Whitewater Investigation

from the ranks of former law enforcement personnel, it is less obvious that a trustee who stands in the shoes of the local's president should be a former prosecutor. Certainly, there is nothing in the prosecutor's training or experience that qualifies him or her to negotiate collective bargaining agreements or handle grievances and enforce contract provisions.

The funding of court-appointed trusteeships is a crucially important matter. The most common funding source in the union cases has been the very union local that was exploited by racketeers in the years leading up to the trusteeship; in some cases this has bankrupted the local union. In a few cases, the international union has paid the bill for the trustee and his staff. The judge can fix the trustee's compensation.

Usually, trustees are compensated at a rate comparable to lawyers in private practice. Ironically, this may be more compensation than was paid to the corrupt union officer whom the trustee replaced. Because RICO trusteeships should not be seen as sinecures that judges hand out to friends and former colleagues, it is imperative that regularized method(s) and mechanisms for choosing and compensating trustees be established.[2]

Even though RICO trusteeships are one of the most important law enforcement innovations of this generation, they have not always been successful. Sometimes the trustees have become bogged down in the details of union administration. Sometimes they have not found the right techniques or not had enough backing from the court. The trustees whose only responsibilities are investigative and disciplinary probably have been more successful than those who have also had to shoulder responsibility for running the union.

RICO trusteeships raise a number of legal and philosophical questions that need to be examined. Trustees have voided elections, replaced union officers, redesigned hiring halls, and expelled union members for associating with organized-crime figures. One might legitimately ask whether such power is fully consistent with a free labor movement based on union members' sovereignty over their unions. Also, one might ask when the trusteeship should end: When new elections have been held? When all traces of organized crime have been eliminated? Not until union democracy is thriving? As in other institutional litigation, there is a tendency for RICO trusteeships to take on a life of their own, accumulating more goals as time passes and all sorts of problems come to the trustee's attention.

Private-Sector Monitors

Drawing on the public sector's experience with inspectors general, the New York State Organized Crime Task Force's *Final Report on Corruption and Racketeering in the New York City Construction Industry*[3] first raised the idea of requiring government contractors to hire a certified investigative auditing firm (CIAF) to assure that the private contractor was not tied to organized crime, covering up criminality, or being victimized by racketeers or public officials.

Ronald Goldstock, director of the New York State Organized Crime Task Force, 1981–1994, in several plea bargains required companies to hire IPSIGs and encouraged regulatory agencies to do the same, in effect, forcing questionable contractors to police themselves. The inspector general's office of the School Construction Authority was the first agency to utilize IPSIGs to monitor contractors, assist them in establishing corruption controls, and to report to the SCA on the firms' conduct.[4] The Trade Waste Commission took monitoring to the next stage by making hiring an IPSIG a condition of licensing for certain firms. The New York City Department of Investigation has recommended IPSIGs to a number of city departments that do business with questionable contractors.

The IPSIG is one of the great contemporary innovations in organized-crime control. It has spawned the formation and growth of private-sector investigation firms run and staffed by former prosecutors, forensic accountants, analysts, and detectives. These firms provide monitoring services for companies that wish to assure clients and government regulators that they are complying with all laws and regulations. Further, under the U.S. Sentencing Commission's Corporate sentencing guidelines, a corporation that can show that it exercised due diligence in designing an internal corruption-control system significantly limits its exposure (i.e., fines) in the event that a crime is uncovered. The monitor, in effect, investigates the company at the company's own expense and reports to the company's top management and to the government on any problems that it finds. The monitor invariably has power to audit the company's books and records, interview employees, and interview subcontractors. If the monitor finds something suspicious, like excessive fees to a questionable "consultant," he informs the government agency, which can demand an explanation from the company. Likewise, if one of the company's subcontractors is known to be mobbed-up or if an employee is a known mob associate, the monitor demands that the company explain why the subcontract should not be terminated and the employee fired.

"Monitoring" is an art, not a science. Success depends upon the skills, persistence, energy, and intelligence of the monitor. In addition, the government agency that has imposed the monitor has to manage the monitor to make sure that the monitor is aggressive enough (but not too aggressive) and must evaluate the accuracy of the monitor's reports. The independent private-sector monitors work best when they are focused on a specific problem, like payoffs to organized crime or defrauding union workers. Likewise, they also are most effective when the company's management is committed to solving the problem and maintaining its reputation and good relationship with the government agency.

Rudolph Giuliani

It is dangerous to personalize history, yet it is difficult to escape the conclusion that Rudolph Giuliani has played an extremely important role in the struggle to defeat New York City's Cosa Nostra crime families. Giuliani's first major contribution to organized-crime control came when he served as associate U.S. attorney general (1981–1983). (He had previously served as an assistant U.S. attorney in New York City.)[5] According to President Reagan, Giuliani helped to convince him and other top officials in the administration that they should commit themselves to a full-scale organized-crime control effort.[6]

In 1983, Giuliani opted to return to New York City as U.S. attorney for the Southern District of New York (1983–1989). During his tenure, he compiled a record as the most active and successful organized crime prosecutor since Thomas Dewey. Giuliani's office brought many of the lawsuits that are featured in Part 2. His office indicted the Cosa Nostra commission for running a racketeering enterprise and, in one blow, brought down a number of the nation's top crime bosses.[7] That case and some associated lawsuits against Biff Halloran brought an end to the concrete cartel.[8] Giuliani's office brought four of the five so-called family RICO prosecutions against key members of all five New York City Cosa Nostra crime families. The theory of each prosecution was that the defendants, in violation of RICO, participated in the affairs of an enterprise (i.e., their crime family) through a pattern of racketeering activity (i.e., their individual and joint crimes).[9] Giuliani's office brought the civil RICO suit against the Romanos and Local 359 at the Fulton Fish Market.[10] As we have seen, it resulted in consent and default judgments and the appointment of a market administrator. Another of Giuliani's most important cases was the unprecedented civil RICO labor-racketeering suit against the General Executive Board of the Teamsters International Union.[11] The suit resulted in a trusteeship that, in various guises, has lasted ten years; made possible the first free elections in generations; and purged hundreds of corrupt national, regional, and local officials from the union.

Regulatory Strategies

Although it builds upon the experiences of the Nevada Gaming Commission, the New Jersey Gambling Commission, and the New York/New Jersey Waterfront Commission, the mobilization of local regulatory authority to attack organized crime is a New York City–specific innovation. Until recently, mayors viewed organized-crime control as the responsibility of law enforcement agencies. The Giuliani administration accepted responsibility for cleaning up racketeer-ridden industries, arguing that they impeded the city's growth and prosperity. The city's regulatory initiatives have significantly expanded the repertoire of organized-crime control strategies.

When Giuliani became mayor of New York City (1994), he immediately set out to complete the work he had started as U.S. attorney. His first organized-crime control initiative built on his previous effort to purge the mob from the Fulton Fish Market. He established a licensing scheme (the jurisdiction of which was eventually extended to all of the city's food markets), which included background checks for many market participants. The city began aggressively managing the market; it threw out the mob-connected unloading companies, signed a contract with an independent firm to provide unloading services, and appointed a market manager to provide day-to-day supervision.

The Giuliani administration's next major organized-crime control initiative sought to eliminate the Cosa Nostra–run waste-hauling cartel by means of the New York City Trade Waste Commission. Giuliani appointed a former assistant U.S. attorney to head that agency. The TWC used its authority to deny business licenses to carters with ties to organized crime. Some companies were allowed to continue participating in the industry only by agreeing to hire an IPSIG to guarantee that the company was operating lawfully and without organized crime contacts.

The Trade Waste Commission is a model that may well be followed around the country and around the world. The TWC has used its licensing authority to purge the carting industry of mob-connected firms. Quite simply, the agency denies a business license to any firm that is connected to organized crime. And it has the expertise and investigative resources to ferret out such information. Furthermore, it has used its rule-making and (maximum) price-setting authority to break down the customer property-rights system and to stimulate competition. The TWC's investigators constantly look for signs of organized crime and act swiftly if any sprouts are sighted.

In his second mayoral term, Giuliani prepared his most ambitious initiative, a regulatory attack on corruption and racketeering in the construction industry. The proposal called for a five-person commission to license the five hundred largest construction contractors in the city. Licenses would be granted on the condition that these contractor-licensees police their subcontractors. As this book goes to press, the proposal is still pending.[12]

The TWC has had great initial success, yet we must sound a note of caution. The history of government licensing agencies is a checkered one. At different points in time in various U.S. states and cities licensing authorities, like the state liquor authorities, have fallen into the hands of political cronies and have been associated with a great deal of corruption. The TWC is currently being run by organized-crime fighters of the highest personal integrity, but who is to say that later mayors will not use the commission to reward political allies and that the TWC won't someday end up being captured by the industry, or worse?

Although the strategy used at the Javits Center was less dramatic, it demonstrated that a little political will goes a long way, especially in conjunction with persistent and ongoing law enforcement efforts. Quite simply, Governor Pataki committed himself to cleaning up the center, changed its governing board and hired a new CEO, who forced the center's entire workforce to resign and apply for positions. Employees with criminal records and/or organized-crime ties were not rehired. Labor relations were revamped. Good management was instituted. Success followed.

IS THE BATTLE WON?

Admittedly, it is not possible to prove definitively that Cosa Nostra is no longer a force, or at least a substantial force, in New York City's core economy. We necessarily have to make inferences from a number of facts and rely on the assessment of observers close to the scene.

What is the evidence that Cosa Nostra's demise is at hand? First, there is the remarkable list of leaders who are in jail for lengthy or life terms. With the 1997 sentencing of Vincent "the Chin" Gigante (boss of the Genovese crime family), there is no longer a single renowned New York City Cosa Nostra leader on the streets.[13] Certainly, there is no John Gotti walking around thumbing his nose at law enforcement, publicly holding court, and collecting homage. Current Cosa Nostra members are maintaining very low profiles. The New York City Cosa Nostra "commission" reputedly has ceased to function.[14]

The mob seems to be eliminated from the Javits Center and the Fulton Fish Market and is nearly gone from the New York City and Long Island carting industries, at least that is the assessment of law enforcement personnel, city officials, and people who do business in these industries. One key indicator is the dramatic decrease in prices in the carting industry and fish market. The Javits Center is also enjoying booming business, reversing a downward trend. The air-cargo industry at JFK Airport has reported a steep decrease in the amount of cargo thefts.

In the construction industry, the cartels in concrete and drywall have completely disappeared. A great deal of progress has been made toward purging organized crime from the Teamsters union. The IBT's General Executive Board no longer contains any known mob members. The national election process is much freer.[15] Union democracy now has a chance. The efforts of the national union to remove the stain of racketeering from its locals has had impact. The Carpenters union has been substantially reformed, and labor racketeering is certainly on the wane in a number of the other previously mobbed-up unions' locals. It is premature to say that there is no organized-crime presence, but there is little doubt that that presence is far less significant than it was in the 1980s.

It takes courage or perhaps foolhardiness to pronounce the death of Cosa Nostra, a crime syndicate that has wielded enormous power in the underworld and upperworld for more than half a century. How can we be sure that new Cosa Nostra leaders will not arise and that Cosa Nostra will not find its way into new industries? The short answer is that we cannot. If law enforcement is not vigilant, if the next New York City mayoral administration turns a blind eye toward organized crime, Cosa Nostra might indeed make a comeback. Administrations come and go. Priorities change. Strong leaders emerge and disappear. It is not in the nature of our governmental system to stay focused on one set of problems and to build upon programmatic and administrative experience, even successes. However, as of this writing, there seems to be a good chance that Cosa Nostra's role as a key player in the New York City economy and power structure will not survive into the twenty-first century.

Notes

NOTES TO CHAPTER 1

1. See Kenneth T. Jackson, ed., *The Encyclopedia of the City of New York* (New Haven: Yale University Press, 1995).

2. See James B. Jacobs, Christopher Panarella, and Jay Worthington, *Busting the Mob: United States v. Cosa Nostra* (New York: New York University Press, 1994).

3. John J. DiIulio Jr. et al., "The Federal Role in Crime Control," in *Crime,* James Q. Wilson and Joan Petersilia (San Francisco: Institute for Contemporary Studies Press, 1995).

4. See Howard Abadinsky, *Organized Crime,* 4th ed. (Chicago: Nelson Hall, 1994); Alan Block, "Organized Crime: History and Historiography," in *Handbook of Organized Crime in the United States,* ed. Robert Kelly, Ko-Lin Chin, and Rufus Schatzburg (Westport, Conn: Greenwood Press, 1994).

5. *United States v. Badalamenti,* 84 Cr. 236 (S.D.N.Y. 1987), convictions aff'd. in 887 *United States v. Casamento* F.2d 1141 (2d Cir. 1989); Shana Alexander, *The Pizza Connection* (New York: Weidenfeld, 1988).

6. Peter Maas, *The Valachi Papers* (New York: G. P. Putnam's Sons, 1968); see also Henry Zeiger, *Sam the Plumber* (Bergenfield, N.J.: New American Library, 1973).

7. Philip Taft, *Corruption and Racketeering in the Labor Movement* (Ithaca: New York State School of Industrial and Labor Relations, 1970).

8. Joseph Bonanno (with Sergio Lalli), *A Man of Honor: The Autobiography of Joseph Bonanno* (New York: Simon and Schuster, 1983).

9. Francis Ianni and Elizabeth Reuss Ianni, *A Family Business: Kinship and Social Control in Organized Crime* (New York: Russell Sage, 1972).

NOTES TO THE INTRODUCTION TO PART 1

1. Alan A. Block and William Chambliss, *Organizing Crime* (New York: Elsevier, 1981), 14–15.

2. Daniel Bell, "The Racket-Ridden Longshoremen: The Web of Economics

and Politics," in *The End of Ideology,* ed. Daniel Bell (New York: Collier, 1961), 175–209.

3. Although brothers, Tony Anastasio and Albert Anastasia chose alternate spellings of their family name. See John H. Davis, *Mafia Dynasty* (New York: HarperCollins, 1993), 58.

4. Virgil W. Peterson, *The Mob: 200 Years of Organized Crime in New York* (Ottawa, Ill.: Green Hill, 1983), 290.

5. Ibid., 291–93.

6. Davis, *Mafia Dynasty,* 115.

7. Jonathan Kwitny, *Vicious Circles: The Mafia in the Marketplace* (New York: Norton, 1979).

8. See Vivian S. Toy, "Deal Expected on Street Fair in Little Italy," *New York Times,* September 10, 1995, A45.

9. *United States v. Bellomo,* 96 Cr. 430 (LAK), Indictment; *United States v. Bellomo,* superceding indictment dispositions (April 23, 1997).

10. John C. Sabetta, *Report to the Mayor Concerning the Society of San Gennaro and the 1995 San Gennaro Feast,* 9, December 1995.

11. Benjamin Weiser, "Brokers and Mob Linked to Swindle," *New York Times,* November 26, 1997, A1.

12. *United States v. Gangi et al.,* 97 Cr. 1215.

NOTES TO CHAPTER 2

1. *Barton Trucking Corp. v. O'Connell,* 173 N.Y.S.2d 464 (N.Y.Sup. 1958).

2. See Robert D. Parmet, "Garments," in *The Encyclopedia of New York,* ed. Kenneth T. Jackson (New Haven: Yale University Press, 1995), 451–53.

3. Ibid., 452. This figure is adjusted to 1995 dollars from $48.4 million, based on *Historical Statistics of the United States, Colonial Times to 1970,* series F 1–5, and *1997 Economic Report of the President* (Washington, D.C.: Government Printing Office, 1997), 481.

4. See Parmet, "Garments," 452.

5. See Franz S. Leichter, "Sweatshops to Shakedowns: Organized Crime in New York's Garment Industry" (unpublished, March 1982), pt. 3, p. 5.

6. See Parmet, "Garments," 450–453; Jenna W. Joselit, *Our Gang: Jewish Crime and the New York Jewish Community, 1900–1940* (Bloomington: Indiana University Press, 1983), 128.

7. See Joselit, *Our Gang,* 128.

8. See Thomas E. Dewey, *Twenty Against the Underworld* (Garden City, N.Y.: Doubleday, 1974), 476.

9. Ibid., 305.

10. See Arthur A. Sloane, *Hoffa* (Cambridge: MIT Press, 1991), 81.

11. See Dewey, *Twenty Against the Underworld,* 309.

12. See Parmet, "Garments," 453.

13. The cutting trade appears to have been pushed to the margins over time. Previously, cutters worked on the premises of Seventh Avenue designers, but now much cutting is done either abroad or across the Hudson River in New Jersey. See James Traub, "Behind All of That Glitz and Glitter, the Garment District Means Business," *Smithsonian,* August 1985, 36.

14. See Franz S. Leichter, "The Return of the Sweatshop: A Call for State Action," in "A Report on New York's Garment Industry" (unpublished, October 1979), pt. 1, pp. 3–5.

15. See ibid.; New Jersey State Commission of Investigation, *A Report on the New Jersey Garment Industry* (April 1991), 28. See also Tony DeStefano, Thomas Moran, and Allen Richardson, "Loanshark Jaws Take Biggest Bite," *Women's Wear Daily,* August 23, 1977, 1.

16. See Leichter, "Sweatshops to Shakedowns," pt. 3, p. 42.

17. See DeStefano, Moran, and Richardson, "Loanshark Jaws Take Biggest Bite," 1.

18. See Ralph Blumenthal, "When the Mob Delivered the Goods," *New York Times,* July 26, 1992, 23.

19. See New Jersey State Commission of Investigation, *A Report on the New Jersey Garment Industry,* 26.

20. See Moran, DeStefano, and Richardson, "Trucks to Bucks It's All for Sale," *Women's Wear Daily,* August 22, 1977, 1; Tony DeStefano, Thomas Moran, and Allen Richardson "Wheeler-Dealers' Code of the Road," *Women's Wear Daily,* August 26, 1977, 1.

21. See Leichter, "The Return of the Sweatshop" (unpublished, February 1981), pt. 2, p. 6.

22. See New Jersey State Commission of Investigation, *A Report on the New Jersey Garment Industry,* 29; Leichter, "The Return of the Sweatshop," pt. 2, p. 9.

23. See Leichter, "The Return of the Sweatshop," pt. 2, p. 14.

24. See Allen Richardson, Tony DeStefano and Thomas Moran, "Trucking Local 102: Who Sat in the Drivers Seat?" *Women's Wear Daily,* August 29, 1977, 1.

25. *United States v. DiLapi,* 651 F.2d 140, 140–143 (2d Cir. 1981).

26. See Richardson, DeStefano and Moran, "Trucking Local 102."

27. See Leichter, "The Return of the Sweatshop," pt. 2, p. 14.

28. *United States v. DiLapi,* 651 F.2d 140, at 143.

29. See Selwyn Raab, "Wiretap Evidence in Gambino Case Links Garment Group to Mob," *New York Times,* April 30, 1989, 38 (estimates five hundred member contractors; Leichter, "Sweatshops to Shakedowns," pt. 3, p. 38 (estimates seven hundred contractors).

30. See Leichter, "Sweatshops to Shakedowns," pt. 3, p. 38.

31. Joseph Nicholas Gallo is often confused with Joseph "Crazy Joe" Gallo,

who was also a member of the Gambino crime family. Joseph N. served as consigliere under Paul Castellano and John Gotti until his conviction and incarceration in 1989. See James B. Jacobs, Christopher Panarella, and Jay Worthington, *Busting the Mob: United States v. Cosa Nostra* (New York: New York University Press, 1994), 226. "Crazy Joe" was a "key figure" in the notoriously violent "Gallo Gang," which he ran with his brothers Lawrence and Albert Jr. until his assassination in 1972. See Virgil Peterson, *The Mob: 200 Years of Organized Crime in New York* (Ottawa, Ill.: Green Hill, 1983), 337; 404–5; 407–8.

32. Thomas F. Gambino was the son of former Gambino crime boss Carlo Gambino. He was also married to the daughter of former Lucchese family crime boss Thomas "Three Fingers Brown" Lucchese. See, e.g., John H. Davis, *Mafia Dynasty: The Rise and Fall of the Gambino Crime Family* (New York: Harper Collins, 1993), 90–91.

33. Ibid; see also Tony DeStefano, Thomas Moran, and Allen Richardson, "U.S. Continues Probe of Organized Crime Links to SA Firms," *Women's Wear Daily*, May 2, 1989, 1.

34. See Leichter, "Sweatshops to Shakedowns," pt. 3, pp. 39–40.

35. Ibid., 40.

36. See DeStefano, Moran, and Richardson, "U.S. Continues Probe of Organized Crime Links to SA Firms"; Leichter, "Sweatshops to Shakedowns," pt. 3, p. 38.

37. See Tony DeStefano, Thomas Moran, and Allen Richardson, "The Rule of the Mob: Keep on Truckin'," *Women's Wear Daily*, August 25, 1977, 18; and idem, "Sherwood: A Look Behind the Door," *Women's Wear Daily*, August 24, 1977, 13.

38. See Leichter, "Sweatshops to Shakedowns," pt. 3, p. 10; *People v. Gambino, Indictment No. 11859-90*, Plea Agreement: 12–13.

39. See Moran, DeStefano, and Richardson, "Trucks to Bucks It's All for Sale."

40. *People v. Gambino, Indictment No. 11859-90*, Plea Agreement: 13–14.

41. *United States v. Amuso*, 21 F.3d 1251, 1254 (2d Cir. 1994).

42. See Moran, DeStefano, and Richardson, "Trucks to Bucks It's All for Sale."

43. Leichter, "Sweatshops to Shakedowns," pt. 3, p. 13.

44. *United States v. Casso*, 843 F. Supp 829, 835 (E.D.N.Y. 1994).

45. See Davis, *Mafia Dynasty*, 290–98.

46. Ibid., 22–23.

47. See, e.g., *United States v. Socony-Vacuum Oil Co.*, 310 U.S. 150, n. 59 (1940) ("Whatever economic justification particular price-fixing agreements may be thought to have, the law does not permit an inquiry into their reasonableness. They are all banned.").

48. *United States v. Cloak and Suit Trucking Ass'n, Inc.*, Civ. No. 66-141, Oc-

tober 24, 1955, reported in *1955 Trade Cases,* Commerce Clearing House, 68, 175, at 70, 835.

49. Ibid.

50. See Moran, DeStefano, and Richardson, "Trucks to Bucks It's All for Sale," and "Wheeler-Dealers' Code of the Road."

51. See *Barton Trucking Corp. v. O'Connell,* 173 N.Y.S.2d 464, 466 (1958) (referring to Section B32-93.0 of the Administrative Code of the City of New York).

52. *Barton Trucking Corp. v. O'Connell,* 197 N.Y.S.2d 138, 141 (N.Y. Ct. of App. 1959).

53. *Barton Trucking Corp. v. O'Connell,* 180 N.Y.S.2d 686, 689 (App. Div. 1958).

54. *Barton Trucking Corp. v. O'Connell,* 10 Misc.2d at 719–20; 173 N.Y.S.2d at 467–78.

55. Ibid., at 718; 466.

56. *Barton Trucking Corp. v. O'Connell,* 180 N.Y.S.2d at 688, 691.

57. Ibid., at 691.

58. *Barton Trucking Corp. v. O'Connell,* 197 N.Y.S.2d at 144.

59. Ibid., at 148.

60. Ibid., at 149.

61. See Marcia Chambers, "8 Indicted for Graft in Garment District," *New York Times,* October 16, 1975, 1.

62. In what was termed "Project Detroit," a coat designer named Harold Whellan also agreed to serve as an informant and to use his own firm, Whellan Coat Company, to develop contacts and engage in recorded discussions with organized-crime figures. See DeStefano, Moran, and Richardson, "The Rule of the Mob." Project St. Louis reportedly consisted of a sting operation selling stolen garment-industry goods. See Martin Tolchin, "Senate Unit Asks Why Crime Inquiry Here Was Ended," *New York Times,* April 7, 1975, 1.

63. *United States v. Provenzano,* 615 F.2d 37, 40 (2d Cir. 1980).

64. See Arnold H. Lubasch, "Four Are Acquitted in Extortion Trial," *New York Times,* November 21, 1976, 36.

NOTES TO CHAPTER 3

1. Frank Wohl, *Midterm Report of Administrator* (August 8, 1990), 11, pursuant to April 15, 1988, Consent Judgment in *United States v. Local 359,* 87 Civ. 7351 (S.D.N.Y. 1992).

2. Compare, e.g., *United States v. Local 359,* 705 F. Supp. 894, 899 (S.D.N.Y. 1989), with Selwyn Raab, "Delay in Tackling Fish-Market Crime," *New York Times,* February 17, 1991, 46.

3. See Selwyn Raab, "Fish Market's Problems Revert to New York City," *New York Times,* March 27, 1994, A1.

4. Frank Wohl, *Notice of Imposition of Sanctions* (June 18, 1992), 5, pursuant to April 15, 1988, Consent Judgment in *United States v. Local 359,* 87 Civ. 7351 (S.D.N.Y. 1992).

5. The description of market operations is based on an interview with Frank Maas, first deputy commissioner, New York City Department of Investigation, October 31, 1995.

6. See Brian Carroll, "Combating Racketeering in the Fulton Fish Market," in *Organized Crime and Its Containment: A Transatlantic Initiative,* ed. Cyrille Fijnaut and James Jacobs (Boston: Kluwer, 1991), 194.

7. *United States v. Romano,* 684 F.2d 1057, 1060 (2d Cir. 1982).

8. See "The Fulton Fish Market: Hearings Before the New York City Council Committee on Economic Development" (May 4, 1992).

9. See *United States v. Local 359,* 705 F. Supp. 894, 906 (S.D.N.Y. 1989).

10. Carroll, "Combating Racketeering in the Fulton Fish Market," 183, 192.

11. See Raab, "Fish Market's Problems Revert to New York City."

12. *United States v. Romano,* 684 F.2d at 1061 (2d Cir. 1982).

13. John S. Martin, "Sentencing Memorandum" (January 4, 1981), 24, following *United States v. Romano,* 81 Cr. 514 (S.D.N.Y. 1981). In 1989, eight individuals, including a captain of the Bonanno crime family, pled guilty to racketeering in connection with a gambling and loan-sharking ring that operated at the Fulton Fish Market. See Paul Moses, "Guilty Pleas on Rackets Charges," *Newsday,* December 21, 1989, 35.

14. *Danielson v. Local 359,* 405 F. Supp. 396 (S.D.N.Y. 1975).

15. "Lanza Is Sentenced to Six Months More," *New York Times,* March 19, 1938, 10.

16. *Report of Judge Samuel Seabury to Honorable Governor Roosevelt Recommending Dismissal of Crain Charges,* reprinted in *New York Times,* September 1, 1931.

17. See Carroll, "Combating Racketeering in the Fulton Fish Market," 185.

18. The trade associations were the Fish Credit Association, Inc., Bronx and Upper Manhattan Fish Dealers Association, Inc., and Brooklyn Fish Dealers Association, Inc. See "54 in Fish Trade Indicted in Racket," *New York Times,* September 1, 1931, 14.

19. See Howard Abadinsky, "Fulton Fish Market," *Organized Crime,* 4th ed. (Chicago: Nelson-Hall, 1994), 393.

20. See Virgil Peterson, *The Mob: 200 Years of Organized Crime in New York* (Ottawa, Ill.: Green Hill, 1983), 314–15.

21. See Martin, "Sentencing Memorandum," 21.

22. *United States v. Romano,* 684 F.2d 1057 (2d Cir. 1982).

23. This and other dollar figures are based on the Consumer Price Index obtained from Bloomberg, Inc. In this case the CPI was the average of the numbers for 1976 and 1977.

24. See Martin, "Sentencing Memorandum," 12–13.

25. Other alleged coconspirators were severed before trial, and the Romanos were tried on a redacted ninety-four-count indictment. See *United States v. Romano*, 684 F.2d 1057, 1059 (2d Cir. 1982).

26. *United States v. Local 359*, 705 F. Supp. 894, 895 (S.D.N.Y. 1989).

27. Complaint, filed October 15, 1987 in *United States v. Local 359*, 87 Civ. 7351 (S.D.N.Y. 1992).

28. See Carroll, "Combating Racketeering in the Fulton Fish Market," 185.

29. See "Crain Tells of Terrorism," *New York Times*, April 9, 1931, 1.

30. See Martin, "Sentencing Memorandum," 11.

31. See "Market Men 'Glad' to Buy Protection," *New York Times*, January 16, 1934, 8.

32. *United States v. Romano*, 684 F.2d at 1060–61.

33. See James Cook, "Fish Story," *Forbes*, April 1982, 60.

34. *United States v. Romano*, 684 F.2d at 1062; see also Arnold H. Lubasch, "Organized Crime Said to Rule Fulton Fish Market," *New York Times*, August 23, 1981, p. 46.

35. See, e.g., *United States v. Nunzio Leanzo*, 80 Cr. 808 (S.D.N.Y. 1981) (sentencing owner of an unloading company to two years in prison for committing perjury before the grand jury).

36. *United States v. Romano*, 684 F.2d at 1065.

37. See Arnold H. Lubasch, "Union Heads Sentenced in Fulton Market Payoffs," *New York Times*, February 6, 1982, 27.

38. See Martin, "Sentencing Memorandum," 13.

39. *United States v. Romano*, 684 F.2d at 1062.

40. See Martin, "Sentencing Memorandum," 14.

41. See ibid.

42. *United States v. Romano*, 684 F.2d at 1061.

43. See "The Fulton Fish Market: Hearings Before the New York City Council Committee on Economic Development."

44. See Wohl, *Midterm Report of Administrator*, 7–8.

45. See Wohl, *Notice of Imposition of Sanctions*, 6.

46. See Carroll, "Combating Racketeering in the Fulton Fish Market," 193.

47. See Wohl, *Midterm Report of Administrator*, 16

48. See Sentencing Memorandum, *United States v. Local 359*, 81 Cr. 514 at 24 (S.D.N.Y. 1981).

49. Interview with Frank Maas.

50. See Cook, "Fish Story," 60.

51. See Martin, "Sentencing Memorandum," 25.

52. See Selwyn Raab, "A Crackdown on Fees at Fulton Fish Market," *New York Times*, January 11, 1987, 28.

53. See Selwyn Raab, "To Fight Mob, Giuliani Proposes Takeover of Fulton Fish Market," *New York Times,* February 1, 1995, A1.

54. *Russo v. Morgan,* 21 N.Y.S.2d 637 (1940). It was alleged that throughout the 1930s, only Joseph "Socks" Lanza could obtain these permits. See Rebecca Rankin, *New York Advancing: A Scientific Approach to Municipal Government* (New York: Gallery Press, 1936), 282.

55. See "Crain Tells of Terrorism."

56. See "Crain Denounces Accusers as Police Official Admits Racketeering City-Wide," *New York Times,* April 14, 1931, 1.

57. See Cook, "Fish Story," 60.

NOTES TO CHAPTER 4

1. Select Committee on Improper Activities in the Labor or Management Field, 85th Cong., 1st sess., 1957, 3597.

2. See Stanley Penn, "Mob Rule: How Mafia Controls Air-Cargo Businesses at Kennedy Airport," *Wall Street Journal,* May 22, 1985, 1.

3. JFK Airport opened on July 1, 1948, as Idlewild Airport; it was renamed in 1963. See Paul Barnett, "John F. Kennedy International Airport," in *The Encyclopedia of the City of New York,* ed. Kenneth Jackson (New Haven: Yale University Press, 1995), 623.

4. See Office of Economic and Policy Analysis, *Port Authority of New York and New Jersey International Air Cargo Statistics: Year End 1993* (1994), 1.

5. Interview with David Krasula, chief investigator of the New York City Teamsters Local 851, April 16, 1997.

6. Ibid.

7. Select Committee on the Impact of Crime on Small Business, 91st Cong., 2d sess. 1970, 545.

8. The *New York Times* and other newspapers have extensively documented the presence of organized crime in the urban economy.

9. See Arthur A. Sloane, *Hoffa* (Cambridge: MIT Press, 1991), 82–83, 86–87; Stephen Brill, *The Teamsters* (New York: Simon & Schuster, 1978), 204; Robert D. Leitner, *The Teamsters Union: A Study of Its Economic Impact* (New York: Bookman, 1957), 122–23.

10. See H.R. 1417, 85th Cong., 2d sess., 1958, 168–72 (1958); Ralph C. James and Estelle Dinerstein James, *Hoffa and the Teamsters: A Study of Union Power* (Princeton: D. Van Nostrand, 1965), 18–21.

11. John "Johnny Dio" Dioguardi, a longtime soldier in the Lucchese crime family, was a convicted felon who had been incarcerated twenty years earlier for extorting money from truck operators in the garment industry. See Sloane, *Hoffa,* 81. In 1956, Dioguardi achieved national notoriety when U.S. Attorney Paul Williams charged him with plotting to throw sulfuric acid in the face of

labor journalist Victor Riesel. The charges were ultimately dropped. See Virgil W. Peterson, *The Mob: 200 Years of Organized Crime in New York* (Green Hill, 1983), 310–11.

12. See Sloane, *Hoffa*, 82–83.

13. Anthony "Tony Ducks" Corallo was a high-ranking member and ultimately boss of the Lucchese crime family. In 1986, he was convicted under RICO of participating in a "commission" of Cosa Nostra bosses through a pattern of racketeering and sentenced to one hundred years in prison. See James B. Jacobs, Christopher Panarella, and Jay Worthington, *Busting the Mob: United States v. Cosa Nostra* (New York: New York University Press, 1994), 81, 86.

14. Select Committee on Improper Activities in the Labor or Management Field, 85th Cong., 2d sess., 1958, 12191, quoted in Peterson, *The Mob*, 339.

15. See James and James, *Hoffa and the Teamsters*, 21, 131.

16. See *United States v. Local 295*, 784 F. Supp. 15 (1992).

17. See Penn, "Mob Rule."

18. Nicholas Pileggi, *Wiseguy: Life in a Mafia Family* (New York: Simon and Schuster, 1985), 181.

19. Interview with Steve Carbone, supervisory special agent of the Federal Bureau of Investigation, March 7, 1997.

20. See Roy Rowan, "The 50 Biggest Cosa Nostra Bosses," *Fortune*, November 1986, 24.

21. See Pileggi, *Wiseguy*, 84, 92.

22. Ibid., 90.

23. Interview with Steve Carbone.

24. See *United States v. Werner*, 620 F.2d 922 (2d Cir. 1979).

25. See Richard Haitch, "$5 Million Holdup," *New York Times*, October 2, 1983, 49; see also Pileggi, *Wiseguy*, 179–81.

26. See Ira Breskin, "Teamsters Strike Emery Facilities in New York," *Journal of Commerce*, July 20, 1989, 4B.

27. See *Local 851 v. Thyssen Haniel Logistics, Inc.*, 1996 WL 5252-48, *6 (E.D.N.Y. September 5, 1996); Selwyn Raab, "U.S. Inquiry Finds Gangsters Hold Grip on Kennedy Cargo," *New York Times*, September 30, 1984, 1.

28. *Local 85 v. Kuehne & Nagel Air Freight, Inc.*, 1998 WL 178873, *1 (E.D.N.Y. March 6, 1998).

29. Interview with Ron DePetris.

30. Interview with David Krasula.

31. New York State Commission of Investigation, "Racketeer Activities in the New York City Freight Industry," in *New York State Commission Report on Organized Crime* (1968), 41.

32. William Ferrante, Port Authority's chief of police at JFK Airport, quoted in Roy Rowan, "How the Mafia Loots JFK Airport," *Fortune*, November 1986, 24.

33. See Joseph P. Fried, "Airport Crime Under Attack in U.S. Drive," *New York Times,* May 17, 1992, 33.

34. See Selwyn Raab, "Kennedy Airport: Mob's Candy Store," *New York Times,* August 3, 1994, B2.

35. See David Firestone, "22 Are Arrested in Thefts of Kennedy Airport Cargo," *New York Times,* August 3, 1994, A1.

36. See *United States v. NAFA,* 1974 WL 903, *1 (E.D.N.Y., August 29, 1974).

37. *United States v. Santoro,* Cr. No. 85-100(S) (E.D.N.Y. November 7, 1986); Joseph Fried, "11 Indicted In Airport Extortion Case," *New York Times,* February 22, 1985, B3.

38. *People v. Davidoff,* Cr. No. 85-100(SS) (E.D.N.Y. December 12, 1986).

39. *United States v. Davidoff,* 845 F.2d 1151 (2d Cir. 1988).

40. See, e.g., *United States v. Local 295,* 784 F. Supp. 15, 21–22 (E.D.N.Y. 1992).

41. See James Cook, "The Worms in the Big Apple," *Forbes,* September 1987, 102.

42. See Selwyn Raab, "U.S. Inquiry Finds Gangsters Hold Grip on Kennedy Cargo," *New York Times,* September 30, 1984, 1.

43. See Cook, "The Worms in the Big Apple."

44. See Fried, "Airport Crime Under Attack in U.S. Drive."

45. See, e.g., *United States v. Santoro,* 647 F. Supp. 153, 158 (1986); Raab, "U.S. Inquiry Finds Gangsters Hold Grip on Kennedy Cargo."

46. See Rowan, "How the Mafia Loots JFK Airport."

47. Interview with Edward McDonald, head of the Brooklyn Organized Crime Strike Force, in Raab, "U.S. Inquiry Finds Gangsters Hold grip on Kennedy Cargo."

48. Local 295, "The Problem of Airborne Management Harassment," *#295 News,* February 1993, 7.

49. *United States v. Local 295,* 784 F. Supp. 15, 21–22 (E.D.N.Y. 1992); see also Fried, "Airport Crime Under Attack in U.S. Drive."

50. See, e.g., Raab, "Kennedy Airport."

NOTES TO CHAPTER 5

1. IBT Independent Review Board, "Report Concerning Proposed Charges Against Local 807 Member Robert Rabbitt, Sr.," December 1993.

2. See New York State Management Division of Management Audit, *An Evaluation of Management Activities and Controls at the Jacob K. Javits Convention Center* (May 1995); Philip Lentz, "Late, Over Budget . . . and Worth It? N.Y. Convention Center Draws Flak," *Chicago Tribune,* April 13, 1986, C6.

3. Brett Pulley, "Senate to Begin Hearings on Operation of Javits Center," *New York Times,* March 16, 1995, B4.

4. See James B. Jacobs, Christopher Panarella, and Jay Worthington III, *Busting the Mob: United States v. Cosa Nostra* (New York: New York University Press, 1994).

5. Pulley, "Senate to Begin Hearings on Operation of Javits Center."

6. George James, "Court Records Say That Schiff Was Informant," *New York Times*, 10 June 1989, A30.

7. *Management and Operations of the Jacob K. Javits Center*, Investigative Hearing before the New York State Senate, March 16, 1995, statement of Governor George E. Pataki, 8–15.

8. The Urban Development Corporation (UDC) was formed as a public benefit corporation for the benefit of the people of the state, for a public purpose, and to perform an essential government function. This status exempts the corporation from all city, state, and local taxes.

9. Of the board members appointed by the legislature, two are chosen by the president of the Senate, one by the Senate minority leader, two by the Assembly speaker, and one by the Assembly minority leader.

10. *Management and Operations of the Jacob K. Javits Center*, statement of Senator Leichter, 21; Wayne Barrett, "Headless Center in Top-Led Scandal," *Village Voice*, March 28, 1995, Metro sec. 12.

11. Barrett, "Headless Center in Top-Led Scandal."

12. Brett Pulley, "Portrait of Javits Center's Chief: Autocratic, Disdainful of Rules," *New York Times*, May 6, 1995, A1.

13. The New York Auto Show, coordinated by the Greater New York Auto Association (a trade association representing five hundred franchised new-car dealers), provides an example of how the center works. See *Management and Operations of the Jacob K. Javits Convention Center*, statement of Mark Schienberg, 82–106.

14. *Management and Operations of the Jacob K. Javits Convention Center*, statement of Governor George E. Pataki, 15.

15. Ibid., statement of Mayor Rudolph Giuliani), 43–45.

16. See ibid., statement of Mark Schienberg, 86.

17. Kenneth Conboy, *Second Interim Report of the Investigations and Review Officer*, Report to Judge Haight, March 13, 1995, 18. Cafaro was the righthand man of Anthony "Fat Tony" Salerno, boss of the Genovese family until his stroke in 1981. *United States v. District Council*, 90 Civ. 5722 (CSH).

18. Conboy, *Second Interim Report of the Investigations and Review Officer*, 5.

19. Contractor requests must be presented in writing. To request a specific union member, the contractor must have employed that member within the past three months.

20. See Conboy, *Second Interim Report of the Investigations and Review Officer*, 8–24.

21. Kenneth Conboy, *First Interim Report of the Investigations and Review*

Officer, Report to Judge Haight, September 1994, 28; *United States v. District Council,* 90 Civ. 5722 (CSH), 1990.

22. Tom Robbins, "Javits List in Chin's HQ," *Daily News,* March 22, 1995, 38; see also Kenneth Crowe, "Smoking List in Javits Hearing; Names May Link Carpenters Rep to Genovese Crime Family," *Newsday,* March 22, 1995, Business sec., A34.

23. The Colombo capo was Salvatore Miciotta. See Conboy, *Second Interim Report of the Investigations and Review Officer,* 13.

24. Salvatore Miciotta tried, and failed, to get his son a job at the center. See ibid., 4.

25. Kenneth Conboy, *Third Interim Report of the Investigations and Review Officer,* Report to Judge Haight, October 31, 1995, 45; *United States v. District Council,* 90 Civ. 5722 (CSH).

26. Conboy, *Second Interim Report of the Investigations and Review Officer,* 6.

27. Damon Stetson, "Carting Trade Has History of Strong-Arm Tactics," *New York Times,* December 11, 1975, 55.

28. Jerry Capeci, "Union Boss to Hammer Mob Link," *Daily News,* March 16, 1995, News, 5. The informant was Alfonse "Little Al" D'Arco, the Lucchese family's former acting boss.

29. Conboy, *Second Interim Report of the Investigations and Review Officer,* Exhibit 5, p. 1.

30. Ibid., 4, 17.

31. See Selwyn Raab, "Former Chief of the Carpenters Union Convicted of Stealing Funds," *New York Times,* March 25, 1998, B3; Barbara Ross and Bill Hutchinson, "Jail for Ex-Carpenter Boss," *Daily News,* August 18, 1998, News sec., 11.

32. Conboy, *First Interim Report of the Investigations and Review Officer,* Exhibit 13, Letter of Frederick W, Devine, dated April 25, 1994.

33. The associate was Attilio Bittondo, who was convicted of conspiracy, and bribery of a labor official in 1990. See Conboy, *Second Interim Report of the Investigations and Review Officer,* 11.

34. See Jerry Capeci and Tom Robbins, "Javits Center a Genovese Show," *Daily News,* March 15, 1995, News sec., 24.

35. Conboy, *Second Interim Report of the Investigations and Review Officer,* 10–11.

36. *Management and Operations of the Jacob K. Javits Center,* statement of Frederick Devine, 117–18.

37. Conboy, *Second Interim Report of the Investigations and Review Officer,* Exhibit 18, p. 3.

38. Kenneth Crowe, "All in the Family," *Newsday,* June 19, 1995, C1.

39. Kenneth Conboy, *Fourth Interim Report of the Investigations and Review*

Officer, Report to Judge Haight, March 15, 1996, 5; *United States v. District Council,* 90 Civ. 5722 (CSH). Some Teamsters members indicated that they went to the Javits Center and took part in the shape before they had become union members.

40. "Trusteeship Recommendation Concerning Local 807," *IBT Independent Review Board Report* (March 1995), 26–37.

41. Ron Scherer, "A Look Under the Hood of Teamsters 807," *Christian Science Monitor,* May 24, 1996, 1.

42. *United States v. International Brotherhood of the Teamsters, et al.,* 708 F. Supp. 1288 (S.D.N.Y. 1989); see "Trusteeship Recommendation Concerning Local 807," 1. For a discussion of the IBT case, see James B. Jacobs, Christopher Panarella, and Jay Worthington, *Busting the Mob: United States v. Cosa Nostra* (New York: New York University Press, 1994), 167–210.

43. Crowe, "All in the Family."

44. See IBT Independent Review Board, *Concerning Proposed Charges Against Local 807 Member Robert Rabbitt, Sr.* (December 1993), for sworn statement of Robert Rabbitt Sr., general foreman of the Javits Center.

45. See Crowe, "All in the Family."

46. IBT Independent Review Board, *Concerning Proposed Charges Against Local 807 Member Robert Rabbitt, Sr.,* sworn statement of Rabbitt Sr., general foreman of the Javits Center, who testified that the position was created by the contractors and Local 807.

47. *People v. Rabbitt,* 506 N.Y.S.2d 983 (1986).

48. IBT Independent Review Board, *Report Concerning Charges Against Local 807 Members Michael Rabbitt, John Hohmann, James Tansey, Donald Rozas, Brian Rittenhouse, James Perrone, Antony Furino and Vincent Michaels* (May 1995); Crowe, "All in the Family."

49. *New York v. Robert Rabbitt Sr.,* Indictments 245–249/92.

50. Plea Agreement, *New York v. Robert Rabbitt Sr.,* Indictments 245–249/92, dated November 9, 1992; Crowe, "All in the Family."

51. IBT Independent Review Board, *Report Concerning Charges Against Local 807 Members Michael Rabbitt* (and others); Crowe, "All in the Family."

52. Plea Agreement, *New York v. Robert Rabbitt Sr.,* Indictments 245–249/92, dated November 9, 1992.

53. Crowe, "All in the Family."

54. IBT Independent Review Board, *Report Concerning Charges Against Local 807 Members Michael Rabbitt* (and others); Crowe, "All in the Family."

55. See Tom Robbins, "Bid to Cut Mob from Javits," *Daily News,* June 21, 1995, 8.

56. See Tom Robbins, "A Daring Undercover Cop," *Daily News,* March 15, 1995, 3.

NOTES TO CHAPTER 6

1. "Ringing in Recycling," *New York Times,* December 30, 1996, A14.

2. Peter Reuter, "The Cartage Industry in New York," in *Beyond the Law: Crime in Complex Organizations,* ed. Michael Tonry and Albert J. Reiss Jr. (Chicago: University of Chicago Press, 1993), 151–52.

3. William Bunch, "Fighting a Trashy Image," *Newsday,* April 12, 1995, A24.

4. "City Ends Monopoly in Waste Collection," *New York Times,* March 15, 1947.

5. The city ended its collection services to commercial establishments in residential areas because it decided such services represented an improper subsidy to a specific class of businesses. See Peter Reuter, *Racketeering in Legitimate Industries: A Study in the Economics of Intimidation* (Santa Monica: Rand, 1987), 8–9; James Cook, "The Garbage Game," *Forbes,* 21 October 1985, 122–23. The Trade Waste Commission, *Report on the Reduction of the Maximum Legal Rate for the Removal of Trade Waste,* March 25, 1997, 6.

6. Reuter, *Racketeering in Legitimate Industries,* 8–9.

7. Reuter, "The Cartage Industry in New York," 154. In Chicago, most waste haulers have been of Dutch origin; in Los Angeles, the firms historically have been predominately Armenian and Jewish.

8. See *United States v. Gotti,* 1997 WL 157549, *15 (E.D.N.Y., April 3, 1997); *United States v. Private Sanitation Industry Assoc. of Nassau/Suffolk, Inc.,* 995 F.2d 375,376 (2d Cir. 1993); *United States v. Casso,* 843 F. Supp. 829, 837 (E.D.N.Y. 1994).

9. Reuter, *Racketeering in Legitimate Industries,* 7.

10. "New York and Cosa Nostra: Clean Streets," *Economist,* March 12, 1994, 33.

11. Reuter, *Racketeering in Legitimate Industries,* 10.

12. Reuter, "The Cartage Industry in New York," 155–56.

13. "City Ends Monopoly in Waste Collection," 11.

14. Selwyn Raab, "He Runs Trash Hauling with Silence and Pastry," *New York Times,* February 20, 1993, 21.

15. John Rather, "U.S. Tries to Bar Crime Families from Carting," *New York Times,* June 18, 1989, 1.

16. Arnold H. Lubasch, "Undercover Concern Used in Garbage Case," *New York Times,* May 20, 1977, A26.

17. "21 Are Indicted on Long Island: Carting Plot Is Alleged," *New York Times,* September 14, 1984, B2.

18. Kevin Flynn, "Mayor to Return Funny Money," *Newsday,* January 11, 1991, 3.

19. See James B. Jacobs and Alex Hortis, "New York City as Organized Crime Fighter," *New York Law School Law Review* 42, nos. 3–4 (1998): 1069–92;

Arnold H. Lubasch, "19 Are Charged in City Racketeering Inquiry," *New York Times,* February 20, 1985, B3.

20. Detective Joseph Lentini, *In Re Warrant to Search the Greater New York Waste Paper Association,* search warrant affidavit submitted to the New York State Supreme Court (June 1995), 4–5.

21. Jonathan Rabinovitz, "Union Local Agrees to Court Monitor to Bar Any Association with Mobsters," *New York Times,* January 12, 1994, B4.

22. Ibid.

23. John McQuiston, "Families of Slain Informers Awarded $10.8 Million," *New York Times,* July 22, 1998, B7.

24. Alan A. Block and Frank R. Scarpetti, *Poisoning for Profit: Cosa Nostra and Toxic Waste in America* (New York: Morrow, 1985), 89.

25. Damon Stetson, "Carting Trade Has a History of Strong-Arm Tactics," *New York Times,* December 11, 1975, 55.

26. Allan Meyerson, "The Garbage Wars: Cracking the Cartel," *New York Times,* July 30, 1995, C1; Greg Goeller, "BFI Intent on Staying in NYC: Garbage Company Facing Heat from Organized Crime," *Houston Post,* March 18, 1995, C1.

27. Raab, "He Runs Trash Hauling with Silence and Pastry," 21.

28. Senate Select Committee on Improper Activities in the Labor or Management Field, *Report No. 1417,* 85th Cong., 2d sess. (Washington, D.C.: Government Printing Office, 1958), 328.

29. Ibid.

30. Ibid., 310; see also Reuter, "The Cartage Industry in New York," 157.

31. Tom Renner and Michael Slackman, "They Defied Cosa Nostra," *Newsday,* September 24, 1989, 5.

32. *United States v. IBT,* 998 F.2d 120, 122 (2d Cir. 1993).

33. Ibid.

34. Block and Scarpetti, *Poisoning for Profit,* 73.

35. Ibid., 74.

36. *People v. Adelstein,* 8 N.Y.2d 998 (N.Y. App. Div. 1960).

37. Ibid.; see also Reuter, "The Cartage Industry in New York," 157.

38. Ibid., 186–87.

39. Ibid.

40. Ibid., 159.

41. Nicholas Gage, "Carting in Brooklyn Is Linked to Crime," *New York Times,* March 19, 1974, 1.

42. See Jacobs and Hortis, "New York City as Organized Crime Fighter," 5; I. Jeanne Dugan, "The Auditor of Your Dumpster," *Business Week,* May 13, 1996, 14; see also Roy Rowan, "The 50 Biggest Media Bosses," *Fortune,* November 10, 1986, 24.

43. Dugan, "The Auditor of Your Dumpster."

44. Selwyn Raab, "To Prosecutors, Breakthrough After 5 Years of Scrutiny," *New York Times,* June 23, 1995, B3.

45. "N.Y.C. Bill Seeks to Curtail Mob Influence in Commercial Hauling," *Integrated Waste Management,* April 26, 1995, 5.

46. John T. McQuiston, "Break-Up of Carters Sought," *New York Times,* 27 January 1985, 8.

47. Gage, "Carting in Brooklyn is Linked to Crime."

48. Reuter, "The Cartage Industry in New York," 180; Frank J. Prial, "55 Carters Are Charged with Brooklyn Monopoly," *New York Times,* March 29, 1974, 1.

49. Reuter, "The Cartage Industry in New York," 164; Damon Stetson, "Carting Trade Has History of Strong-Arm Tactics."

50. "State Seeks to Curb Brooklyn Carter," *New York Times,* November 21, 1974, 38; Stetson, "Carting Trade Has History of Strong-Arm Tactics."

51. Peter Reuter, "The Cartage Industry in New York," in *Crime and Justice: An Annual Review of Research,* ed. Michael Tonry 18 (1994): 149–201.

52. David Bird, "City May Take Indicted Carters' Routes," *New York Times,* July 22, 1974, A1.

53. Ibid.

54. Ibid.

55. See *People v. Vespucci,* 553 N.E.2d 965, 966 (N.Y. 1990); "21 Are Indicted on Long Island."

56. "21 Are Indicted on Long Island."

57. *People v. Vespucci,* 553 N.E.2d, at 966–67.

58. "21 are Indicted on Long Island."

59. *People v. Private Sanitation Indus. of Nassau/Suffolk, Inc.,* 136 Misc. 2d 612, 613 (Suffolk County Ct. 1987).

60. *People v. Sail Carting & Recycling Co., Inc.,* 158 A.D. 2d 724, 724 (N.Y. App. Div. 1990).

61. "9 Garbage Haulers Face Jail or Work," *New York Times,* January 13, 1987, B5; Don Smith, "Judge Fines Carting Firms $1.01 M," *Newsday,* January 26, 1988, 25.

62. *State v. Salem Sanitary Carting Corp.,* 1989 WL 111597 (E.D.N.Y. Aug. 9, 1989), at 1: John T. McQuiston, "Breakup of Carters Sought," *New York Times,* January 27, 1985, 8.

63. 15 U.S.C. 12–27.

64. *State v. Salem Sanitary Carting Corp.,* 1989 WL 111597, at 1.

65. McQuiston, "Breakup of Carters Sought."

66. See *Jerry Kubecka, Inc. v. Avellino,* 898 F. Supp. 963, 966 (E.D.N.Y. 1995). The Kubecka and Barstow families brought a civil-racketeering and wrongful-death suit against Avellino, Lucchese crime family member Anthony Casso, and two carting companies that Avellino owned. The families next brought suit

against the state of New York, alleging that the New York State Organized Crime Task Force, with which Kubecka and Barstow had been cooperating, failed to protect the two men from being murdered. See *Kubecka v. State,* 1996 WL 766553, *1 (N.Y.Ct.Cl. December 20, 1996). The New York Court of Claims ruled for the plaintiffs, finding that the OCTF failed in its duty to provide reasonable protection to the decedents. In June 1998, New York State was ordered to pay $10.8 million to the families of Kubecka and Barstow. John T. McQuiston, "Families of Slain Informers Awarded $10.8 Million," *New York Times,* July 22, 1998, B7.

NOTES TO CHAPTER 7

1. New York State Organized Crime Task Force, *Corruption and Racketeering in the New York City Construction Industry* (hereinafter OCTF Final Report) (New York: New York University Press, 1990), 83.
2. See ibid., 16–17.
3. Ibid., 225–26.
4. See OCTF Final Report.
5. Joseph Trerotola, in his eighties at the time, died later that year. Jerry Seper, "Organized Labor Fights Family Ties," *Insight on the News,* November 21, 1994, 6.
6. See OCTF Final Report, 81.
7. See *United States v. Cody,* 722 F.2d 1052 (2d Cir. 1983), cert. denied, 467 U.S. 1226 (1984).
8. See *United States v. Sasso,* Cr. 92-1344 (IBT Local 282 F.O.R.E. Collection, Tamiment Library, Robert F. Wagner Labor Archives, New York University); Robert Kessler, "Union Boss Sentenced," *Newsday,* September 10, 1994, A13.
9. See *United States v. Petito,* 671 F.2d 68 (2d Cir.), cert. denied, 459 U.S. 824 (1982); *United States v. Sanzo,* 673 F.2d 64 (2d Cir.), cert. denied, 459 U.S 858 (1982).
10. See OCTF Final Report, 21, 81 (citing *United States v. Sherman,* 84 Cr. 205 (S.D.N.Y. 1984)).
11. Ralph Scopo died in prison in March 1993. See *United States v. LIUNA,* draft complaint at 15(1).
12. In March 1987, pursuant to a civil RICO suit brought by the U.S. attorney for the Southern District of New York, Local 6A of the District Council of Cement and Concrete Workers agreed to replace many of its leaders and accept supervision by a court-appointed trustee. *United States v. Local 6A, Cement and Concrete Workers,* 86 Civ. 4819 (S.D.N.Y. 1986).
13. See ibid.; *United States v. Local 6A, Cement and Concrete Workers,* 832 F. Supp. 674 (1993) (noting that monitorship was to end 1990 but was extended to 1992); see also OCTF Final Report, 79.

14. In September 1989, LaBarbara and Abbatiello pled guilty to multiple counts of accepting payoffs totaling $18,000 from seven Long Island contractors. Abatiello also pleaded guilty to obstructing justice by instructing a witness to lie to the grand jury. Vario resigned from the union in December 1988. In March 1990, he was convicted on thirty-eight federal counts. See *United States v. Vario,* 88 Cr. 719 (E.D.N.Y. 1988).

15. See *United States v. Gallo,* 671 F. Supp. 124 (E.D.N.Y. 1987); *United States v. Daly,* 842 F.2d 1380 (2d Cir. 1988); Kevin Flynn and Michael Weber, "Blast Firms' Tangled Mob Ties," *Newsday,* April 9, 1983, News sec., 3.

16. *People v. Pagano,* Indictment No. 120/89 (Rockland County 1989). In this case, Daniel and his son Joseph pleaded guilty to loan-sharking and gambling charges.

17. See *United States v. LIUNA,* Draft Complaint at 13(z).

18. *United States v. Cervone,* 907 F.2d 332 (2d. Cir. 1990).

19. See *United States v. Mason Tenders District Council of Greater New York,* 94 Civ. 6487 (RWS), 1997 WL 97836 at *1 (S.D.N.Y. March 16, 1997).

20. See *United States v. Mason Tenders District Council of Greater New York,* 94 Civ. 6487 (RWS), 1995 WL 679245 (S.D.N.Y. November 15, 1995); Richard Bernstein, "Papers Diagram Mob's Grip on a Union," *New York Times,* November 2, 1994, B1.

21. See *United States v. Mason Tenders District Council of Greater New York,* 1997 WL 97836 at *1.

22. See *United States v. District Council,* 90 Civ. 5722 (CSH), Government's Memorandum in Support of Its Motion for Preliminary Relief (hereinafter Government's Memorandum), 1–15; Selwyn Raab, "Former Chief of Carpenters' Union Convicted of Stealing Funds," *New York Times,* March 25, 1998, B3.

23. As a reaction to the federal investigation of Maritas, the international union imposed a trusteeship over the District Council from 1981 to 1984. See *United States v. McGuinness,* 764 F. Supp. 888, 891 (S.D.N.Y. 1991); Jerry Gray, "Union Leader Wins Acquittal in a Bribe Case," *New York Times,* July 25, 1991, B1.

24. Kenneth Conboy, *Fifth Interim Report of the Investigations and Review Officer,* Report to Judge Haight, September 30, 1996; *United States v. District Council,* 90 Civ. 5722 (CSH); Raab, "Former Carpenters' Union Chief Convicted of Stealing Funds." Devine was later sentenced to a fifteen-month prison term. Barbara Ross and Bill Hutchinson, "Jail for Ex-Carpenter Boss," *Daily News,* August 18,1998, News sec., 11.

25. OCTF Final Report, 50–51.

26. Interview with James McNamara, former director of the Mayor's Office of Construction Industry Relations, former consultant to the Manhattan District Attorney's Office and to the OCTF, on September 8, 1998.

27. See Selwyn Raab, "New York Officials of Plumbing Union Charged in Bribery," *New York Times*, October 15, 1993, A1; *People v. Moscatiello*, 566 N.Y.S.2d 823.

28. See *United States v. Daly*, 842 F.2d 1380 (2d Cir. 1988); *United States v. Gallo*, 671 F. Supp. 124 (E.D.N.Y. 1987), Cr. 86-452(S); Selwyn Raab, "Court Aide and 15 Others Indicted in Move Against Gambino Group," *New York Times*, June 21, 1986, A1.

29. See *People v. Salzarulo*, 639 N.Y.S.2d 885 (1996).

30. See Manhattan District Attorney, news release, April 22, 1996 (James McNamara collection, Tamiment Library, Robert F. Wagner Labor Archives, New York University); Selwyn Raab, "Ex-Plumbers' Union Officials Guilty in Extortion," *New York Times*, April 23, 1996, B4. Paul Martello was later acquitted. Interview with James McNamara on September 8, 1998.

31. See *People v. Capaldo*, 572 N.Y.S.2d 989 (1991).

32. See Selwyn Raab, "Painters Union Officials Admit Links to Mob," *New York Times*, March 10, 1991, A31.

33. Association for Union Democracy, "Jimmy Bishop Murdered in Painters District Council 9," *Union Democracy Review*, No. 77 (August 1990): 4.

34. See *United States v. McGowan*, 58 F.3d 8 (2d Cir. 1995).

35. See *United States v. Gigante*, 39 F.3d 42 (2d Cir. 1994); *United States v. McGowan*; *United States v. Mangano*, 90 Cr. 0446 (E.D.N.Y.).

36. OCTF Final Report, 31–51.

37. OCTF Final Report, 64, 93–94 (citing President's Commission on Organized Crime, *Organized Crime and Labor-Management Racketeering in the United States, Record of Hearing VI, Chicago, Illinois* (Washington, D.C.: Government Printing Office, April 1985)).

38. OCTF Final Report, 28.

39. Rich Blake, "NY Carpenter's Reportedly Reviewing Mandates Totaling $1.3 Billion," *Money Management Letter*, May 5, 1997, 9, 1.

40. See Tom Robbins, "Carpenters' Ex-Prez Hit in Fund Theft," *Newsday*, October 25, 1996, News sec., 2.

41. See *United States v. District Council*, 90 Civ. 5722 (CSH), Declaration of Jesse Hyman, at 9.

42. See OCTF Final Report, 23.

43. Ibid., 84–85.

44. Hearings on Organized Crime and the Laborer's International Union of North America, before the Subcommittee on Crime, of the House Judiciary Committee, 104th Congress, 2d session, July 24, 1996, at 47 (testimony of James E. Moody, former Deputy Assistant Director, Criminal Investigations Division, FBI).

45. Michael Oreskes, "Corruption Is Called a Way of Life in New York Construction Industry," *New York Times*, April 25, 1982, A1.

46. *United States v. Salerno,* 86 Cr. 245 (S.D.N.Y. 1986); *United States v. Salerno,* 85 Cr. 139 (S.D.N.Y. 1985).

47. M. A. Farber, "Concrete Contractors Tell of Payoffs to a Union Leader for Labor Peace," *New York Times,* December 18, 1985, B1; M. A. Farber, "Colombo Jury Hears Tapes of '83 Conversations about Payments," *New York Times,* April 21, 1985, A31; Ronald Smothers, "Jury Is Told Crime Families Control Concrete Business," *New York Times,* January 15, 1986, B3.

48. Roy Rowan, "The Mafia's Bite of the Big Apple," *Fortune,* June 6, 1988, 128.

49. Selwyn Raab, "Key Teamster Leader Is Convicted of Labor Racketeering by Long Island Jury," *New York Times,* October 9, 1982, A1.

50. See *United States v. Halloran,* 86 Cr. 245, 1989 WL 2691 (S.D.N.Y. 1989).

51. Rowan, "The Mafia's Bite of the Big Apple," 128.

52. See OCTF Final Report, 87; *United States v. Salerno,* 937 F.2d 797 (2d Cir. 1991), rev'd., 505 U.S. 317 (1992); *United States v. Salerno,* 974 F.2d 231 (2d Cir. 1992), rev'd. in part sub nom., *United States v. DiNapoli,* 8 F.3d 909 (2d Cir. 1993) (en banc); *United States v. Migliore,* 104 F.3d 354 (2d Cir. 1996) (noting that all five remaining defendants pled guilty by 1995).

53. See Selwyn Raab, "Trouble for New York's Concrete Venture," *New York Times,* May 30, 1993, A29; Selwyn Raab, "Irregularities in Concrete Industry Inflate Building Costs, Experts Say," *New York Times,* April 26, 1982, A1.

54. See *United States v. Vario,* 88 Cr. 719 (E.D.N.Y. 1988).

55. For a detailed description of this conspiracy, see Robert W. Greene, "The LI Concrete Trial," *Newsday,* March 11, 1990, Long Island ed., 3; Tom Morris, "LI Prices among Highest," *Newsday,* March 11, 1990, Long Island ed., 3; Steve Wick, "How a Small Firm Became the Island's Largest Supplier," *Newsday,* March 11, 1990, Long Island ed., 27.

56. See Government's Memorandum, 12.

57. See Selwyn Raab, "Investigators Charge Contractors Formed 'Club' for Tax Fraud," *New York Times,* July 6, 1983, A1.

58. Interview with James McNamara on September 8, 1998; Memorandum regarding conversations with Michael Gedell (Jim McNamara Collection, Tamiment Library, Robert F. Wagner Labor Archives, New York University Library).

59. See Government's Memorandum, 1–15.

60. See OCTF Final Report, 84; *United States v. District Council,* 90 Civ. 5722 (CSH), Svedese Affidavit, 7.

61. Government's Memorandum, 12; *United States v. District Council,* 90 Civ. 5722 (CSH), Declaration of Salvatore Gravano at 3; 90 Civ. 5722 (CSH), Affidavit of Marcello Svedese, 4–6.

62. See OCTF Final Report, 50–51.

63. See Rowan, "The Mafia's Bite of the Big Apple"; Government's Memorandum, 12; OCTF Final Report, 85.

64. See *United States v. Maritas,* 81 Cr. 122 (E.D.N.Y. 1981); see also Selwyn Raab, "Contractor on U.S.-Backed Projects in Bronx Is Tied to Organized Crime," *New York Times,* March 1, 1981, A1.

65. Government's Memorandum, 15; *United States v. District Council,* 90 Civ 5722 (CSH), Declaration of Vincent Cafaro, 6.

66. See OCTF Final Report, 84.

67. See Government's Memorandum, 16–17.

68. See *United States v. McGuinness,* 764 F. Supp. 888, 891 (S.D.N.Y. 1991); Gray, "Union Leader Wins Acquittal in a Bribe Case."

69. Conboy, *Fifth Interim Report of the Investigations and Review Officer,* 21–24; Selwyn Raab, "Former Carpenters' Union Chief Convicted of Stealing Funds," *New York Times,* March 25, 1998, B3.

70. See *United States v. Gigante,* 39 F.3d 42 (2d Cir. 1994).

71. See Pete Bowles, "'Window' Trial Gets Rackets Buildup," *Newsday,* April 24, 1991, News sec., 21.

72. See *United States v. Gigante,* 39 F.3d at 44.

73. See *United States v. McGowan,* 854 F. Supp. 176, 182 (E.D.N.Y. 1994), aff'd. 58 F.3d 8 (2d. Cir. 1995). Thomas McGowan, acquitted in the "windows" case, was convicted of related conspiracies in 1994. See *United States v. McGowan,* 58 F.3d 8, 11 (2d Cir. 1995). Belief that John Morrissey might testify for the government led to his murder in 1989 (before the trial began) by another defendant in the "windows" case. Peter Chiodo, who later become a government witness, admitted responsibility. See *United States v. Gigante,* 39 F.3d at 46 (referring to Chiodo's testimony in *United States v. Fatico,* 579 F.2d 707 (2d Cir. 1978)).

74. See *United States v. Fatico,* 579 F.2d 707 (2d Cir. 1978); *United States v. Gigante,* 39 F.3d at 45.

75. Arnold H. Lubasch, "US Says Mob Gained Grip on Window Trade," *New York Times,* April 24, 1991, B3 (quoting prosecutor's opening statement).

76. See *United States v. Gigante,* 39 F.3d at 45.

77. See ibid.

78. See Pete Bowles, "Mobster: I Bribed City Housing Chief," *Newsday,* May 8, 1991, News sec., 33.

79. *Newsday* reported that unions assigned "drunks and derelicts" to competitors. See ibid.

80. Ibid. (quoting testimony of Savino).

81. See Pete Bowles, "Window Opened on Alleged Mob Scam," *Newsday,* May 7, 1991, News sec., 23.

82. See *United States. v. Gigante,* 39 F.3d at 45.

83. Selwyn Raab, "12 Indicted as Mob Rulers of Painting," *New York Times,* June 22, 1990, B1; *People v. Capaldo,* 572 N.Y.S.2d 989 (1991) (holding that OCCA was not unconstitutionally vague); U.S. Dept. of Labor, press release, June 26,

1990 (Jim McNamara Painters Collection, Tamiment Library, Robert F. Wagner Labor Archives, New York University).

84. Raab, "12 Indicted as Mob Rulers of Painting."

85. See Association for Union Democracy, "Jimmy Bishop Murdered in Painters District Council 9."

86. See Raab, "Painters Union Officials Admit Links to Mob," A31.

87. Robert E. Tomasson, "Documents Describe Corruption in Painters' Union," *New York Times*, April 21, 1991, A1.

88. "Painters Union Double-Dipped in Green Deals," *Engineering News-Record* (231, no. 15) (October 11, 1993): 18; Arnold H. Lubasch, "13 Indicted in U.S. Drive Against Mob," *New York Times*, November 1, 1992, A64.

89. Raab, "Ex-Plumbers' Union Officials Guilty in Extortion."

90. Selwyn Raab, "Top Plumbing Company Cited in Tax Evasion Case," *New York Times*, April 14, 1994, B3; Raab, "New York Officials of Plumbing Union Charged in Bribery," A1.

91. *Morgenthau v. Salzarulo*, Affirmation in Support of Plaintiff's Application for a Temporary Restraining Order and Motion for a Preliminary Injunction and Appointment of a Temporary Receiver (Jim McNamara Collection, Tamiment Library, Robert F. Wagner Labor Archives, New York University); Raab, "New York Officials of Plumbing Union Charged in Bribery." Louis Moscatiello Jr. was later acquitted.

92. *Morgenthau v. Salzarulo*, Affirmation in Support of Plaintiff's Application for a Temporary Restraining Order and Motion for a Preliminary Injunction and Appointment of a Temporary Receiver (Jim McNamara Collection, Tamiment Library, Robert F. Wagner Labor Archives, New York University).

93. *Trustees of Plumbers and Pipefitters National Pension Fund, v. Transworld Mechanical, Inc.*, 886 F. Supp. 1134, 1138 (S.D.N.Y. 1995).

94. Interview with Perry Carbone, former assistant district attorney in Manhattan.

NOTES TO CHAPTER 8

1. See John Landesco, *Organized Crime in Chicago* (Chicago: University of Chicago Press, 1968; originally published in 1929).

2. Cf. Peter Maas, *Underboss: Sammy "The Bull" Gravano's Story of Life in the Mafia* (New York: HarperCollins, 1997), 43, 65–66.

3. There is some dispute as to whether a national "commission," ostensibly made up of the most powerful representatives of the major Italian crime families, ever existed. Compare Maas, *Underboss*, 33–34, with James B. Jacobs, Christopher Panarella, and Jay Worthington, *Busting the Mob: United States v. Cosa Nostra* (New York: New York University Press, 1994), 79–91.

4. Other reports hold that by the early 1980s, the Bonanno family had dropped out of the "commission" because of internal warfare. The leaders of the Bonanno family were indicted in a separate RICO prosecution for conducting a criminal enterprise (the crime family) through a pattern of racketeering activity (supplied by information gathered from Operation GENUS). See Jacobs, Panarella, and Worthington, *Busting the Mob*, 81.

5. See Peter Reuter, *Racketeering in Legitimate Industries: A Study in the Economics of Intimidation* (Santa Monica: Rand 1987).

6. Peter Reuter, "Regulating Rackets," *American Enterprise Institute Journal on Government and Society*, September/December 1984, 34.

7. Maas, *Underboss*, 61–63, 105, 135–36, 167.

8. Ibid., 232–33, 277.

9. Ibid., 283.

10. Many newly made Cosa Nostra members married into the family, or had blood ties to the mob. See generally, ibid.

11. John H. Davis, *Mafia Dynasty: The Rise and Fall of the Gambino Crime Family* (New York: HarperCollins, 1993), 114.

12. There is no definitive study of the history of organized-crime's involvement in the American labor movement. But see Philip Taft, *Corruption and Racketeering in the Labor Movement*, 2d ed. (Ithaca: New York State School of Industrial and Labor Relations Press, 1970); John Hutchinson, *The Imperfect Union* (New York: Dutton, 1970; Stephen Fox, *Blood and Power: Organized Crime in the Twentieth Century* (New York: Morrow, 1989).

13. Notably, union reformer Frank Schonfeld won control of Painters District Council 9 in 1967, but without government assistance in rooting out corruption, his six-year term failed to liberate the union from organized-crime's influence. See Association for Union Democracy, "Painters, Roofers, Fish Market," *Union Democracy Review* 90 (October 1992): 6.

14. Jacobs, Panarella, and Worthington, *Busting the Mob.*

15. Maas, *Underboss*, 279.

16. Perhaps rank-and-file indifference to the possibility of reform can be explained by the fact that union democracy is not important to most union members. See James Coleman, Seymour Martin Lipset, and Martin A. Trow, *Union Democracy, The Internal Politics of the International Typographical Union* (Glenco, Ill.: Free Press, 1956).

17. Landesco, *Organized Crime in Chicago*, 152.

18. Robert W. Snyder, "Organized Crime," in *Encyclopedia of New York City*, ed. Kenneth Jackson (New Haven: Yale University Press, 1995), 866–68.

19. *United States v. Corallo*, 413 F2d 1306 (2d Cir. 1969).

20. See ibid., 1312.

21. See ibid., 1315; 1319.

22. See ibid., 1318.

23. See ibid., 1306–7.

24. See George Walsh, *Public Enemies: The Mayor, the Mob and the Crime That Was* (New York: Norton, 1980).

25. Earlier in the twentieth century, other ethnic organized-crime groups did engage in industrial racketeering. For example, notorious Jewish ganglord Lepke Buchalter, aided by his violent sidekick Gurrah Shapiro, ran rackets in the garment industry in the 1930s, until the state convicted and executed him for murder. See chapter 2; Jonathan Kwitny, *Vicious Circles: The Mafia in the Marketplace* (New York: Norton, 1979) 65, 236, 267.

NOTES TO THE INTRODUCTION TO PART 2

1. Thomas E. Dewey, *Twenty Against the Underworld* (Garden City, N.Y.: Doubleday, 1974), 475–76 (Lepke conviction) and 262–70 (Luciano case)

2. John Kobler, *Capone: The Life and World of Al Capone,* (New York: De Capo, 1992), 270–82.

3. See chapter 2.

4. See chapter 3.

5. Gary W. Potter, *Criminal Organizations: Vice, Racketeering and Politics in an American City* (Prospect Heights, Ill.: Waveland Press, 1994), 182–84.

6. U.S. Senate Special Committee to Investigate Organized Crime in Interstate Commerce (Kefauver Committee), *Final Report,* 82d Cong., 1st sess., 1951, S. Rept. 725.

7. *U.S. Senate Select Committee on Improper Activities in the Labor or Management Field* (McClellan Committee), *Final Report,* 86th Cong., 2d sess. 1960, S. Rept. 1139.

8. Anthony Summers, *Official and Confidential: The Secret Life of J. Edgar Hoover* (New York: G. P. Putnam's Sons, 1993), 237–59. See also Arthur M. Schlesinger Jr., *Robert Kennedy and His Times* (Boston: Houghton, Mifflin, 1978), 264–66.

9. Schlesinger Jr., *Robert Kennedy and His Times,* 266–72.

10. U.S. Task Force on Organized Crime, *Task Force Report: Organized Crime, Annotations, and Consultants' Papers,* (Washington D.C.: Government Printing Office, 1967).

11. James B. Jacobs, Christopher Panarella, and Jay Worthington, *Busting the Mob: United States v. Cosa Nostra* (New York: New York University Press, 1994), 14.

12. Attorney General Order No. 136-89, December 26, 1989 ("Order Directing Realignment of Organized Crime Program Resources").

13. Part of Title III of the Omnibus Crime Control and Safe Streets Act of 1968. 18 U.S.C. 2510-20 (1982)

14. 18 U.S.C. 1961.

15. 18 U.S.C. 1961 (d).

16. 18 U.S.C. 1963 (a).

17. *United States v. Salerno,* 85 Cr. 139 (S.D.N.Y. 1985).

18. See Bonanno family: *United States v. The Bonanno Organized Crime Family,* 87 Civ. 2974 (E.D.N.Y. 1987); Colombo family: *United States v. Persico,* 832 F.2d 705 (2d Cir. 1987), *United States v. Colombo,* 616 F. Supp. 780 (E.D.N.Y. 1985); Gambino family: *United States v. Gotti,* 641 F. Supp. 283 (S.D.N.Y. 1986); Genovese family: *United States v. Salerno,* 868 F.2d 524 (2d Cir. 1989).

19. 18 U.S.C. 1964 (c).

20. 18 U.S.C. 1964 (a).

21. The Witness Security Program was created by the Organized Crime Control Act of 1970. Public Law 91–452, *United States Statutes at Large* 84, secs. 922, 922–23 (1970).

22. Personal interview, Robert Stewart, July 28, 1998.

23. Personal interview, James Kossler, July 9, 1998.

24. Jacobs, Panarella, and Worthington, *Busting the Mob,* 80–81.

25. Peter Maas, *The Valachi Papers* (New York: Putnam, 1968).

26. Jacobs, Panarella, and Worthington, *Busting the Mob,* 13–14.

NOTES TO CHAPTER 9

1. Arthur Friedman, "Gambino Trial: SA to Take Witness Stand," *Women's Wear Daily,* February 5,1992, 1.

2. See, for example, *United States v. Cloak and Suit Trucking Ass'n, "Undercover Cop Tells of Trucker's Threats,"* *Women's Wear Daily,* February 7, 1992, 13.

8. Manhattan district attorney Robert Morgenthau announced that the prosecutions reflected a comprehensive, industry-wide approach and a break with past law enforcement efforts. "This time we are focusing on the major entrenched players. And we are doing our level best to get rid of these illicit activities." Selwyn Raab, "Police Say Their Chinatown Sting Ties Mob to the Garment Industry," *New York Times,* March 20, 1990, A1.

9. Thomas Ciampi, "Gambino Trucking Trial Hears How SA Apportioned," *Women's Wear Daily,* February 11, 1992, 28.

10. Friedman, "Gambino Trial."

11. Friedman and Struensee, "Undercover Cop Tells of Trucker's Threats."

12. Ibid.; Raab, "Police Say Their Chinatown Sting Ties Mob to the Garment Industry."

13. Friedman and Struensee, "Undercover Cop Tells of Trucker's Threats."

14. Selwyn Raab, "7 Held in Extortion of Mob Clothiers," *New York Times,* October 19, 1990, B3.

15. Raab, "Police Say Their Chinatown Sting Ties Mob to the Garment Industry," 13.

16. John DiSalvo, Raymond Buccafusco, Clothing Carriers Corp., Consolidated Carriers Corp., Greenberg's Express, Inc., and GRG Delivery Corp. were also named in the indictment. *People v. Gambino,* Indictment No. 11859-90.

17. Ibid.

18. The second indictment named David Stuart, Mark Stuart, Michael Voulo, AAA Garment Delivery, Inc., J. R. Garment Delivery, Inc., IMC Carriers, Ltd., FM & J Delivery Service, Inc., Lucky Apparel Carriers, Inc., Lucky Garment Transportation Co., Inc. *People v. David Stuart,* Indictment No. 11858-90.

19. Raab, "7 Held in Mob Extortion of Clothiers."

20. *People v. Gambino,* in *New York Law Journal,* May 1, 1991, 23.

21. Ibid.; Cerisse Anderson, "OCCA Counts Stand in Trucking Case," *New York Law Journal,* April 30, 1991, 1.

22. Ronald Sullivan, "Gambino Gained 'Mob Tax' with Fear, Prosecutor Says," *New York Times,* February 5, 1992, B3.

23. Ronald Sullivan, "Gambino Trial: Trucks and 'Guys in Trenchcoats,'" *New York Times,* February 6, 1992, B2.

24. Friedman and Struensee, "Undercover Cop Tells of Truckers' Threats."

25. Chuck Struensee, "Ex-Gambino Rep Testifies He Didn't Threaten Firms," *Women's Wear Daily,* February 20, 1992, 9.

26. Ralph Blumenthal, "When the Mob Delivered the Goods," *New York Times Magazine,* July 26, 1992, 23.

27. Ronald Sullivan, "2 Gambinos Go on Trial, Very Quietly," *New York Times,* February 23, 1992, A1.

28. Specifically, the Gambinos pled guilty to violating New York's General Business Law 340, 341, as did John DiSalvo, Clothing Carriers Corp., Consolidated Carriers Corp., Greenberg's Express, Inc., and GRG Delivery Corp. Jonathan M. Moses and Milo Geyelin, "Legal Beat," *Wall Street Journal,* February 27, 1992, B8.

29. Michael Vuolo, AAA Garment Delivery, Inc., J. R. Garment Delivery, Inc., IMC Carriers, Ltd., FM & J Delivery Service, Inc., Lucky Apparel Carriers, Inc., and Lucky Garment Transportation Co., Inc. pled guilty to violating the same state business laws as the Gambinos. Both David Stuart and Raymond Buccafusco pled guilty to violating New York State Penal Law sec. 100.05 (criminal solicitation). The charges against Mark Stuart were dropped. *People v. Gambino,* Indictments 11859-90 and 11858-90, Plea Agreement, 2–3 (1992).

30. DiSalvo and Buccafusco also were forced out of the garment industry. *People v. Gambino,* Indictments 11859-90 and 11858-90, Plea Agreement, 4 (1992). Voulo and David Stuart, along with the other companies mentioned in the second indictment, agreed to cease anticompetitive practices. *People v. Gambino,* Indictments 11859-90 and 11858-90, Plea Agreement, 3 (1992).

31. *People v. Gambino,* Indictments 11859-90 and 11858-90, Plea Agreement, 4 (1992).

32. Gay Jervey, "Waltzing with the Wise Guys," *American Lawyer,* May 1992, 86.

33. *People v. Gambino,* Indictments 11859-90 and 11858-90, Plea Agreement, 6 (1992).

34. Ibid., 5.

35. Arthur Friedman, "Robert McGuire Says He Aims to Nurture Competitive Trucking on SA; Court-Appointed Special Master Over Garment Industry Trucking," *Women's Wear Daily,* March 29, 1993, 8.

36. Arthur Friedman, "McGuire: SA Trucking on a Level Playing Field," *Women's Wear Daily,* November 29, 1993, 3.

37. "Gambinos Get Extension on Sale of Truck Companies," *Women's Wear Daily,* March 17, 1993, 16.

38. Friedman, "McGuire: SA Trucking on a Level Playing Field."

39. "Gambinos Get Extension on Sale of Truck Companies."

40. Arthur Friedman, "McGuire: The Trucks Are Rolling," *Women's Wear Daily,* March 7, 1995, 8.

41. "Gambinos Get Extension on Sale of Truck Companies."

42. Friedman, "Robert McGuire Says He Aims to Nurture Openly Competitive Trucking on SA."

43. Chuck Struensee, "Court Approves New SA Trucking Rules," *Women's Wear Daily,* April 6, 1993, 14.

44. Robert J. McGuire, *Report of the Special Master,* April 7, 1995, 10–11, pursuant to *People v. Gambino,* Indictments 11859-90 and 11858-90, plea agreement.

45. Friedman, "McGuire: The Trucks Are Rolling."

46. Ibid.

47. Arthur Friedman, "McGuire: More Probes Needed," *Women's Wear Daily,* April 30, 1998, 1.

48. Office of the Inspector General, press release, April 28, 1998 http://www.dol.gov/dol/opa/public/media/press/oig/oig98181.htm.

49. *United States v. Defede,* Indictment No. 98 Cr. 373 (S.D.N.Y. 1998), 19.

50. Ibid., 6.

51. Ibid., 5; Sharon Edelson and Arthur Friedman, "Probe into Mob Might Also Aim at Apparel Union," *Women's Wear Daily,* April 30, 1998, 1.

52. Al Guart, "Feds Bust Mob Boss; Garment Center Rackets Unraveling, FBI Claims," *New York Post,* April 29, 1998, 5.

53. *United States v. Defede,* Indictment No. 98 Cr. 373 (S.D.N.Y. 1998), 6.

54. Edelson and Friedman, "Probe into Mob Might Also Aim at Apparel Union."

55. 18 U.S.C. 1963 (a)(1), (a)(2), and (a)(3).

56. *United States v. Defede,* Indictment No. 98 Cr. 373 (S.D.N.Y. 1998), 19.

57. Edelson and Friedman, "Probe into Mob Might Also Aim at Apparel Union."

58. Ibid.; Patricia Hurtado, "A Dressing Down; Indictment Alleges Mob Has Control of Garment Dist.," *Newsday*, April 29, 1998, 5.

59. Selwynn Raab, "Curb on Mob Aids Garment Makers," *New York Times*, June 12, 1995, A1.

60. Friedman, "McGuire: The Trucks Are Rolling."

61. Guart, "Feds Bust Mob Boss."

62. Friedman, "McGuire: More Probes Needed," 1.

NOTES TO CHAPTER 10

1. Administrative Code of the City of New York, Title 16A, sec. 1, January 26, 1994. (Hereinafter Local Law 50.)

2. 705 F. Supp. 894, 900 (S.D.N.Y. 1989).

3. Brian Carroll, "Combating Racketeering in the Fulton Fish Market," in *Organized Crime and Its Containment: A Transatlantic Initiative*, ed. Cyrille Fijnaut and James Jacobs (Boston: Kluwer, 1991), 183, 186.

4. *United States v. Local 359*, 705 F. Supp. 894, 900 (S.D.N.Y. 1989).

5. Benjamin Ward, *A Former Commissioner's View on Investigating Corruption, New York Law School Law Review* (1995): 45, 46.

6. Eileen V. Quigley and Bob Drogan, "U.S. Seeks Control of Fish Market under Rackets Law," *Los Angeles Times*, October 16, 1987, 30.

7. The three previous suits seeking union trusteeships involved Local 560 of the International Brotherhood of Teamsters, Local 6A of the New York District Council of Cement and Concrete Workers, and Local 814 of the International Brotherhood of Teamsters. Arnold H. Lubasch, "Mafia Runs Fulton Fish Market, U.S. Says in Suit to Take Control," *New York Times*, October 16, 1987, 1.

8. The court dismissed the government's claims against Local 359, the executive administrator of the union welfare and pension fund, and two trustees of the welfare and pension fund. Carroll, "Combating Racketeering in the Fulton Fish Market," 187.

9. *United States v. Local 359*, 705 F. Supp. 894, 895–96 (S.D.N.Y. 1989).

10. Carroll, "Combating Racketeering in the Fulton Fish Market," 188.

11. *United States v. Local 359*, 87 Civ. 7351, (S.D.N.Y. 1987), Consent Judgment, April 15, 1988, 2. (Hereinafter Local 359 Consent Judgment.)

12. Peter Romano, Robert and Thomas La Carrubba, Joseph Macario, Camine Russo, and Elia Albanese, *Local 359 Consent Judgment*, 3.

13. Ibid., 1–9.

14. *United States v. Local 359*, 705 F. Supp. 894, 897 (S.D.N.Y. 1989).

15. Ibid., 917.

16. *Local 359 Consent Judgment*, 13–14.

17. Ibid., 10–14.

18. Anemona Hartocollis, "A History of Mob's Influence at Market," *Newsday*, December 24, 1990, 3.

19. Frank Wohl, *Second Report of the Administrator* (February 21, 1989), 1, pursuant to *Local 359 Consent Judgment*.

20. *United States v. Local 359*, 87 Civ. 7351 (S.D.N.Y. 1991).

21. *United States v. Local 359*, 87 Civ. 7351 (S.D.N.Y. 1991).

22. Frank Wohl, *Midterm Report of the Administrator* (August 10, 1990), 16, pursuant to *Local 359 Consent Judgment*.

23. Joseph F. Sullivan, "Union Overseers Seek More Time and Support in Curbing Mob Ties," *New York Times*, April 9, 1989, 30.

24. Administrator Wohl claimed that the market manager "has done an excellent job and has achieved some improvements with regard to sanitation, garbage removal, traffic patterns, police presence and collection of overdue rents." However, Wohl pointed out that the market manager's staff of two employees was too small to run the market efficiently. Wohl, *Midterm Report of the Administrator*, 9.

25. Selwyn Raab, "Curbs Due on Rackets at Fish Market," *New York Times*, August 10, 1990, B3.

26. Wohl, *Midterm Report of the Administrator*, 21.

27. Jeanne Nathan, spokeswoman for the New York City Office of Business Development, quoted in *Associated Press*, "Racketeering Rampant at Fulton Fish Market," August 8, 1990.

28. Selwyn Raab, "Fulton Panel Gets Details on Violence," *New York Times*, May 5, 1992, B1.

29. By the 1990s, the majority of seafood retailers were Korean Americans. The administrator's office provided Korean translations of all written communication with market retailers.

30. Frank Wohl, *Notice of Imposition of Sanctions* (June 18, 1992), pursuant to *Local 359 Consent Judgment*.

31. Frank Wohl, *Fulton Fish Market Administrator's Statement of Reasons Supporting Imposition of Sanctions* (June 18, 1992), pursuant to *Local 359 Consent Judgment*.

32. Wohl, *Notice of Imposition of Sanctions*.

33. See *United States v. Local 359*, 87 Civ. 7351 (S.D.N.Y. 1991); *United States v. Local 359*, 88 Civ. 7351 (S.D.N.Y.1990).

34. Wohl, *Notice of Imposition of Sanctions*; the administrator's sanctions were upheld on appeal. See *United States. v. Local 359*, 87 Civ. 7351 (S.D.N.Y. 1994); *United States v. Local 359*, 55 F.3d 64 (2d Cir. 1995).

35. *United States. v. Local 359*, 1994 WL 387679 (S.D.N.Y. 1994), 2–3.

36. Selwyn Raab, "U.S. Administrator Seeks Funds to Stay at Fulton Market," *New York Times*, May 23, 1992, 6.

37. M. P. McQueen, "Feds Send Funds to Market," *Newsday,* July 22, 1992, 35.

38. Selwyn Raab, "Curbs Due on Rackets at Fish Market."

39. Selwyn Raab, "Delay in Tackling Fish Market Crime," *New York Times,* February 17, 1991, 46.

40. Selwyn Raab, "Fish Market's Problems Revert to New York City," *New York Times,* March 27, 1994, 1.

41. *New York City Council Hearing on the Fulton Fish Market,* May 4, 1992, remarks by Richard M. Weinberg, general counsel for the Legal Division of the City Council, 13.

42. Ibid., 5, 10, 23–25, 49.

43. Ibid., remarks by Robert Brackman, deputy commissioner of the New York City Department of Investigation, 135–51.

44. John Shanahan, "New York Mayor to Fish Market Mobsters: Cut Bait," Associated Press, February 1, 1995.

45. See New York City Council, *Committee on Economic Development Meeting,* March 27, 1995.

46. Ibid., remarks by Michael Driansky, president of The Committee to Preserve the Fulton Fish Market, 159–68.

47. Joe Sexton, "Fulton Market Fire Investigators Find Blaze Was Deliberately Set," *New York Times,* March 31, 1995, 4.

48. Joe Sexton, "Fire Sweeps Through Major Building at Fulton Fish Market," *New York Times,* March 30, 1995, B1.

49. Selwyn Raab, "Fish Dealers May Abandon Fulton Market," *New York Times,* April 18, 1995, B1.

50. Selwyn Raab, "Giuliani Seeks Fish Sellers for Market," *New York Times,* April 29, 1995, 25.

51. These observations and criticisms are contained in sec. 22-201 of Local Law 50.

52. In 1989, the Dinkins administration established the Market Manager's Office within the Department of Ports and Trade to regulate the Fulton Fish Market. Subsequently, under the City Charter, sec. 1301(2)(a), the Department of Business Services is responsible for regulating city markets, including the Fulton Fish Market. New York City Council, *Hearing on the Fulton Fish Market,* May 4, 1992.

53. New York City Council, *Committee on Economic Development Meeting,* March 27, 1995, remarks by Randy Mastro, mayor's chief of staff, 10–11.

54. Local Law 50, sec. 22-216(a)(i). The commissioner may, after notice and the applicant's opportunity to be heard, refuse to issue a photo identification card. Local Law 50 provides that the commissioner may consider, among other factors, (1) a pending indictment or criminal action against the applicant, which would provide a basis for denial of a business license or photo identification

card; and (2) a conviction of such applicant of a crime, which, under article 23 of the correction law, would provide a basis for denial of a business license. Local Law 50, sec. 22-216(b).

55. Local Law 50, sec. 22-203 (ii).

56. *Committee to Save the Fulton Fish Market v. City of New York,* 95 Civ. 8759 (S.D.N.Y. 1996).

57. Raab, "Fish Market's Problems Revert to New York City."

58. Selwyn Raab, "New Fulton Market Lease Includes Big Rent Increase," *New York Times,* May 4, 1995, B3.

59. Selwyn Raab, "Second Group of Fish Dealers Agrees to Lease at Fulton Market," *New York Times,* June 1, 1995, B2.

60. Selwyn Raab, "Five Fish Dealers Face Eviction from Market," *New York Times,* July 22, 1995, 21

61. Ibid.

62. "Fish Market Ouster Upheld," *New York Times,* July 21, 1996, B3.

63. Selwyn Raab, "Six Companies Lose Control at Market," *New York Times,* October 13, 1995, B3.

64. "L.I. Firm to Help Clean Up Fish Market," *Newsday,* October 14, 1995, A17.

65. Selwyn Raab, "Crackdown on Mob at Fish Market Brings Chaos," *New York Times,* October 17, 1995, 1.

66. *Committee to Save the Fulton Fish Market v. City of New York,* 95 Civ. 8759 (S.D.N.Y. 1996).

67. Dan Barry, "At the Fulton Fish Market, Traditions Give Way to Tension," *New York Times,* October 18, 1995, B1.

68. *Committee to Save the Fulton Fish Market v. City of New York,* 95 Civ. 8759 (S.D.N.Y. 1996).

69. Selwyn Raab, "Several Fulton Fish Workers Ousted in Background Checks," *New York Times,* December 10, 1995, 1.

70. "Mayor's Pick for Market Omitted Data," *New York Times,* December 2, 1995, 5.

71. Raab, "Several Fulton Fish Workers Ousted in Background Checks."

72. Ibid.

73. Tom Robbins, "City Unloads on Six Fishy Firms," *Newsday,* October 14, 1995, 2.

74. "Carters Dropped at Fish Market," *Crain's New York Business,* October 16, 1995, 1.

75. *Crivelli & Crivelli v. City of New York* (N.Y. Cty. Sup. Ct.) in *New York Law Journal,* August 30, 1996, 22. In an unrelated suit, the U.S. District Court for the Southern District of New York had just previously upheld Local Law 50 as a valid exercise of police powers. See *Committee to Save the Fulton Fish Market v. The City of New York,* 95 Civ. 8759 (S.D.N.Y. 1996).

76. Selwyn Raab, "Two Loaders Are Evicted from the Fulton Market," *New York Times,* December 31, 1995, 4.

77. Selwyn Raab, "Fish Market Disrupted for Second Day," *New York Times,* January 4, 1996, B4.

78. "Security Firm Ousted at Fulton Fish Market," *New York Times,* May 18, 1996, B4.

79. Selwyn Raab, "Man Linked to Mob Loses Spot at Market," *New York Times,* July 11, 1996, B6.

80. "Fish Market Ouster Upheld," *New York Times,* July 31, 1996, B3.

81. Selwyn Raab, "A Crackdown on Fees at Fulton Market," *New York Times,* January 11, 1997, 2.

82. Selwyn Raab, "Mayor Seeks to End Link of Mob to Food Markets," *New York Times,* October 27, 1996, 37.

83. The markets account for more than $3 billion in annual sales and provide for roughly eight thousand jobs. Randy Kennedy, "Bill Gives City New Powers to Fight Crime at Markets," *New York Times,* April 16, 1997, B3.

84. Grant McCool, "New York Presses for New Anti-Mafia Laws," Reuters North American Wire, June 25, 1996.

85. Raab, "Mayor Seeks to End Link of Mob to Food Markets."

86. Administrative Code of the City of New York, Title 22, May 16, 1997. (Hereinafter Local Law 28.)

87. Raab, "Mayor Seeks to End Link of Mob to Food Markets."

88. Selwyn Raab, "Gains Seen in Fish Market Crackdowns," *New York Times,* November 11, 1996, B3.

89. Greg B. Smith, "Breaking the Mob's Back," *Daily News,* May 3, 1998, 5.

NOTES TO CHAPTER 11

1. *United States v. Local 295,* 784 F. Supp. 15, 18, 19, 22 (E.D.N.Y. 1992).

2. When the consent decree was entered into in 1989, the IBT was the nation's largest union with 1.6 million members. Leo Abruzzese, "Judge Names Watchdogs to Monitor Teamsters," *Journal of Commerce,* June 1, 1989, 2B. By 1998, the National Education Association was the nation's largest union, with a membership of 2.3 million, the IBT was second, with 1.4 million members. Steven Greenhouse, "Teacher Groups to Merge, Creating Largest U.S. Union," *New York Times,* January 27, 1998, A12.

3. *United States v. Int'l. Brotherhood of Teamsters,* 1991 U.S. Dist. LEXIS 11256 (S.D.N.Y. 1991).

4. James B. Jacobs, Christopher Panarella, and Jay Worthington, *Busting the Mob: United States v. Cosa Nostra* (New York: New York University Press, 1994), 167–81.

5. *United States v. Int'l. Brotherhood of Teamsters,* 1992 U.S. Dist. LEXIS 795,

802 (S.D.N.Y. 1992). The IBT independent administrator also permanently expelled Patrick Dellorusso, a Local 295 member and associate of the Lucchese crime family, from the IBT in 1994. This debarment was upheld by the District Court. *See United States v. Int'l. Brotherhood of Teamsters,* 853 F. Supp. 757, 758 (S.D.N.Y. 1994).

6. *United States v. Int'l. Brotherhood of Teamsters,* 90 Civ. 0970 (E.D.N.Y. 1990).

7. For an in-depth discussion and analysis of the IBT case, see Jacobs, Panarella, and Worthington, *Busting the Mob,* 167–81.

8. *United States v. Int'l. Brotherhood of Teamsters,* 803 F. Supp. 761, 786 (S.D.N.Y. 1994).

9. The district court approved Ferchak's appointment in September 1991. Ibid.

10. *United States v. Int'l. Brotherhood of Teamsters,* 803 F. Supp. 761 (S.D.N.Y. 1994).

11. Kenneth C. Crowe, "Teamsters Leader Accused of Misusing Dues," *Newsday,* January 12, 1994, 35.

12. Kenneth C. Crowe, "Teamster Boss at JFK Quits," *Newsday,* February 16, 1990, 51.

13. "Teamsters Union Names Trustee to Oversee New York Local," *Journal of Commerce,* February 2, 1994, 2B.

14. *United States v. Local 295 of the Int'l. Brotherhood of Teamsters,* CV-90-970, (E.D.N.Y. 1990), amended complaint.

15. Both Davidoff's and Calise's convictions stem from *United States v. Santoro* 647 F. Supp. 153 (E.D.N.Y. 1986). Calise pled guilty to RICO conspiracy and was sentenced to nine years in prison. Davidoff was found guilty of RICO conspiracy and four extortion-related charges. These convictions were subsequently overturned by the U.S. Court of Appeals for the Second Circuit because the district court had erred in refusing Davidoff's request for a bill of particulars. *United States v. Davidoff* 845 F.2d 1151 (2d Cir. 1988). On retrial in 1989, Davidoff was again found guilty and sentenced to a ten years prison term. 85 Cr. 100 (s) (E.D.N.Y. 1989)

16. 18 U.S.C. 1964 (b).

17. *United States v. Local 295,* 90 Civ. 0970 (E.D.N.Y. 1990).

18. Edward Frost, "U.S. Judge Authorizes Trustee to Oversee Teamsters Local," New York Law Journal 207 (1992): 1, 2.

19. *United States v. Local 295,* 90 Civ. 0970 (E.D.N.Y. 1990).

20. Frederick Lacey, former IBT independent administrator, and later IBT Independent Review Board member, sent a letter to the court urging the appointment of a permanent trustee, citing the institutional and personal limitations of the temporary trustee. He argued that the temporary trustee lacked the skills and experience necessary to investigate and remediate corruption plaguing Local 295. *United States v. Local 295,* 784 F. Supp. 15, 17 (E.D.N.Y. 1992).

21. Ibid., 20, 18, 22.

22. *United States v. Local 295,* 784 F. Supp. 15, 17 (E.D.N.Y. 1992).

23. Ibid.

24. Joseph P. Fried, "Airport Crime Under Attack in U.S. Drive," *New York Times,* May 17, 1992, 33.

25. Ibid.

26. Michael Tobin replaced Mike Moroney as deputy trustee of Local 295.

27. Jeff Girth and Tim Weiner, "Despite Change, Reform Is Slow in the Teamsters," *New York Times,* June 28, 1993, A1; Kenneth Crowe, "Friction Drives the Hearings in Judge's Watch Over Teamsters," *Newsday,* October 4, 1992, 82.

28. Selwyn Raab, "Obstacles to Cleanup: Mob Hinders, Teamster Trustee Says," *New York Times,* June 29, 1993, B1.

29. "Trustee Puccio Identifies Companies as Organized Crime Controlled and Demands Employer Action," *#295 News,* May 1993, 4.

30. "Local 295 By-Laws To Be Rewritten," *#295 News,* October 1992, 7; "News You Can't Use But Might Want to Know," *#295 News,* February 1993, 15.

31. "News You Can't Use But Might Want to Know," 14, 15.

32. "Trustee Puccio Identifies Companies as Organized Crime Controlled and Demands Employer Action."

33. Michael Tobin claims that the trustee has curbed costs and that the union local will sson be back "in the black." Personal Interview, Michael Tobin, deputy trustee, Teamsters Local 295, March 10, 1997. On the cost of the trusteeship, see also Ronald Goldstock, Leslie Skillen, Barry DeFoe, and Wilda Hess, *Report of Working Group of the International Association of Private Sector Inspectors General* (1996), Appendix.

34. Raab, "Obstacles to Cleanup."

35. *United States v. Dello Russo and Razza,* 93 Cr. 1012 (E.D.N.Y. 1993)

36. *Local 851 of the Int'l. Brotherhood of Teamsters v. Kuehne & Nagel Air Freight Inc.,* 97 Civ. 0378 (E.D.N.Y. 1997), Complaint 12–13; "Razza Pleads Guilty," *#295 News,* April 1994, 1.

37. "Corruption Is Cited in Suit on Dismissals," *New York Times,* December 17, 1995, 55.

38. Raab, "Obstacles to Cleanup."

39. Kenneth C. Crowe, "Puccio Trusteeship Questioned," *Newsday,* August 26, 1994, 59.

40. *United States v. Local 295,* 90-CV-1012 (E.D.N.Y. 1990) Consent Decree, September 1994. (Hereinafter *Local 295 Consent Decree.*)

41. Eileen Sullivan replaced Ostrander as union trustee in November 1996.

42. *Local 295 Consent Decree.*

43. Where a member of Local 851 who is an officer or steward asserts his

Fifth Amendment privilege against self-incrimination in the course of an investigation by the independent supervisor, the independent supervisor may refer the case to the IBT Review Board for appropriate action.

44. An amendment to the consent decree was required because the independent supervisor lacked authority to discipline members qua members. The independent supervisor could remove lead agents from the union, but not from their jobs.

45. *Local 295 Consent Decree,* 10–11.

46. The Local 851 treasury was completely depleted at the time of DePetris's appointment in November 1994. Personal interview, Ron DePetris, independent supervisor, Teamsters Local 851, April 16, 1997.

47. *Local 851 of the Int'l. Brotherhood of Teamsters v. Kuehne & Nagel Air Freight, Inc.,* 97 Civ. 0378 (E.D.N.Y. 1997) and *Local 851 of the Int'l. Brotherhood of Teamsters v. Thyssen Haniel Logistics, Inc.,* 95 Civ. 5179 (E.D.N.Y. 1995).

48. Personal interview, Ron DePetris.

49. Sec. 725 New York Labor Laws.

50. *Local 851 of the Int'l. Brotherhood of Teamsters v. Thyssen Haniel Logistics, Inc.,* 95 Civ. 5179 (E.D.N.Y. 1995), Compl.

51. Ibid., 19, 20, discussing *United States v. Dello Russo and Razza,* 93 Cr. 1012 (E.D.N.Y. 1993).

52. Ibid., 21, discussing *People v. Niehenke,* Superior Court Information #86218.

53. Ibid., 19–23.

54. *Local 851 of the Int'l. Brotherhood of Teamsters v. Thyssen Haniel Logistics, Inc.,* 95 Civ. 5179, Consent Order, June 2, 1998, 2.

55. Ibid., 3.

56. *Local 851 v. Kuehne & Nagel Air Freight, Inc.,* 97 Civ. 0378 (E.D.N.Y. 1997), Compl.

57. *Local 851 v. Kuehne & Nagel Air Freight, Inc.,* 1998 WL 178873 (E.D.N.Y. 1998), Civil RICO Report, vol. 13, no. 22, 29 April 1998.

58. Personal interview, Ron DePetris.

NOTES TO CHAPTER 12

1. *Management and Operations of the Jacob K Javits Center: Investigative Hearing Before the State Senate* (New York, 1995), 11–12.

2. *United States v. District Council of New York and Vicinity of the United Brotherhood of Carpenters and Joiners of America,* 90 Civ. 5722 (S.D.N.Y. 1990). (Hereinafter *United States v. District Council.*)

3. *United States v. District Council,* 1995 U.S. Dist. LEXIS 8229, at *2.

4. *United States v. District Council,* 90 Civ. 5722, Consent Decree 2. (Hereinafter *District Council Consent Decree.*)

5. Ibid., 3–12. The Independent Hearing Committee comprised Patrick Barth, Paul Curran, John Fried, Helen Gredd, and Alan Kaufman.

6. Ibid., 13.

7. Kenneth Conboy, *Third Report of Investigations and Review Officer,* Report to Judge Haight, October 31, 1995, 6.

8. Ibid., 44.

9. Selwyn Raab, "Javits Union Boss Says He Just Scrapes By," *New York Times,* April 7, 1995, B3.

10. Selwyn Raab, "Mob's Man? No, Says Javits Hall Union Chief," *New York Times,* April 6, 1995. The Independent Hearing Panel (IHP) found Fiorino's version of events "implausible." Conboy, *Third Report of Investigations and Review Officer,* 45.

11. Conboy, *Third Report of Investigations and Review Officer,* 43.

12. Kenneth Crowe, "Smoking List in Javits Hearing; Names May Link Carpenters Rep to Genovese Crime Family," *Newsday,* March 22, 1995, A34.

13. Conboy, *Third Report of Investigations and Review Officer,* 6.

14. Ibid., 46.

15. *United States v. District Council,* 941 F. Supp. 349, 1996.

16. Douglas J. McCarron, testimony before the House and the Workforce Committee Employer-Employee Relations Subcommittee, June 25, 1998.

17. Selwyn Raab, "Head of Carpenters' Union Is Dismissed in an Office Raid," *New York Times,* June 27, 1996, B3.

18. Selwyn Raab, "Former Chief of Carpenters' Union Convicted of Stealing Funds," *New York Times,* March 25, 1998, B3; "Carpenter Leader Is Found Guilty," *Engineering-News Record,* April 6, 1998, 18.

19. Barbara Ross and Bill Hutchinson, "Jail for Ex-Carpenter Boss," *Daily News,* August 18, 1998, 11.

20. *United States v. Int'l. Brotherhood of Teamsters,* 998 F.2d 1101, 1105 (S.D.N.Y. 1993).

21. *United States v. Bonanno LCN Family, IBT Local 814,* Civ. 87-2974 (E.D.N.Y. August 25, 1987).

22. Leonard Buder, "Judge Approves Decree to Help Rid Teamster Local of Mob Control," *New York Times,* October 10, 1987, 34.

23. *United States v. Bonanno LCN Family, IBT Local 814,* Civ. 87-2974 (E.D.N.Y. 1987), Consent Judgment.

24. *Investigations Officer v. Senese et al.,* independent administrator decision at 37, aff'd. *United States v. Int'l. Brotherhood of Teamsters,* 745 F. Supp. 908 (S.D.N.Y. 1990), aff'd. *United States v. Int'l. Brotherhood of Teamsters,* 941 F.2d 1292 (2d Cir. 1991).

25. The list is derived from *IBT Independent Review Board Report,* Trusteeship Recommendation Concerning Local 807, March 6, 1995, 26–37.

26. Kenneth C. Crowe, "The Rabbitts of Brooklyn May Soon Lose Their Grip on Union Hiring at the Javits Center," *Newsday*, June 19, 1995, B1.

27. *United States v. Int'l. Brotherhood of Teamsters*, 908 F. Supp. 139, (S.D.N.Y. 1995).

28. Ibid. quoting Independent Review Board, *Investigative Report in Re: Costabile Lauro*, 17.

29. *United States v. Int'l. Brotherhood of Teamsters*, 910 F. Supp. 139 (S.D.N.Y. 1996), aff'd. IRB decision.

30. *United States v. Int'l. Brotherhood of Teamsters*, 946 F. Supp. 318, (S.D.N.Y. 1996).

31. IBT *Independent Review Board Report*, Trusteeship Recommendation Concerning Local 807, March 6, 1995.

32. Ibid., 16–26.

33. Ibid., 52–58.

34. Kenneth C. Crowe, "Trustee Named to Oversee Javits Teamsters Local," *Newsday*, March 29, 1995. Carey appointed Johnnie Brown trustee of Local 807. Brown had just served a two-year stint as trustee of an IBT concrete drivers local. Al Fernandez, a retired New York Police lieutenant, who also was an investigator for Fulton Fish Market Administrator Frank Wohl, was appointed one of Brown's aides. See also Joel Siegel and Tom Robbins, *Daily News*, March 9, 1995, 8.

35. Lawrence Van Gelder, "Teamsters Seize Local on Costs at Javits Center," *New York Times*, March 9, 1995, 1.

36. Brett Pulley, "Senate to Begin Hearings on Operation of Javits Center," *New York Times*, March 16, 1995, B4.

37. *People v. Rabbitt Sr.*, Indictments 245–249/92 (February 5, 1992).

38. Ibid.

39. Ibid.

40. Ibid.

41. *People v. Robert Rabbitt Sr.*, Indictments 245–249/92, Plea Agreement (November 9, 1992).

42. Crowe, "The Rabbitts of Brooklyn May Soon Lose Their Grip on Union Hiring at the Javits Center."

43. *People v. Potts*, Indictment 254-92 (1992), Certificate of Conviction (January 29, 1992).

44. Ibid.

45. This is an excellent illustration of the new structure of intergovernmental law enforcement that has been stimulated by organized crime control.

46. District Attorney, New York County, news release, June 20, 1996; Tom Robbins, "10 Union Bigs Are Charged; Stole Benefits, DA Says," *Daily News*, June 21, 1996, 30.

47. *People v. McNamee,* Indictment 4293-96 (1996).

48. *People v. Gardner,* Indictment 4032-96 (1996); *People v, Falco,* Indictment 4033-96 (1996); *People v. McCann,* Indictment 4292-96 (1996); *People v. McNamee,* Indictment 4293-96 (1996).

49. *People v. McCann,* Indictment 4035/96 (1996).

50. *People v. McCann,* Indictment 4034/96 (1996).

51. *People v. McCann,* Indictment 4292-96 (1996); *New York v. Falco,* Indictment 4033/96 (1996).

52. *People v. Gardner,* Indictment 4032/96 (1996).

53. *People v. McCann,* Indictment 4031-96 (1996)

54. *People v. Gardner,* Indictment 4031-96 (1996) (pled guilty to conspiracy in the fifth degree and received a conditional discharge); *People v. Gardner,* Indictment 4032-96 (1996)(pled guilty to grand larceny in the third degree and received a conditional discharge); *People v. Falco,* Indictment 4033-96 (1996)(pled guilty to forgery in the second degree and grand larceny in the third degree); *People v. McCann,* Indictment 4034-96 (1996) (pled guilty to promoting gambling in the first degree); *People v. McCann,* Indictment 4035-96 (1996) (pled guilty to criminal usury in the first degree and received a $5,000 fine*); People v. McCann,* Indictment 4292-96 (1996) (pled guilty to falsifying business records in the first degree); *People v. McNamee,* Indictment 4293-96 (1996) (McNamee's case was abated; the others pled guilty to conspiracy in the second degree and insurance fraud in the third degree).

55. Tom Robbins, *Daily News,* April 19, 1995, 10.

56. New York State Management Division of Management Audit, *An Evaluation of Management Activities and Controls at the Jacob K. Javits Convention Center,* Report 95-S-25 (May 1995), 9.

57. "Inspector for Javits Center," *New York Times,* February 15, 1991, B2.

58. Selwyn Raab, "Cuomo Guard Defends Actions in Assault Inquiry," *New York Times,* November 30, 1987, B3.

59. Jim Dwyer, "He Did Well, but Got Boot," *Newsday,* March 13, 1995, A2.

60. *Management and Operations of the Jacob K Javits Center: Investigative Hearing Before the State Senate* (New York, 1995), 169.

61. Ibid., 171; Dwyer, "He Did Well, but Got Boot," A2.

62. Dwyer, "He Did Well, but Got Boot."

63. *Management and Operations of the Jacob K Javits Center: Investigative Hearing Before the State Senate* (New York, 1995), 171; John Connolly, "The Mob's Glass House," *New York Magazine,* January 9, 1995, 31.

64. Tom Robbins, *Daily News,* March 12, 1995, 16.

65. Lawrence Van Gelder, "Pataki Asks Board of Javits Convention Center to Resign," *New York Times,* March 10, 1995.

66. Letter to William Mack, chairman, New York Convention Center Operating Corporation, regarding New York State Management Division of Man-

agement Audit, *An Evaluation of Management Activities and Controls at the Jacob K. Javits Convention Center,* (May 1995); Kevin Sack, "Audit Assails Former Chief of Javits Hall," *New York Times,* March 13, 1995.

67. New York State Management Division of Management Audit, *An Evaluation of Management Activities and Controls at the Jacob K. Javits Convention Center,* 1–3.

68. Ibid., 5–7, 19–23.

69. According to Governor Pataki, the Board of Directors is not intended to run the day-to-day operations of the center but should be aggressively involved in the oversight of the management team. *Management and Operations of the Jacob K Javits Center: Investigative Hearing Before the State Senate* (New York, 1995), 24.

70. New York State Management Division of Management Audit, *An Evaluation of Management Activities and Controls at the Jacob K. Javits Convention Center,* 13–16.

71. Ibid., 15–16.

72. Kenneth C. Crowe, "Security a Joke," *Newsday,* May 5, 1995, A26.

73. Kyle Hughes, "Cuomo Legacy Lives On," Gannett News Service, May 9, 1995.

74. New York State Management Division of Management Audit, *An Evaluation of Management Activities and Controls at the Jacob K. Javits Convention Center,* 19–21.

75. Ibid., Executive Summary.

76. Ibid., 1.

77. Ibid., 9–11.

78. *Management and Operations of the Jacob K Javits Center: Investigative Hearing Before the State Senate* (New York, 1995).

79. New York Public Authorities Law, Art. 8, Title 27, sec. 2562.

80. *Management and Operations of the Jacob K Javits Center: Investigative Hearing Before the State Senate* (New York, 1995), 14.

81. Kenneth C. Crowe, "Pataki Ally Named Head of Javits," *Newsday,* April 4, 1995, A35.

82. Phyllis Furman, Phillip Lentz, and Gerri Willis, "Betting on Board at Javits Center," *Crain's New York Business,* 14 October 1996, 6. Paul O'Neil, the managing director of the Sheraton New York Hotel and chairman of the New York Convention and Visitors Bureau, was also named to the board.

83. New York Public Authorities Law, Art. 8, Title 27, sec. 2563.

84. Selwyn Raab, "State to Hire a Work Force at Javits Hall," *New York Times,* June 24, 1995, 21.

85. Randy Kennedy, "Javits Is Hiring, and Crowds Turn Up," *New York Times,* July 1, 1995, 21.

86. Randy Kennedy, "About 500 Workers Are Hired for New Force at Javits Center," *New York Times,* July 6, 1995, B4.

87. Tom Robbins, "Fiorino Blasts Javits Sweep," *Daily News,* July 13, 1995, 8.

88. "Two Unions Reinstated at the Javits Center," *New York Times,* July 19, 1995, B6.

89. Ibid.

90. *Devine v. New York Convention Center Operating Corp.,* 639 N.Y.S.2d 904 (N.Y. Sup. Ct. 1996).

91. David L. Lewis and Tom Robbins, "Coliseum Comeback? Carpenters Union Eyes Purchase," *Daily News,* November 20, 1995, 5.

92. Tom Robbins and David L. Lewis, "Rudy Hammers Union's Coliseum Plan," *Daily News,* November 21, 1995, 7.

93. Selwyn Raab, "Assembly Speaker Attacked on Crime Checks for Javits Center," *New York Times,* July 2, 1996, B4.

94. Assembly Bill 11135, 219th General Assembly 1996.

95. Assembly Bill 11135, sec. 7, 219th General Assembly 1996.

96. Ibid., sec. 2.

97. Melinda Jensen, "Javits Anti-Mob Bill: Too Diluted?" *Successful Meetings* 45, no. 10 (September 1996): 16.

98. Assembly Bill 11244, 219th General Assembly, 1996.

99. Office of the State Comptroller, *Report No. 96-F-13,* 2.

100. Ibid.

101. Paul Tharp, "No Longer Married to the Mob, Javits Will Show Profit," *New York Post,* December 30, 1997, 32.

102. Frederick Gabriel, "After Chasing Out the Mob, Exec Moves to a New Port," *Crain's New York Business,* April 14, 1997, 18.

103. Melissa Ng, "Javits Center: Back on Top," *Travel Agent,* October 14, 1996, 123.

104. Charles V. Bagli, "Bid to Expand Javits Center Loses Ground," *New York Times,* June 10, 1998, B4.

NOTES TO CHAPTER 13

1. 928 F. Supp. 407, 424 (S.D.N.Y 1996).

2. *United States v. Private Sanitation Indus. Assoc. of Nassau/Suffolk, Inc.,* 793 F. Supp. 1114, 1120 (E.D.N.Y. 1992).

3. Ibid., 1121.

4. Leslie Gevirtz, "Gotti Targeted in Fed's Attack on Trash Hauling Cartel" U.P.I., June 7, 1989.

5. John Rather, "U.S. Tries to Bar Crime Families from Carting," *New York Times,* June 18, 1989, Long Island sec., 1.

6. *United States v. Private Sanitation Indus. Assoc. of Nassau/Suffolk, Inc.,* 793 F. Supp. 1114, 1120–21 (E.D.N.Y. 1992).

7. Ibid., 1149. Judge Glasser's ruling was based on the Second Circuit's interpretation of the language of 28 U.S.C. 1964(c), under which a RICO plaintiff seeking monetary damages must have suffered injury to his business or property. See *United States v.* Bonanno LCN Family, 683 F. Supp. at 1456 (E.D.N.Y. 1987) aff'd. 879 F.2d at 27 (2d Cir. 1989). In Glasser's opinion the government had not demonstrated such injury.

8. *United States v. Private Sanitation Indus. Assoc. of Nassau/Suffolk, Inc.,* 811 F. Supp. 808, 810 (E.D.N.Y. 1992)

9. Ibid., 815. Judge Glasser referred to Avellino's 1992 guilty pleas in *People v. Salem Sanitary Carting Corp.,* CV-85-0208 (E.D.N.Y. 1985), where he agreed to pay $231,000 and to refrain from conspiring to restrain trade. In 1986, he pleaded guilty to coercion in the first degree and to conspiracy to commit bribery.

10. Ibid., 818.

11. *United States v. Private Sanitation Indus. Assoc. of Nassau/Suffolk, Inc.,* 899 F. Supp. 974 (E.D.N.Y. 1994). Glasser relied on Ferrante's guilty pleas to coercion and bribery.

12. Robert Kessler, "U.S. Monitors to Oversee Carting on LI; Aim Is to Shut Out the Mob," *Newsday,* March 3, 1994, 4.

13. Personal interview with Michael Cherkasky, June 12, 1998; Kossler, "U.S. Monitors to Oversee Carting on LI."

14. Michael Cherkasky, *Report VII From the Compliance Officer,* (January 26, 1998), 2, pursuant to *United States v. Private Sanitation Indus. Assoc.,* CV-89-1848, (E.D.N.Y. 1992).

15. Cherkasky's monitorship is to conclude in the year 2002.

16. "Carting Judgment Is Filed," *New York Law Journal,* March 3, 1994, 4.

17. Robert E. Kessler, "Ex-Prosecutor Eyed for Carting Monitor," *Newsday,* April 28, 1994, A26; John McDonald, "New Monitor Assures East End Carters," *Newsday,* July 15, 1994, A27.

18. Robert E. Kessler, "Striking at Corrupt Carters; Syosset Man Barred from Trash Industry," *Newsday,* October 18, 1994, A3.

19. More often than not the threat of charges before the magistrate leads to a settlement. The largest settlement has been $65,000. Personal interview with Michael Cherkasky, June 12, 1998.

20. Ibid.

21. Michael Cherkasky, *Report VI from the Compliance Officer,* July 11, 1997, 2.

22. Elizabeth Moore, "Cartel Out, Now Buyers In," *Newsday,* June 22, 1997, A8.

23. Cherkasky, *Report VI from the Compliance Officer,* 1–2, fn. 1.

24. Personal interview with Michael Cherkasky.

25. Cherkasky, *Report III from the Compliance Officer,* December 22, 1995, 5.

26. Ibid.

27. Daniel Fisher, "Mr. Clean Ruckelshaus Helps BFI Get Ahead in Garbage Game," *Houston Post*, December 5, 1994, E2.

28. Larry Black, "New York Tidies Up Garbage Image," *Independent*, February 7, 1991, 24.

29. Fisher, "Mr. Clean Ruckelshaus Helps BFI Get Ahead in Garbage Game."

30. Ironically, California prosecutors have also charged WMX with links to organized crime. WMX strongly disputes the allegation and has filed suit against the prosecutors. See *WMX Technologies v. Miller*, 104 F.3d 1133 (9th Cir. 1997).

31. Allan R. Gold, "U.S. Acts to End Monopolies in New York Trash Hauling," *New York Times*, February 6, 1991, A1.

32. Kevin Flynn, "Violations May Trash Efforts of Firm to Crack Into Carting," *Newsday*, May 19, 1992, 23.

33. Matthew L. Wald, "Trash Giant Makes Plans to Expand in New York," *New York Times*, October 7, 1993, B5.

34. Greg Groeller, "BFI Intent on Staying in N.Y.C.; Garbage Company Facing Heat from Organized Crime," *Houston Post*, March 18, 1995, C1; Philip Angell, "Competition vs. Corruption: Reforming New York's Garbage Waste Industry," *Civic Bulletin*, October 1996, 2.

35. "Solid Waste: Supreme Court Decision May Trigger Price War," *Greenwire*, February 28, 1994.

36. Wald, "Trash Giant Makes Plans to Expand in New York."

37. Allen R. Myerson, "The Garbage Wars," *New York Times*, July 30, 1995, 1.

38. The officer also posed as a relative of the owner. Selwyn Raab, "When the Mafia Got Greedy, a Garbage Hauler Went Undercover," *New York Times*, June 9, 1996, 37.

39. *In re a Warrant to Search the Greater New York Waste Paper Ass'n.* (N.Y. Sup. Ct. 1995), Search Warrant Affidavit of Det. Joseph Lentini.

40. See *United States v. Mongelli*, 2 F.3d 29, 30 (2d Cir. 1993); "Browning-Ferris Expands with Purchase of Mob Haulers," *Reuter Business Report*, October 20, 1994. The companies were formerly owned by Louis and Robert Mongelli, both of whom pled guilty to racketeering in 1992.

41. Angell, "Competition vs. Corruption," 1.

42. James C. McKinley, Jr., "Big Private Garbage Haulers, Linked to Mafia, Are Indicted," *New York Times*, June 23, 1995, A1.

43. Indictment No. 05614/95 (1995), *People v. Association of Greater Trade Waste Removers* (Supreme Court, New York County), at 1–2.

44. See New York Penal Law 460.20(1)(a).

45. Indictment No. 05614/95 (1995), *People v. Association of Greater Trade Waste Removers* (Supreme Court, New York County), at 2.

46. Each of these 113 was also charged as an independent criminal violation. Indictment No. 05614/95 (1995), *People v. Association of Greater Trade Waste Removers* (Supreme Court, New York County), at 69–149.

47. Indictment No. 05614/95 (1995), *People v. Association of Greater Trade Waste Removers* (Supreme Court, New York County), at 3.

48. Joe Sexton, "Monitors to Oversee Finances of Indicted Trash Haulers," *New York Times*, September 16, 1995, 23; "Watchdogs Can't Do Much Watching," *Crain's New York Business*, September 18, 1995, 1.

49. The monitors were two former New York State appellate division judges, Sidney Asch and Bentley Kassal; four former State supreme court judges, Thomas Galligan, Michael Dontzin, Burton Sherman, and Seymour Schwartz; and three lawyers, Harold J. Reynolds, Lawrence Goldberg, and Murray Greenspan. George James, "Monitors Appointed for Trash Haulers," *New York Times*, December 23, 1995, 31.

50. *Morgenthau v. Allocca*, in *New York Law Journal*, September 25, 1995, 25.

51. Selwyn Raab, "Arson Case Turned Into an Offer He Couldn't Refuse," *New York Times*, June 23, 1997, 3.

52. Selwyn Raab, "Trash Carter Pleads Guilty to Corruption," *New York Times*, January 28, 1997, B2.

53. "USA Waste's Acquisitions Sharply Boost NY Volume: Company Grabs Top Market Share; Other National, Local Firms Buy Too," *Crain's New York Business*, 21 April 1997, 60.

54. Raab, "Trash Carter Pleads Guilty to Corruption."

55. A seventh defendant, Patrick Pecoraro, and the Kings County Trade Waste Association had their trials severed because of the death of their attorney. Eventually, both pled guilty on January 21, 1998: Pecoraro to three antitrust violations and attempted enterprise corruption; the trade association to one antitrust violation. "More Guilty Pleas Entered; Sentences Handed Down in New York Carting Trial," *Solid Waste Report* 29, no. 5 (January 29, 1998).

56. Selwyn Raab, "Testimony to Start in Trash Carting Trial," *New York Times*, May 27, 1997, B3.

57. Selwyn Raab, "Trash Haulers Plead Guilty in Cartel Case," *New York Times*, July 23, 1997, B3.

58. Francolino was found guilty of all thirty-four charges against him, including grand larceny by extortion, coercion, and antitrust violations. Malangone was convicted on all ten charges. "Last Two Defendants Convicted on All Counts in New York City Carting Trial," *Solid Waste Report* 28, no. 42 (October 23, 1997).

59. "Defendants in New York City Carting Trial Hit with Prison Terms and Fines," *Solid Waste Report* 28, no. 50 (December 18, 1997).

60. "More Guilty Pleas Entered, Sentences Handed Down in New York Carting Trial."

61. Pete Bowles, "Feds Indict 6 Pals of Gotti in Death of a Mob Witness," *Newsday*, April 20, 1993, 18.

62. *United States v. Failla*, 1993 WL 547419 (E.D.N.Y. December 21, 1993), at *1. The other defendants were Daniel Marino, Joseph Watts, Louis "Louis Fats" Astuto, Philip "Philly Dogs" Mazzara, and Dominick "Fat Dom" Borghese. Astuto, Mazzara, and Borghese were soldiers in the Gambino family and Watts was an associate. Watts was also charged with the conspiracy and subsequent murder of former Gambino family boss Paul Costellano and Gambino capo Thomas Bilotti.

63. *United States v. Failla*, 1993 WL 547419 at *1.

64. Joseph P. Fried, "Judge Says He May Reject Plea Deal in Garbage Hauling Case," *New York Times*, April 5, 1994, B3. The sixth defendant, Joseph Watts, decided to go to trial but pled guilty to conspiracy to murder Spinelli and was sentenced to six years in prison. See Joseph P. Fried, "Plea Deal Keeps 'Sammy Bull' Off Stand," *New York Times*, February 16, 1996, B3.

65. Jonathan Rabinovitz, "Union Local Agrees to Court Monitor to Bar Any Association with Mobsters," *New York Times*, January 12, 1994, B4.

66. Ibid.

67. See *United States v. Int'l. Brotherhood of Teamsters*, 998 F.2d 120, 121 (2d Cir. 1993).

68. Rabinovitz, "Union Local Agrees to Court Monitor to Bar Any Association with Mobsters."

69. Robert E. Kessler, "New Teamsters Job: Rackets-Buster," *Newsday*, January 12, 1994, 6; Rabinovitz, "Union Local Agrees to Court Monitor to Bar Any Association with Mobsters."

70. Jonathan Rabinovitz and Annette Fuentes, "The Polsinelli Family Wants Wood to Burn," *Daily News*, May 7, 1995, 1. (Mentions Foy as Local 813's trustee.)

71. Mark Green, "Competition in Sanitation: How to Reduce Costs and Improve Service for Businesses and Residences," drafted January 11, 1994 and introduced at the January 26, 1994, New York City Council meeting.

72. Philip Lentz, "Mayor Aiming at Mob Carters: Breaking Silence, Rudy Eyes Licenses, Background Checks and a New Post," *Crain's New York Business*, November 13, 1995, 3.

73. Local Law 42 is officially entitled "A Local Law to Amend the Administrative Code of the City of New York in Relation to Commercial Waste Removal." Local Law 42 added Title 16-A to the Administrative Code, setting forth new regulations for commercial waste hauling in New York City. We refer to Title 16A as Local Law 42.

74. Local Law 42, 16-501 to 16-525.

75. James B. Jacobs and Alex Hortis, "New York City as Organized Crime Fighter," *New York Law School Law Review* 42, nos. 3–4 (1998): 1069–92.

76. *Sanitation and Recycling Indus., Inc. v. City of New York*, 928 F. Supp. 407 (S.D.N.Y. 1996)

77. Ibid., 412.

78. Declaration of Randy M. Mastro, June 17, 1996, *Sanitation and Recycling Indus., Inc. v. City of New York*, 96 Civ. 4131 (MP) (S.D.N.Y.), at 2.

79. *Sanitation and Recycling Indus., Inc. v. City of New York*, 928 F. Supp. 407, 424 (S.D.N.Y. 1996).

80. *Sanitation and Recycling Indus., Inc. v. City of New York*, 107 F.3d 985, (2d. Cir. 1997).

81. Ibid., 985.

82. *Universal Sanitation Corp. v. Trade Waste Comm'n.*, 940 F. Supp. 656, 659 (S.D.N.Y. 1996).

83. Ibid., 660–61.

84. Local Law 42, 11-iii (June 3, 1996).

85. The firms denied exemption were V. Ponte & Sons Company, Vaparo Company, Vigliotti & Sons, AVA Carting, Duffy Waste and Recycling, Rutigliano Paper Stock, All City Paper Fibers, V.A. Sanitation, Litod Paper Stock, Professional Recycling, Crest Carting, and Yankee Continental Carting. Selwyn Raab, "City's New Waste Agency Flexes Regulatory Muscles," *New York Times*, August 10, 1996, 27; David Medina, "Companies Raise a Stink over Haulers' Contracts," *Crain's New York Business*, August 26, 1996, 33.

86. Personal interview with Chad Vignola, deputy commissioner for licensing and operations, New York City Trade Waste Commission, December 11, 1997.

87. Selwyn Raab, "Trash Haulers Told: No Mobsters or Odors," *New York Times*, September 1, 1996, 43.

88. New York City Trade Waste Commission, "Notice of Promulgation of Final Rule"; see also *Rules of the City of New York*, Title 17, ch. 1, 5-02(a) and 5-02(b); Selwyn Raab, "New York Cuts Hauling Rates for Garbage," *New York Times*, March 26, 1997, B1.

89. City of New York Trade Waste Commission; *The Trade Waste Commission's Report on the Reduction of the Maximum Legal Rate for the Removal of Trade Waste*, March 25, 1997, 17.

90. Philip Lentz, "Back to Garbage Cartel? Giants to Merge; Prices May Jump Here," *Crain's New York Business*, March 16, 1998, 1.

91. Juan Gonzalez, "New Cartel Cashing in on Trash," *Daily News*, July 7, 1998, 10.

92. Abby Goodnough, "Hauling Rates for Garbage Rising Again, Shops Report," *New York Times*, July 15, 1998, B5.

93. Douglas Martin, "Settlement Allows Trash Companies to Merge After Divesting," *New York Times*, July 17, 1998, B5.

94. Sharon McDonnell, "Trash-Carting Outsider Slowly Gains Foothold," *Crain's New York Business,* March 20, 1995, 28.

95. Philip Lentz, "Garbage Rivals Ignore NY Despite Mob Bust," *Crain's New York Business,* June 26, 1995, 1.

96. Philip Lentz, "Out-of-Towner Faces Down Tainted New York Industry," *Crain's New York Business,* April 8, 1996, 32.

97. Selwyn Raab, "Texas Company Agrees to Buy Mafia-Linked Waste Hauler," *New York Times,* January 23, 1996, B1.

98. Thomas J. Lueck, "Major U.S. Recycler to Buy Large New York Trash Company," *New York Times,* 1 March 1996, B5.

99. Trade Waste Commission, *Estimated Annual Savings from Reductions in Trade Waste Collection Costs* (1997).

100. Philip Lentz, "Big Companies Abandon Cartel for New Players," *Crain's New York Business,* June 26, 1996, 3.

NOTES TO CHAPTER 14

1. New York State Organized Crime Task Force, *Corruption and Racketeering in the New York City Construction Industry* (hereinafter OCTF Final Report) (New York: New York University Press, 1990), 1, quoting a June 25, 1985, letter from Governor Mario M. Cuomo to Mayor Edward I. Koch.

2. OCTF Final Report, 169.

3. *United States v. Cody,* 722 F.2d 1052 (2d Cir. 1983), cert. denied, 467 U.S. 1226 (1987).

4. *United States v. Langella,* 804 F.2d 185 (2d Cir. 1986).

5. James B. Jacobs, Christopher Panarella, and Jay Worthington, *Busting the Mob: United States v. Cosa Nostra* (New York: New York University Press, 1994), 79–87; *United States v. Salerno,* 85 Cr. 139 (S.D.N.Y. 1985). Ralph Scopo died in prison in March 1993.

6. *United States v. Halloran,* 1989 WL 2691 (S.D.N.Y. January 11, 1989); *United States v. Salerno,* 937 F.2d 797, (2d Cir. 1991), rev'd. 505 U.S. 317 (1992); *United States v. Salerno,* 974 F.2d 231 (2d Cir. 1992), rev'd. in part sub nom., *United States v. DiNapoli,* 8 F.3d 909 (2d Cir. 1993) (en banc); *United States v. Migliore,* 104 F.3d 354 (2d Cir. 1996) (noting that all five remaining defendants pled guilty by 1995).

7. *United States v. Halloran,* 1989 WL 2691; *United States v. Salerno,* 937 F.2d 797; Selwyn Raab, "Big Concrete Supplier Faces U.S. Inquiry into Possible Mob Tie," *New York Times,* March 5, 1990, B1.

8. Interview with Herman Benson of the Association for Union Democracy on July 14, 1998; Kenneth Crowe, "New Trustee for Powerful Union Group," *Newsday,* March 27, 1996, A47; Association for Union Democracy (AUD), "Federal Trusteeship over Cement Workers." *Union Democracy Review,* May 1987, 13;

Michele Galen, "N.Y.–Based Union Agrees to Less-Radical Approach." *National Law Journal,* August 31, 1987, 30; David M. Halbfinger, "Corporate Cops: They're Private, They're Crime Busters and They're Proliferating," *Newsday,* March 26, 1995, Money & Careers sec., 1.

9. A year earlier there had also been an important, albeit unsuccessful state civil antitrust action alleging that the ready-mix producers were monopolizing concrete production in New York City. *Palmieri v. State of New York,* 779 F.2d 861 (2d Cir. 1985); see also *Big Apple Concrete Corp. v. Abrams,* No. 82/27293 (Sup. Ct., N.Y. Co. June 9, 1983), rev'd. in part, 481 N.Y.S.2d 335; see also President's Commission on Organized Crime, *The Edge: Organized Crime, Business, and Labor Unions* (Washington, D.C.: Government Printing Office, March 1986), 226–27.

10. *Quadrozzi v. City of New York,* 127 F.R.D. 63, 66 (S.D.N.Y. 1989).

11. Ally allegedly misrepresented his "financial background, experience, assets and ability to run a concrete plant" according to former deputy mayor Robert Esnard. He also attempted to make a $10,000 contribution to Mayor Koch through former senator George McGovern. Howard Kurtz, "George McGovern, $10,000 in Cash and a Donation That Wasn't Made: Ex-Senator's Only Activity as Lobbyist Tangles Him in Legal Dispute," *Washington Post,* April 5, 1990, A10; Suzanne Daley, "Ad Spurs a 'Bored' Guyanese to Build City Concrete Plant," *New York Times,* August 31, 1986, A45; *Quadrozzi v. City of New York,* 127 F.R.D. at 66.

12. While the court ultimately dismissed the suit, holding that the city had a "duty . . . to take action" in light of monopolistic underworld domination of concrete production," investors backed out of the project. *Quadrozzi v. City of New York,* 127 F.R.D. at 66; Kirk Johnson, "City Project on Concrete Threatened," *New York Times,* April 13, 1987, B1.

13. In July 1987, West 57th produced its first one hundred cubic yards of concrete, barely avoiding contract cancellation. However, the fledgling company was unable to meet further production requirements. See Bruce Lambert, "Concrete Company Given 2d Chance by Koch," *New York Times,* July 28, 1987, B3; Elizabeth Kolbert, "New York City Cancels Concrete Plant Deal," *New York Times,* August 19, 1987, B3.

14. Selwyn Raab, "Trouble for New York's Concrete Venture," *New York Times,* May 30, 1993, A29.

15. Selwyn Raab, "Mob Allegation Clouds New York Concrete Deal," *New York Times,* September 23, 1994, B1.

16. Selwyn Raab, "City Tries Again to Set Up Manhattan Concrete Plant," *New York Times,* April 15, 1996, B5.

17. Selwyn Raab, "Big Concrete Supplier Faces U.S. Inquiry into Possible Mob Tie," *New York Times,* March 5, 1990, B1.

18. Ronald Sullivan, "Businessman Is Accused of Mob Ties," *New York Times,* May 30, 1983, A29.

19. *United States v. District Council,* 90 Civ. 5722 (CSH), Government's Memorandum of Law in Support of Its Motion for Preliminary Relief (hereinafter Government's Memorandum), 12.

20. *United States v. District Council,* 90 Civ. 5722 (CSH), Declaration of Marcello Svedese, 7.

21. Government's Memorandum, 14.

22. *United States v. Standard Drywall Corporation,* 617 F. Supp. 1283 (E.D.N.Y. 1985); Selwyn Raab, "Investigators Charge Contractors Formed 'Club' for Tax Fraud," *New York Times,* July 6, 1983, A1; President's Commission on Organized Crime, *Report to the President and Attorney General: The Edge—Organized Crime, Business, and Labor Unions* (Washington, D.C.: Government Printing Office, 1986), 234–35; OCTF Final Report, 27.

23. Murray Kempton, "Customs of Accommodation," *Newsday,* July 30, 1989, News sec., 4; *United States v. Salerno,* 937 F.2d 797 (2d Cir. 1991); *United States v. Migliore,* 104 F.3d 354 (2d Cir. 1996).

24. Selwyn Raab, "Carpenter Union Official Is Linked To Extortion Plot." *New York Times,* July 20, 1987, B1; Selwyn Raab, "5 Carpenters' Union Leaders Indicted in Extortion," *New York Times,* October 14, 1987, A1.

25. OCTF Final Report, 20, 50; Government's Memorandum, 20–21; *People v. Schepis,* 614 N.Y.S.2d 719 (1994).

26. *United States v. District Council,* 90 Civ. 5722 (CSH), Consent Decree (1994).

27. Kenneth Conboy, *Fifth Interim Report of the Investigations and Review Officer,* Report to Judge Haight, September 30, 1996; *United States v. District Council,* 90 Civ. 5722 (CSH).

28. *United States v. Gigante,* 39 F.3d 42, 45 (2d Cir. 1994).

29. Ibid.; Pete Bowles, "Window Opened on Alleged Mob Scam," *Newsday,* May 7, 1991, News sec., 23.

30. One juror was dismissed for talking with her jailed boyfriend. The boyfriend later pleaded guilty to conspiring with other inmates to tamper the jury. Pete Bowles, "2 Plead Guilty in Windows Case," *Newsday,* November 3, 1992, News sec., 76.

31. Patricia Hurtado, "Reputed Mobster Mentally Unfit to Go on Trial," *Newsday,* March 12, 1991, News sec., 6.

32. Arnold Lubasch, "US Says Mob Gained Grip on Window Trade," *New York Times,* April 24, 1991, B3; Peter Bowles, "Mistrial Asked in Mob Case; Defendants' Alleged Ties to the Mob," *Newsday,* August 13, 1991, News sec., 4.

33. Mangano's sentence was increased from 27 to 33 months to 188 months; Aloi's from 27 to 33 months to 200 months. *United States v. Gigante,* 39 F.3d at 46–47.

34. Chiodo himself was the target of an assassination attempt not thought

to be related to his testifying. *United States v. Gigante,* 39 F.3d at 46; *United States v. Amuso,* 21 F.3d at 1251, 1255 (2d Cir. 1994).

35. *United States v. Gigante,* 39 F.3d at 42; *United States v. Amuso,* 21 F.3d at 1254.

36. *United States v. McGowan,* 58 F.3d 8 (2d Cir. 1995).

37. *United States v. Amuso,* 21 F.3d at 1254.

38. *United States v. Gigante,* 989 F. Supp. 436, 438 (E.D.N.Y. 1997).

39. Selwyn Raab, "Reputed Crime Boss Is Said to Have Stored Cash in Hideaway," *New York Times,* January 21, 1993, B2; Pete Bowles, "Mobster Dropped As Witness," *Newsday,* July 1, 1998, A29; Devlin Barrett, "Rubout King 'Gaspipe' Gets Life 15 Times," *New York Post,* July 9, 1998, News sec., 10.

40. *People v. Capaldo,* 572 N.Y.S.2d 989 (1991).

41. Selwyn Raab, "A Corrupt Alliance in New York Clenches the Construction Trade," *New York Times,* June 23, 1990, A25.

42. *People v. Capaldo,* 572 N.Y.S.2d 989 (1991) (upholding OCCA charges as not unconstitutionally vague).

43. "Painters Union Double-Dipped in Green Deals," *Engineering News-Record* 231, no. 15, October 11, 1993, News sec., 18.

44. Associated Press, "10 Indicted in Plumbing Industry Probe," *Record,* April 14, 1994, A4; John Jordan, "Accounting Firm Charged under New State Racketeering Law," *Westchester County Business Journal* 33, no. 17 (April 25, 1994): sec. 1, 3.

45. Interview with James McNamara on September 9, 1998.

46. James McNamara, "Democracy Buffeted by Backlash," *Union Democracy Review,* no. 113, July 1997, 5; Justice Fried, "Surveillance of Defendants Reveals They Are Not Too Ill to Be Jailed," *New York Law Journal,* October 21, 1996, Court Decisions, 25; Selwyn Raab, "Ex-Plumbers' Union Officials Guilty in Extortion," *New York Times,* April 23, 1996, B4.

47. Justice Fried, "Provisional Remedies Are Denied Because of Actions by Union's Parent," *New York Law Journal,* April 4, 1994, Court Decisions, 25.

48. Interview with Herman Benson of the Association for Union Democracy on July 14, 1998; James McNamara, "Democracy Buffetted by Backlash," *Union Democracy Review,* no. 113, July 1997, 5.

49. *United States v. District Council,* 90 Civ. 5722 (CSH), consent decree (1994); see also 880 F. Supp. 1051 (S.D.N.Y. 1995) (upholding IRO's election rules).

50. Susan Jennik, "U.S. RICO Suit and Union Democracy Disturb Carpenter Officials," *Union Democracy Review,* no. 89, August 1992, 1–2.

51. Kenneth Conboy, *Ninth Interim Report of the Investigations and Review Officer,* Report to Judge Haight, June 28, 1998, 26–33; *United States v. District Council,* 90 Civ. 5722 (CSH).

52. Conboy, *Fifth Interim Report of the Investigations and Review Officer,* 2.

53. According to Douglas McCarron, the international president, Devine "bought his 1995 reelection by providing pension benefit increases that neither the pension nor welfare benefit funds could afford." Moreover, Devine's corrupt practices largely contributed to the funds' impoverished state. Prepared Statement of Douglas J. McCarron, General President, Before the House and the Workforce Committee Employer-Employee Relations Subcommittee, June 25, 1998.

54. Conboy, *Fifth Interim Report of the Investigations and Review Officer,* 2.

55. Prepared Statement of Douglas J. McCarron, General President, Before the House and the Workforce Committee Employer-Employee Relations Subcommittee.

56. Ibid. Some observers believe that the restructuring reduces union democracy by converting elected positions to appointed positions. Interview with James McNamara, former director of Mayor's Office of Construction Industry Relations, former consultant to the Manhattan DA's Labor Racketeering Unit, on September 8, 1998; see also OCTF Final Report.

57. Conboy, *Ninth Interim Report of the Investigations and Review Officer,* 19.

58. Ibid., 26–33; Kenneth Conboy, *Eighth Interim Report of the Investigations and Review Officer,* Report to Judge Haight, November 29, 1997, 3–4; *United States v. District Council,* 90 Civ. 5722.

59. Conboy, *Ninth Interim Report of the Investigations and Review Officer,* 35.

60. Prepared Statement of Douglas J. McCarron, General President, Before the House and the Workforce Committee Employer-Employee Relations Subcommittee.

61. Kenneth Crowe, "Teamsters Seize Locals Suspected of Ties to Mob," *Newsday,* July 16, 1992, Business sec., 47.

62. "Teamsters Officials Face Extortion Charges," *New York Times,* July 2, 1993, B6.

63. Samson Mulugeta, "Feds to Monitor Union," *Daily News,* March 24, 1995, 7.

64. Kenneth Crowe, "New Trustee for Powerful Union Group; Stony Brook Man Picked for Teamsters Local 282 for Trusteeship of Local," *New York Times,* March 27, 1996, A47.

65. Kenneth Crowe, "Mob-Linked Teamsters Removed in Crackdown," *Newsday,* October 4, 1995, A46.

66. Kenneth Crowe, "Trustee Named to Oversee Javits Teamsters Local," *Newsday,* March 29, 1995, A37.

67. Crowe, "New Trustee for Powerful Union Group."

68. Interview with Herman Benson.

69. Ibid.; James S. Newton, "Concrete Workers Wary of U.S. as Union Boss," *New York Times,* March 22, 1987, A1.

70. *United States v. Local 6A, Cement and Concrete Workers,* 832 F. Supp. 674, 677 (S.D.N.Y. 1993).

71. Association for Union Democracy, "Federal Trusteeship over Cement Workers," *Union Democracy Review,* no. 58, May 1987, 13.

72. Alan Barnes, "Suit Seeks Federal Trusteeship Over Cement Workers Local." *Union Democracy Review,* no. 55, November 1986, 8.

73. Association for Union Democracy, "Federal Trusteeship over Cement Workers"; Michele Galen, "N.Y.–Based Union Agrees to Less-Radical Approach," *National Law Journal,* August 31, 1987, 30.

74. *United States v. Mason Tenders District Council,* 94 Civ. 6487 (RWS), 1997 WL 97836 at *1 (S.D.N.Y. March 6, 1997); 1995 WL 679245 at *2 (S.D.N.Y. November 15, 1995).

75. *United States v. Mason Tenders District Council,* 94 Civ. 6487 (RWS), 1996 U.S. Dist. LEXIS 13231 (S.D.N.Y. August 14, 1996) (upholding ban against Lanza); 1998 U.S. Dist. LEXIS 237, *19 (S.D.N.Y. January 12, 1998) (upholding Vario's expulsion and fine for improper severance pay).

76. *United States v. Mason Tenders District Council,* 1997 U.S. Dist. LEXIS 8715, *10–11 (S.D.N.Y. June 19, 1997).

77. Testimony of Michael S. Bearse, general counsel, Laborers International Union of North America, before the House Education and the Workforce Committee Subcommittee on Employer-Employee Relations Impediments to Union Democracy, May 4, 1998.

78. *Mason Tenders District Council v. Laborers International Union of North America,* 924 F. Supp. 528 (S.D.N.Y. 1996).

79. LIUNA has hired an independent team of former federal prosecutors and FBI agents to combat corruption in the union. The 1995 agreement was originally supposed to last three years, but it was extended for one year. See Testimony of Michael S. Bearse, general counsel, LIUNA, Before the House Subcommittee on Employer/Employee Relations, May 4, 1988; Testimony of Jim Moody, former deputy assistant director, Criminal Investigations Division, FBI, Before the Crime Subcommittee of the House Judiciary Committee, July 24, 1996.

80. Rael Jean Isaac, "A Corrupt Union Escapes Justice" (editorial), *Wall Street Journal,* July 27, 1998.

81. Interview with Herman Benson.

82. Testimony of Michael S. Bearse, General Counsel LIUNA, Before the House Subcommittee on Employer/Employee Relations, May 4, 1988.

83. Interview with Herman Benson.

84. *People v. Capaldo,* 572 N.Y.S.2d 989 (1991).

85. Frank Schonfeld, "A Failed Trusteeship in Painters District Council," *Union Democracy Review,* no. 90, December 1993, 7; Kenneth C. Crowe, "Painters Union Put into Trusteeship," *Newsday,* March 5, 1991, News sec., 28.

86. Ibid.

87. Interview with Herman Benson.

88. The Association for Union Democracy (AUD) wrote in 1997 that "[t]he Local's notoriety for race discrimination is matched only by its reputation for organized crime connections." AUD, "Discrimination in Ironworkers Local 580," *Union Democracy Review,* no. 110, January 1997, 7.

89. Raab, "Ex-Plumbers' Union Officials Guilty in Extortion."

90. Fried, "Provisional Remedies Are Denied Because of Actions by Union's Parent."

91. Raab, "Ex-Plumbers' Union Officials Guilty in Extortion"; Paul Martello was later acquitted.

92. Interview with Herman Benson.

93. McNamara, "Democracy Buffeted by Backlash."

94. Thomas D. Thacher II, "Institutional Innovation in Controlling Organized Crime," in *Organized Crime and Its Containment: A Transatlantic Initiative,* ed. Cyrille Fijnaut and James B. Jacobs (Boston: Kluwer, 1991), 169–82.

95. James B. Jacobs and Frank Anechiarico, "Blacklisting Public Contractors as an Anti-Corruption and Racketeering Strategy," *Criminal Justice Ethics* 11, no. 2 (summer/fall 1992): 64–76.

96. Thomas D. Thacher II, "Combating Corruption and Racketeering: A New Strategy for Reforming Public Contracting in NYC's Construction Industry," *New York Law School Law Review* 15, nos. 1–2 (1995): 113–42, 133.

97. Selwyn Raab, "Top Plumbing Company Cited in Tax Evasion Case," *New York Times,* April 14, 1994, B3.

98. See Thacher, "Combating Corruption and Racketeering," 136–38.

99. See Frank Anechiarico and James B. Jacobs, *Pursuit of Absolute Integrity: How Corruption Control Makes Government Ineffective* (Chicago: University of Chicago Press 1996).

100. A description of VENDEX (Vendor Information Exchange System) is set out in City of New York, Mayor's Office of Contracts, *VENDEX: Policies and Procedures* (March 1990).

101. See James B. Jacobs and Frank Anechiarico, "Purging Corruption from Public Contracting: The 'Solutions' Are Now Part of the Problem," *New York Law School Law Review* 15, nos. 1–2 (1995): 143–75.

102. Anechiarico and Jacobs, *Pursuit of Absolute Integrity,* 128–30.

103. See Jacobs and Anechiarico, "Purging Corruption from Public Contracting," 156.

104. Charles V. Bagli, "Bid-Rigging Case Engulfs an Elite Who Built the Interiors of Offices," *New York Times,* March 27, 1998, A1.

105. Charles V. Bagli, "After Guilty Plea in Bribe Case, Company Calls the Payments Legal," *New York Times,* June 18, 1998, B10.

106. Barbara Stewart, "Consultants Investigated Over Bribes for Buildings," *New York Times,* August 8, 1998, B2.

NOTES TO CHAPTER 15

1. James B. Jacobs, Christopher Panarella, and Jay Worthington, *Busting the Mob: U.S. v. Cosa Nostra* (New York: New York University Press, 1994), i.

2. Steve Greenhouse, "G.O.P. in a Jam over Move against Teamster Election," *New York Times,* June 29, 1998, A14.

3. New York State Organized Crime Task Force, *Final Report on Corruption and Racketeering in the New York City Construction Industry* (New York: New York University Press, 1990).

4. Ronald Goldstock, "How to Reform a Fishy Business," *Newsday,* March 3, 1995, A34.

5. From Mayor Giuliani's webpage at http://www.ci.nyc.ny.us/html/om/html/bio.html

6. Ronald Reagan, "Declaring War on Organized Crime," *New York Times,* January 12, 1986, 6–26.

7. *United States v. Salerno,* 85 Cr. 139 (S.D.N.Y. 1985).

8. See *United States v. Halloran,* 1989 WL 2691 (S.D.N.Y. 1982); *United States v. Salerno,* 937 F.2d 797 (2d Cir. 1991), rev'd. 505 U.S. 317 (1992); *United States v. Salerno,* 974 F.2d 231 (2d Cir. 1992) rev'd. in part sub nom. *United States v. DiNapoli,* 8 F.3d 909 (2d Cir. 1993)(en banc); see also *United States v. Migliore,* 104 F.3d 354 (2d Cir. 1996)(noting that all remaining defendants entered into plea agreements).

9. See Bonanno family: *United States v. The Bonanno Organized Crime Family,* 87 Civ. 2974 (E.D.N.Y. 1987); Colombo family: *United States v. Persico,* 832 F.2d 705 (2d Cir 1987), *United States v. Colombo,* 616 F. Supp. 780 (E.D.N.Y. 1985); Gambino family: *United States v. Gotti,* 641 F. Supp. 283 (S.D.N.Y. 1986); Genovese family: *United States v. Salerno,* 868 F.2d 524 (2d Cir 1989).

10. *United States v. Local 359,* Civ. 7351 (S.D.N.Y. 1987).

11. *United States v. Int'l. Brotherhood of Teamsters,* 708 F. Supp. 1388 (S.D.N.Y. 1989).

12. Selwyn Raab, "New Rules Sought for Contractors," *New York Times,* June 20, 1998, A1.

13. *United States v. Gigante,* 989 F. Supp. 436 (E.D.N.Y. 1997).

14. Selwyn Raab, "Mob's 'Commission' No Longer Meeting, as Families Weaken," *New York Times,* April 27, 1998, B1.

Glossary of Names

Robert Abrams New York State attorney general, 1979–1993.

Bernard Adelstein Founder and secretary-treasurer (top position) of Teamsters Local 813 from 1951 to 1992. Linked with the Gambino and Lucchese crime families.

Benedetto Aloi Underboss of the Colombo crime family. Organized the window-replacement cartel with Venero Mangano. He was convicted in 1991 for his participation in the cartel.

Mustapha Ally Maryland resident who in 1986 won the contract to start a concrete-batching plant that would supply concrete for all New York City public construction projects. Because his West 57th Street Concrete Corporation was unable to produce significant amounts of concrete, the contract was terminated.

Herbert Altman New York State justice who upheld the constitutionality of Organized Crime Control Act (OCCA), the state racketeering statute.

Vittorio Amuso Boss of the Lucchese family who fled to avoid prosecution in the windows case. Ultimately, he was apprehended and convicted of murder and racketeering.

Eugene R. Anderson Former federal prosecutor who served from 1987 to 1993 as the court-appointed trustee for Local 6A and the District Council of Cement and Concrete Workers. He concluded that the trusteeship was largely unsuccessful due to inadequate legal powers and insufficient funding.

William Aronwald Head of the U.S. Department of Justice's Joint Strike Force Against Organized Crime in Manhattan in the 1970s. He coordinated Project Cleveland, a large-scale sting operation in the garment center from March 1973 to August 1974.

Salvatore Avellino Lucchese family capo who dominated waste hauling on Long Island through the Private Sanitation Industry Association of Nassau/Suffolk from the 1960s to the 1980s. Owned Salem Sanitary Carting Corporation. He was convicted of murder conspiracy and racketeering in 1994.

Liborio "Barney" Bellomo Genovese family capo and reputedly the family's acting boss in the mid-1990s. In February 1997, he pled guilty to extortion related to the carting and construction industries and received a ten-year prison term.

G. Robert Blakey Principal draftsman of RICO statute, criminal law professor, and key advisor to the FBI in the 1980s.

Robert Boyle Appointed by Governor George Pataki as Javits Center president and CEO in 1995 with a mandate to purge organized crime. He implemented major reforms in the administration of the center. He resigned in 1997 to become executive director of the Port Authority of New York and New Jersey, and chairman of the Javits Center Board.

William Bratton New York City police commissioner, 1994–1996.

Raymond Buccafusco Codefendant with the Gambino brothers in the 1992 Garment Center racketeering case. He entered into a plea agreement.

Louis "Lepke" Buchalter In 1928, with Jacob "Gurrah" Shapiro, he took over Arnold Rothstein's labor rackets in the garment industry. He owned design firms and controlled trade associations and the truckers' union. He was convicted of murder and executed in 1944.

Vincent "the Fish" Cafaro Genovese family soldier who played a key role at the Javits Center and in the Carpenters' union. He became a cooperating witness and testified in several prosecutions and in the civil RICO suit against the Carpenters District Council.

Anthony Calagna Picked by Lucchese crime family in 1990 to run International Brotherhood of Teamsters Local 295 after Frank Calise was convicted of labor racketeering. He pled guilty in 1991 to extorting payoffs from a trucking company at JFK Airport.

Frank Calise Picked by Lucchese crime family to run International Brotherhood of Teamsters Local 295 when the Davidoffs were driven from power. In 1990, along with Harry Davidoff, Calise was convicted of labor racketeering involving payoffs from freight-forwarding companies at JFK Airport. He was sentenced to a nine-year prison term.

Charles Carberry Former federal prosecutor who was appointed investigations officer pursuant to the 1989 consent decree that established a three-person monitorship over the general executive board of the International Brotherhood of Teamsters. His investigations led to disciplinary charges against hundreds of Teamsters officials and members. Most charges resulted in expulsions and resignations from the union.

Ronald Carey Teamsters union reformer who campaigned against corruption and organized crime and was elected president of the International Brotherhood of Teamsters in 1991. He imposed trusteeships on several corrupt locals and stripped several local officers of their positions. He was charged with campaign finance fraud in the 1996 Teamsters election, was removed from office, and was expelled from the union.

U.S. Attorney Zachary Carter U.S. attorney for the Eastern District of New York, 1993 to present.

Anthony "Gaspipe" Casso Lucchese underboss who went into hiding in 1991 after being indicted in the windows case. While on the lam, he was also charged with involvement in the painters cartel. Apprehended in 1993, he pled guilty and served as a government witness. However, his untruthful testimony led to his removal from the Witness Security Program and ultimately to several life sentences for murders and other crimes.

Paul Castellano Carlo Gambino's successor as boss of the Gambino crime family. He was heavily involved in construction-industry racketeering, including the concrete cartel. He was assassinated in 1985 by a Gambino crew headed by capo John Gotti, who then became his successor as boss.

Michael Cherkasky Chief of Manhattan D.A. Office's investigations division who led the investigation of the Gambinos garment-industry racketeering. Later, as an executive of a private-sector security firm, he assisted Special Master Robert McGuire in the remedial phase of the Garment Center case. In 1994, he was appointed monitor for the Long Island waste-hauling industry. In 1997, he was appointed to monitor the 1998 International Brotherhood of Teamsters election.

John Cody Gambino associate and president of International Brotherhood of Teamsters Local 282 from 1976 to 1982. One of the most powerful labor figures in New York City, he was convicted of racketeering in 1982 and sentenced to five years in prison.

Kenneth Conboy Former New York City commissioner of investigation and federal judge who was appointed to be the investigations and review officer over the Carpenters District Council in 1994. His efforts led Carpenters International president Douglas McCarron to place the District Council under trusteeship in 1996. Conboy also serves (as of January 1999) as the court-appointed election officer in the International Brotherhood of Teamsters case.

Paul Coscia Chief shop steward and later vice-president of the Exhibition Employees Union Local 829, which represented workers at the Javits Center. Reputed to be an associate of the Genovese crime family.

Mario Cuomo Governor of New York State from 1983 to 1995.

Alphonse "Little Al" D'Arco Acting boss of the Lucchese crime family who exerted influence on the Carpenters union and received payoffs from businesses that employed members of the union, ghost payrolled family members, and defrauded employee pension funds. Became a government witness.

Harry Davidoff Lucchese family associate whom Jimmy Hoffa appointed president of International Brotherhood of Teamsters Local 295 in 1956. He dominated Local 295 until 1989, when he was convicted on racketeering, extortion, and conspiracy charges. He was sentenced to twelve years in prison and banned from participating in the affairs of Local 295 and Local 851. In 1991, he and Frank Calise were convicted of collecting payoffs from freight-forwarding companies at JFK Airport. He was fined nearly $1 million.

Mark Davidoff Harry Davidoff's son, secretary-treasurer of International Brotherhood of Teamsters (IBT) Local 851. He resigned in 1990 when the IBT Review Board began investigating racketeering in New York City Teamsters locals.

Steven "Beansy" Dellacava Chief shop steward, with Paul Coscia, for the Exhibition Employees Union at the Javits Center until mid-1995. Reputed to be an associate of the Genovese crime family. After leaving the

Javits Center, he controlled job distribution for exhibition and trade shows in other New York facilities.

Ron DePetris Former chief assistant U.S. attorney, Eastern District of New York, who, pursuant to a 1994 consent decree, was appointed independent supervisor of International Brotherhood of Teamsters Local 851, which represented workers in the JFK air-cargo industry. He hired David Krasula as his chief investigator.

Frederick Devine President of the Carpenters District Council from 1991 to 1996. Mob turncoats, including Vincent Cafaro and Sammy Gravano, testified that he was associated with several Cosa Nostra families. He was ousted from his position in 1996 by the International union president. In 1998, he was convicted of embezzling union funds and sentenced to fifteen months in prison.

Thomas E. Dewey Assistant U.S. attorney for the Southern District of New York from 1931 to 1933. Special prosecutor for the State of New York from 1935 to 1937. Manhattan district attorney from 1938 to 1942. He prosecuted several organized-crime figures, including garment-industry racketeers Louis "Lepke" Buchalter, Jacob "Gurrah" Shapiro, and John "Johnny Dio" Dioguardi. He was New York State governor from 1943 to 1952.

Vincent DiNapoli Genovese family capo who organized the drywall cartel. He controlled Cambridge Drywall and Inner City Drywall. He was also responsible for creating Plasterers Local 530, which was run by Louis Moscatiello. In 1980, he was convicted of racketeering and sentenced to a five-year prison term. In 1988, he was convicted in the Genovese family RICO case and sentenced to a long prison term.

John "Johnny Dio" Dioguardi Capo in the Lucchese crime family who was associated with Thomas Lucchese in the Garment Center. He was convicted on racketeering charges in the 1930s but served only a brief sentence. He worked as a trucking "consultant" for the Metropolitan Import Truckmen's Association (MITA), later known as the National Association for Air-Freight, Inc. (NAFA). He assisted Jimmy Hoffa in taking control of Teamsters Joint Council 16, which includes Local 295 and many other locals. He was convicted in 1958 for conspiracy and extortion in connection with labor racketeering at JFK Airport. He went to prison in 1973 on a stock-fraud conviction and died there in 1979.

John DiSalvo Owner of trucking interests in the Garment Center who was named as a codefendant with the Gambino brothers. He entered a plea agreement in 1992.

Natale "Joe Diamond" Evola Longtime member and nominal boss of the Bonanno crime family in the early 1970s. He owned several Garment Center trucking companies and was a major racketeer in the Garment Center. He died of natural causes in 1973 while under federal investigation.

James "Jimmy Brown" Failla Managed Association of Trade Waste Removers of Greater New York for more than thirty years. Exerted influence over International Brotherhood of Teamsters Local 813. Capo in the Gambino family. In 1994, he pled guilty to charges of conspiracy to commit murder and received a seven-year prison term.

William A. Ferchak Longtime officer of International Brotherhood of Teamsters (IBT) Local 732 whom Frederick Lacey appointed temporary trustee of IBT Local 295 in 1991.

Edward T. Ferguson III Former federal prosecutor who, in 1997, was appointed executive director of New York City Trade Waste Commission.

Anthony Fiorino Genovese crime-family associate and Liborio Bellomo's brother-in-law. In 1982 he became a member of Carpenters Local 257 and was named shop steward in 1985. He was assigned to the Javits Center in 1988 and four weeks later appointed to the supervisory position of "timekeeper." He was soon promoted to be the chief of carpenters at the center. Frederick Devine appointed him to succeed Ralph Coppola as District Council representative in 1994. He was the first union member to face disciplinary charges under the consent decree. He was expelled from the union for life for knowingly associating with members of the Genovese crime family and for enforcing a corrupt "pool-list" referral system.

Dominic Froncillo International Brotherhood of Teamsters Local 807 member and Javits Center employee whom the Independent Review Board charged with knowingly associating with a member of organized crime. He testified to a fifteen-year friendship with Alphonse Malangone, reputed Genovese family capo. In 1996, he was permanently barred from the union.

Thomas Galligan New York State justice who presided over *People v. Gambino et al.* (1992). He appointed Robert McGuire as special master of the Gambinos' trucking interests in the Garment Center.

Joseph N. Gallo Gambino family consigliere who controlled the Greater Blouse, Skirt and Undergarment Association. He was convicted of bribery in 1987 and sentenced to a long prison term.

Carlo Gambino Boss of Gambino Cosa Nostra crime family. Father of Thomas and Joseph Gambino. He selected Paul Castellano as his successor. He died in 1976.

Joseph Gambino Carlo Gambino's son and Thomas Gambino's brother. The Gambino brothers were the dominant figures in Garment Center trucking until in a 1992 plea bargain they agreed to withdraw from the industry and pay a $12 million fine.

Thomas Gambino Carlo Gambino's son and Joseph Gambino's brother. The Gambino brothers were the dominant Cosa Nostra figures in the New York City garment industry until their 1992 plea bargain, in which they agreed to withdraw from the industry and pay a $12 million fine. Thomas's wealth was estimated as $100 million. He was convicted in 1993 on unrelated racketeering charges in Connecticut and was sentenced to a five-year prison term.

William F. Genoese Officer of International Brotherhood of Teamsters (IBT) Local 732. He was nominated by IBT president Ron Carey in 1992 to replace William Ferchak as temporary trustee of Local 295. After an investigation uncovered ties to the Lucchese crime family and inaction in the face of corruption at JFK Airport, his nomination was vetoed by IBT Independent Administrator Frederick Lacey. President Carey ultimately stripped him of his Local 732 position.

Vincent "the Chin" Gigante Boss of the Genovese family who was known to walk the streets in his bathrobe while mumbling to himself. Government prosecutors argued that he was faking mental illness. Sammy Gravano testified that Gigante was in full control of his wits and the Genovese family. Gigante avoided trial in the windows RICO case when found mentally unfit to stand trial. In 1997, he was convicted of RICO and sentenced to twelve years in prison.

Rudolph Giuliani Associate attorney general of the United States, 1981–1983. U.S. attorney for the Southern District of New York, 1983–1989. His office prosecuted the Gambino, Bonanno, and Genovese family RICO cases and *United States v. Salerno,* the "commission" case. He also brought civil RICO suits against the general executive board of the International Brotherhood of Teamsters, and against Local 359 and the Genovese family at the Fulton Fish Market. As mayor (1994–present), he established a licensing system to free the Fulton Fish Market of mob control and a Trade Waste Commission to break up the waste-hauling cartel.

Leo I. Glasser United States district judge, Eastern District of New York, who presided over several organized-crime cases, including *United States v. Private Sanitation Industry Assoc. of Nassau/Suffolk, Inc.,* and *United States v. Gotti.*

John Gleeson Assistant U.S. attorney, Eastern District of New York, and chief of that office's organized crime section, 1990–1993. Federal court judge, 1994 to present.

Ronald Goldstock Director of New York State's Organized Crime Task Force, 1981–1994, who directed the comprehensive investigation of corruption and racketeering in the New York City construction industry. He first advocated use of private monitors as an organized-crime control strategy. He played a key role in investigating the Long Island carting cartel. In 1996, he was appointed to the Board of Directors of the New York Convention Center Operating Corporation, which operates the Javits Center.

John Gotti Boss of the Gambino crime family in the 1980s after the assassination of Paul Castellano. In the 1960s, he spent three years in prison for hijacking trucks from JFK Airport. He was convicted in 1992 of RICO violations and various predicate offenses, including the murder of Paul Castellano. He was sentenced to life in prison.

Victor Grande Pled guilty in 1982 to failure to pay taxes on money received from a vehicle-protection racket at the Fulton Fish Market.

Sammy "the Bull" Gravano Gambino underboss who cooperated with the government and testified against John Gotti in 1992 and against several other important mob figures.

Mark Green Commissioner of Department of Consumer Affairs from 1990 to 1992. With Deputy Commissioner Richard Schreder, he undertook a number of initiatives to purge organized crime from the carting industry. In 1993, he was elected public advocate.

Thomas Griesa U.S. district judge for the Southern District of New York who presided over a number of cases involving the Fulton Fish Market, including *United States v. Local 359.*

Charles Haight Federal judge who presided over the civil RICO suit against the Carpenters District Council. He appointed Kenneth Conboy investigations and review officer.

Edward "Biff" Halloran Genovese associate who monopolized all ready-mix concrete suppliers in the 1980s. He was convicted in the Genovese family RICO case in 1988, and the companies he owned were forfeited to the government.

Henry Hill Lucchese associate turned government witness. He claims to have masterminded the 1978 Lufthansa heist with Jimmy Burke and Paul Vario. He testified against various Lucchese members and associates and entered the Witness Security Program. The story of his life, written with Peter Maas, was published as *Wiseguy* and later adapted into the movie *Goodfellas.*

James R. Hoffa Turned over several New York City–area International Brotherhood of Teamsters (IBT) locals to Cosa Nostra in exchange for the mob's support in his 1956 campaign for the IBT presidency. President of IBT from 1956 to 1958, and from 1961 until his conviction in 1964 for pension fraud and jury tampering. Disappeared in 1975, presumed the victim of a mob assassination, while campaigning to regain control of the IBT on a platform of freeing the union from mob domination.

Samuel H. Hofstadter New York State justice who, in the 1950s, upheld New York City's denial of a license to James Plumeri's garment-industry trucking company because of Plumeri's ties to organized crime.

Michael Holland Labor lawyer appointed elections officer pursuant to 1989 consent decree that established a three-person trusteeship over the International Brotherhood of Teamsters.

Matthew "Matty the Horse" Ianniello Longtime capo in the Genovese crime family. He was involved in several rackets, including working as

Frank Wolf's assistant in the Master Truckmen of America and as a business agent for International Ladies Garment Workers Union Local 102. In 1976, he was acquitted of conspiracy to commit extortion in Garment Center. Convicted in 1986 on unrelated racketeering charges and sentenced to a long prison term.

Paul Kamen President of Painters District Council 9 until 1991, when he pled guilty to Organized Crime Control Act (OCCA) enterprise corruption related to the painters cartel. His plea confirmed prosecutors' suspicions that he was associated with the Lucchese crime family.

Gerald Kelty Member of Carpenters Local 257 who alleged that Anthony Fiorino had ordered him set on fire and had metal studs dropped on him because he had complained about union-contract violations.

Edward I. Koch Mayor of New York City, 1978–1989. He joined with Governor Cuomo in calling for an investigation of corruption and racketeering in the construction industry.

James Kossler Coordinating supervisor, organized crime branch, New York City FBI office, late 1970s to late 1980s. One of the key figures in designing and implementing the FBI's organized-crime control program.

David Krasula Longtime investigator with the U.S. Postal Inspection Service and U.S. Department of Labor. He was hired by Ron DePetris as chief investigator of International Brotherhood of Teamsters Local 851, pursuant to the October 1994 consent decree in a case involving racketeering in the air-cargo industry at JFK Airport.

Frederick B. Lacey Former federal judge who, pursuant to 1989 Teamsters consent decree, served as independent administrator in the trusteeship over the International Brotherhood of Teamsters. Later he served as a member of the Independent Review Board in that same case.

Joseph "Socks" Lanza Genovese crime family capo who controlled Fulton Fish Market and exerted much influence on the entire New York City waterfront from the 1920s to the 1950s. In 1923, he organized Local 359 of the United Seafood Workers representing workers in the Fulton

Fish Market. Despite criminal convictions and prison terms, he remained on the local's payroll and served as its business agent until his death in 1968.

Nunzio "Harry" Lanza Capo in the Genovese crime family and brother of Joseph Lanza. He served as a Local 359 official throughout the 1960s.

Franz Leichter New York State senator who, in 1981, issued a comprehensive report on Cosa Nostra's involvement in the New York City garment industry.

Thomas "Three-Finger Brown" Lucchese Successor to Jacob Shapiro and Louis Buchalter. As boss of the Lucchese crime family, he had several ownership interests in and was involved in managing rackets in the garment industry. His garment-industry interests were passed on to his son-in-law Thomas Gambino and to Joseph Gambino.

Andrew J. Maloney U.S attorney for Eastern District of New York from 1986 to 1992.

Venero Mangano Genovese underboss in the late 1980s who organized the window-replacement cartel with Benedetto Aloi and conspired to murder potential witnesses. He was convicted in 1991 and received a 188-month sentence.

Theodore "Teddy" Maritas President of the Carpenters District Council from 1977 to 1981. He allegedly helped Vincent DiNapoli organize and enforce the drywall cartel. The prosecution against him and DiNapoli for drywall racketeering ended in a hung jury. He disappeared in 1992, presumed murdered to prevent cooperation with the government against his codefendants.

Paul Martello Business agent of Plumbers Local 2 who was reelected in 1996 despite pending charges of enterprise corruption and other crimes related to the painters cartel. He was acquitted of those charges.

Randy Mastro Assistant U.S. attorney in the Southern District of New York under Rudolph Giuliani. Lead attorney on the civil RICO suit against the International Brotherhood of Teamsters general executive board and Cosa Nostra members. Chief of staff and deputy mayor of the City of New York, 1994–1998. First (temporary) director of the Trade Waste Commission, 1996–1997.

H. Carl McCall New York State comptroller whose 1995 audit criticized the Javits Center's management and financial controls.

Edward McDonald Director of Brooklyn Organized Crime Strike Force from 1982 to 1989.

Thomas McGowan President of Local 580 of the Architectural and Ornamental Ironworkers Union. He was acquitted in the windows prosecution. He was convicted in 1994 for crimes, related to the windows cartel, involving payoffs from a private contractor.

Robert McGuire New York City police commissioner who was appointed special master over the Gambino brothers' Garment Center trucking interests from 1992 to 1997. He instituted several reforms to break up the trucking cartel's "marriage system" and established a $3 million victims' compensation fund from the Gambinos' $12 million fine.

Gerald McQueen Former investigator in the Manhattan district attorney's organized crime and labor racketeering unit. In 1995, Governor Pataki appointed him inspector general of Javits Center. In 1997, the governor appointed him chief executive officer of the center. He carried forward the organized-crime-control and administrative-reform program of Robert Boyle.

John Mitchell U.S. attorney general, 1969–1972. He brought antitrust suits in 1971 against several New York City trucking companies and the National Association for Air-Freight, Inc. (NAFA), leading to the 1974 dissolution of the corrupt trade association.

Robert Morgenthau U.S. attorney for Southern District of New York, 1961–1970. Manhattan district attorney 1975 to present.

Michael Moroney Former official in the U.S. Department of Labor's Office of Labor Racketeering who in April 1992 was hired by Thomas Puccio as deputy trustee of International Brotherhood of Teamsters Local 295.

Louis Moscatiello President of Plasterers Local 530, which was created by Vincent DiNapoli. He was convicted in 1991 for his role as a bribe broker in the drywall industry and sent to prison.

Eugene H. Nickerson Federal judge who presided over cases dealing with JFK Airport racketeering.

Curt Ostrander Appointed trustee of Local 851 in 1994 by International Brotherhood of Teamsters President Ron Carey. He was replaced by Eileen Sullivan in November 1996.

Fabian Palomino Javits Center's president and CEO, 1991–1995. The state comptroller charged that he mismanaged the center and tolerated corruption.

George Pataki Governor of New York State, 1994 to present. He committed his administration to an all out attack on organized crime at the Javits Center. He appointed Robert Boyle as CEO of the Javits Center and Gerald McQueen as the center's inspector general.

Sebastian Pipitone Javits Center inspector general, 1994–1995, under CEO Fabian Palomino.

James Plumeri Lucchese crime-family member who held ownership interests in the Garment Center, including, Ell-Gee Carriers Corp. and Barton Trucking Company. He unsuccessfully challenged the New York City commissioner of licenses for denying a business license to Barton Trucking in the 1950s. He was murdered in 1971.

Angelo Ponte Member of the carting cartel. Owner of CV Ponte & Sons, one of the largest waste-hauling firms in the city, and allegedly a business partner of the Genovese crime family. Pled guilty to attempted enterprise corruption and was sentenced to two to six years in prison, fined $7.5 million, and permanently barred from the waste-hauling industry.

Michael Porta Jr. International Brotherhood of Teamsters member employed at the Javits Center. In 1995, he was charged with knowingly associating with members of organized-crime families and permanently barred from the union.

Anthony "Tony Pro" Provenzano Longtime president of International Brotherhood of Teamsters Local 560 and capo in the Genovese crime family. In 1978, as a result of the Project Cleveland investigation, he was convicted of illegally obtaining a loan from a union pension fund. In 1978, he was convicted of murder and later died in prison.

Thomas Puccio Former assistant U.S. attorney and former chief of the Brooklyn Organized Crime Strike Force. As a private lawyer, he was appointed trustee of IBT Local 295 in April 1992.

Michael Rabbitt Son of Robert Rabbitt Sr. In 1994, he headed Teamsters' contract-negotiating team with the decorator companies. The contract redefined the general foreman as a management position. He left the union and assumed the new general foreman position. He was indicted for conspiracy to extort money from the president of a company doing business at the Javits Center, receiving bribes, grand larceny through extortion, criminal possession of stolen property, and falsification of business records with the intent to defraud. All the charges were dropped after Rabbitt Sr. pled guilty. He subsequently relinquished the general foreman position to Rabbitt Sr. upon the latter's release from prison.

Robert Rabbitt Sr. With sons Michael and Robert Jr., led International Brotherhood of Teamsters Local 807 for almost three decades. Business agent of Teamsters Local 807 charged with bringing reproach upon the union by taking money from an exhibitor at the Javits Center. Upon settlement, he resigned from the union for five years. He was indicted for conspiracy to extort money from the president of a company doing business at the Javits Center, receiving bribes, grand larceny through extortion, criminal possession of stolen property, and falsification of business records with the intent to defraud. He pled guilty to falsification of business records, and all the other charges were dropped. He was convicted of second-degree manslaughter in 1985 and banned from the union for five years. The general foreman position was held open until he was released from prison in 1988. In 1992, he pled guilty to falsifying business records and, after serving one year in prison, returned to the position of general foreman. Under threat of bribery charges, he accepted a five-year suspension from the union, and his son Michael took over his position.

Robert Rabbitt Jr. Son of Robert Rabbitt Sr. who succeeded his father as International Brotherhood of Teamsters (IBT) Local 807 business agent. He was removed from this position in 1985 by IBT President Ron Carey.

Anthony Razza Secretary-treasurer (the top position) of International Brotherhood of Teamsters Local 851, which represented employees in the JFK air-cargo industry. In 1994, he was convicted of labor racketeering and tax fraud and sentenced to twenty-one months in prison. He was barred from the IBT for life.

Armando Rea Teamster member employed at the Javits Center who in 1994 was charged with violating the International Brotherhood of Teamsters oath by being a member of an organized-crime family and associating with organized-crime figures. The Independent Review Board permanently barred him from the union.

Salvatore Reale Associate of the Gambino crime family who served as director of security for a trucking company at JFK Airport. He was John Gotti's "on-stage guy" at JFK Airport. Named Man of the Year by the Patrolmen's Benevolent Association in 1978. In 1987, he pled guilty to extortion and was sentenced to a fifteen-year suspended prison term.

Ronald Rivera New York State Police officer who ran Chrystie Fashions during yearlong undercover sting operation in the Garment Center. He testified for the prosecution against the Gambino brothers.

Carmine Romano "Socks" Lanza's successor as the Genovese family's boss at the Fulton Fish Market. He served as secretary-treasurer of United Seafood Workers, Smoked Fish and Cannery Union Local 359 from 1974 to 1980, when he received a twelve-year prison sentence for violating RICO and the Taft-Hartley Act.

Peter Romano Brother of Carmine Romano. He was appointed business agent of Local 359 in 1974 when Carmine became secretary-treasurer. In 1981, he was convicted of obstruction of justice and perjury and sent to prison for eighteen months.

Vincent Romano Brother of Carmine and Peter and member of the Genovese crime family. He assumed control of the Fulton Fish Market in 1981 following his brothers' convictions. He took over as secretary-treasurer of United Seafood Workers, Smoked Fish and Cannery Union Local 359 in 1980. A 1988 consent judgment permanently barred him from working in the market.

Arnold Rothstein First major organized-crime figure involved in New York City's garment industry. He employed thugs for and against designers in their battles with unions. He was murdered in 1928.

William Ruckelhaus Chief executive officer of Browning, Ferris, Inc. (BFI), who led BFI into the New York waste-hauling market in 1991, and cooperated with District Attorney Morgenthau.

Anthony "Fat Tony" Salerno Genovese family's ostensible boss. FBI later considered him to be Vincent Gigante's subordinate. He was convicted in the 1986 "commission" case, among other things, of rigging Javits Center bids, inflating the center's concrete bids, and inflating the center's construction costs by approximately $12 million. He died later in prison while under indictment in the Genovese family RICO case.

Robert Sasso President of International Brotherhood of Teamsters Local 282. He resigned as a result of an investigation by the International union's court-appointed investigations officer, Charles Carberry, into allegations that Sasso was influenced by the Gambino crime family. He pled guilty to racketeering involving an extortion conspiracy with organized crime in 1994.

Peter Savino Genovese associate implicated in the windows cartel. He started Arista Windows with Lucchese drug money and used Cosa Nostra's domination of the window-replacement industry to advance the company. He became a government informant, and surreptitiously recorded several hours of conversations regarding the windows cartel.

Irwin Schiff Owner of electrical contracting company that did business at the Javits Center. He was murdered in a Manhattan restaurant after informing the FBI of an alleged contract killing at the center and of a money-laundering scheme.

Ralph Scopo Colombo soldier who enforced the concrete cartel through his position as the president of the District Council of Cement and Concrete Workers. He was convicted in both the "commission" and Colombo family RICO cases and sentenced to one hundred years in prison.

Jacob "Gurrah" Shapiro Along with Louis "Lepke" Buchalter, took over Arnold Rothstein's labor rackets in the New York City garment industry. He expanded into ownership of design firms, controlled the trade associations and the International Ladies Garment Workers Union's local. Shapiro was convicted of extortion in 1938.

Gerald Shargel Prominent criminal defense lawyer who represented John Gotti in his 1990 state case and the Gambino brothers in their 1992 case. He negotiated a plea agreement with the Manhattan District Attorney's Office in which the Gambino brothers agreed to withdraw from the industry and to pay a $12 million fine.

Elliot Spitzer Assistant district attorney (New York County) who served as lead prosecutor in the Garment Center racketeering case in 1992 against Thomas and Joseph Gambino. Elected New York State attorney general in 1998

Marcello Svedese Carpenter's union official who, as a cooperating witness, testified in several cases, including the civil RICO suit against the Carpenters District Council.

Brian Taylor FBI agent who played an important part in both the fish market and carting investigations. He succeeded James Kossler as coordinating supervisor, organized-crime branch, New York City FBI office.

Thomas D. Thacher II Director of the Construction Industry Strike Force in the late 1980s and first inspector general of the School Construction Authority in 1989.

Paul Vario Capo in the Lucchese crime family who, according to Henry Hill, directed the Lufthansa heist. He was convicted and sentenced to four years in prison for conspiring to secure the early release of a Lufthansa employee who had been convicted for involvement in that heist. He was convicted in 1986 of extorting from trucking companies operating at JFK Airport, and was sent to prison. He died in prison in 1988.

Peter "Butch" Vario Nephew of Paul Vario, cousin to Peter "Jocko" Vario, and an associate of the Lucchese crime family. Business manager of Mason Tenders Local 46 from 1984 to 1989. In 1988, he was convicted of RICO conspiracy involving labor payoffs in Queens. He was sentenced to three and a half to ten and a half years in prison in 1989.

Peter "Jocko" Vario Nephew of Paul Vario. Cousin to Peter "Butch" Vario. Lucchese soldier. Vice-president of Laborer's International Union of North America Local 66, which policed the Long Island concrete cartel. He was convicted in 1990 for RICO conspiracy involving labor payoffs in Queens and was sentenced to a forty-six-month prison term.

Mary Jo White Former acting U.S. attorney, Eastern District of New York. U.S. attorney for Southern District of New York from 1993 to present.

Frank Wohl Former federal prosecutor appointed administrator of the Fulton Fish Market by Judge Griesa following the 1988 *United States v. Local 359* consent and default judgments. He issued fourteen reports from 1988 to 1992, including a 1990 midterm report calling on New York City to pass comprehensive regulatory reforms. He hired Brian Carroll as assistant administrator.

Frank Wolf President of the Master Truckmen of America (MTA) representing trucking companies in the garment center. As a result of the Project Cleveland sting operation, he was indicted for extortion. His acquittal in 1976 was a major blow to the Project Cleveland effort.

John C. Zancocchio Member of International Brotherhood of Teamsters (IBT) Union who worked at Javits Center. He was charged with violating the IBT oath by knowingly associating with members of organized crime. In 1994, IBT's Independent Review Board found him to be a member of the Bonanno crime family and barred him from the IBT.

List of Indictments and Judicial Decisions

Barton Trucking Corp. v. O'Connell, 173 N.Y.S.2d 464 (N.Y.Sup. 1958).
Big Apple Concrete Corp. v. Abrams, 481 N.Y.S.2d 335 (1983).
Comm. to Save the Fulton Fish Mkt. v. City of New York, 95 Civ. 8759 (S.D.N.Y. 1996).
Danielson v. Local 359, 405 F. Supp. 396 (S.D.N.Y. 1975).
Devine v. New York Convention Center Operating Corp., 639 N.Y.S.2d 904 (N.Y. Sup. Ct. 1996).
Jerry Kubecka, Inc. v. Avellino, 898 F. Supp. 963 (E.D.N.Y. 1995).
Local 85 v. Kuehne & Nagel Air Freight, Inc., 1998 WL 178873 (E.D.N.Y. March 6, 1998).
Local 851, IBT v. Kuehne & Nagel Air Freight, Inc., 97 civ. 0378 (E.D.N.Y. 1997).
Local 851, IBT v. Thyssen Haniel Logistics, Inc., 95 Civ. 5179 (E.D.N.Y. 1995).
Palmieri v. State of New York, 779 F.2d 861 (2d Cir. 1985).
People v. Adelstein, 8 N.Y.2d 998 (N.Y. App. Div. 1960).
People v. Association of Trade Waste Removers, Indictment No. No. 05614/95 (Sup. Ct., N.Y. County 1995).
People v. Capaldo, 572 N.Y.S.2d 989 (1991).
People v. Davidoff, 85 Cr. 100 (SS) (E.D.N.Y. December 12, 1986).
People v. Falco, Indictment No. 4033-96.
People v. Gambino, Indictment No. 11859-90.
People v. Gardner, Indictment No. 4032-96.
People v. McCann, Indictment No. 4292-96.
People v. McNamee, Indictment No. 4293-96.
People v. Moscatiello, Indictment No. 8081/89 (N.Y. County 1989).
People v. Pagano, Indictment No. 120/89 (Rockland County 1989).
People v. Potts, Indictment No. 254-92.
People v. Private Sanitation Industry of Nassau/Suffolk, Inc., 136 Misc.2d 612 (Suffolk County Court, 1987).
People v. Robert Rabbitt Sr., Indictment Nos. 245–249/92.
People v. Sail Carting & Recycling Co., Inc., 158 A.D.2d 724 (N.Y. App. Div. 1990).
People v. Salzarulo, 639 N.Y.S.2d 885 (1996).

People v. Schepis, 614 N.Y.S.2d 719 (1994).
People v. Stuart, Indictment No. 11858/90 (October 1990).
People v. Vespucci, 553 N.E.2d 965 (N.Y. 1990).
Quadrozzi v. City of New York, 127 F.R.D. 63 (S.D.N.Y. 1989).
Russo v. Morgan, 21 N.Y.S.2d 637 (1940).
Sanitation and Recycling Indus. v. City of New York, 923 F. Supp. 407 (S.D.N.Y. 1996).
State of New York v. Salem Sanitary Carting Corp., 1989 WL 111597 (E.D.N.Y. August 9, 1989).
Trustees of Plumbers and Pipefitters Nat'l. Pension Fund v. Transworld Mechanical, Inc., 886 F. Supp. 1134 (S.D.N.Y. 1995).
United States v. Amuso, 21 F.3d 1251 (2d Cir. 1994).
United States v. Badalamenti, 84 Cr. 236 (S.D.N.Y. 1987).
United States v. Bonanno Organized Crime Family, 87 Civ. 2974 (E.D.N.Y. 1987).
United States v. Bellomo, 96 Cr. 430 (LAK).
United States v. Casso, 843 F. Supp. 829 (E.D.N.Y. 1994).
United States v. Cervone, 907 F.2d 332 (2d Cir. 1990).
United States v. Cloak and Suit Truckin Ass'n, Civ. No. 66-141 (1955).
United States v. Cody, 722 F.2d 1052 (2d Cir. 1983).
United States v. Colombo, 616 F. Supp. 780 (E.D.N.Y. 1985).
United States v. Corallo, 413 F.2d 1306 (2d Cir. 1969).
United States v. Daly, 842 F.2d 1380 (2d Cir. 1988).
United States v. Defede, 98 Cr. 373 (S.D.N.Y. 1998).
United States v. Dello Russo, 93 Cr. 1012 (E.D.N.Y. 1993).
United States v. Dilapi, 651 F.2d 140 (2d Cir. 1981).
United States v. DiNapoli, 8 F.2d 909 (2d Cir. 1993) (en banc).
United States v. District Council of New York City and Vicinity of the United Brotherhood of Carpenters and Joiners of America, 90 Civ. 5722 (CSH) (S.D.N.Y. 1990).
United States v. Failla, 1993 WL 547419 (E.D.N.Y. December 21, 1993).
United States v. Gallo, 671 F. Supp. 124 (E.D.N.Y. 1987).
United States v. Gangi, Indictment No. 97 Cr. 1215.
United States v. Gigante, 39 F.3d 42 (2d Cir. 1994).
United States v. Gotti, 1997 WL 157549 (E.D.N.Y. April 3, 1997).
United States v. Gotti, 641 F. Supp. 283 (S.D.N.Y. 1986).
United States v. Guerrieri, 89 Cr. 307(S) (E.D.N.Y. 1991).
United States v. Halloran, 86 Cr. 245 (S.D.N.Y. 1989).
United States v. IBT, 708 F. Supp. 1288 (S.D.N.Y. 1989).
United States v. Langella, 804 F.2d 185 (2d Cir. 1986).
United States v. Lanza, Cr. 86-90 (S.D.N.Y. 1938).
United States v. Local 6A, Cement and Concrete Workers, 86 Civ. 4819 (S.D.N.Y. 1986).
United States v. Local 295, IBT, 90 Civ. 0971 (E.D.N.Y. 1991).

United States v. Local 359 of the United Seafood Worker, Smoked Fish and Cannery Union, 87 Civ. 7351 (S.D.N.Y.).
United States v. Mangano, 90 Cr. 0446 (E.D.N.Y. 1990).
United States v. Maritas, 81 Cr. 122 (E.D.N.Y. 1981).
United States v. Mason Tenders District Council of Greater New York, No. 94 Civ. 6487 (RWS).
United States v. McGowan, 58 F.3d 8 (2d Cir. 1995).
United States v. McGuinness, 764 F. Supp. 888 (S.D.N.Y. 1991).
United States v. Migliore, 104 F.3d 354 (2d Cir. 1996).
United States v. Mongelli, 2 F.3d 29 (2d Cir. 1993).
United States v. NAFA, 1974 WL 903 (E.D.N.Y. August 29, 1974).
United States v. Nunzio Leanzo, 80 Cr. 808 (S.D.N.Y. 1981).
United States v. Persico, 832 F.2d 705 (2d Cir. 1987).
United States v. Petito, 671 F.2d 68 (2d. Cir. 1982).
United States v. Private Sanitation Industry Assoc. of Nassau/Suffolk, Inc., 995 F.2d 375 (2d Cir. 1993).
United States v. Provenzano, 615 F.2d 37 (2d Cir. 1980).
United States v. Reale, 86 Cr. 302 (E.D.N.Y. 1988).
United States v. Romano, 684 F.2d 1057 (2d Cir. 1982).
United States v. Salerno, 86 Cr. 245 (S.D.N.Y. 1986); 85 Cr. 139 (S.D.N.Y. 1985).
United States v. Salerno, 868 F.2d 524 (2d Cir. 1989).
United States v. Salerno, 937 F.2d 797 (2d Cir. 1991).
United States v. Santoro, Cr. No. 85-100(s) (E.D.N.Y. November 7, 1986).
United States v. Sanzo, 673 F.2d 64 (2d Cir. 1982).
United States v. Sasso, Cr. 92-1344.
United States v. Sherman, 84 Cr. 205 (S.D.N.Y. 1984).
United States v. Socony-Vacuum Oil Co., 310 U.S. 150 (1940).
United States v. Standard Drywall Corp., 617 F. Supp. 1283 (E.D.N.Y. 1985).
United States v. Vario, 88 Cr. 719 (E.D.N.Y. 1988).
United States v. Werner, 620 F.2d 922 (2d Cir. 1979).
Universal Sanitation Corp. v. Trade Waste Comm'n, 940 F. Supp. 656 (S.D.N.Y. 1996).
WMX Technologies v. Miller, 104 F.3d 1133 (9th Cir. 1997).

Select Bibliography

Abadinsky, Howard. *Organized Crime.* 4th ed. Chicago: Nelson Hall, 1994.

Alexander, Shana. *The Pizza Connection: Lawyers, Money, Drugs, Mafia.* New York: Weidenfeld, 1988.

Anechiarico, Frank, and James B. Jacobs. *Pursuit of Absolute Integrity: How Corruption Control Makes Government Ineffective.* Chicago: University of Chicago Press, 1996.

Bell, Daniel. "The Racket-Ridden Longshoremen: The Web of Economics and Politics." In *The End of Ideology,* edited by Daniel Bell. New York: Collier, 1961.

Blakey, G. Robert, and Ronald Goldstock. "On the Waterfront: RICO and Labor Racketeering." *American Criminal Law Review* 17 (1980): 341.

Block, Alan A. *Organizing Crime.* New York: Elsevier, 1981.

Block, Alan, and Frank R. Scarpetti. *Poisoning for Profit: Cosa Nostra and Toxic Waste in America.* New York: Morrow, 1985.

Bonanno, Joseph (with Sergio Lulli). *A Man of Honor: The Autobiography of Joseph Bonanno.* New York: Simon and Schuster, 1983.

Brill, Stephen. *The Teamsters.* New York: Simon and Schuster, 1978.

Carroll, Brian. "Combating Racketeering in the Fulton Fish Market." In *Organized Crime and Its Containment,* edited by Cyrille Fijnaut and James B. Jacobs. Boston: Kluwer, 1991.

Coleman, James, Seymour Martin Lipset, and Martin A. Trow. *Union Democracy: The Internal Politics of the International Typographical Union.* Glenco, Ill.: Free Press, 1956.

Davis, John H. *Mafia Dynasty: The Rise and Fall of the Gambino Crime Family.* New York: HarperCollins, 1993.

Dewey, Thomas E., *Twenty against the Underworld.* Garden City, N.Y.: Doubleday, 1974.

DiIulio, John J., Jr., et al. "The Federal Role in Crime Control." In *Crime,* edited by James Q. Wilson and Joan Petersilia. San Francisco: Institute of Contemporary Studies Press, 1995.

Fijnaut, Cyrille, and James B. Jacobs, eds. *Organized Crime and Its Containment: A Transatlantic Initiative.* Boston: Kluwer, 1991.

Fox, Stephen. *Blood and Power: Organized Crime in the Twentieth Century.* New York: Morrow, 1989.

Goldstock, Ronald. "IPSIG: The Independent Private Sector Inspector General Program." *Corporate Conduct Quarterly* 4 (1996): 38.

Hutchinson, John. *The Imperfect Union.* New York: Dutton Press, 1970.

Ianni, Francis, and Elizabeth Reuss Ianni. *A Family Business: Kinship and Social Control in Organized Crime.* New York: Russell Sage, 1972.

Jackson, Kenneth T., ed. *The Encyclopedia of the City of New York.* New Haven: Yale University Press, 1995.

Jacobs, James B., and Frank Anechiarico. "Purging Corruption from Public Contracting: The 'Solutions' Are Now Part of the Problem." *New York Law School Law Review* 15, nos. 1–2 (1995): 143–75.

Jacobs, James B., and Lauryn P. Gouldin. "Cosa Nostra: The Final Chapter?" In *Crime and Justice: An Annual Review of Research,* edited by Michael Tonry. Vol. 25. Chicago: University of Chicago Press, 1999.

Jacobs, James B., and Alex Hortis. "New York City as Organized Crime Fighter." *New York Law School Law Review* 42, nos. 3–4 (1998): 1069–92.

Jacobs, James B., Christopher Panarella, and Jay Worthington. *Busting the Mob: United States v. Cosa Nostra.* New York: New York University Press, 1994.

James, Ralph C., and Estelle D. James. *Hoffa and the Teamsters: A Study of Union Power.* Princeton: D. Van Nostrand, 1965.

Joselit, Jenna W. *Our Gang: Jewish Crime and the New York Jewish Community, 1900–1940.* Bloomington: Indiana University Press, 1983.

Kelly, Robert, Ko-Lin Chin, and Rufus Schatzburg. *Handbook of Organized Crime in the United States.* Westport, Conn.: Greenwood Press, 1994.

Kenney, Dennis J., and James O. Finckenauer. *Organized Crime in America.* New York: Wadsworth, 1995.

Kobler, John. *Capone: The Life and World of Al Capone.* New York: De Capo, 1992.

Kwitny, Jonathan. *Vicious Circles: The Mafia in the Marketplace.* New York: Norton, 1979.

Landesco, John. *Organized Crime in Chicago.* Chicago: University of Chicago Press, 1968; originally published in 1929.

Leichter, Franz. "Sweatshops to Shakedowns: Organized Crime in New York's Garment Industry." Unpublished. March 1982.

Leichter, Franz, "The Return of the Sweatshop: A Call for State Action." In "A Report on New York's Garment Industry." Unpublished. February 1981.

Leiter, Robert D. *The Teamsters Union: A Study of its Economic Impact.* New York: Bookman, 1957.

Maas, Peter. *Underboss: Sammy "The Bull" Gravano's Story of Life in the Mafia.* New York: HarperCollins, 1997.

Maas, Peter. *The Valachi Papers.* New York, G. P. Putnam's Sons, 1968.

New Jersey State Commission of Investigation. *A Report on the New Jersey Garment Industry.* April 1991.

New York State Commission of Investigation. *New York State Commission Report on Organized Crime.* 1968.

New York State Organized Crime Task Force. *Corruption and Racketeering in the New York City Construction Industry.* New York: New York University Press, 1990.

Peterson, Virgil W. *The Mob: 200 Years of Organized Crime in New York.* Ottawa, Ill.: Green Hill, 1983.

Pileggi, Nicholas. *Wiseguy: Life in a Mafia Family.* New York: Simon & Schuster, 1985.

Potter, Gary W. *Criminal Organizations: Vice, Racketeering and Politics in an American City.* Prospect Heights, Ill.: Wakeland Press, 1994.

President's Commission on Organized Crime. *The Edge: Organized Crime, Business and Labor Unions.* Washington D.C.: Government Printing Office, March 1986.

Rankin, Rebecca B. *New York Advancing: A Scientific Approach to Municipal Government.* New York: Gallery Press, 1936.

Reuter, Peter. "The Cartage Industry in New York." In *Crime and Justice: An Annual Review of Research,* edited by Michael Tonry. Vol. 18. Chicago: University of Chicago Press, 1994.

Reuter, Peter. *Racketeering in Legitimate Industries: A Study in the Economics of Intimidation.* Santa Monica: Rand, 1987.

Reuter, Peter. "Regulating Rackets." *AEI Journal on Government and Society* (September/December 1984): 34.

Schlesinger Jr., Arthur. *Robert Kennedy and His Times.* Boston: Houghton, Mifflin, 1978.

Sloane, Arthur A. *Hoffa.* Cambridge: MIT Press, 1991.

Summers, Anthony. *Official and Confidential: The Secret Life of J. Edgar Hoover.* New York: G. P. Putnam's Sons, 1993.

Taft, Philip. *Corruption and Racketeering in the Labor Movement.* 2d ed. Ithaca: New York State School of Industrial and Labor Relations Press, 1970.

Thacher II, Thomas D. "Combating Corruption and Racketeering: A New Strategy for Reforming Public Contracting in NYC's Construction Industry." *New York Law School Law Review* 15, nos. 1–2 (1995): 113–42.

Tonry, Michael, and Albert J. Reiss, eds. *Beyond the Law: Crime in Complex Organizations.* Chicago: University of Chicago Press, 1993.

U.S. Senate Select Committee on Improper Activities in the Labor or Management Field (McClellan Committee). Final Report. 86th Cong., 2d sess. 1960. S. Rept. 1139.

U.S. Senate Special Committee to Investigate Organized Crime in Interstate Commerce (Kefauver Committee). *Final Report,* 82d Cong., 1st sess. 1951. S. Rept. 725.

U.S. Task Force on Organized Crime. *Task Force Report; Organized Crime, Annotations, and Consultants' Papers.* Washington, D.C.: U.S. Government Printing Office, 1967.

Walsh, George. *Public Enemies: The Mayor, the Mob and the Crime That Was.* New York: Norton, 1980.

Ward, Benjamin. "A Former Commissioner's View on Investigating Corruption." *New York Law School Law Review* 40 (1995): 45.

Zeiger, Henry. *Sam the Plumber.* Bergenfield, N.J.: New American Library, 1973.

Index

Note: *Italicized* letters *n*, *m*, and *t* following page numbers indicate notes, maps, and tables, respectively.

About the Authors

JAMES B. JACOBS is Professor of Law and Director of the Center for Research in Crime and Justice at New York University. He is also co-author of *Busting the Mob: United States v. Cosa Nostra* and, most recently, *Hate Crimes: Criminal Law and Identity Politics.*

COLEEN FRIEL and ROBERT RADICK, former Glass Fellows in Crime & Justice at NYU School of Law, are currently in private law practice in Washington, D.C. and New York City.